Wrestling Angels into Song

Penn Studies in Contemporary American Fiction

A Series Edited by Emory Elliott,
University of California at Riverside

A complete listing of the books in this series appears at the back of this volume

Wrestling Angels into Song

The Fictions of Ernest J. Gaines and James Alan McPherson

Herman Beavers

University of Pennsylvania Press

Philadelphia

Grateful acknowledgment is made to the following publishers and individuals for permission to cite from published materials:

Random House: Ralph Ellison, *Invisible Man*, *Shadow and Act*, and *Going to the Territory*; Ernest J. Gaines, *In My Father's House*, *A Gathering of Old Men*, and *A Lesson Before Dying*.

Little, Brown and Company: James Alan McPherson, *Hue and Cry* and *Elbow Room*.

JCA Literary Agency: Ernest J. Gaines, *Of Love and Dust*, *Bloodline*, and *Catherine Carmier*.

Doubleday, Inc.: Ernest J. Gaines, *The Autobiography of Miss Jane Pittman*.

William Morris Literary Agency: international rights to cite from the works of Ralph Ellison.

Michael S. Harper: Harper, *Images of Kin: New and Selected Poems* and *Healing Song for the Inner Ear*.

Library of Congress Cataloging-in-Publication Data
Beavers, Herman.
Wrestling angels into song : the fictions of Ernest J. Gaines and James Alan McPherson / Herman Beavers.
p. cm. — (Penn studies in contemporary American fiction)
Includes bibliographical references and index.
ISBN 0-8122-3150-3
1. Gaines, Ernest J., 1933– —Criticism and interpretation. 2. McPherson, James Alan, 1943– —Criticism and interpretation. 3. American fiction—Afro-American authors—History and criticism. 4. American fiction—20th century—History and criticism. 5. Afro-Americans in literature. I. Title. II. Series.
PS3557.A355Z594 1994
813′.5409—dc20 94-24523
CIP

Contents

Preface

It has occurred to me, over the course of writing this book, that questions would arise concerning the title I have chosen. However, after much internal wrangling I have decided to remain true to this title, and I want to take space here to explain the why and how of it. Those who are familiar with the figure of Jacob in the Bible will remember, of course, his battle with the angel.[1] The battle results, not in Jacob's victory, but in an act of renaming. Jacob becomes Israel, and thus he remains himself, but also something more: the focal point, the signifier, if you will, of nationhood. Let Jacob stand for the African American presence in the United States. And consider the time we have spent in this country to be indicative of both the wrestling match and the act of renaming. For in so many ways the African American struggle to belong is likewise a struggle for identity. As Kenneth Karst has pointed out, "The most heartrending deprivation of all is the inequality of status that excludes people from full membership in the community, degrading them by labeling them as outsiders, denying them their very selves."[2] What this suggests is that the African American presence is one that calls attention to and references the process of conceptualizing who Americans are and how they engage in a process of knowing.

But if much time has been spent considering the process of "denying Blacks their very selves," this book came into being because I recognized that so many African Americans had constructed creative niches in order to combat this process—places where, as James Alan McPherson might suggest, African Americans could "remain free enough . . . to take chances, to be ridiculous, perhaps even try to form [their own] positive stories out of whatever [those] experiences provided."[3] As I ruminated on the force of African American music, its impact on American culture-at-large, I began to think about how this struggle for identity has often been carried on in symbolic spaces. In the blues, for example, the relationship between performer and audience is rendered complex, largely because misery, reflection, and responsibility are configured into a dynamic whole. What this means to the project at hand is that I began to recognize that the end result was of little importance. What matters is the process—an investment in acts not destinations.

It is this sensibility that I have gleaned from the works of Ralph Ellison and that can be found in the works of Ernest J. Gaines and James Alan McPherson. To be sure, there are other writers whose work has been influenced by Ellison's literary personage. But, as I argue here, what attracted me to the triad of Ellison, Gaines, and McPherson was that each has found creative ways to situate their Southernness, to posit circumstances that, in the popular view, indicate despair and squalor as the site of cultural vitality. The other, perhaps less clear, aspect of this is that this study works in a smaller unit of literary history. Though they are not peers, Gaines and McPherson are, in literary terms, contemporaries. As such, I hope it is clear to readers the debt this study owes to those previous foundational endeavors in African American literary studies: to name but a few, Houston Baker's *The Journey Back*, Robert B. Stepto's *From Behind the Veil*, Barbara Christian's *Black Women Novelists*, Michael S. Harper's and Robert Stepto's *Chant of Saints*, and of course even further back, Sterling A. Brown's and Ulysses Lee's seminal anthology, *The Negro Caravan*. I cite these particular studies for no reason other than to suggest that each in its fashion attempts to cover large units of literary history.

In that sense, *Wrestling Angels into Song* can be said to make much smaller claims (though, I think, no less important ones), if only because I have not attempted to be comprehensive: my interests in ancestry are much more tightly focused. When I began this project as a dissertation, neither Gaines nor McPherson had received much in the way of critical attention; the former had become a representative figure in the sense that his writing is often used to portray life in the South (as evidenced by the three films based on his fiction) but the latter had only been mentioned in the chapters of several books (most notably Keith Byerman's fine study, *Fingering the Jagged Grain*) and some scattered articles. And few scholars had begun to consider either writer's work in terms of how he addressed matters of citizenship or, for that matter, the issue of how to "place" them. It has not been my intention here to suggest that Gaines or McPherson should be neatly "boxed." If anything, in reading their work one finds that they resist this impulse with great fervor. But I did want to find new ways to read them, and in doing so to begin to see African American literary production in terms that were not so monolithic. For it is most certainly the case that as McPherson and Gaines were making aesthetic choices other writers were as well. That those choices were, and are, different means that there is still much to do in terms of the analytical project I attempt here.

In order to facilitate my efforts, the book is divided into three parts: "Innovations of Kin," "Trueblood Echoing," and "The Lower Frequencies." Chapter 1 is devoted to Ellison's aesthetic posture and the manner in which that posture situates the blues as a way of formulating a coherent American identity, one that can contain the kinds of contradictions inherent in the American experience. In talking about this, I suggest that Gaines's and McPherson's fictions participate in a wider tradition, one that posits acts of storytelling (and, as Robert Stepto might argue, "telling off") as sites of intervention (and invention) in the American dilemma. Chapter 2 works out the particularities of the literary kinship of Ellison, Gaines, and McPherson, not only in terms of their strategies of asserting authorial control over their artistic production, but also in terms of the manner in which the subject of innovation is addressed in their fictions. They situate their origins outside the confines of conventionality, and innovation and resourcefulness (especially as demonstrated in expressive culture) become important tropes for their works. Thus, African American identities need not be formulated on the basis of their victimization within the societal mainstream because African American expressive culture points to improvisation and agency.

Part II, "Trueblood Echoing," uses Ellison's Trueblood as a representative figure, one whose coupling of memory and performance make him, on the one hand, a source of communal shame, and on the other, a coherent figure whose resourcefulness leads him to self-acceptance. As a figure who finds his voice, and in finding it discovers that he is censored by his own community, Trueblood helps us to understand the manner in which certain forms of address in the African American community threaten the collective identity, requiring more silence than sympathy. In Chapter 3 I examine Gaines's novels *Of Love and Dust* and *In My Father's House* as fictions which utilize characters who dramatize the difficulties that arise when storytelling and memory are enjoined. Cultural integrity, for these protagonists, rests on their ability to displace "texts" that silence them and prevent them from connecting memory and voice. Jim Kelly and Phillip Martin are characters who demonstrate the need to reassess their resources and thus find forms of solitude that will allow them to speak. The loss of community they experience makes them liminal characters, but as such they provide useful examples of Gaines's preoccupation with characters who seek the middle ground between active (e.g., violent) resistance and passive acceptance of their plight. Chapter 4 focuses on McPherson's classic short story, "A Solo Song: For Doc." As in the previous chapter, we see how the narrator of the story posits the importance of displacing a written text with an oral one that casts him as the site where memory and performance form a viable confluence. The relationship of McPherson's story and Ellison's novel arises out of both writers' depictions of the greenhorn's journey from innocence to insight.

I have chosen to call Part III of this study "The Lower Frequencies" because both chapters address the issue of "speaking for" others in ways that are adequately representative. In Chapter 5 I discuss the relationship between storytelling and community, beginning with Gaines's *Catherine Carmier*; continuing with *The Autobiography of Miss Jane Pittman*, *A Gathering of Old Men*, and several stories from *Bloodline*; and concluding with a discussion of Gaines's latest novel, *A Lesson Before Dying*. These fictions each offer protagonist/narrators who bring private upheaval into public space. Their importance is manifested via strategies Gaines employs to manumit his fictional voice from the pervasive authority of William Faulkner. Gaines's characters use call and response to achieve self-recovery and thus distance themselves from the characters who people Faulkner's endurance narrative. Though they often begin in states of hibernation, these protagonists revise Faulkner's vision of the South (as doomed landscape) by using storytelling to create an intimacy that has rejuvenating possibilities. Gaines's characters are "articulate witnesses" whose voices rupture their respective forms of confinement by breaking the connection between experience and unspeakability while insisting on the value of kinship ties.[4]

In the final chapter of this study I examine storytelling as it unfolds in what I like to refer to as McPherson's "legal fiction trilogy," three stories that harken back to Ellison's exploration of law in *Invisible Man*. As I will demonstrate, Ellison and McPherson both dramatize the American inability to read beyond surfaces. Indeed, McPherson's stories portray the legal confrontation (his "legal fictions" all utilize courtroom settings) as a discourse of surfaces locked in place by a "persuasive community" that erases difference (as it accrues in the form of race or gender) in order to carry out its function. These stories dramatize the difficulty of representation (of a legal sort) by illuminating the conspiratorial nature of legal practice. As McPherson demonstrates, the legal arena often falls into a state of incoherence because of the failure of imagination, the inability to utilize new stories to revitalize the legal process.

In completing this project, it becomes clear that I still have much to do with these authors, with McPherson's short stories in particular. For as I have learned from these writers, the idea of completion is a fiction. There is, finally, only process: the struggle to know and remember our own names, to seek the blessing to be found in the making.

Herman Beavers,
Philadelphia

Acknowledgments

The act of writing a book, as many writers before me have recognized, is a collaborative enterprise and results from contributions that flow from many levels of interaction. I have plumbed the depths of my memory and concluded that there are so many people to thank for their input into the project that I do not have space to thank them all. Thus it is my hope that all those individuals who do not find their names on these pages will know they are recorded in a space much more secure. But there are a number of people whose names I feel compelled to call, whose presence must be conjured. Jerry Singerman and Alison Anderson, my editors at the University of Pennsylvania Press, have seen this manuscript through each storm and trial with grace and wit. Rudolph P. Byrd, John Lowe, Vera Kutzinski, John Callahan, Lani Guinier, Vincent Peterson, Elizabeth Alexander, Marjorie Levenson, Rita Barnard, Dana Phillips, Craig Saper, John Roberts, Valerie Smith, and Bob Perelman all took time from their own work to read portions of the manuscript and offer valuable comments and suggestions. Leslie Collins, Charles Austin, Ericka Blount, Kia Brookins, and Nicole Brittingham provided invaluable support as research assistants. The members of my graduate seminar on Ellison, Gaines, and McPherson—Tim Waples, Crystal Jones Lucky, Jeanine DeLombard, Dana Jackson, Amy Korn, Giselle Anatol, and Joe Watts—sharpened my thinking and challenged me to see the works from a variety of perspectives. To each of you, let me say that the only thing I possess that outdistances your commitment is my gratitude.

I also wish to thank Hazel Carby, John Szwed, and Michael G. Cooke for their guidance during this project's beginnings as a dissertation. Though Professor Cooke did not live to see the project's completion, I must acknowledge him for his words at the end of what turned out to be our last encounter; they are words I continue to live by and cherish.

I must also acknowledge some of the people who are, and always shall be, sources of safe harbor: Douglas Banks, Johnny Jones, Carolyn

Beard Whitlow, Lester Barclay, George Barnwell, Louis E. Green, Mencer Donahue Edwards, Dwight D. Andrews, bell hooks, Farah Griffin, Sharon Bryant, Dawn Terrell, David A. Thomas, Kali Tal, Cathy McKinley, Kai Jackson, Ajana Mebane-Cruz, Joyce Delaney, Dean Robinson, Caroline Jackson, Robert and Jackie O'Meally, Alice A. Deck, Jim Miller, Deborah McDowell, Richard Yarborough, Thadious Davis, Bill Lowe, Mark Sanders and Kimberly Wallace-Sanders, Gwen Williams, Meghan and Nzadi Kieta, Peter Vaughan, Valerie Swain Cade-McCoullom, Al Green, Ken Shropshire, Pam Robinson, Vivian Gadsden, Gay Wilentz, Al Filreis, Inez Salazar, Lisa New, and students past and present. If I but had the words . . .

Of Michael S. Harper I can only say that, if we are allowed one person to serve as the guardian of our faith, he is my unequivocal choice. Mentor, confidant, nurturer, and nemesis: it was Professor Harper who guided me to the works of James Alan McPherson, a gift that has sustained me through trouble of every sort. In Robert Hayden's words, "This man, superb in love and logic, this man / shall be remembered." To Professor Robert B. Stepto, who piloted this work along its journey as a dissertation, his wisdom and commitment to excellence are a blessing to live up to. To Houston A. Baker, invaluable colleague and guiding light, and Charlotte Pierce Baker, kindred spirit, your labors instruct me, on all levels, in the matter of "love's instruments."

I would end by thanking my family, both immediate and extended; at their peril they have guided me to this place without adequate recompense and loved me all the more. Above all, I want to thank my wife, Lisa James-Beavers. Daily, I witness her unshakable belief in human justice and know I am renewed.

And in this quiet place I own these words and know that, come what may, the blessing lies in the opportunity to share them.

Introduction

1

In an interview with James Alan McPherson in 1970, Ralph Ellison had this to say about the idea of a specifically "black" awareness:

> I think too many of our assertions continue to be in response to whites. . . . I think we're polarized by the very fact that we keep talking about "black awareness" when we really should be talking about black American awareness, an awareness of where we fit into the total American scheme, where our influence is. I tell white kids that instead of talking about black men in a white world or about black men in white society, they should ask themselves how black they are because black men have been influencing the values of the society and the art forms of the society . . . We [African Americans] did not develop as a people in isolation. We developed within a context of white people.[1]

What makes Ellison's comments so richly problematic is that he argues for an American identity that issues from cultural collaboration, even in instances where the participants are less than willing to acknowledge it as such. This position calls for different assumptions, which do not focus on *who* belongs, but *how.*

A unique feature of Ellison's comments, then, is his refusal to acknowledge the existence of either an hermetically sealed "black awareness" or "black culture," or such a thing as "white culture":

> I don't recognize any white culture. . . . I recognize no American culture which is not the partial creation of black people. I recognize no American style in literature, in dance, in music, even in assembly-line processes, which does not bear the mark of the American Negro.[2]

American culture, then, was the result of collisions between different racial groups; the result, as Robert Penn Warren says, in light of slavery, of "every possible, every *imaginable* combination of human social relationships," the country could manifest.[3] This led, Ellison suggests, to a crisis of identity for white Americans that could be traced back as far as the nation's beginnings; and thus he argues that whites "simplif[ied] the answer," using the African American presence

> as a marker, a symbol of limits, a metaphor for the "outsider." Many whites could look at the social position of blacks and feel that color formed an easy and reliable gauge for determining to what extent one was or was not an American.[4]

This posture allowed white Americans to engage in a cultural politics the goal of which was to render "American culture" recognizable, homogeneous, and intentional. As Ellison saw it, the resulting conflict took the form of the "older, dominant groups of white Americans, especially the Anglo-Saxons, on the one hand, and the newer white and non-white groups on the other, over the major group's attempt to impose its ideals upon the rest, insisting that its exclusive image be accepted as *the* image of the American."[5]

While this has been a position articulated by scholar and layperson alike, what interests me for the moment is the manner in which Ellison touches on the inherent anxiety of this enterprise, the longing for an essential American reality whose intensity leads those who "belong" to exclude with vigor those who do not. As Wernor Sollors has ably demonstrated, American literature has often attempted "to construct a sense of natural family cohesion in the new world, especially with the help of naturalizing codes and concepts such as 'love' and 'generations.'"[6] But for all this groping for intentionality, the result was that those who sought to articulate American identity became even more deeply mystified. Thus, in answering why he wrote *Invisible Man,* Ellison observed:

> I felt that there was a great deal about the nature of American experience which was not understood by most Americans. I felt also that the diversity of the total experience rendered much of it mysterious. And I felt that because so much of it which appeared unrelated was actually most intimately intertwined, it needed exploring. In fact, I believed that unless we continually explored the network of complex relationships which bind us together, we would continue being the victims of various inadequate conceptions of ourselves, both as individuals and as citizens of a nation of diverse peoples.[7]

Ellison's work speaks to (or for?) a shared destiny, a plight Americans, black and white alike (among other groups who fit neither of these designations) must ponder within the context of an ongoing experiment characterized as much by its failures as its successes. What distinguishes Ellison's remarks most, however, is his insistence on the accidental nature of American identity: its incompleteness. When he describes American culture as an "experiment," or argues that America is an "undiscovered country," he suggests that the nation is characterized by the anomalous, the liminal, and the unfinished. If this aspect of American experience threatened national self-esteem and endangered the ability to assess and utilize American strengths, these issues were resolved in part through the "emergence of a new principle or motive in the drama of American democracy,"[8] which proved to be race. Ellison continues:

> [R]ace became a major cause, form, and symbol of the American hierarchical psychosis. As the unwilling and unjust personification of that psychosis and its major victim, the Afro-American took on the complex symbolism of social health and social sickness. He became the raw labor force, the victim of social degradation, and symbolic of America's hope for future perfection. He was to be viewed at least by many whites, as both cause and cure of our social malaise.[9]

Ellison's analysis points to, but does not name directly, the manner by which African Americans became a resource whose purpose was one of providing white Americans with the raw materials necessary to formulate a contingent identity. What was called for was a vision that could dramatize the accidental, the improvisatory nature of American identity and thus valorize the process of becoming an American. And by taking up Mark Twain's project, which made distinctions between American ideals and American conduct, if Ellison sought to use the novel as a way to confront American chaos, he also improvised a protagonist who recognized the need to be his own best resource.[10]

Invisible Man fuses vernacular storytelling and cultural reflection to spawn one of the most pervasive metaphors in American letters. In order to accomplish this, Ellison employs the figure of the greenhorn, a figure who is at once arrivant and aspirant, to work out his exploration of American identity. It is this figure who will become important to this study, largely because the greenhorn emerges as that figure in American letters whose arrival in unfamiliar circumstances is characterized by the attempt to belong: to discover, first, the resources necessary for sustenance, and later, the processes by which those resources can be transformed into power and influence.[11] Ellison's hero, in wanting to make himself, fails again and again because he insists on labels and strategies not of his own choosing. His journey through the novel is thus one of both making and unmaking; the story he narrates demonstrates his failures, or better, his success in recognizing that he is a failure.

But the issue of resourcefulness is important to the hero's numerous reversals of fortune. For the greenhorn is a literary figure whose value lies not only in examining the process by which American identities are formed, but also in examining the codes and mores of the dominant culture and how the past configures life in the present. As Ellison's hero demonstrates, his discovery of a usable past renews his prospects in the present. That "usable past" takes the form of African American expressive culture, first in the form of his grandfather and later in the form of Louis Armstrong. Ellison's depiction of the greenhorn thus codifies the manner in which improvisation, indeed, the willingness to submit to an improvisatory mode, moves the individual from object to subject.

What is also lifted up, of course, is what Robert Stepto has established as the quest for freedom and literacy. For the greenhorn's success hinges on his or her ability to navigate the cultural codes swirling about. And, as the invisible man comes to understand, this does not mean the mere aping of dominant styles. Rather, the challenge is one of mastering language and behavioral codes in ways that allow one to become an innovator in one's own right. The resourcefulness called for to achieve this goal represents a state in which the greenhorn moves from assimilation to innovation, acquiring the sense that his circumstance is not reified but fluid. I call this state of being "coherence." And by this I mean that we find characters whose failures lead them to reassess their resources in ways which allow for self-determination. Part of this reorganization of resources comes through the act of storytelling. As an instance of oral performance where one is required to negotiate with an audience for narrative space, storytelling is also a site of representative power: Ellison's narrator, over the course of *Invisible Man,* learns how to perform symbolically what he set out to do literally: to become a voice that can accommodate unpredictability and "speak for" other voices. But in recognizing that he is nobody but himself, the narrator also demonstrates a coherence which allows him to embrace optimism and thus prepare himself for that day when he leaves hibernation in order to carry out an overt action.

When I use the term "coherent," then, I mean not that one can necessarily control outcomes, but that one is in position to utilize resources in ways that can make use of failure as readily as success. A way to understand this comes through Lucius Outlaw's observations on an African American cultural hermeneutic:

> Without question one of the most significant features of the multifaceted struggle on the part of African peoples and people of African descent for a liberated existence has been and is the struggle to achieve cultural integrity: to embrace where available, to construct where unavailable, those productions and expressions of meaning which serve to reflect the self-affirmations of black people, our views of the world, in concepts and forms which we have projected for these purposes.[12]

As Outlaw suggests, this is a decisive struggle: for it centers on issues of meaning and meaningfulness, the ways African American existence becomes a self-defined concept. "Thus," Outlaw concludes, "the struggle for cultural integrity . . . creates a different (and opposing) constellation of symbols and assertions."[13] Hence, when I use the term "coherence," I am referring both to the drive for cultural integrity and to the effect of the artistic forms which result, however transient those forms may be. As Outlaw asserts, cultural struggle involves what he terms "endeavors in symbolic reversal," which allude to the manner by which one "moves . . . from imposed determination of one's (a people's) existence to those [symbols] generated oneself." The reversal of meaning creates possibility, which serves to make the American landscape a more lucid entity. In short, as African American writers reverse the symbolic meaning of blackness (as negative valence) in American cultural space, they likewise disclose the "uncreated features" of American identity. I should caution the reader, however, that the term coherence is not meant to suggest a romanticized (or totalized) American cultural landscape, only one which suggests a process open to new forms of negotiation and improvisation.

Ellison's virtuosity refers not to politics but to jazz; and an effective way to launch a discussion on artistic innovation and symbolic reversals can be gleaned when Ellison articulates the antagonistic relationship he describes as "the jazz moment":

> There is . . . a cruel contradiction implicit in the art form itself. For true jazz is an art of individual assertion within and against the group. Each true jazz moment (as distinct from the uninspired commercial performance) springs from a context in which each artist challenges all the rest; each solo flight, or improvisation, represents . . . a definition of his identity: as individual, as member of the collectivity and as a link in the chain of tradition. Thus, because jazz finds its very life in an endless improvisation upon traditional materials, the jazzman must lose his identity even as he finds it.[14]

The jazz musician's struggle to be an innovator collides with the innovations of his or her predecessors, and what crystallizes is a coherent tradition, not only in terms of technical invention but also in the levels of virtuosity he or she must achieve to stand as a watershed in the tradition. This dialogue assumes guises that can be celebratory or revisionary (at times, radically so), as successive examples of innovative skill dramatize the strain and grind of tradition.

2

Ellison's depiction of the antagonistic cooperation contained within the accidental nature of American identity and citizenship creates the conceptual niche for the writers whose work I examine in this volume, Ernest J. Gaines and James Alan McPherson. Though a discussion on the "mysteries of American citizenship" could easily include many more writers than just these two, I was attracted to Gaines's and McPherson's fictions because, as Southern writers, they seemed to devote themselves to an interrogation of American experience in ways that resemble Ellison's refusal to accept narrow definitions of diversity. But more than this, their fiction was peopled by characters who valued acts of storytelling and whose stories were attempts to understand their lives in terms larger than those afforded by race. These characters valued resourcefulness in ways that reflected the influence of the African American trickster, on the one hand, and a desire to belong on the other. As both Gaines and McPherson demonstrate, this is problematic, for on what terms does one settle in order to be accepted? What kinds of communities result from the kinds of negotiations called for by a segregated (if only figuratively) culture.

These questions, it seemed to me, were ones that Ellison had grappled with in his novel—as well as in his stories and occasional pieces. As I decided, therefore, that this was, in fact, a book on Gaines's and McPherson's fictions, I also realized that Ellison provided the resources to "open up" their work for analysis. What I mean by this is by no means simple: in some instances I talk about how Gaines and McPherson actually rework scenes or tropes from *Invisible Man,* in others I use moments from the novel to frame my discussion because I wish to acknowledge these authors' attempts to continue Ellison's investigation of the American mystery.

But there is also the relationship of Gaines to McPherson, and here I find one of the latter's observations most useful in articulating how one might place these writers together as literary relatives. In his essay "On Becoming an American Writer," McPherson observes American society's trajectory as one moving from status to contract. Gaines's depictions of life in Louisiana span the period from the Civil War to the post-Civil Rights Movement and exemplify such an imperative: his characters work largely in a space that does not offer protection of a contractual sort, though it is nonetheless governed by very strict codes of behavior that determine the quality of interactions between black and white. McPherson depicts this imperative in a very different way. His characters' odyssey is over the American landscape characterized by their attempts to locate themselves (or others) within racial or sexual categories whose dictates are status-driven but are enacted as contractual arrangements. Their journeys often work out the contradictions to be found in American culture, demonstrating the fluidity of American identity and the fact that we have not, as yet, begun to grasp American experience as a coherent phenomenon.

While it is the pervasive impact of Ralph Ellison's literary innovation that has led me to bring a critical eye to the fiction of Ernest J. Gaines and James Alan McPherson, let me suggest that their literary kinship with the older writer clearly demonstrates Ellison's notion of "antagonistic cooperation." This is to say that Gaines and McPherson simultaneously make and unmake their connection to Ellison's novel and aesthetic so that one sees both revoicing and resistance taking place in their fictions. What finally makes Ernest Gaines and James McPherson central to this discussion is that their fiction often embodies the impulse toward symbolic reversals, disclosing aspects of American experience that exist outside conventional forms of representation. As he endures one set of reversals after another, Ellison's protagonist discovers the necessity of improvising on received materials to become part of a tradition of innovators that includes Louis Armstrong. By "agreeing his enemies to death and destruction," Ellison's narrator begins to unravel the mystery of African American citizenship. One finds this discovery reflected in Gaines and McPherson's authorial postures. Neither eschews his connections to Western literary or legal traditions (which often obscure African American contributions), but both clearly enact reversals on some of the assumptions these traditions may embody in order to subvert reified notions of American society. By combining "the methods of modern fiction making with the materials of Black folk culture," Keith Byerman notes, Gaines and McPherson have created literary voices that are authentically African American and yet fully engaged with American literature as a whole.[15]

But in achieving such an engagement, neither Gaines nor McPherson eschews the depiction of African American characters who reflect the diversity to be found in black communities. One finds, for example, that both writers recuperate the South as a site, not only of expressive culture, but also of African American resistance. This resistance takes many forms, and I want to suggest that the readers of their fiction find themselves in a place where relationships are, as Albert Murray has demonstrated in *South to a Very Old Place,* difficult to categorize and impossible to elude. This suggestion is not an attempt to diminish brutality and loss, of which we have become so much aware; rather it is a reprise of what Ellison, quoting Henry James, argued in 1969: as Americans, we "have an on-going quarrel with our lives, with the condition that we live in."

Part I
Innovations of Kin

Chapter 1

Relative Politics: The Literary Triumverate of Ralph Waldo Ellison, Ernest J. Gaines, and James Alan McPherson

"The first true phrase sings out in barnyard; the hunt in books for quail."

—Michael S. Harper, "Goin to the Territory"

1

The Prologue of Ralph Ellison's *Invisible Man* finds the protagonist offering testimony to his acquisition of inventive skill. "Though invisible," he states, "I am in the great American tradition of tinkers. That makes me kin to Ford, Edison, and Franklin." After surviving the novel's near-calamitous episodes, he reaches the conclusion that he is, in his estimation, a "thinker-tinker." Ellison's play on language illuminates the manner in which intellect and action are components of a project whose goal is reflection, recuperation, and self-invention. It also refers to the diadic nature of African American consciousness; the necessity to apply acts of symbolic reversal to conventional formulations of African American enactments of identity.[1]

But this begs the question why Ellison's hero chooses to associate himself with Ford, Edison, and Franklin. The choice could be interpreted as one of great temerity, but I submit that the decision is no accident of insolence, nor is it an arbitrary one. Ellison's conceptual strategy intends to valorize a particular social posture, one that he shares with the aforementioned American "tinkers." Each successfully harnesses power (mechanical or electrical) and puts it to work in the service of self-creation; this is what makes them such important symbols for the narrator, who is himself involved in a project of self-formulation that involves the use of electricity tapped from the lines of Monopolated Light & Power. Ford, Edison, and Franklin each offer a unique combination of mechanical know-how, persistence, and public presence, which they employ in dilemmas of a technical or scientific sort. Their skill at negotiation, as the forces of disorganization swirl around, marks their passage into the ranks of self-made men.[2]

But there is yet another, more basic, trait that makes them important symbolic devices for both Ellison and his hero, namely that these American inventors have crystallized in the national memory as figures of resourcefulness. While I need not recount here the details behind the "discovery" of electricity or its use in the invention of the light bulb and the automobile, what is essential to our discussion is the fact that each of these events represents the ability to bring resources to bear, in the most efficient manner, on the production of a desired social result. Join this resourcefulness with the fact that all Ellison's "thinker-tinkers" can be characterized by technological/scientific action of an evolutionary (and not a revolutionary) sort,[3] and what becomes clear is that American "innovation" is situated in the interstice between marketplace and social myth.[4]

Ellison's hero, then, adopts a posture that is best characterized by his ability to recognize opportunities and mobilize the resources necessary to navigate the public sphere by using his "invisibility" to his advantage. As one who "tinkers," the hero calls to our attention the relationship between exegesis and action, insight and improvement. Engaged in the act of self-repair, the hero wires his hole with light and sound using 1,369 light bulbs and Louis Armstrong's horn. In the process he realizes that he alone must bear responsibility for his image, however unstable it may prove to be. Armed with "a theory and a concept," the narrator sets about the task of verifying his form by relying on the process storytelling affords. Before he reaches such a state of awareness, however, the hero is battered, chased, and ostracized. His failures result because he insists on replacing thought with ideology, imagination with sloganeering. As one who has realized his hibernation is a temporary state, the hero discerns that the remedy lies in recognizing attempts to negate him and in using these situations to his own advantage by seeing the affirmation to be found there. This likewise means that he needs to find a process that will ensure this affirmation; he must produce—and consistently *reproduce*—this quality of consciousness.

The hero's dilemma throughout *Invisible Man* is one, simply, of developing self-reliance. As many critics have argued, Ellison's narrator repeatedly talks himself into corners until he develops the ability to "see around" them. But what does it mean to "see around" corners? Certainly the phrase refers to the hero's awareness that he must ascertain reality differently. But more than this, it has to do, if one examines the novel closely, with how the individual comes to understand how to manage resources in an attempt to discern what is tangible and what is illusory. While the hero no doubt wants to be free, we need to understand how Ellison's novel investigates this notion. This idea has value in the abstract, but finally one has to engage the idea of citizenship: what constitutes and ensures it. In writing a novel like *Invisible Man,* Ellison interrogates the malfunction of American democracy. This, in itself, is not a new revelation. What makes this a point of departure for this study is that Ellison's novel does not use his hero as a strategy to metaphorize resourcefulness as the beginning of American democratic practice. Rather, *Invisible Man* abounds with instances where the hero fails to recognize exactly what he possesses in the way of resources. Indeed, his grandfather's advice comes to him while he is young and ill-equipped to make use of it in his everyday dealings. Time and again, he refuses to acknowledge and utilize this resource as he embraces someone else's mock-up of reality.

Numerous commentators on Ellison's novel have spoken of the manner in which it creates the most exact terms for the description of African American experience.[5] While I find no cause to disagree with this assessment, let me state that this is not Ellison's ultimate goal. For to conclude that Ellison's task was solely to represent African American experience inevitably diminishes the impact of the novel's last sentence: "Who knows but that, on the lower frequencies, I speak for you?" If we are to agree with R. W. B. Lewis's assessment that *Invisible Man* is the "greatest American novel in the second half of the twentieth century," then we must recognize the conceptual bridge that Ellison wants to create between African American experience, as an isolated idea, and American citizenship as a holistic idea. What makes this connection such a radical departure from the notion that African Americans are excluded from democratic practice is that it attempts to locate African American enactments of citizenship in places where the individual often fails to look. Characters like Mary Rambo, Peter Wheatstraw, the Vet, and Jim Trueblood are in their respective fashions individuals who have found ways to "change the joke and slip the yoke."[6] Through their example, Ellison's hero comes to describe himself as "one of the most irresponsible beings that ever lived." His irresponsibility, however, is the sign of the resistant, self-redemptive posture he has adopted, so that the decision to utilize these "invisible" figures culminates in his use of Louis Armstrong as a paradigmatic figure. I will discuss Armstrong further in the pages that follow, but for now let me suggest that Ellison's hero, by telling his story of displacement and hibernation, is not articulating his pain for its own sake. What he suggests is that the democratic process embraces both the painful and the celebratory, and the novel's last words are meant primarily to adjust the reader's sense of where American citizenship occurs: that is, as the characters above suggest, in the most unexpected circumstances. The hero's story is also imbued with resources that make the democratic process viable as an enterprise of inquiry, rather than simply as an end in itself. Indeed, as I will show, the crux of the matter is that Ellison's novel works out the manner in which the failure to utilize cultural resources adequately is the ultimate cause of the malfunction of American democracy.

2

If there is a sense of doublespeak here, perhaps the best way to unravel it is to look at Ralph Ellison himself. For one can conclude, after examining his essays and occasional pieces, that he returns again and again to the problems of American consciousness and identity, and that the recurrent subtext in Ellison's writing has to do with the resources we bring to bear on these problems. Like his protagonist, Ellison values thought and action. In order to understand the significance of this, it is important to understand Ellison's syncretic approach to being both an American and a novelist.[7] In both guises, he can be characterized as a figure of rebellion.[8] This is not easily discerned if one looks for the conventional set of social cues. For Ellison's rebellion is based on his ability to see the possibility for transformation using all the resources available. Like the scientist described in Thomas Kuhn's *The Structure of Scientific Revolutions,* Ellison is committed to seeing the anomaly embedded inside convention and improvising upon it.[9] But in order to be innovative, one must first be willing to part with the known, to travel into the symbolic territory that divides convention and chaos. Looking at Ellison's career shows clearly that he confronts the familiar in order to find new approaches to technique. He situates his aesthetic rebellion within the task of utilizing resources to the fullest extent possible.

Ellison's aesthetic pose functions in close range of the American literary mainstream. This is not to suggest that he accepts its premises blindly. He has written too eloquently about the jazz musician's struggle for artistic identity (he, himself, had been a trumpeter) to settle for mere imitation of his forbears. But like his hero, he has chosen his own models and what value their examples hold for his work. Thus writers like T. S. Eliot, William Faulkner, Ernest Hemingway, and André Malraux are described as "ancestors," while he refers to African American writers Richard Wright and Langston Hughes as "relatives." Consider alongside this dichotomy his response to an observation made by African American novelist Leon Forrest, who stated: "I guess you might say that McPherson, Toni Morrison, Albert Murray, Ellison, and I constitute a crowd." Though he acknowledged the possibility of a "collectivity of sensibilities," regarding the writers mentioned, Ellison countered by noting that he was "by instinct (and experience) a loner" and continued that

> as to our constituting a school, that kind of thing—no, I don't think its desirable even though it offers some relief from the loneliness of the trade. For when writers associate too closely there is a tendency to control one another's ideas . . . they do their thinking and I do mine.[10]

This begs the question, of course, of how Ellison can dub white, modernist writers as ancestors while distancing himself from other African American writers? The key is his desire to participate in a wider field of inquiry than that afforded by race. Indeed, his first foe, as an artist engaged in symbolic rebellion, is the narrowing circumstance of categorization. In this instance, race is the most inadequate of categories; in Ellison's view writers do not spring from purely racial traditions. To rely solely on racial categories as a way of establishing an aesthetic sensibility is to draw on a resource that prohibits one's ability to see the complexity, the cultural hybridity that American life affords. That he (and thus, his protagonist) seeks to formulate kinship ties outside the African American tradition intimates his belief in the dynamic nature of American culture, which results from "the creation of many, many people." This viewpoint expresses Ellison's view that in America there "is no absolute separation of groups." But more importantly, Ellison believed that he could use African American experience to portray American cultural and moral strength. In his estimation this was an idea that had not found expression in twentieth-century literature. "Unfortunately, many Negroes have been trying to define their own predicament in exclusively sociological terms," he observed, "a situation I consider quite short sighted."[11]

Ellison's unwillingness to acknowledge African Americans solely as victims was often interpreted as an apolitical stance because it seemed to assert apathy. Consider these remarks by John Henrik Clarke:

> When Ellison's book was published, we had every expectation that his talent would extend beyond literary creation and would be given over at least in part, to his people's struggle for survival. At a time when some of our major writers took time to lend their voices and their monies to our people's struggles, it was to their everlasting disappointment that they called on Ellison and got no answer because he seemed to stand aloof.[12]

Clarke's observations invoke the notion that the African American writer is a public figure whose success in the literary world demands that he or she translate that energy into civic effort. But because Ellison postulates the mysteries of African American citizenship more broadly, African American writing, by nature, was dialogic. He saw the need to reinstate African Americans into the discussion on American democracy, because white men had for so long used them as a "human natural resource" so that the whites "could become more human." Thus writing becomes a political ritual that must, if one is to understand protest, maintain the link between ideas and action.[13] When Ellison asserts, "I recognize no dichotomy between art and protest," he challenges the assumptions surrounding the political labor that African American writers are called to perform outside the literary sphere. While many see public demonstrations as the way to express dissatisfaction, an assertion that democracy has failed, Ellison's remarks see them as part of a larger process. Thus his role on numerous boards and cultural commissions in the 1960s and 70s, while attacked as tokenism, was part of his insistence that African Americans could not afford to abandon a system into which their identities were so intimately woven.

Clarke and others have misread Ellison's intentions, I believe, because they construct literary success as the predecessor to civic responsibility; symbolic action is, finally, not enough. In this alignment, writing is not a sufficient display of social awareness. But this points to a misreading of *Invisible Man,* where Ellison's hero shuns the role of racial spokesperson to embrace the role of writer. The expectations to which Clarke alludes suggest that Ellison's status as "spokesman" rests on the fact that his novel is a weapon of dissent, that it argues from a stance of opposition and marginality rather than one of participation. But as Albert Murray has argued, the protest novel turns on this one-dimensionality, where the writer's task is to persuade the reader of racial oppression's negative consequences.[14] *Invisible Man* eschews this project, which turns, after all, on narrow acts of reading and still narrower acts of writing. Hence, Ellison observes,

> the white reader draws his whiteness around him when he sits down to read. He doesn't want to identify himself with Negro characters in terms of our immediate racial and social situation, though on the deeper human level, identification can become compelling when the situation is revealed artistically. The white reader doesn't want to get too close, not even in an imaginary recreation of our society. Negro writers have felt this and it has led to much of our failure.[15]

Ellison describes an instance where "Negro experience" as dramatized by African American writers failed to exercise the artistic tenacity necessary to bridge the distance between themselves and their white readership. And because a sociological approach to fiction relegates African American characters to the role of the "Negro Problem" emplotted unimaginatively, white readers' unwillingness to embrace African American fiction is likewise a failure to see it as a viable resource to be harnessed within the space of their own experience.[16] W. E. B. Dubois provides insight into the posture Ellison adopts. In *The Souls of Black Folk,* DuBois poses the rhetorical question, "How does it feel to be a problem?" and responds, "I answer seldom a word." DuBois's silence points to his unwillingness to construct African American identity in the narrow terms offered by victimization. *The Souls* anticipates Ellison's novel because it, too, attempts to formulate a plan for *communitas.*[17] His refusal to dissociate art from protest likewise challenges the assumptions that undergird the idea of social protest. To understand Ellison's approach, consider the remarks of Albert Murray, who asserts that it "is all but impossible for a writer of serious fiction to engage his craft as such in a political cause." The reason for this, he maintains, is that the serious artist "has what amounts to an ambivalence toward the human predicament." Thus, Murray concludes,

> There is first of all the serious novelist's complex awareness of the burdensome but sobering fact that there is some goodness in bad people however bad they are, and some badness or at least some flaw or weakness in good people however dear. In fact, the artist comes pretty close to being politically suspect; because on the one hand he is always proclaiming his love for mankind and on the other he is forever giving the devil his due![18]

The challenge as Ellison saw it was how to investigate American identity in search of its complexity. "Who knows but on the lower frequencies I speak for you?" By ending his novel with a question and not a declarative statement, Ellison offers an important rhetorical consideration. Not only does the narrator avoid closure, opting instead to assume an inquisitive, open posture, he forces the reader to shift from simply receiving a narration to being the narrative's subject, the source of the narration itself. The use of the word "for," instead of "to," forces the reader to imagine the novel's often nightmarish twists as self-referential episodes where the task of "finding oneself" takes on a double meaning. Suddenly, the novel makes reference to two "texts" to be evaluated, one resonating inside the other. Additionally, the Prologue ends with the statement, "Bear with me." This is a call for the reader to identify with the narrator's experience and as such, it is an assertion that American democracy is, in spite of race (or perhaps *because* of it), a shared experience. However, because "the end is in the beginning and lies far ahead," the reader does not yet have the critical equipment to make full sense of this call, and so it serves merely to create the performative niche for the narrative to come.

The sentence prior to the Prologue's last, "What did I do to be so blue?" offers a clue to the full significance of the close. This variant on Louis Armstrong's "What Did I Do To Be So Black and Blue?" is not a statement meant to evoke pity, rather it is an assertion of transcendence. Again, the reader lacks the necessary tools to discern this since the narrator has not yet told his story. However, the last sentence (the "end" that lies in the beginning) opens the space through which the reader may enter this transcendent state. The fact that the episodes found in chapters 1 through 25 work out the narrator's confusion, which is then framed by the Prologue and Epilogue, suggests that the form of the novel itself is attuned to the *ritual* of citizenship rather than its material substance.

Not only does Ellison attempt to articulate the intertextual nature of American citizenship, but the whole of *Invisible Man* can be seen as a cross-examination of the reader. Readers are forced to breach the surface of their assumptions, to "tinker" with their conclusions. Ellison explores the politics of rupture as it assumes both personal and social form. Thus, the coincidence of closure and inquiry calls attention to the stated and the unstated, confusing the boundaries between reader and writer. His task is on the same order as that of DuBois's *Souls,* that is, he wants to suggest

> that a journey of immersion into the "deeper recesses" of [blackness] conducted by a group of blacks and whites alike will indeed be a moment in and out of time, an occasion of communitas, a "ritual transition" to a true America.[19]

Like DuBois's "race-conscious and self-conscious narrator" in *Souls,* Ellison's hero adopts the role of remembrancer, addressing himself to the "tradition of forgetfulness," that characterizes American culture.[20] Because Ellison wants to participate in the discussion of American democracy and citizenship, he has to choose artistic models operating in that same field. He characterizes the crisis in contemporary American writing as a disillusionment in the future.[21] Writing a novel is a return to the same struggles with form and morality (or perhaps, the morality of form?) that marked American literature in the nineteenth century, where

> writers of that period took a much greater responsibility for the condition of democracy and, indeed, their works were imaginative projects of the conflicts within the human heart which arose when the sacred principles of the Constitution and the Bill of Rights clashed with the practical exigencies of human greed and fear, hate and love.[22]

The vision of the novelist that Ellison offers here is that of moral and cultural leader.[23] However, that leadership is manifest in the imagination, not in the public persona. This set of observations allows him to critique the literary strategies of his contemporaries. His call for a return to the artistic consciousness that produced the literature in the nineteenth century insists that American writers see literature as a form of social inquiry. Because slavery (and its aftermath) is the counterpoint against which American citizenship must be juxtaposed, utilizing such works from the American literary canon as *Huckleberry Finn* and "Benito Cereno" allowed Ellison to propose a new paradigm of the novel. That paradigm envisioned the novel as an instrument capable of recording the transient and unstable nature of American citizenship, as a way of harnessing cultural resources in the service of making "citizenship" a verb rather than a noun.

Because a discursive category such as race reifies literary persona and leads to the creation of characters who do not reflect the fluidity of American life, Ellison's hero represents a conceptual move in the opposite direction. Thus he states in the Epilogue, "I condemn and affirm, say no and say yes, say yes and say no. . . . So I approach it through division. So I denounce and I defend and I hate and I love" (*Invisible Man,* 580). While this statement could be read as the narrator's inability to adopt a political stance, such a conclusion would be misguided. The narrator articulates the simultaneity of chaos and civilization. His "escape" is likewise a leap into disorder, and the "hole" becomes a space of inquiry, a site of investigation. One can conclude, then, that it is instability that enables, rather than hinders, the practice of democracy.

This investigation is made possible because the narrator sees the trap of ideology, of static positioning. However, the notion that American citizenship is an unstable enterprise couched in contradiction is interpreted as the failure of the democratic project. The American dilemma, as Ellison sees it, is to recast this instability as a sign that the democratic project is an experiment yet unfinished. This thinking undergirds his assertion that "America remains an undiscovered country." In his acceptance speech for the National Book Award, Ellison posits his efforts in *Invisible Man* as a break from literary convention. As rebel and innovator, he saw the need to create a prose style that would reflect not only certain issues of literary style, but also the wider issues inherent in the search for a national identity. To that end, Ellison's critical project called attention to the relationship between literary style and cultural wastefulness.

Consider, then, this survey of novelistic approaches to language, style, and structure:

I became gradually aware that the forms of so many of the works which impressed me were too restricted to contain the experience which I knew. The diversity of American life with extreme fluidity and openness seemed too vital and alive to be caught for more than the briefest instant in the tight well-made Jamesian novel which was, for all its artistic perfection, too concerned with good manners and stable areas. Nor could I safely use the forms of the "hard-boiled" novel, with its dedication to physical violence, social cynicism, and understatement. Understatement depends, after all, upon commonly held assumptions and my minority status rendered such assumptions questionable. ("Brave Words," 103)

The clearest references in this passage are to Henry James and Ernest Hemingway. But there is a less explicit reference to Richard Wright as well. While it is clear that Ellison values the literary contributions of all three writers, none fit his purposes. What is most striking about the passage above, however, is that Ellison characterizes American fiction as an instrument that fails to take full advantage of the resources available. None of the writers to which Ellison refers put forth coherent models of American culture; indeed, they chose literary strategies that avoided an engagement with the complexity of American life. What he saw as signs of a nation that had not completed the task of formulating an identity were for many of his contemporaries reasons to be cynical and pessimistic. Hemingway's and Wright's failure to couple an experimental posture with the "personal responsibility for democracy," meant "that something vital had gone out of American fiction after Mark Twain."

What makes this an important consideration is exemplified in Hemingway's belief that "all modern American fiction" emanated from Twain's *Huckleberry Finn.*[24] However, if we look at two of Hemingway's short stories, "The Battler" and "The Killers," fictions that include black characters, a concern arises as to the roles the characters play. In her insightful study of American literary depictions of Africanism, Toni Morrison observes that Hemingway's black characters, "articulate the narrator's doom and gainsay the protagonist-narrator's construction of himself."[25] Thus, in the former story, Hemingway creates the character of Bugs, the companion of Ad Francis, a former boxing champion prone to violent outrage. When Nick Adams, the story's hero, is threatened by the boxer, Bugs hits Ad over the head with a blackjack, stunning the fighter long enough for Nick to leave their camp. Before he leaves, Bugs tells him the story of how he came to be Ad Francis's companion. "I met him in jail," he says, noting that he was "in for cutting a man."[26] After the two are released from jail, they take up traveling around the country. Enjoying his new-found lifestyle, Bugs states, "He [Ad] thinks I'm crazy and I don't mind. I like to be with him and I like seeing the country and I don't have to commit no larceny to do it. I like living like a gentleman" ("The Battler," 137).

What is striking about this story is its recapitulation of the relationship between Huck and Jim. In this instance, however, what begins as a symbiosis in Twain becomes in Hemingway's revision a parasitic relation: Francis is the lens that allows Bugs "to see the country." But on this picaresque journey, he is outside, marginal. This is evidenced by Hemingway's refusal to provide Bugs with a story of his own, a deeper set of motivations. His function in the story is to provide Nick Adams with the information to explain his presence, a narrative embedded in Ad Francis's story. Thus Bugs is a caricature, made interesting only because Ad Francis's insanity gives credence to his existence. What binds him finally to Ad is not their affinity, a mutually recognized humanity. Their mutual terrain is achieved through violence; indeed, their act of lighting out for the territory is an instance where mobility embraces violence. The cycle of violence that entraps Ad and Bugs signals Hemingway's literary construction of purgatory: a white man hovering on the knife-edge of insanity, "rescued from the pit" again and again by a black man. This has to do with the manner in which Hemingway uses Ad's diminished state as the polished surface in which Nick Adams can see his own reflection; and Bugs's coupling of "unfailing politeness" and violence parodies the "good nigger," on one hand, but inevitably it points at Ad's loss of virility.

"The Battler" offers no less a caricature in Sam, the black cook in the diner in which the story is set. When two men come into the diner to kill Ole Andreson, they tie up Nick and Sam in the kitchen and wait for their victim to arrive. He fails to show up and they leave. Nick offers to go to the boarding house to warn Andreson, but Sam tells him to stay out of it. While I agree with Morrison's reading of Sam as one who comments "with derision on Nick's manhood," what I wish to call attention to here is the way Sam's presence in the story makes the reader aware of the boundaries of the story's moral field. ("The Battler," 83). Sam is most certainly outside the moral dilemma of the event and wants to remain so, as if his blackness marks off valuelessness. He gives voice to his unwillingness to take responsibility; "I don't want any more of that." While his statement alludes to the physical discomfort of being confined, it also intimates his lack of participatory energy. He is the canvas against which the white characters are projected. Like "The Battler," this story displays Hemingway's propensity to describe blacks as "niggers," as if the description provides a cultural shorthand. But though one could conjecture as to Hemingway's real intent—for example, that his use of the epithet is meant to suggest that he views racism, like the rest of American life, cynically—the characters do not offer evidence that they are more than props. Like Bugs, Sam's lack of personal history makes him the perfect surface on which to map moral agency. Neither Bugs nor Sam, as two of the very few black characters one finds in Hemingway, occupies the same "essential humanity" as Twain's Jim. As Ellison asserts, "Hemingway was alert only to Twain's technical discoveries—the flexible colloquial language, the sharp naturalism, the thematic potentialities of adolescence. Thus, what was for Twain a means to a moral end, became for Hemingway an end in itself."[27] Coupled with Wright's depiction of Bigger Thomas as "a near sub-human indictment of white oppression," and the fact that "Bigger Thomas possessed none of the finer qualities of Richard Wright," it seemed that black characters in American fiction were either comic props or pathological monsters. None of these figures were, in Ellison's view, recognizable. Both Hemingway's and Wright's fictions were examples of identification with defeat, rather than the democratic process.[28]

So, while Hemingway could be a literary model in terms of his ability to capture an event's visceral qualities, neither he nor Wright offered through "the hard-boiled stance and monosyllabic utterance" of naturalism anything more than a vision of American cultural austerity. Thus, in wanting to portray American life, Ellison saw that American speech had been relatively unexplored in the twentieth century:

> Our speech I found resounding with an alive language swirling with over three hundred years of American living; a mixture of the folk, the Biblical, the scientific and the political. Slangy in one stance, academic in another, loaded poetically with imagery in one moment, mathematically bare of imagery in the next. ("Brave Words," 104)

Ellison concluded that a "novel whose range was broader and deeper was needed." Language offered the site at which the experimental, improvisational nature of American democracy could be seen in its surest guise. Ellison's blueprint for the novel offered a site where the disparate elements of American reality could be brought together into a chaotic whole. Assessing those portions of literary innovation that had been discarded or ignored called him to reappraise the energizing paradigms of writers he had begun his career imitating and now would have to abandon. Reality, Ellison concluded, "was far more mysterious and uncertain, and more exciting, and still . . . more promising." When those aspects of American life were held up to his conceptual light, he realized that limitations of form called for an innovative posture, the invention of a novel that could

> express [the] American experience which has carried one back and forth and up and down the land, and across again the great river, from freight train to

Pullman car, from contact with slavery to contact with advanced scholarship, art, and science ("Brave Words, 104).

Achieving this form would essentially, "burst . . . the understated forms [of the modernist] novel asunder." This novel, as Ellison saw it, would be capable of rendering American experience more coherently than had the works of his predecessors, because it would employ resources previously thought to be useless. As an African American writer, he would be able to express the same concern with democracy and form as his nineteenth-century models, and at the same time use the novel to resituate the discussion, moving it away from static rhetoric into the more energizing realm of inquiry: democracy as question rather than answer.

But how was this to be achieved? And in the achievement was there the risk that African American experience (in all its diversity) would be trivialized or dismissed? What finally makes *Invisible Man* such a watershed event in American literary history was its insistence that American experience, when viewed through the ennobling lens of the blues, was one that could achieve—and sustain—symbolic affirmation. The conceptual break Ellison envisioned from twentieth-century American letters was one that required him to examine and actualize the blues idiom as a form of literary practice. As Albert Murray describes them, the blues move beyond sociological conclusions, which posit black victimization in its myriad forms. Rather than serving the purpose of avoidance, the blues idiom's intent is "to make human existence meaningful," an African American art form that could "acknowledge the essentially tenuous nature of all human existence."

Ellison's novel, like Zora Neale Hurston's *Their Eyes Were Watching God* and Langston Hughes's blues poems, was situated in a matrix that issued from those people Sterling A. Brown would have referred to as "the folk." But what *Invisible Man* actualizes is that the blues idiom, which had always served the purpose for African Americans of "sizing up the world . . . [as] a mode and medium of survival," could be viewed as an operative metaphor for American democratic practice. Hence its failures were merely indicators of the difficulties of making "a theory and a concept" into substance. The irresponsibility to which the narrator alludes in the Prologue is a conceptual inversion; it represents his awareness that it is "irresponsible" to attempt to see realistically, given the large numbers of people who wish to adhere to illusion. Thus Ellison wanted to portray, not only the failures of American democracy as it pertained to racial equality, but also the failure inherent in an unwillingness to confront the problem of national identity. Consider these remarks from *Going to the Territory:*

Being committed to optimism, serious novels have always been troublesome to Americans, precisely because of their involvement with our problems of identity. If they depict too much of reality, they frighten us by giving us a picture of society frozen at a point so far from our optimistic ideal (for in depiction there is a freezing as well as a discovery and a release of possibility) that we feel compelled to deny it. . . . Another way of putting it is that we are a people who, while desiring identity, have been reluctant to pay the cost of its achievement. We have been reluctant since we first suspected that we are fated to live up to our sacred commitments or die, and the Civil War was the form of that fateful knowledge. Thus we approach serious [fiction] with distrust until the moment comes when the passage of time makes it possible for us to ignore their moral cutting edge.[29]

Ellison demonstrates an understanding that is both a return to the energy exerted by nineteenth-century novelists in their depiction of the nation's "moral evasion," and an approach to metaphor that would resonate in twentieth-century experience. His use of the blues, and more specifically Louis Armstrong, is what makes his narrator's decision to align himself with the engineers of "American know-how" so poignant. For, as Albert Murray observes, Armstrong's gift as a cultural innovator lay, not in his "invention [of] the form but his assimilation, elaboration, extensions, and refinement of its elements."[30] Hence Ellison's hero chooses Edison, Ford, and Franklin because each bears the title of "inventor." An even more correct rendering of each man, particularly Edison and Ford, is that their achievements lay, not only in the invention of the light bulb and the automobile, but in the improvements that led, as Daniel Boorstin asserts, to the "democratization" of these products: they were successful in producing them cheaply enough for the masses to acquire them.[31] As "the touchstone for all who came after him," Armstrong becomes the model for the hero's inquiry because he configures the hole, not as an instrument of escape (the hole, as he states, is a space of "preparation") but rather as one of stylization. Moreover, Armstrong's achievements as a musician are raised to the level of democratic inquiry: that the hero likes Armstrong "because he's made poetry out of being invisible" is also the assertion that, for all his public clowning, what came out of his trumpet was deadly serious.[32] It is there where the hero embraces stylization and becomes a blues-idiom dancer; his approach to identity is analogous to Armstrong's approach to the trumpet:

The blues-idiom like the solo instrumentalist turns disjunctures into continuities. He is not disconcerted by intrusions, lapses, shifts in rhythm, intensification of tempo, for instance; but is inspired by them to higher and richer levels of improvisation. As a matter of fact (and as the colloquial sense of the word suggests) the "break" in the blues idiom provides the dancer his greatest opportunity—which, at the same time, is also his most heroic challenge and his moment of greatest jeopardy.[33]

Many issues are harnessed and put to work here: the creative risks inherent in Ellison's artistic choices, the symbolic agency imbedded in the hero's need to tell his tale, the attempt to associate art-making with innovation, the decision to use the metaphorization of experience as the ground for action, and finally the novel's capitulation of democracy as both risk and question. What Murray (and also Ellison in his ruminations on the blues) suggests is that the blues offers an instance where negative happenstance occurs with such frequency it becomes, finally, a site of creativity.[34] Ellison realized that this occasioned storytelling, and the work Ellison began in his novel, to frame the "complex fate" of American identity continues. Like Armstrong, he improvises on notions of African American citizenship: he did not articulate the original fact of American democracy, but he has attempted to capture African American improvisation on that fact, placing American experiences at-large inside the boundaries of mystery and the incomplete. In this respect, one can look at *Invisible Man* as a novel that looks both backward as revisionist tale and forward as blueprint.

3

The question that must now occupy our critical attention is whether writers following in Ellison's wake have improvised on his authorial posture. Ellison's novel called attention to the manner in which an African American presence was a legible presence ignored, and thus cited the need to recognize African American experience as a legitimate portion of all American (including white American) experience. When African Americans spoke they "spoke for" their white counterparts as well. Are there writers who have been as concerned with rendering the question of American citizenship, whose work likewise attempts to "speak for" a multiplicity of sensibilities? Moreover, are there writers who have tried to revise Ellison's ideas? What I am gesturing toward, of course, is the notion of literary kinship. And by kinship I do not mean to suggest that writers identified as "kin" are engaged in the act of merely parroting their predecessors. Rather, influence can occur across generational lines; one might find the faintest echo of one writer's ideas in the works of another, or one might find writers holding themselves aloof from any association with other writers (remember here Ellison's response to the Forrest observation). However, kinship, or tradition, is a useful critical tool, one that Robert Stepto suggests is finally best discerned by looking at the works of one writer in relation to another:

An author's place in tradition depends on how he reveals that tradition. It is not simply a matter of when his works were published but also how they illuminate—and in some cases honor—what has come before and anticipate what will follow. In African-American literature particularly the idea of a tradition involves certain questions about the author's posture not only among his fellow writers but also within a larger artistic continuum.[35]

Stepto's observations are necessary if we are to ruminate on the relationship between younger writers, in this instance Ernest Gaines and James Alan McPherson, and Ralph Ellison. As per Stepto's observation, there are numerous moments in the fiction of the former writers where Ellison's work is the call to which they respond. Both men intimate that American identity politics achieve coherence through new forms of recognition that eschew denial. Moving forward from this posture, Gaines and McPherson have been concerned with acts of telling and reading. Moreover, as writers who originate in geographical settings where segregation was a conventional mode, the younger writers share a kinship with Ellison in that they, too, demonstrate a ritualistic political sensibility that explicates rituals of race in terms of strategies of negotiation and inquiry.

Let me assert, however, that neither Gaines nor McPherson is engaged in any form of impersonation. McPherson's and Gaines's fictions are most certainly capable of standing on their own merits. Because of this, the literary kinship I have proposed does not represent a random association, but a deeper impulse which proceeds from a profound set of beliefs that crystallize around issues of belonging, resourcefulness, and innovation. In this sense, what allows us to locate Gaines and McPherson in Ellison's orbit are their respective approaches to the identity politics addressed in *Invisible Man.* Gaines's fiction is driven by its strong sense of place, its use of ritual sites. But if this is so, what makes these sites significant is Gaines's deep investment in an oral tradition in which people's lives are rendered through the act of telling stories. The oral narratives Gaines's narrators tell and retell are necessary if one is to begin to identify the connective forces of a community. Hence Gaines captures storytelling as it unfolds within the web of communal activity. This is not, in itself, a revelation. What makes it significant is that storytelling works toward a deeper purpose: the quarters, as Gaines depicts them, are most often places where to talk about racial injustice is to risk one's life. Telling stories, as Gaines asserts, has a great deal to do with intervening on conspiratorial, exclusive forms of history, though the act of storytelling is often dismissed as no more than an instance of quaint entertainment. But as Gaines's narrators utilize it, storytelling ultimately has a great deal to do with how communities are formed and sustained, a process that occurs across barriers of race. And ambivalent though they may be, failure to tell their stories leads to a far worse fate than breaking silence. For despite, or perhaps because of, its complex racial politics and intermingled cultural streams, Louisiana is a resonant microcosm on which to focus a discussion on African American citizenship. This is a place where conspiracy and intimacy exist in an almost indistinguishable relationship, and it is the process of living with the contradictions that finally allows the individual to proceed.

Certainly there are echoes of Ellison here, especially when he observes that the moral predicament of the United States rests on the nexus formed by literature and what he refers to as the Sacred Documents: for example, the Declaration of Independence, the Bill of Rights, and the Constitution. Because the South represents a setting where these documents were put to the most strenuous of trials, Gaines's attempts to portray life in Louisiana, his concern with portraying the dignity and moral resiliency of its African American inhabitants, needs to be seen within a national context. This is particularly so in light of Ellison's assertion that "[the Sacred Documents] form the ground of assumptions upon which our social values rest; they inform our language and our conduct with public meaning, and they provide the broadest frame of reference for our most private dramas."[36] The implication here is that Gaines's storytellers render stories that, however esoteric, dramatize the question of American identity (and within that, of course, African American citizenship). To address issues of community via the use of symbolic sites and the acts of storytelling that give them credence, then, is simultaneously to address modes of belonging, even under the guise of dissent. Gaines recognizes the manner in which the national literature has been shaped by this conflation of place and voice when he notes:

> I think a writer writes about what he is part of. I think he has to. I don't know that he could do it if he does not have this kind of background. I don't know that Faulkner could have written what he wrote if he had not come from that kind of background, where people squatted around the stores or the courthouse square. I don't know if Twain could have done it had he not been part of that traditional Mississippi River storytelling crowd. . . . And I don't know if you can do the same thing if you don't have that kind of tradition.[37]

It is this notion of writers writing about what they are "part of" that most interests me here. For in talking about how symbolic spaces provide the basis for acting out community, Gaines also refers to the way his own fiction resonates as part of a larger imperative: the formulation of a coherent sense of national identity.

An example can be found in Gaines's short story, "Three Men." In jail for killing a man, Procter Lewis is placed in a cell where he is faced with a choice: he can be bonded out of jail by Roger Medlow, the owner of the plantation where he lives, or he can serve his time in the penitentiary. He turns himself in to the sheriff to wait to be bonded out. Procter waits along with two other men, Munford and Hattie, for his uncle to get in contact with Medlow. He has been bonded out once before, and thus he understands neither the nature of confinement, nor what it means to be freed by Medlow.[38]

What he fails to discern is that, in the South, African American lives lack value within the Jim Crow legal system and thus they are not protected under the same laws that protect whites. What is legally enforced is their otherness. It is Munford who gives voice to the inherent inequities to be found within this matrix. Like Procter, Munford began his life by being bonded out after killing a man, "Been going in and out of these jails here, I don't know how long . . . forty, fifty years" ("Three Men," 137). It has taken him nearly his entire life to understand his predicament and he concludes:

> They need me to prove they human—just like they need that thing (Hattie) over there. They need us. Because without us, they don't know what they is—they don't know what they is out there. With us around, they can see us and know what they ain't. They ain't us. ("Three Men," *Bloodline*, 137–38)

Munford elucidates the philosophical foundations of Jim Crow: white humanity achieves meaning at the expense of African American humanity.[39] What he suggests is that Jim Crow is a parasitic relation, where white humanity is sustained by its repeated acts of negation. Munford portrays this as an illusion of surfaces:

> They think they men. They think they men 'cause they got me and him in here who ain't men. But I got news for them—cut them open; go 'head and cut one open—you see if you don't find Munford Bazille or Hattie Brown. Not a man one of them. 'Cause face don't make a man—black or white. Face don't make him and fucking don't make him and fighting don't make—neither killing. None of this prove you a man. 'Cause animals can fuck, can kill, can fight—you know that? (138)

Munford reconfigures the moral degradation in blackface that sustains Jim Crow. But what I also wish to point out here is that Gaines implies that "whiteness" as a category is composed beneath its surface of African elements. While those elements are denied, ignored, and devalued, we see Gaines recapitulating Ellison's idea of "speaking for" the Other. He proposes an intertextuality that can only be discerned by radical intervention ("go 'head cut one open") into a seemingly univocal text.

However, because the concept of race locates meaning at the level of surfaces, it annihilates the impulse to examine moral substance and integrity more deeply.[40] Munford's speech decodes the shorthand of race by which morality is inscribed and codified on the surface, held in place by confounding all attempts to erase or penetrate that inscription. The only solution, in Munford's view, is to go into hibernation.

While he knows that his own life is locked into a cycle of violence which functions in the service of white men, Munford knows Procter has yet another opportunity to recover his selfhood. While the world outside jail wages numerous assaults on selfhood, hibernation (in the form of going to prison) offers an opportunity to achieve a new integrity. Like Ellison's hole and Dostoevsky's Underground (we can include Wright's "underground man" as well), Procter's prison becomes a performance space; it offers him the opportunity to take responsibility for the presentation of self. In light of this, consider Munford's observations:

> But you don't go to the pen for the nigger you killed. Not for him—he ain't worth it. They told you from the cradle—a nigger ain't worth a good grey mule. Don't mention a white mule: fifty niggers ain't worth a good white mule. So you don't go to the pen for killing the nigger, you go for yourself. You go to sweat out all the crud you got in your system. You go saying... "I want to be a man... For once in my life I will be a man." (141)

What is striking about this passage is that Gaines uses Munford as the voice of anomaly. In order to understand his plight, Procter needs Munford to deconstruct the idea of freedom. The convention, as he understands it upon his arrival in the jail cell, is physical mobility's equivalence to freedom. But, as Munford makes clear, that mobility is based on several assumptions, the first being that African American lives have less value than white ones. Moreover, it assumes the only responsibility black men can demonstrate is to white men, not to one another, not even to themselves. Because so many black men fail in this endeavor, Munford suggests, whites use this failure to fuel a paradigm of difference (difference being synonymous with superiority).

What finally makes the character of Munford such a brilliant stroke is that he represents the type of anomaly to be found in Ellison's characterizations of Trueblood and of the Vet at the Golden Day. As Gaines portrays it, confinement can be a form of freedom if that confinement is entered into on one's own terms. Let me make clear, however, that while Munford is the necessary element in Procter's maturation, he also represents the anomaly necessary to enact a paradigm shift. He recognizes how he comes to be entrapped in the cycle of violence and drunkenness that lead to his perpetual incarceration, but he has not worked out a strategy which would break this cycle. The solution he proposes for Procter is one he, himself, has only partially considered. But we must, here, pay attention to the name "Procter," and conjecture as to why Gaines chooses such a name. The word "proctor" is used to describe anyone in a supervisory position, particularly one who oversees an examination or test. Procter's importance rests on his ability to carry out the experiment Munford has proposed: that the task of valuing other lives begins with valuing one's own life. What I would suggest, then, is that seen within the context of a Jim Crow system, the idea of self-valuation becomes a radical gesture.

But we need also to pay attention to Gaines's allegorical message here. This story celebrates the paradigm that underscores African American strategies in the Civil Rights Movement. Procter's decision to stay in jail and to accept a prison term for murder, is, in an ironic turn, an act of civil disobedience. This is important because the concept of "disobedience," as Gaines's story proposes it, rests on the ability to reverse societal polarities. Procter decides to stay in jail because Munford's counsel decodes—and then, recodes—African American strategies of self-valuation. What makes this story such a powerful allegory for the Civil Rights moment is that, once protest acquires a basis in the blues, where "impromptu heroism" becomes regarded as "normal procedure,"[41] the assumption that a just cause is worth imprisonment is in line with an innovative posture. Like Ellison's Brother Tarp, whose chain link says "yes and no," and contains "a heap of signifying," Gaines's Procter signals the necessity of reclaiming symbolic territory; transforming the jail cell into a site of resistance and resilience is an act of reclamation. What is most important in a comparison to Ellison is Gaines's enactment of African American humanity on ritualistic grounds. Like Ellison's hole, the jail cell becomes a site of self-realization. Though the story does not contain overt resistance and its indictment of the "legal system" is merely implicit, what Gaines suggests here is that a spiritual posture needs to be assumed before resistance can take place.

Though he uses the conventional category of "manhood" to describe this space, it can just as easily be thought of as a construct where resistance and consciousness come together to create a self-realized individual. Munford has reached a high level of lucidity with regard to his situation. However, he lacks the ability to resist its force. Hattie, whose homosexuality is dismissed by Munford as the sign of failed manhood, is perhaps best understood as the resistant posture Procter needs to assume. For Hattie represents the kind of tenderness and compassion men must demonstrate to create a new kind of community. Indeed, Munford's problems rest on his inability to enact compassion, while Hattie's resistant posture—for example, his decision to represent an alternative form of masculinity—lacks the self-consciousness necessary for him to articulate a coherent critique of the system that confines black men.[42] He can recognize and sympathize with individual forms of suffering, he can even resist Munford's advances, but he does not appear willing to assert himself as a figure who resists the system's corruption (here, a system that jails a person because of who he is). Though Gaines's story offers us a narrator who reaches a new level of self-awareness, this self-awareness allows him to incorporate aspects of what must be considered as less successful paradigms into a more resistant, reflective posture. And while I would not assert that "Three Men" is intended as a revision of Ellison's novel, what I would argue is that Gaines clearly resituates Ellisonian hibernation as a way of successfully negotiating, and thus negating, a highly charged symbolic site in Southern race ritual. There is also, through the use of Munford and Hattie as paradigms of masculine behavior, the same kind of move Ellison enacts in the Golden Day section of *Invisible Man,* where men like the Vet are vehicles of insight whose messages require new forms of literacy to decode them.[43] But perhaps most dramatic is Gaines's decision to invest Procter with a mixture of ambivalence and improvisatory energy reminiscent of Ellison's hero (the story ends with Procter's uncertainty about his ability to survive prison and his conclusion, "I don't know, I thought to myself, I'll just have to wait and see."

We see this use of place repeated in Gaines's fiction, from his first novel, *Catherine Carmier,* to his latest novel, *A Lesson Before Dying,* where he reprises the jail cell as a site of symbolic action and, in ways reminiscent of Ellison, uses writing to explicate the act of self-discovery that Jefferson, the novel's hero, experiences there. Thus the novel turns on the interaction between Grant and Jefferson who, as black men battered by the vagaries of segregation, find a way to engage in a dialogue that transforms them from a disillusioned school teacher and a nearly illiterate young man falsely accused of murder into men whose brief symbiosis empowers them both. Though Jefferson's death is certain, Grant's task—which becomes Jefferson's legacy—is to impart some of himself, to demonstrate to Jefferson a way to improvise upon a negative situation till he discovers dignity and purpose. Gaines's preoccupation with his character's dignity is a gesture toward another branch on his literary family tree, namely Ernest Hemingway. As did Ellison, Gaines claims Hemingway as an ancestor. He notes:

> I admire Hemingway because of this grace under pressure thing which I think is more accurate of the black man in this country than the white man. Hemingway, without his knowing it, without a lot of younger blacks knowing it, was writing as much about Joe Louis or Jackie Robinson as he was about any white

man. The bull ring, the fight, the war, blacks do this sort of thing all the time, daily. Not all of them come out gracefully under pressure, but many of them do, especially those who accomplish anything.[44]

This sensibility informs all of the characters in the Gaines canon. As I will discuss in greater detail in the chapters to follow, his characters—both black and white—signal his adherence to a poetics of opposition. His fiction explores the conflagration that results when opposing ideas come into contact. Rather than dramatizing a violent explosion embodying radical change, Gaines's fiction depicts a slower reaction, one that is no less disruptive, largely because the participants continue to adhere to conventions, despite the pervasive nature of the changes taking place. Thus his characters do not represent the futility of change as much as the ambivalence that accompanies it. Gaines's characters often find solace in the familiar, they know that their lives are driven more by that which they can improvise upon than that which they can plan.

It is this improvisational quality of American culture that forms the major concerns in James Alan McPherson's fiction. Unlike Gaines, whose fiction is so deeply rooted in a geographical circumstance, McPherson's fiction is less driven by geography than it is by the *ideology* of place, the nexus of consciousness and geography. Which is to say that his fiction is often at its most insightful when he is able to capture the absurdities to be found in postures of regional identity. Thus one does not find McPherson creating images of physical landscapes or descriptions of rooms merely for their own sake. Rather, his fiction is oriented toward a rendering of the emotional and psychological significance of physical place as a key to his character's respective states of mind. Thus, physical landscape is always a layer of reality that must be stripped away to reveal its power source. Indeed, one often finds that McPherson's fiction is as concerned with the proverbial fish out of water fighting to make sense of his or her surroundings as he is with what happens when opposites exert gravitational pull, one upon the other.

This is not to suggest that McPherson displays a lack of concern for characters who revel in telling stories. The oral tradition is, indeed, central to his fiction; characters tell stories characterized by disjointedness or just plain wackiness. But the other element that is so important to the fiction is the act of reading. By "reading" I refer not only to instances of simple literacy but also to those moments when characters fail either because they lack tribal literacy—or because they rely too heavily upon it. Indeed, McPherson's fiction suggests that "tribal literacy" is simultaneously America's boon and curse. For while the adherence to race as a viable category of description and practical shorthand for social motivation continues to shape American experience, we find that McPherson sets out to embody Ellison's observation that all Americans share a sensibility that is grounded in certain forms of conduct ("Society, Morality, and the Novel," 249). Clearly, McPherson moves from Gaines's more implicit wranglings with the question of democracy into a realm where to delight in its contradictions is likewise to suggest its experimental, inconclusive nature. Thus, Ellison's discussion regarding the way fiction imitates democracy offers an apt description of the latter's fictional project:

> Indeed, these assumptions [about human possibility] have been questioned and resisted from the very beginning, for man cannot simply say, "Let us have liberty and justice and equality for all," and have it; and a democracy more than any other system is always pregnant with its contradiction. ("Society, Morality, and the Novel," 249)

Thus "democracy" as McPherson attempts to portray it in his fiction is not noun but verb. Like Gaines, who writes out of a profound sense that (were he to articulate it in such explicit terms) his audience crosses racial and generational lines, McPherson, too, exhibits an impulse toward the indissoluble aspects of American identity. He carries the argument toward its logical conclusion when, in his essay entitled "On Becoming an American Writer," he discusses his realization that many of his friendships were the epitome of contradiction:

> Some of these people and their values were called "black" and some were called "white," and I learned very quickly that all of us tend to wall ourselves off from experiences different from our own by assigning to these terms greater significance than they should have. Moreover, I found that trying to maintain friendships with, say, a politically conservative white Texan, a liberal-to-radical classmate of Scottish-Italian background, my oldest black friends, and even members of my own family introduced psychological contradictions that became tense and painful as the political climate shifted.[45]

Then, in a move that takes Ellison's observations and relocates them in personal experience, McPherson suggests that the combative nature of democratic practice takes up residence within his own mind and body, resonating inside all his relationships until he is forced to find a new way to contain the tangle of contradiction. Thus he concludes:

> There were no contracts covering such friendships and such feelings, and in order to keep the friends and maintain the feelings I had to force myself to find a basis other than race on which such contradictory urgings could be synthesized. I discovered that I had to find, first of all, an identity as a writer, and then I had to express what I knew or felt in such a way that I could make something whole out of a necessarily fragmented experience. ("On Becoming an American Writer," 56)

As a law student at Harvard, McPherson began to conceptualize what he refers to as a "model of identity." He writes, "I began to play with the idea that the Fourteenth Amendment was not a legislative instrument devised to give former slaves legal equality with other Americans. . . . I saw that through the protean uses made of the Fourteenth Amendment, in the gradual elaboration of basic rights to be protected by federal authority, an outline of something much more complex than 'black' and 'white' had been begun" ("On Becoming an American Writer," 57). This is an important move, one as much concerned with a coherent vision of American identity as that outlined by Ellison in "Brave Words for a Startling Occasion." It carries Ellison's discussion into the realm of citizenship, where (using the legal brief Albion Tourgee argued during the *Plessy v. Ferguson* trial before the Supreme Court) he concludes that the Fourteenth Amendment created a new paradigm of citizenship, one that called for "each United States citizen . . . to approximate the ideals of the nation, be on at least conversant terms with all its diversity, carry the mainstream of the culture inside himself."[46] Thus, McPherson concludes, "As an American, by trying to wear these clothes he would be a synthesis of high and low, black and white, city and country, provincial and universal. If he could live with these contradictions, he would be simply a representative American" (57).

McPherson's narrators often dramatize the "great . . . mistakes" involved in the attempt to create an alternative model of identity. Here, the "mainstream" is reconfigured from a racial construct to a cultural one that crosses racial and caste lines. To use Michael S. Harper's phrase, McPherson's fiction often "puts the reader to work."[47] Unlike Gaines's narrators, whose authority as tellers issues from the fact that, because of race rituals, telling stories places them under great peril as they enter the realm of transgressive speech, McPherson's narratives are characterized by speech that is oddly conventional. But this means it is often a mistake to identify too strongly with McPherson's narrators. One could easily read the stories as mere framed narratives were it not for the fact that details appear that provide clues that the narratives are contaminated by mixed intentions.

In McPherson's work, this takes the form of narrators who are, themselves, totally unreliable sources of veracity. *Hue and Cry* and *Elbow Room* contain stories like "The Story of a Dead Man," "The Story of a Scar," "A New Place," "A Loaf of Bread," "Problems of Art," and "A Sense of Story," where McPherson uses narrative personas who enact instances of failed literacy. Viewed as part of a project meant to portray an American culture that has yet to be fully realized, these faulty narrators demonstrate that "American identity" is as much the result of failures of literacy and the sign of incompetence and unwillingness as it is the fruit of insight and cooperation. Embracing a ritualistic identity politics, McPherson's fiction depicts the manner in which secular identity politics are doomed to fail. However, as "The Story of a Dead Man" suggests, what is more important in McPherson's fiction is for the reader to discern the process by which narrators come to voice, the assumptions that inform those voices. The reader's task is one of watching McPherson's narrators reassemble the world. What makes the stories I have cited above so poignant is that each involves instances where the narrators fail because they either jumble, ignore, or lose altogether the necessary elements of complexity.

For example, in "Widows and Orphans," McPherson proffers a story that, on its face, is merely a tale of unrequited love; a man encounters a former lover and finds his desire rekindled. However, this masks a deeper, more complex fiction laden with postmodern overtones. Set in Los Angeles (Watts, to be exact), the story dramatizes the act of lighting out for the territory; but this "frontier spirit" gives way to the more fearful realization that one arrives there only to find darkness, a situation in which, as Irving Howe once observed, its characters cannot "dream themselves out of the shapeless nightmare of California."[48]

The story's protagonist, Louis Clayton, is black and Southern born. But this fact is juxtaposed against the sensibility to be found at a formal banquet he attends in honor of Clair, his former lover. While Ellison's hero enjoyed the luxury of 1,369 light bulbs, all of which signaled his achievement of a transcendent posture and situated him as the source of intertextuality, the only light available to Louis Clayton is that which powers cinematic illusion. In a situation where the "lower frequencies" can only be accessed via a script from some forgotten B-movie, Louis's journey is characterized by a familiarity he cannot name. And because he cannot utilize the resources from his Southern background, or perhaps because he lacks the ability to make use of anything else, film is the only way to "descend" into the depths. Louis looks around him and sees the following:

> To his left, several tables away, sat a thin man, whose tight-pressed mouth and steady-eyed expression of understated strength reminded [him] of Gregory Peck. Across the room, at a table near the glass wall, he watched a plump little brown woman, whose bulging eyes and nervously waving cigarette, while she talked, recalled to his mind the abysmally lonely intensity of Bette Davis.[49]

and glimpses further

> a man whose face expressed the corruption-comfortable look and the energetic meanness of Edward G. Robinson. . . . He saw Marlon Brando's full cheeks, set mouth, and unabashed eyes. He was convinced it was Brando as he looked in

his prime. But just then the man laughed, and he heard the irrepressible rhythms of the barbershop. Then Louis remembered that this was only a banquet honoring the achievements of the Progressive Association of Greater Watts. *Everyone in the room had accepted and defined himself in terms of caste distinction. They were all black, except for the guest speaker and his wife seated at the head table.* ("Widows," 164; emphasis mine)

What makes this story so important to the discussion is McPherson's insistence that the cultural identity—at least as Louis conceptualizes it—of the African Americans at the banquet is generated as much by the influence of Hollywood as it is by their racial identification. Though they choose to identify merely with their racial status, McPherson suggests that Louis, as spectator, sees much more than race at work in the self-presentation of the audience. In a room where he lacks the outward manifestations of a Los Angeles persona (in the words of one character, he "dresses funny"), Louis can only gain his bearings by seeing the encounter as scripted and its participants as mirror images of film personalities. This begs the question, are the individuals who look like film stars acting out roles, or is Louis manufacturing their resemblance? Certainly, that the majority of them are black does not erase their affinity for visibility. The best evidence of this is Louis's former lover, Clair. Though he remembers her as "completely self-sustained," a person whose "toughness . . . test[s] relentlessly the toughness of others," the persona she constructs is one so finely controlled that, on receiving a civic award, she can feign love and appreciation for the mother she has often mistreated. A consummate politician, Clair has mastered her life within the space of public spectacle. Though she and Louis have been intimate, the story ends with Clair introducing him as her "former teacher," a signal that she has neatly compartmentalized his contribution to her life. But as Louis looks on Clair, he realizes that he, too, is trapped at the level of mythic encounter: his desire for Clair is heightened by her inaccessibility; he is attracted to the illusion she presents, even as he remembers the woman it obscures.

This story suggests that McPherson's ancestral ties to Ellison are best understood in the context of the former's insistence that, just as race functions as a point of separation, other cultural manifestations—especially those generated by mass culture—tie Americans into a coherent whole. While one could most certainly read "Widows and Orphans" as a postmodern tale chronicling the disorienting effects of a culture whose system of referentiality is foregrounded in the mass media, let me propose that McPherson's first priority is to work out a way of looking at American cultural dynamics in terms other than racial ones. I would myself assert that this story has very serious implications, offering as it does such a cynical critique of mass culture.

However, I would also argue that the story's main impulse is oriented toward the assertion that American identity, by virtue of mass culture, has been rendered so fluid, so permeable, that men like Louis Clayton (who is born in Baxter, North Carolina and leaves there to become a college professor in Chicago, who writes "bawdy poems, in the Elizabethan style, to the broad and truant wife of a departmental colleague" while they are in bed) can throw off their Southern identities and create new ones. Indeed, the process Louis endures is relatively painless; "It had seemed to him an easy process," McPherson writes, "much like shedding old skins" ("Widows," 172).

We must remember Louis's background, for it is there that we can locate the past in the form of racial and cultural memory mediated by what he refers to as "old world rules." The story's post-sixties setting argues for an identity politics that is purely experimental and noncontractual. As McPherson observes, "Old identities were thrown off, of necessity, but there were not many new ones of a positive nature to be assumed." Louis's rootlessness is indicative of a culture whose rules are so flexible that the quest for familiarity becomes truncated. No longer do individuals look to the familial past for answers about who they are; they merely create a new persona incorporating as much of the past as they can safely assimilate into these disposable narratives without jeopardizing the opportunity for upward mobility.

If, as Sir Henry Maine observes, society's progress is from "status to contract,"[50] the unkindness Clair displays toward Louis suggests that she values the former over the latter. Indeed, the story presents them as polar opposites: Clair's life is oriented toward the acquisition of status and thus it is a life stripped clean of the encumbrances of the past; Louis, though he embraces a new life as a Southerner transplanted in Chicago, is at heart a romantic, which means he sustains a longing for the past when contracts were more readily established. At first ambivalent about such a contract during their romance, Clair finally refuses such an arrangement altogether.

These conflicting views are, allegorically speaking, a pervasive dilemma within the American democratic project. Clair Richards and Louis Clayton are metaphors for the dilemma that is American identity: the ancestral past, for both, is rendered inert, a public spectacle that is either quaint, reduced to a few words at a testimonial, or immobile, incapable of moving beyond the limitations of caste and class. Further, they represent the cost of identity; the process of establishing identities distant from their respective pasts leaves them unmoored to any reliable tradition. And yet, their respective successes indicate the shift in the terms upon which identity are established: a situation which both liberates them and locks them into a purely experimental mode.

And yet, for all its bleakness, McPherson's story is not without optimism. For it also asserts that what is divisive, what seems to stand as irreconcilable difference, pales in comparison to the task the nation faces as it tries to make itself whole. When Louis announces to Clair's mother that "These mixed marriages don't always work out," he refers to the difficulties pertaining to the act of reconciling the viewpoints that stem from African American Southern experience with its contractual condition and those borne of experiences outside the South, which McPherson suggests are intimately tied to the acquisition of status. Because of this, the story revoices Ellison's assertion that "America remains an undiscovered country," an experiment far from conclusion. This is not a reason for resignation, for if we return to the paragraph from which the assertion above originates, we find that Ellison concludes, "We're only a partially achieved nation, and I think this is good because it gives the writer of fiction a role beyond that of entertainer."[51]

As we will see in the chapters that follow, neither McPherson nor Gaines chooses the role of entertainer. Rather, in ways that I plan to elaborate upon below, I find them to be deeply interested in performing fictions that engage the notion of a usable present. If, as Dell Hymes has asserted, a performer is anyone who takes responsibility for presentation to an audience,[52] what we find is that acts of telling and reading are necessary ingredients in the enactment of citizenship. And what renders them so necessary is that they point, implicitly, to the transformative and the communal. Emulating Ford, Edison, and Franklin, I suggest that Gaines and McPherson, like Ellison, are "thinker-tinkers," and what they attempt to invent for public use is a viable notion of our process of becoming. And so, despite the persistence of the nation's shameful racial dramas, as portrayed by Gaines and McPherson even within the context of brutality and failure there is a collective thread to be discerned and utilized.

Chapter 2

The Possible in Things Unwritten: Kinship and Innovation in the Fictions of Ellison, Gaines, and McPherson

> Our mode is our jam session
> of tradition,
> past in this present moment
> articulated, blown through
> with endurance . . .
>
> —Michael S. Harper, "Corrected Review"

1

In an interview with Marcia Gaudet and Carl Wooten, Ernest J. Gaines asserts with great finality, "No black writer had influence on me."[1] Moreover, in his essay "On Becoming an American Writer," James Alan McPherson, while discussing his Pulitzer Prize-winning collection of short stories, *Elbow Room,* notes that his first intention was to discover his identity as a writer, a project that forced him to "find a basis other than race" to synthesize his experiences as an American, to "make something whole out of a necessarily fragmented experience."[2] Both writers disconnect their artistic projects from the enactment of African American identity. However, as Keith Byerman has pointed out, this seemingly abrupt act of distancing themselves from African American literary tradition is finally itself part of the tradition:

> Each generation of African-American writers seems to need to create a space for itself by claiming kin to no black predecessor or by citing the influence of European and white American artists, such as Joyce, Hemingway, or Turgenev. By defining their background in such a way, Gaines and McPherson, as well as

others, can use a variety of techniques to render African-American experience without being seen as limited to a particular racial tradition.[3]

Byerman observes that writing by African American men follows a paradigm that calls for them to view their work as a distinct rupture from the preceding literary moment. This act of negating the influence of earlier African American writers, or de-emphasizing the importance of race to literary enterprise altogether, likewise functions as affirmation. These writers intimate their connection to tradition as innovators as they dissociate themselves from its more confining aspects.

Like science, literary practice responds to the call of innovation, and writers, no less than scientists, are judged on their ability to articulate further the substance of literary innovation. In light of Ralph Ellison's achievement in *Invisible Man,* it is not difficult to understand the efficacy of Gaines's and McPherson's denial of African American influences.[4] Indeed, there is a scene in Ellison's novel that resonates in the aesthetics of both. As the novel's protagonist prepares to head North to seek his destiny, he encounters one of the "insane" black veterans from the Golden Day, who tells him,

Now is the time for offering fatherly advice . . . but I'll have to spare you that—since I'm nobody's father except my own. Perhaps that's the advice to give you: Be your own father, young man. And remember the world is possibility if only you'll discover it.[5]

The young protagonist is unable to decode Vet's underlying message, lacking the experience necessary to decipher its hidden meaning as a formula for self-awareness and integrity. In making a reference to the need for an innovative approach to selfhood, he warns the narrator to avoid making others the sign of his destiny, the pivots on which his success will turn. Perhaps most important, however, is his attempt to make the hero aware of his own resources. What lies beyond this scene's importance in the novel is its resonance in the careers of Gaines and McPherson. By denying racial ancestry as the enabling force for their creativity, they dramatize Ellison's call for the writer to generate an identity of his or her own, to utilize resources to their best advantage.

It is the manner by which these writers have accomplished this task that generates kinship between them. This is evidenced in two ways: in their portrayal of geographical origins and in their fictive themes. In the former instance, each writer locates his origins outside the North. This pattern begins in Ellison, with his claim that he is, in fact, not a Southerner but a Southwesterner born in the "wild state of Oklahoma." In choosing this mode of self-presentation, he distances himself from the pathology that marks Richard Wright's portrayal of his Mississippi childhood. Ellison's Oklahoma represents possibility, a territory that originates in the twentieth century, peopled by ex-slaves. These folk, Ellison's parents among them, recognized that "geography is fate," and left the South to "light out for the territory" in the West. Born in Louisiana, Gaines follows a slightly different geographical trajectory. His childhood involves its own form of "lighting out": he spent his adolescence in California, another state that evokes possibility. He describes Vallejo, the California town where he lived, as a

> place where you had all these races. I mean my teammates, my playmates were Japanese, Chinese, Filipino, whites, other blacks, the Latinos. I went to a place where you constantly heard different languages, kids going home to eat different kinds of dishes, talking about different things in school together. If I had been sent to Watts where you had a total black ghetto, maybe the other thing could have happened to me. If I had gone to Harlem, it could have happened. If I had gone to the south side of Chicago, it could have happened. But I was lucky.[6]

Gaines's description of his childhood evokes the very essence of diversity. He suggests that he grew up in a geographical circumstance that belied the segregation of his early childhood. He recapitulates Ellison's strategy, characterizing California as a space where his artistic sensibility was freed from the constraints that segregation categorically imposes on the African American writer. More, he cites locations where African American writers like Wright and Baldwin locate much of their writing. By relating Vallejo's differences, he likewise distances himself from the figurative constraints of the North. Thus, in being "lucky," Gaines suggests that his literary voice is a unique formulation, one which has benefited from a variety of cultural resources.[7]

Though raised in the heart of the South, McPherson, like Ellison and Gaines, characterizes his childhood in non-traumatic terms. McPherson observes of his childhood:

> I lived in a lower-class black community in Savannah, Georgia, attended segregated public schools, and knew no white people socially. I can't remember thinking of this last fact as a disadvantage. . . . There was in those days a very subtle, but real, social distinction based on gradations of color, and I can remember the additional strain under which darker-skinned people lived. But there was also a great deal of optimism, shared by all levels of the black community. . . . there was a belief in the idea of progress, nourished, I think now, by the determination of older people not to pass on to the next generation too many stories of racial conflict, their own frustrations and failures. ("On Becoming an American Writer," 54)

Here, we can also find McPherson working to present a dialectical view of the South. While he alludes to the difficulties of racial caste, what is more clearly rendered is the South as a nurturing space. One would not conclude, reading the passage above, that McPherson endured the same level of personal degradation that Wright describes in, say, "The Ethics of Living Jim Crow." Like Ellison and Gaines, McPherson conceptualizes his childhood as one of possibility. The older generation he refers to is characterized by its belief in the "benign intentions of the Federal government" and its faith that the next generation would fare better than they. McPherson alludes to the silence of the elders, rather than their acts of voice, as the force shaping a new generation. He observes that the older folk

> censored a great deal. It was as if they had made basic and binding agreements with themselves, or with their ancestors, that for the consideration represented by their silence on certain points they expected to receive, from either Providence or a munificent federal government, some future service or remuneration. . . . And because they did tell us less than they knew . . . many of us remained free enough of the influence of negative stories to take chances, be ridiculous, perhaps even try to form our own positive stories. (54)

Each writer is engaged in a project of self-disclosure. They reflect on their respective childhoods and give voice to the nurturing aspects of those years. That is, each constructs childhood as a period when they were initiated into the possibilities of being both black *and* American. They all refer to the presence of resources, beyond those found in a racially inflected domain, that allow them to utilize their resources in wider spheres of endeavor. Moreover, the discussion occurs as a postscript to their literary efforts. Thus, each writer, beginning with Ellison, works out "the uniqueness of his experience."

Thus, in stating plainly the lack of African American influence, Gaines and McPherson are empowered to use a conceptual shorthand that builds on Ralph Ellison's work in *Shadow and Act* where he scolds Irving Howe for limiting his artistic possibilities to those presented by Richard Wright in the protest novel. Ellison's response to Howe is characterized, once more, by his unwillingness to enclose himself in provincialism:

> If *Invisible Man* is even "apparently" free from the "ideological and emotional penalties suffered by Negroes in this country," it is because I tried to the best of my ability to transform these elements into art. My goal was not to escape, or hold back, but to work through; to transcend, as the blues transcend the painful conditions with which they deal. The protest is there, not because I was helpless before my racial condition, but because I *put* it there. If there is anything "miraculous" about the book it is the result of hard work undertaken in the belief that the work of art is important in itself, that it is a social action in itself.[8]

Ellison's notion of "working through" is an important one because it illustrates his ability to bring resources to bear, first and foremost, on the problem of the novel. The desire to "transcend" painful circumstance, to breathe meaning into it, likewise meant that protest was not a goal in and of itself, but, as his hero comes to discern, a process leading to new formulations of consciousness.

Ellison's claims are sufficiently open-ended to allow Gaines and McPherson to fuse geography and voice on their own terms. This nexus functions differently in each writer's work. Gaines tells us that one of his strengths is a "sense of place." McPherson is more concerned, it seems, with these categories as signs of cultural specificity; more than an actual geographical space, geography and voice are acted out in small gestures that clarify the eclectic nature of becoming an American. Ellison, Gaines, and McPherson all work to belie the notion that Southern origins are in any way a constraint on personal achievement. Ellison does this by assuming the guise of the Southwesterner; Gaines by becoming one of a large group of immigrants experiencing a new place through cross-cultural germination; and McPherson by invoking the nurturing web of a folk community oriented toward the future instead of the past.[9] This is important as a form of affirmation rather than denial, however. Largely because the South is so often seen as a debilitating space, each writer's revision alters our sense that the region is, as Wright suggests in *Black Boy,* devoid of resources.

The second level where the kinship between Ellison, Gaines, and McPherson can be most clearly located is in the latter two writers' revisions of Ellisonian tropes. As Kuhn observes, a paradigm does not cancel, in one fell stroke, the contradictions or inconsistencies that surround a particular field of endeavor. It merely offers a more precise, consistent means of description. Thus it is not my position here that *Invisible Man* is the realization of a text that confronts and dispels all the contradictions or failures in American culture. I would argue, however, that it represents a gesture toward a more coherent articulation of the syncretic nature of American culture and history. As I discuss in the pages to follow, Gaines and McPherson offer moments in their fiction where they recapitulate and revise numerous moments in Ellison's fiction, not the least of which is resourcefulness as a literary theme.

2

While Gaines's and McPherson's respective claims for their authorial identities demonstrate a sensibility that can be traced back to Ellison, it is important to see how their authorial postures translate into their fictional projects. I want to turn to the manner by which Ellison, Gaines, and McPherson use innovation as a literary theme in their fiction. In each, one finds their protagonists moving from a reliance on convention toward a stance characterized by innovation and utilization.

Ellison's *Invisible Man* is full of instances where the invisible protagonist must break from an adherence to convention. His desire to be a great orator, his hope to replicate the achievements of Booker T. Washington, means that he wants to become a master of rhetorical skill. As a speaker he feels that his voice can have the greatest impact on the largest number of lives. What he fails to realize, however, is that oration is markedly different from oral performance. The orator can function in a conceptual vacuum, without having to acknowledge the presence or needs of an audience. The oral performer, however, must adjust to the audience, to listen to the audience listening in return to the speaker. To render a message successfully, to reach the listeners, the speaker must, in effect, use them. The result of this difference is a struggle for the narrator to use his voice to uphold the status quo or to create possibility, to become a vehicle for introspection and thus transformation. As an orator, the narrator uses his voice as the instrument of the Brotherhood; as an oral performer, he must listen to the audience, utilize them as a conceptual vehicle, before he can use his voice to inspire them to action.

One of the instances in the novel where Ellison's protagonist-narrator must move from conventionality to innovation can be found in the Tod Clifton/Sambo-doll sequence in chapters 20 and 21. The scenario begins when Tod Clifton, his co-worker in the Brotherhood, disappears in Harlem. The narrator uses all the resources available to locate him, with no success. By accident, the narrator comes upon Clifton selling "Sambo-dolls" on the sidewalk downtown, using a salesman's pitch he can barely recognize as belonging to Clifton. He wonders, seeing Clifton, "How on earth could he have dropped from Brotherhood to this in so short a time?" (*Invisible Man,* 438). Though he begins the encounter confused about Clifton's sudden "fall" from an adherence to Brotherhood ideology, it is his own acceptance of that ideology that is ultimately decentered.

The narrator is so incensed by the spectacle of Clifton's sidewalk performance, that he spits on the doll. In a key figuration, the narrator picks up one of the Sambo-dolls and puts it in his pocket along with Tarp's chain link (434). Though he does not realize it, innovation begins to assume a concrete, tangible form. However, he lacks the ability to read this confluence of symbols as a coherent text; he does not understand the two objects, doll and chain, as metaphoric openings into an innovative posture. Tarp tells the narrator that he thinks of the chain link in terms of only two words, "yes and no." But when the narrator slips the link over his knuckles, it realizes Tarp's other claim for the link, namely that "it signifies a whole heap more." Seeing the link around the narrator's knuckles, Tarp responds, "Now there's a way I never thought of using it." The link moves from artifact to weapon, which points at the narrator's innovative ability, but his adherence to the Brotherhood's scientific program prevents him from fusing innovation and action.

Moreover, I would like to suggest that there is yet another way to view the link: not as weapon but as magic circle. In this instance, as an instrument of affirmation and negation, the link is Tarp's symbolic representation of the "yes" of the Constitution and the "no" imposed by race ritual. The act of bequeathing the link to the narrator means that Tarp has literally handed him the task of "completing the link." The gap the ex-prisoner created in order to escape from the chain gang signifies the state of American democracy, and thus the narrator's act of slipping it over his knuckles is one that, in effect, bridges the gap between intention and result. In completing this circle, the narrator creates a new design, a new loop of history. But the narrator does not acquire insight into the link until he is able to enact the paradigm shift prefigured by Tod Clifton and the Sambo-doll. Clifton's Sambo-doll, which he claims will kill "depression and . . . dispossession," likewise symbolizes his escape from the entrapment of Brotherhood ideology. When the narrator considers a combination of the doll and the chain link along with Clifton's sales-spiel and Tarp's limp, he becomes confused. He reads them as reductions of ability, not as the signs of empowerment they actually imply. Hence, when he wonders how Clifton could "fall outside of history," his inquiry is based on discipline and control as vehicles of progress. But, as Tarp and Clifton suggest, they can just as easily be illusory, a fact which escapes the narrator in his present state of awareness, which is characterized by

> the all-embracing idea of Brotherhood. The organization had given the world a new shape, and me a vital role. We recognized no loose ends, everything could be controlled by our science. Life was all pattern and discipline; and the beauty of discipline is when it works. (*Invisible Man,* 382)

Clifton's apparent loss of discipline, his plunge outside the Brotherhood, unveils the conceptual slippage in the group's program. The Sambo-doll represents a way of thinking that is lost on the narrator. He fails to realize that the Brotherhood leaves no space for the highest form of innovation possible: improvisation. By positing discipline as the sign of progress and resistance, linearity and exclusiveness are privileged over cyclicality and inclusiveness. In short, the Brotherhood's program relies on a truncation of personal resources, rather than their fullest use.

The employment of the Sambo-doll as a form of resistance alludes to the need to acknowledge ritual over discipline, where the liminal moment fuses the inclusive and the exclusive and, like Tarp's chain link, "signifies a heap more" than what science can reveal. The Sambo-doll calls for the narrator to avoid the reductive, to seek liberation from the limitations of surfaces. But the Brotherhood's scientific discipline is the ultimate surface; it is "beautiful"—and therefore visible—only when it "works." It is a conditional form of beauty, then, reliant on its ability to create an illusion that masks total containment. Thus the narrator's "domination" of the environment blinds him. He cannot read the Sambo-doll as a figure of innovation because it seems to him to be a symbol of false consciousness. But he has failed, as he has at other points in the novel, to ascertain the doll as a signpost left to guide him. Throughout the novel, perception comes only after he has failed to heed a warning. This moment is certainly no different; it prefigures another perceptual awakening. After Clifton is arrested and killed by a policeman, the narrator leaves the scene of the murder and descends into a subway station wondering:

> Why should a man deliberately plunge outside of history and peddle an obscenity, my mind went on abstractedly. Why should he choose to disarm himself, give up his voice and leave the only organization offering him a chance to "define" himself? (*Invisible Man,* 438)

From his position "inside" history, the narrator regards Clifton's sudden ahistoricity as a form of disempowerment, an abandonment of resources. What he does not recognize is that Clifton meets his demise on his own terms. The opportunity the Brotherhood's ideology offers is, finally, unacceptable to him. The task of the narrator becomes one of trying to find out why, and this knowledge is what powers him into invisibility.

Thus, the narrator's descent into the subway foreshadows his transformative plunge into the "hole" from where he narrates his tale. In this particular moment, however, the narrator confronts history as an instrument which "records the patterns of men's lives." When three young men, wearing their zoot suits with a defiant style, enter the subway behind him, the narrator discovers a metahistorical posture that one can assume outside history. Indeed, he realizes that the three boys, whose suits have shoulders "far too broad to be those of natural western men," are "outside of historical time . . . untouched." Like Clifton's Sambo-doll, their presence questions the assumptions of conventional renderings of history. Though they seem to be caricatures of a form, Ellison's protagonist can reach this conclusion only because he cannot recognize innovation when he encounters it. What he sees is that the suits are "too-hot-for-summer" and concludes that the young men are merely out of step with time. The narrator begins to ponder the significance of the boys in their suits when he asks, "Do they come to bury the others or to be entombed, to give life or receive it?" (481). What he is weighing is whether they represent total marginality or the cutting edge of culture, or simultaneously both these categories. Though he fears the boys will soon be men "out of time, who [will] soon be gone and forgotten," his apprehension rests, again, on the conventional impulse to dominate history through scientific means. But when he reconfigures history not as scientist but gambler, a figure of utmost chance, the narrator begins to understand Clifton and his relationship to the boys and their zoot suits:

> What if history was not a reasonable citizen, but a madman full of paranoid guile and these boys his agents, his big surprise! His own revenge? For they were outside, in the dark with Sambo, the dancing paper doll; taking it on the lambo with my fallen brother, Tod Clifton . . . running and dodging the forces of history instead of making a dominating stand. (*Invisible Man,* 441)

The task for the protagonist is to see Clifton's Sambo-doll and the zoot suits as a new form of discourse. Clifton's decision to utilize the Sambo-doll is not a break in the continuity of rebellious discourse as the narrator imagines it. Rather it attempts to rupture the illusory surface of historical discourse as Brotherhood ideology presents it. The boys in their zoot suits, who see their reflections in the windows of the subway train and communicate "ironically with their eyes" distort conventional notions of design. This distortion brings the margin and cutting-edge of culture into a state of overlap. The narrator must see his relationship to these forms of resistance if he is to resist convention. Thus, he conjectures:

> What was I in relation to the boys, I wondered. Perhaps an accident, like Douglass. Perhaps each hundred years or so men like them, like me, appeared in society, drifting through and yet by all historical logic we, I, should have disappeared around the first part of the nineteenth century, rationalized out of existence. (*Invisible Man,* 442)

This is an important moment, one when the narrator is on the verge of an innovative posture. Indeed, he realizes that Clifton and the zoot-suited boys are a form of resistance that predates the scientific rationalism that emerged in the early stages of the nineteenth century. The resistance they represent is not new, rather it "has been there all along, but somehow [he has] missed [it]." The narrator is forced to acknowledge that history has myriad forms. To dramatize this, Ellison's narrator walks on the sidewalk outside a record shop in Harlem as he ponders the "groove of history." "I moved with the crowd," he observes, "the sweat pouring off me, listening to the grinding roar of traffic, the growing sound of a record shop loudspeaker blaring a languid blues" (433). Having performed such difficult mental labor, the narrator is positioned between two "grooves" indeed. He hears the "grinding roar" of industrial society being slowly overwhelmed by the "growing sound" of the blues, which points to a new kind of opposition. On the one side there is the Brotherhood's scientific program, which—as rhetoric—can be learned and rendered by rote. On the other, the blues straddles binary opposition, it relies on what the musician can bring to the performance, not as mere technician, but as visionary, as innovator. The narrator is forced to examine the variations:

> I stopped. Was this all that would be recorded? Was this the only true history of the times, a mood blared by trumpets, trombones, saxophones and drums, a song with turgid, inadequate words? My mind flowed. (443)

Loosed, at least momentarily, from the rigidity of ideological discipline, the narrator can measure the distance between the Brotherhood and himself. Feeling that he is in the presence of "everyone [he has] ever known," he concludes that it is he, not Clifton or the zoot-suited hipsters on the train, who is at odds with his surroundings. Thus, he concludes, "I'd been so fascinated by motion that I'd forgotten to measure what it was bringing forth. I'd been asleep, dreaming." The protagonist has been a victim of convention, where "no great change has been made" in the living conditions in Harlem. If anything, he is forced to confront, as if for the first time, the static nature of his political life.

Tod Clifton's Sambo-doll teaches the narrator that he can, in fact, achieve a sense of duality; he can straddle theoretical boundaries and reconfigure history into a purely musical "groove." This harkens back to the narrator's use of Louis Armstrong's "What Did I Do To Be So Black and Blue?" as the framing device for his tale in the Prologue. The Sambo-doll is a commodity that ruptures the smooth surface the Brotherhood deploys to explain the degradation found in Harlem. As a scientific discourse, history stands as an objective discipline that is ostensibly free of subjective bias. But herein lies the problem: Harlem is a conceptual vehicle for the Brotherhood, not a community. Clifton's doll "riffs" on the Brotherhood's claim that they accept "the other as a Brother." Selling a doll controlled by an invisible black string, Clifton unmasks the Brotherhood's manipulation of the "race question." Indeed, the doll names the narrator as the agency through which the black community in Harlem is ideologically exploited, even as their position vis-à-vis the old order remains unchanged.

Clifton's commodification of this distortion of African American identity has a two-fold dimension: it disrupts the Brotherhood's version of the dispossessed present and brings the illusion into the capitalist marketplace under his control. The doll, as a reductionist double, achieves true "for-profit" status. The invisible strings controlling the doll, which "keep [the] nigger boy" dancing, demonstrate the Brotherhood's relationship to Harlem: a system of exchange whereby the Brotherhood advances its ideological position at the black community's expense. The Sambo-doll heightens the contradiction of the Brotherhood's stance by unveiling its racism and making it a commodified symbol.

Clifton and the zoot-suited boys represent a system, a paradigm of resistance. This system turns on nothing less than a determination to distort historical form, to manipulate it to their own ends. Thus, they are not historical, but instead metahistorical. Hayden White articulates how important a recognition of this difference can be when he observes:

> In order to write the history of any given scholarly discipline or even of a science, one must be prepared to ask questions about it of a sort that do not have to be asked in the practice of it. One must try to get behind or beneath the presuppositions that sustain a given type of inquiry and ask the questions that can be begged in its practice in the interest of determining why this type of inquiry has been designed to solve the problems it characteristically tries to solve.[10]

White posits the necessity of querying historical practice in order to unveil anomalies which may render its conclusions incoherent. Clifton and the boys provide a model of innovation that allows the narrator to abandon his adherence to conventional notions of historical inquiry and to assume a metahistorical presence.

This is evidenced in the narrator's eulogy for Tod Clifton, where he works out the difference between oration and oral performance. While the former can be characterized as "formal speech," the latter has much more to do with call and response, an awareness of the audience. Thus, when the narrator begins planning for Clifton's funeral, not yet having broken from Brotherhood ideology, he relies on organizational discipline as a way of making Clifton's funeral a political statement. As political event, the funeral will "put [Clifton's] integrity together again." What the narrator hopes is that, by using the Brotherhood as a vehicle, he can politicize the Harlem community and make Clifton's death coherent within the space of organizational policy. The integrity he hopes to restore has to do with reintegrating Clifton's actions with Brotherhood ideology. He seeks to recuperate the Sambo-doll episode as ideological juncture rather than as rupture.

The crowd that gathers in the park for the funeral becomes a "singing mass" when they begin to sing "There's Many a Thousand Gone." The nature of the event shifts from the purely secular to the ritualistic. The crowd is no longer a political force; it is rendered incoherent in that context, as evidenced when the narrator observes that he "looked into that face, trying to plumb its secret, but it told me nothing" (452). The narrator's act of reading fails largely because he brings strategies of organization, of textuality, to bear when he should rely on what he can hear. When a horn begins to accompany the singers, the narrator shifts into an aural mode:

> I looked at the coffin and the marchers, listening to them, and yet realizing that I was listening to something within myself, and for a second I heard the shattering stroke of my heart. Something deep had shaken the crowd, and the old man and the man with the horn had done it. (*Invisible Man,* 453)

The narrator recovers his self-consciousness, which prefigures the manner in which he is about to use his voice. By conjoining the act of listening to the crowd to an elemental force within himself, he moves into a sermonic mode for the eulogy. As he stands before the crowd, however, Ellison's protagonist realizes that he has "no words," nor does he have any idea of the Brotherhood's funeral rituals. It is in this conceptual break that he finds his voice. Indeed, without thinking he asks, "What are you waiting for me to tell you?"

The launching point for his utterance is the site at which the narrator fuses his indecision and turmoil. Where he has had to "speak scientifically" for the Brotherhood, to dominate an audience with organization, here he has to improvise. He begins with indeterminacy which leads him to tell the crowd to go home, to forget about the events that have led to Clifton's death. When the crowd remains, he has no choice but to respond to their continued presence. Thus the speech, or the sermon if you wish, builds on this rhetorical inversion. As the narrator erects each conceptual unit of the speech (for instance, he provides Clifton's biographical information and moves from there into a more critical posture from which he contextualizes Clifton's death), the gravity of the murder grows from the death of one man to the plight of a community. My contention here is that the conceptual shape of the speech can be likened to the Sambo-doll in that it, too, unfolds to assume symbolic consequence. The "fine black thread" the narrator finds to make his words dance, that holds his audience's attention, is the sermonic mode, not Brotherhood ideology. However, because he continues to consider his speech from the point of view of the Brotherhood's rhetorical strategy, he believes he has failed. "I had let it get away from me, had failed to bring in the political issues. And they had stood there, sun-beaten and sweat-bathed, listening to me repeat what was known" (459).

The narrator does not recognize his own shift from the stiff, rhetorical posture of oration to the innovative and regenerative space of oral performance. He misreads the crowd's silence as his failure to move them, which it would be if one considers the event a political gathering. A eulogy at a funeral requires no less than what he has accomplished: that he evoke the essence of Tod Clifton and his connection to the community. The crowd he has spoken to is not a mass, but a gathering of individuals. After he completes his eulogy, the narrator takes "one last look at the crowd [and sees] not a crowd but the set faces of individual men and women." He recovers the specificity of Harlem; it becomes a community rather than a political space. The crowd's silence, then, is completely appropriate in the context of a funeral.

The effectiveness of the narrator's eulogy is demonstrated in Chapter 22, when he must answer to the Brotherhood leadership for his actions. This chapter illuminates the extent to which he has broken from convention and embraced—if unconsciously—a posture of innovation. One has to compare this moment, then, to the eviction speech in Chapter 14, which brings him into the Brotherhood's orbit.[11] The Clifton euology inverts the final result of the eviction scene. In the latter, the crowd is galvanized into a form of collective action when they take the old people's possessions back into the apartment building. However, this action collapses into mob violence when they attack the policeman. This negative energy, which the narrator is finally incapable of harnessing, is what the Brotherhood seizes upon to coopt the narrator into its circle and gain a foothold in Harlem. His voice, which has created a brief form of coherence, is subverted by scientific discipline. The hero is transformed, through the Brotherhood's tutelage, into an orator whose only tool is rhetoric.

The eulogy by contrast is a moment when the narrator performs. He tells Clifton's story and how that story impacts on the community. He shifts from a posture that seeks to manifest coherence through the mass to one which recognizes the crowd's individuality. He throws off the mantle of secular politics for the ritualistic; the rhetorical for the rhythmical. The negative reaction from the Brotherhood leadership suggests the scale of his innovative break from convention.

3

Ernest Gaines offers moments in his fiction where acts of innovation are no less important to his characters. For example, in *Bloodline,* a set of related short stories, Gaines's protagonists are figures of innovation who strain against convention. While resistance does not always lead to large-scale transformation, it often implies the presence of a new social design, imminent change. In "The Sky Is Grey," James is taken to the dentist by his mother to have a tooth pulled. In the dentist's office, a young man, well dressed and articulate, is debating with a preacher about black life in the South. "We don't question is exactly our problem," the young man asserts. "We should question and question and question—question everything" ("The Sky Is Grey," 95). By challenging the preacher, a symbol of stability in the black community, the young man likewise challenges the community's adherence to convention. When the young man argues that God's existence should be questioned, the preacher's anger begins to rise. He says, "When I come into this room and seen you there with your book, I said to myself, 'There's an intelligent man.' How wrong a person can be" ("Sky," 96). When the young man asserts that the preacher's ignorance is exemplified by the fact that he believes in God because he's been told to do so by white men, the preacher's only recourse is to strike the young man in the face and leave. Because the younger man has used "cold logic" to refute the older man's worldview, violence becomes the preacher's only means of ending the debate.

Further, the fact that the young man argues for the need to "question everything" suggests that race ritual in the South reifies citizenship, forcing black and white to conform to proscribed social roles in a drama that replays itself so many times till all the participants reach the outcome by rote. However, in formulating his life around the act of inquiry, the young man proposes a new way of perception, one that relies on open-endedness rather than closure. The preacher's view of the world, which eschews the secular in favor of blind faith, cannot contain this new posture: it functions as a threat to his authority and thus he cannot discern its usefulness. His dismissal of the young man and his books stems from his inability to discern the type of literacy the latter has achieved. Their encounter provides a clear example of the clash of paradigms.

When a woman engages the same young man in conversation, he tells her the grass is black rather than green, another instance where he challenges conventional assumptions about the world. He is reminiscent of Ellison's protagonist, if only because he asserts, "Words mean nothing. Action is the only thing. Doing. That's the only thing." The woman concludes that the young man is a "lunatic," but what she and the preacher fail to understand is that his achievement of literacy has left him in a state of perpetual agitation that makes him an anomaly in the eyes of the folk. But even as he represents a break from convention, the young man is finally frozen by his loss of faith. "Unfortunately," he tells the old woman, "I was born too late to believe in . . . God. Let's hope that the ones who come after will have your faith—if not in your God, then in something else, something definite that they can lean on. I haven't anything. For me, the wind is pink, the grass is black" ("Sky," 102). Though the young man has intellectual intensity, his achievement is that he has learned to question the nature of reality. But the old woman observes that he has "forgot[ten] the heart absolutely." This is problematic because his inability to utilize emotion alienates him from those who share his racial plight; he can destabilize reality, but he is incapable of managing a strategy that allows him to act on it or persuade others to action.

But there is a moment in the scenario that illustrates the nature of the paradigm shift. James, in observing the young man, concludes, "When I grow up I want be just like him. I want clothes like that and I want keep a book with me, too" ("Sky," 100). This is significant, largely because it is James who represents the likelihood of fusing intellect and emotion. Though his mother attempts to instruct him on "how to be a man," James's fascination with the young intellectual suggests that he resists her imposition of conventional manhood on him. While the story does not offer concrete evidence that James will grow into a leader, what I see here is his recognition and attraction to anomaly, a break from convention.

When we consider this story alongside the last story in the collection, "Just Like a Tree," we can see a conceptual progression at work. Told from several points of view, the story concerns an old woman about to leave her family in order to head up North. After civil rights activity takes place in the quarters, a bombing kills a woman and her two children there. When Emmanuel, the leader of the demonstrations, comes to say goodbye to Aunt Fe, the house gets silent. Gaines allows Etienne, a minor character in the story, to relate what happens after Emmanuel arrives. The older people blame the younger man for bringing violent reaction down on the community. This feeling exemplifies the conventional attitude that a misstep by one person can bring punishment down onto the entire community. Thus race ritual is never challenged because the people in the quarters fear collective reprisal. As the bombing evidences, the innocent are often the victims. But Emmanuel represents a new sensibility. He sees the bombing for what it is, as Etienne relates:

> Sure, they bombed the house, he say; because they want us to stop. But if we stopped today, then what good would we have done? What good? Those who have already died for the cause would have just died in vain. ("Just Like a Tree," 245)

The significance of what Emmanual observes lies in his act of reconfiguring the violence that characterizes black life in the community. Rather than viewing the violence as instances in need of repression, he links them into a "cause," a conceptual whole; he formulates the deaths within a tradition of resistance which he attempts to carry onward: the memory of the bombing becomes a resource to be utilized in further activity. The community's fear leads them to equate Emmanuel's actions with Aunt Fe's departure. But Emmanuel challenges this reading of events by making Aunt Fe the source of his resistance.

Unlike the young man in "The Sky Is Grey," who lacks the ability to love or act, Emmanuel connects his struggle with his love for Aunt Fe. "Nobody in here love her more than I do," he asserts. "Not one of you" ("Tree," 245). After he relates the story of his great-grandfather, who has been lynched and decapitated, he frames this horrible tale with another:

> Just the two of us were sitting here beside the fire when you [Aunt Fe] told me that. I was so angry I felt like killing. But it was you who told me get killing out of my mind. It was you who told me I would only bring harm to myself and sadness to the others if I killed. Do you remember that, Aunt Fe? (246)

Clearly, Emmanuel has chosen non-violent resistance as his course as a direct result of his conversation with Aunt Fe. In this, he affirms his kinship with her, even as he extends and articulates resistance in a new way. Moreover, he represents the conceptual progression from the young man in the dentist's office because he conjoins the former's intellectual determination with communal love. Thus he can say, "I'm not going to stop what I've started" because he recognizes that to do so would be to break his kinship with Aunt Fe. She understands implicitly. (She does not speak in this sequence; she merely nods.) When Emmanuel leaves, Aunt Fe's response is "Goodbye, Emmanuel . . . God be with you." This suggests that she does not think of herself, that she sees the importance of his task. There are numerous cues that demonstrate Gaines's depiction of a paradigm shift, of innovation. The song "Just Like a Tree," is at once an old spiritual sung in the quarters and a song used in the civil rights movement by the people attempting to desegregate Jim Crow facilities. It is important to point out, then, that Aunt Fe and Emmanuel are not given their own sections in the story, moments when they render their own points of view. They represent a tradition of resistance be, but at a deeper level, they are the old and new centers of communal activity. The story's characters are arranged in narrative space around them because of their relationship to one another; it is a soul-deep connection. Emmanuel articulates this when he says that he can walk in Aunt Fe's house in the dark, he "can go anywhere in the house without bumping into anything." While the other voices in the story are Aunt Fe's consanguineal kin, Emmanuel is her spiritual kin. Their closeness resists explanation; hence the people in the quarters see Aunt Fe's departure as Emmanuel's lack of concern. But, in actuality, it is the movement from one paradigm into another. The time has arrived for a more direct form of resistance. Significantly, Aunt Fe never leaves the South. At story's end, she dies. But this suggests that, like Emmanuel, she "will not be moved." Thus her death is her final act of resistance; by being buried in the place where she has lived, Aunt Fe protects the continuity of resistance, she remains rooted in a geographical space as she maintains its symbolic importance.

There are clearly relationships to be established between "The Sky Is Grey" and "Just Like a Tree," because together they offer a means by which to read *Bloodline* as a set of tales chronicling the transformation of a community. But I hope it is also clear that Gaines is dramatizing the movement from convention to innovation in ways that mirror Ellison's project, not only in *Invisible Man,* but also in his short story, "Flying Home." Both texts offer instances where the protagonists must recover the past in the form of voices they have previously ignored or misunderstood. Gaines's collection ends with a figure who engages in rebellion as he maintains his tie to the past. Indeed, he is energized by his ancestral connection in ways that are, for him, implicit and organic (hence, the tree as image); where Ellison's protagonist must stumble upon this connection, using an inorganic means (light) to illuminate his ancestral modalities.

4

James Alan McPherson's fictions take up the trope of innovation in ways that revise elements of both Ellison and Gaines. What distinguishes his work is his attempt to reposition the reader's relationship to his protagonists. McPherson, too, is enamored of the greenhorn as a figure of transformation. Indeed, several of the stories that appear in his second collection of stories, *Elbow Room,* use various incarnations of the greenhorn as a way of exploring innovation. Often, however, McPherson's stance toward the protagonists in his fiction makes it hard to conclude that one is, in fact, encountering the greenhorn. Because he often presents events from the consciousness of the protagonist, the reader "looks out on" the world, not necessarily aware of the limitations of insight the character may possess. More, McPherson utilizes characters whose status or age belie the term greenhorn, though their actions affirm such a reading.

For example, in "The Faithful," McPherson presents John Butler, a barber and preacher. His career in both areas is on the decline. His barber shop is losing business because he refuses to cut hair in the Afro hairstyle. He stubbornly adheres to convention, refusing to accept the value of cultural innovation. His unwillingness to acknowledge the shift in cultural paradigms that longer hair indicates demonstrates his loss of contact with the community.

The story opens with Butler looking out his shop window at people passing the shop. The "colors are blurred because the window is in need of a cleaning; the red lettering has been allowed to fade, almost to a mere outline." Both the window and the red letters are symbolic of Butler's dislocation, his shop is a point of discontinuity. For a preacher, the barber shop is the perfect place for him to place himself in the center of the community's cultural identity. But his failure to adopt an innovative posture makes it impossible for him to understand the cultural significance of longer hair. In a profound misreading, Butler offers this explanation of the Afro:

> These whites have bullshitted our young men. . . . Now, me, I'm as proud as the next man. But our boys didn't stop gettin' haircuts until these white boys started that mess. That's a fact. Wasn't no more than a couple years ago, they'd be lined up against that wall on a Saturday night, laughin at the white boys. But soon as they see these white kids runnin' round wild, all at once they hair ain't long enough no more. ("The Faithful," 78)

This interpretation is misguided, largely because Butler fails to recognize the new cultural awareness and self-esteem the Afro symbolizes. It is a break from mainstream convention rather than a capitulation to it. It is the assertion of a new identity that separates itself from things white. But he places whites at the conceptual center, thus their long hair becomes, in his view, the motivation for blacks to grow longer hair.

Butler's church is no less threatened by his loss of contact. The sermons he preaches to his dwindling congregation can be characterized as both proud and self-righteous. His sermons perform a "different work," his self-interest subverting his task of trying to lead his congregation toward self-awareness. In contrast, Reverend Tarwell's more showman-like style of preaching (he renders his Easter sermon while "crucified" on a cross) has attracted many former members of Butler's church. The other contrast lies in Butler's adherence to the Old Testament. His rival Tarwell preaches from the New Testament, and Butler's refusal to acknowledge the innovation and transformative power to be found in the latter is the source of his demise. Thus, Butler's references to Jacob and Esau and Cain and Abel are designed to dramatize disunity. But again, this indicates an incorrect reading of history and culture on Butler's part. In his mind, the times are exemplified by "the rift there is . . . between father and son . . . son and son and daughter and daughter" ("The Faithful," 80). This misinterpretation ignores the call for unity in communal activity. Previously, men and women had addressed one another as "brother" or "sister" only in the context of religious enterprise, but the new awareness has made this a secular phenomenon as well.

It is tempting to read this fiction as a portrait of a pitiful old man who is simply out of touch, but what we have, more precisely, is a study of a man who embodies the conservative element in the African American community. In this regard Butler reminds us of Ellison's Bledsoe, particularly in the sense that both men represent the power that confines rather than the power that liberates. However, Butler is a revision of Bledsoe in that his life is marked by impotence, given his diminishing flock both in his church and in his barber shop. His failure to recognize the advent of change decenters his position as a mediator of cultural identity. His failure as barber and preacher demonstrates his inability to stay in touch with the community's vitality. Both professions call for him to adhere to a stance of innovation rather than conformity. "You can shape a boy's life by what you do to his hair," he asserts, unaware that this is an argument for stasis, not transformation, that it confines rather than liberates ("The Faithful," 67). After he cuts a young boy's hair in the old fashioned "schoolboy" style instead of the Afro the boy has requested, the boy's father angrily refers to the haircut as that of a "plantation Negro." The haircut is emblematic of political impotence, which characterizes the community Butler envisions.

Reverend Tarwell ponders a political career and is able to do so because he fuses sacred and secular energies that result in political power for the community. The story's ending confirms the disjunctive state of Butler's life when his wife complains, "Lord, why I had to marry a man with such a hard head" (93). His response is telling: "Because you couldn't do no better." Again, it refers to impotence and resignation. His life and the way that that life affects others is organized around incapacity. Clearly, McPherson's use of point of view here brings the reader into contact with powerlessness personified. Butler's relationship to Bledsoe (who is powerful in a certain context) arises out of both men's adherence to conventions which, finally, are sources of self-delusion and exteriority. Neither chooses a path that is regenerative in a new communal matrix.

In his exploration of innovation as a fictive theme, McPherson offers variations on the greenhorn. Butler is a greenhorn because he is "country" in a setting that is clearly urban. He is out of step with the new innovations to be found in such a space. In two other stories from *Elbow Room* McPherson presents the greenhorn in yet another guise. In "The Story of a Scar" and "The Story of a Dead Man," we find characters who embody the greenhorn as an "educated fool." These narrator/protagonists dramatize their literacy not only as a form of cultural myopia, but as naiveté and innocence as well.

In "The Story of a Scar," McPherson proffers, in a doctor's office, a man with a broken nose and a woman with a disfiguring facial scar. The man, who also narrates the story, asks the woman how she received her scar. But, rather than listen to her, the narrator usurps her partially rendered version and reaches his own biased conclusions about the tale and the woman. The narrator does not recognize a connection to the scarred woman. Rather, he assumes an observant posture toward her. She is a source of titillation, but her story holds no deep interest for him.

The woman finally ruptures this preconceived story and view of women, calling both the result of "paper and movie plots." Like Trueblood, she knows she is "nobody but [her]self"; her inner state is one of coherent self-awareness. The story she tells is one of how she received her scar, not a symbol of her woundedness. However, the narrator misses the distinction, which prompts his misreading of her presence. Storytelling on the scarred woman's part creates a space for self-recovery (or perhaps self-discovery) on the part of the narrator.

Innovation unfolds in two ways in McPherson's story. First, it is evidenced in the narrator's transformation. After hearing the woman's story, the narrator achieves a deeper understanding of female experience. The last words of the story, "Sister, what is your name?" demonstrate the extent to which the narrator has been changed. Rather than attempting to "name" her by usurping her story, the narrator realizes that the woman is fully capable of naming herself, thus her "name" is left outside the story's frame. Though she is a victim of male violence, the scarred woman has nonetheless experienced an inner recovery, because she can tell her tale and likewise admonish the narrator for his characterization of abused women as victims who deserve blame rather than empathy.

McPherson revises Ellison's Trueblood scene, where his wife and daughter never assert their own voices to tell their respective versions of the tale. His scarred woman corrects the misreading of the female body by the narrator through her act of storytelling. Moreover, her story takes the scar that Trueblood receives from his wife and inscribes it in the woman's face, both as the mark of male domination and as the sign around which her self-awareness coalesces. The unconscious incestual liaison between Trueblood and his daughter is reread in McPherson's fiction to dramatize the implicit nature of patriarchal domination. This is evidenced by the narrator's constant referrals to the scarred woman as "sister." In Ellison's novel, Trueblood's daughter never achieves the status of reporting subject; her dilemma is discerned by her mother. McPherson's scarred woman tells her own story, despite the protestations of the narrator, leaving him changed.

The second way we find innovation functioning in McPherson's story is in its transformation of the framed tale. He improvises on the framed tale by ending the story with a question. In a manner reminiscent of Ellison's novel, this strategy creates possibility rather than closure. Moreover, the decision to jettison the closing apparatus at story's end alludes to the new territory the narrator has discovered. Whereas closure in the framed tale conventionally addresses the narrator's *arrival* at the point from which he or she narrates, here McPherson's narrator's question functions as *departure,* not only in his relationship with the scarred woman, but also in terms of his own identity. The open-endedness of the tale, then, reenacts the same type of ambivalence that would pertain if Ellison's narrator were to step out of his hole and move toward his "socially responsible role." The framed tale stands here as a sign of embarkation rather than as a sign of foreclosed positionality.

"The Story of a Dead Man" uses a narrator who attempts to debunk the hyperbolic tales of his cousin, which he construes as "lies." At least this is his stated claim. Though his cousin Billy asserts the fact that he is "dead," what the story presents is not one "dead" man, but two.[12] William Renfro, much like Butler in "The Faithful," exemplifies delusion and an overreliance on convention. His aspiration to "settle into the good life in Los Angeles" is never realized in the story largely because he cannot link identity and action coherently. Unlike Billy, who would rather die than be falsely portrayed, William lacks coherence; he is a symbol of self-erasure.

In contrast to Butler, William wants no part of his Southern background, his plan is to remake himself into his idea of the representative Northerner. So intent is he on breaking from his past, he seeks to become "satisfied that no one [can] mistake him for a refugee from the South." Like Ellison's narrator, his invisibility impedes him, but unlike his fictional predecessor, we find, William uses his invisibility to conceal his need to discredit Billy and maintain his familial status. This is a reversal on Ellison's invisible protagonist: the former battles against erasure, the latter revels in it. Again, because McPherson's protagonist tells us the story, the reader must work to become extricated from the web of the character's "fiction." This is best evidenced in the narrator's account of Billy's first—and only—encounter with his in-laws. Because the narrator is himself a figure of stealth and hidden origins, he must likewise attempt to hide Billy's identity. But the plan backfires when Billy strips off the shades and business suit William has furnished to carry out the plan. After he tells a bawdy tale about his adventures as a gun-toting "repo man," Billy claims William as family, much to the dismay and disgust of the in-laws, who misinterpret the tale as a form of exotica, when it stands, in fact, as a sign of Billy's self-realization.

The story's reversal of Ellison centers, then, on the ways upward mobility leads to the collapse of identity rather than to the discovery and assertion of self-awareness. The danger, as in *Invisible Man,* lies in the loss of self-regenerative power. William's version of the story places him at the center of controversy as victim, not as victimizer. This is a key figuration, largely because the reader can be likewise seduced into reading the story as being about Billy's "lies." But the story calls for a more incisive and innovative act of reading in order to see the reductive nature of William's narration. In other words, McPherson's protagonist is in reality an antagonist, but we must utilize an innovative form of reading to reach this conclusion. While the two stories offer similar narrators, what separates them is that the narrator in "Scar" learns how to listen to—and thus tell—a story. William, in "Dead Man," fails to understand the weight of Billy's "lies." It is not a question of truth, rather it is a matter of acquiring the means to create and regenerate an identity in an urban environment where, to paraphrase Ellison, one is "surrounded by . . . hard, distorting glass."

In this and several other McPherson stories, we see him relying on what James H. Kavanaugh (citing Althusser) refers to as "internal distanciation."[13] This means that the innovative posture these stories often achieve rests in McPherson's ability to hold in tension the "I" of his first-person narrators and their "eyes," which provide clues to their blindness. Hence, McPherson's "Dead Man" offers us a narrator whose narrative progression not only furthers his intent, but also immerses the reader within the narrator's vision in such a way that the act of reading becomes, in and of itself, an instance of performative labor. That is, the reader must destabilize the narrator's view of the world in order to perceive the blind spots inherent in that worldview. In this sense, McPherson's William Renfro is kin to Melville's Amasa Delano. Both can be characterized by their simultaneous portrayals of innocence and blindness. Because of this, they never shift their respective positions, despite the fact that they endure (or ignore) what are essentially illusion-destroying events. It is left to the reader to take responsibility for discerning the failure of vision these characters represent. What this means is that the act of reading is likewise an act of antagonistic cooperation where the protagonist of the story is not a mirror but a lens through which to view the dilemma of American citizenship.

What is true of "The Story of a Scar" and "The Story of a Dead Man" is also true for the several other fictions in McPherson's *Elbow Room.* Many of the stories reflect the tension between the rural and urban sensibilities that often clash in the African American community. In this regard they present characters who explore the need to contain the contradictions inherent in a struggle for a coherent identity, and conclude, as does Ellison's narrator, that "all of it is part of me."

This necessitates a discussion of McPherson's "Why I Like Country Music," which opens the *Elbow Room* collection. The story offers a fictional critique of how African Americans conceptualize cultural activity. Because that activity is articulated within what McPherson suggests are very narrow parameters, the narrator's claim that he likes country music is met with disbelief and disdain.

> No one will believe that I like country music. Even my wife scoffs when told such a possibility exists. "Go on!" Gloria tells me. "I can see blues, bebop, maybe even a little buckdancing. But not bluegrass." Gloria says, "Hillybilly stuff is not just music. It's like the New York Stock Exchange. The minute you see a sharp rise in it, you better watch out. ("Country Music," 3)

The narrator's wife draws a relationship between country music and Southern race ritual, where the music acts as a narrative vehicle for black victimization. Thus, the narrator's love for country music becomes the equivalent of self-hatred. The fact that country music is "not just music" implies that the performance of such music enacts the symbolic drama of white supremacy. But we must consider that McPherson's narrator sees the music as a site of African American creativity and agency. He notes, "Of course I do not like all country stuff; just the pieces that make the right connections. I like banjo because sometimes I can hear ancestors in the strumming. I like the fiddlelike refrain in "Dixie" for the very same reason" ("Country Music," 3–4). McPherson's narrator subverts the status of "Dixie" as the "national anthem" of the white South (and thus a signifier for white supremacy) and makes it a site of black cultural activity.

McPherson's fiction forces us to acknowledge that African Americans have diverse tastes that are often the result of a regional rather than a racial identity. It particularly articulates African American identity within a profoundly Northern bias. That so many African Americans, like the narrator's wife, associate the South with victimization and misery means that they can find no way to see it as a nurturing, culturally viable space. McPherson's narrator observes that his wife "hates the South and has capitulated emotionally to the horror stories told by refugees from down home." He also concludes that "while the two of us are black, the distance between us is sometimes as great as that between Ibo and Yoruba" ("Country Music," 3). This statement anticipates the contemporary discussion that has arisen with regard to intra-racial difference and the dilemma that springs from an essentialized racial identity.

To accomplish this move, McPherson uses his narrator as a vehicle to return to an intellectual discussion initially articulated by Ralph Ellison on tensions between blacks from the North and South. In an interview, Ellison referred to Harlem as the paradigmatically "black" American space:

> Harlem has always been a difficult place for Negroes to gain perspective on the national experience because it has sponsored a false sense of freedom. It has also sponsored a false sense of superiority regarding Negroes who live elsewhere. I remember getting into an argument during World War II with a fellow who insisted that Southern Negroes had no knowledge of boxing or baseball. This came from refusing to use his eyes around New York.[14]

What becomes clear, of course, is that among blacks urban experience is privileged as the site of both mobility and cultural insight, so much so that it leads to a failure to see Southern rural life as a viable resource. But this act of privileging begs the question: If this is so, why does African American fiction continually foreground the rural (Southern) experience as the source of cultural identity? Certainly, Ellison's adversary alludes to the manner in which baseball and boxing were sites of heroic activity for the African American community. But, as McPherson's narrator suggests, it is dance, rather than athletics where one is likely to find the individual "coming to voice." As symbolic action, dancing (in this instance, square dancing) works out of what McPherson posits as narrative agency. Thus, the narrator observes that

> proficiency in dance was a form of storytelling. A boy could say, "I traveled here and there, saw this and fought that, conquered him and made love to her, lied to them, told a few others the truth, just so I could come back here and let you know what things out there are really like." He could communicate all this with smooth, graceful jiggles of his round bottom, synchronized with intricately coordinated sweeps of his arms and small, unexcited movements of his legs. Little girls could communicate much more. ("Country Music," 4)

What prevents dance from becoming the racially laden signifier here is that the use of the body in dance is part of a larger narrative imperative. In this instance, the body in motion is a dehiscence through which narrative agency flows. Thus, even as the image of African Americans dancing is encoded within popular culture as a sign which yokes physicality and inferiority in an indestructible relation, the "joke" here is that the narrator relates a much wider range of discourse than mere sexual innuendo.

Though the narrator is blessed with two left feet, he states even more certainly that dancing, like all forms of culture, is transmitted through geographical mobility, that

> most new dances came from up North, brought to town usually by people returning to *riff* on the *good life* said to exist in those far Northern places. They prowled our dirt streets in *rented* Cadillacs; paraded our brick sidewalks exhibiting styles *abstracted* from the fullness of life in Harlem, South Philadelphia, Roxbury, Baltimore, and the South Side of Chicago. They confronted our provincial clothes merchants with the arrogant reminder, "But people ain't wearing this in New Yokkk!" Each of their movements, as well as their world-weary smoothness, told us locals meaningful tales of what was missing in our lives. ("Country Music," 5; emphasis mine)

McPherson's narrator intimates in his choice of words that the dances that filter back South from Northern immigrants visiting "down home," encode the response to confinement rather than prosperity and sophistication. As texts issuing from geographical spaces that, in verbal exchange at least, are sites of racial possibility, the dances are the story made into physical activity; they are texts that capture the disappointment and despair that accompany Northern racism. Each of the places mentioned is an instance of racial segregation that likewise reflects class stratification. The South becomes, for the "world-weary" Northern emigrant, a site where masking (in this instance in the form of "lying") obscures the failed promise of life above the Mason-Dixon line.

McPherson's framed tale, in which his narrator relates his "schoolboy crush" on one Gweneth Lawson, a girl from "the South Carolina section of Brooklyn," is likewise a space that suggests that acts of memory can rupture the illusion of white supremacy that seems to surround country music. Perhaps without recognizing it as such, the narrator offers an innovative account of the complexity of American cultural identity. By relating his tale, the narrator destabilizes the notion that there are aspects of American culture that "belong" to one group or another. The narrator's wife, who never accepts country music as a valid site of African American creative agency, forces him to argue his point, "mostly to [him]self." The story is clearly a "riff" on the kind of "solitary confinement" Ralph Ellison has endured in his quest to find an innovative way to contain the contradictions of American life, its enactment of a set of "delicately poised unity of divergencies."[15]

Placing McPherson's fiction alongside that of Ellison and Gaines makes it clear that what each writer calls for the reader to consider is the necessity of innovation within the "complex fate" of being an American. As we will see in the chapters to follow, storytelling—the ability to improvise on the idea of narrative—becomes the tool each of these writers employs to construct a more coherent model of American identity in a country seeking to make itself whole: to see itself as it is and as it can be.

Part II
Trueblood Echoing

Chapter 3
Tilling the Soil to Find Ourselves: Conversion, Labor, and [Re]membering in Gaines's *Of Love and Dust* and *In My Father's House*

In those empty spaces, times intersect and our relation with things is reversed: rather than remembering the past, we feel the past remembers us. Unexpected rewards: the past becomes present, an impalpable yet real presence.

—Octavio Paz, "The Tree of Life"

say it for nightmare, say it loud
panebreaking heartmadness:
nightmare begins responsibility.

—Michael S. Harper, "Nightmare Begins Responsibility"

1

Community functions in numerous fictional narratives by African American authors as the repository of memory, a space where the individual's redemption hinges upon collective acts of remembering. In this respect, these communal acts of reconstructing the past are vehicles of identity for those who choose to harness them as such. One thinks here, for example, of Toni Morrison's *Song of Solomon,* where Milkman engages in what begins as a materialistic quest for gold and ends as a genealogical journey that leaves him face to face with the knowledge that he is part of an ancestral legacy that includes self-generated flight. Morrison's novel operates within a corpus of novels in which we find a protagonist who, individually, fails to utilize the personal resources necessary to constitute a viable identity.[1] It is the community (or figures in the community who represent the collective memory of the group) that often provides the cultural and historical impetus that leads the individual to a state of recovery and rebirth, often because information passed down from elder to progeny allows the individual to reassess the present, to confront its dilemmas with a renewed sense of purpose.

I would like to propose, however, that it is equally important to bring our critical energies to bear on fictions in which the individual, in order to reach a new state of awareness or self-recovery, must break free from repressive paradigms of folk memory. For there is likewise a need to consider fiction that follows this second impulse: where the protagonist must break out of an older, restrictive circle of memory in order to move into a space where he or she can begin to utilize the past in new ways.[2] In examining this narrative pattern, I hope to clarify the necessity of considering fictional black communities in a context of greater complexity. To argue that the individual will always find him or herself within the space of the collective is likewise to propose that personal forms of struggle become meaningful only in such spaces.[3] We must remember that the blues represent a moment of disjuncture, a break from the group that brings greater clarity than the collective is capable of furnishing at the time.[4] The blues assert that the value of community lies not in the loss of individuality but in the maintenance of processes that valorize acts of individualism, even when those actions appear antithetical to communal interests.[5]

One example of this trajectory in African American literature is to be found in the Trueblood scene (Chapter 2) in *Invisible Man*. There neither the act of remembering nor the storytelling that memory prompts is sanctioned by the community. Trueblood emerges as a figure engaged in unsanctioned activity, a member of the community who inspires both shame and distance on the part of the community. He is described as an individual who brings "disgrace upon the black community." "Several months before," the narrator continues, "he had caused quite a bit of outrage up at the school, and now his name was never mentioned above a whisper" (*Invisible Man,* 46). The narrator withholds the nature of Trueblood's transgression, though it is clear that the sharecropper is a source of communal humiliation emanating directly from the collective's awareness of the white community's negative perceptions of black behavior. Members of the college community, in particular, are embarrassed by his crude ways but tolerate them because white visitors are "awed" by the "primitive spirituals" Trueblood sings. But after he commits his disgraceful act this attitude changes, and what on the part of the school officials had been an attitude of contempt blunted by tolerance, had now become a contempt sharpened by hate. I didn't understand in those pre-invisible days that their hate, and mine too, was charged with fear. How all of us at the college hated the black-belt people, the "peasants," during those days! We were trying to lift them up and they, like Trueblood, did everything it seemed to pull us down. (*Invisible Man,* 47)

While the narrator does not elaborate on it, I want to call attention to the fear a man like Trueblood evokes. We are first made aware of Trueblood's "sin," his incest with his daughter that leads to her pregnancy, when the narrator provides Mr. Norton with a truncated version of the tale. But this serves only to pique the latter's curiosity and he feels compelled to hear the tale from the original source. As Houston Baker has pointed out, the sharecropper's story inspires fear and shame in the college community because they construct themselves in opposition to Trueblood and "his kind." As figures of upward mobility, members of the college misinterpret men like Trueblood as symbols of the past in need of repression. Their sense of themselves, mediated by the vision of the college's white patrons, is almost wholly oriented toward the future. The implication is that Trueblood satisfies a longing for the plantation past, at the expense of black progress. Mr. Norton's insistance that African American achievement and identity are yoked to his destiny makes this unacceptable, given what the narrator concludes is the former's sophistication, success, and power. To break from Trueblood, therefore, is also to break from what the college community remembers as a history of victimization. This, in order to move into a space of acceptability. However, as Baker asserts,

In the Trueblood episode, blacks who inhabit the southern college's terrain assume that they have transcended the peasant rank of sharecroppers and their cohorts. In fact, both the college's inhabitants and Trueblood's agrarian fellows are but constituencies of a single underclass.[6]

Baker goes on to suggest that "expressive representation is the only means of prevailing" in this instance. What we know, of course, is that Trueblood, at that point when he is farthest down, ostracized, and a disgrace to friends and family alike, decides to sing the blues.

I thinks and thinks, until I thinks my brain go'n bust 'bout how I'm guilty and how I ain't guilty. I don't eat nothin' and I don't drink nothin' and cain't sleep at night. Finally, one night, way early in the morning', I looks up and sees the stars and I starts singing. I don't mean to, I didn't think 'bout it, just start singin'. I don't know what it was, some kinda church song, I guess. All I know is I ends up singin' the blues. I sings me some blues that night that ain't never been sang before, and while I'm singin them blues I makes up my mind that I ain't nobody but myself and ain't nothin I can do but let whatever is gonna happen, happen. (*Invisible Man,* 65–66)

Trueblood's decision is likewise an act of remembering, in this instance, a moment where he reconfigures his shattered life as blues metaphor and thus accepts himself and his plight. By doing so, Trueblood positions himself to confront the future, however precarious it may prove to be. This has serious implications, for he concludes that he will view the circumstances as an instance of creative possibility where he chooses symbolization over self-reproach. Hence, as Ellison's language alludes to Trueblood's achievement of a position betwixt and between (his performance occurs at a moment "one night, way early in the morning"), it also proposes a way to "read" experience via a paradigm the community at large refuses to implement. By contrast, Trueblood's predicament equivocates guilt and innocence, his journey from the sacred to the secular collapses his former status as entertainer, moving him directly into a self-constituted performance space. What I am most concerned with here is the manner in which Trueblood's liminal blues and, later, his telling and subsequent retellings of his tale, all occur in a space the black community is loathe to sanction. But that refusal arises because they do not know how to construct an unmediated identity capable of filtering out the negative assessments of the white community. While they cannot will Trueblood into oblivion, they can ignore him, reduce him to the equivalent of a secret discourse maintained by communal consensus.[7] The fact that Trueblood receives "more help than they ever give any colored man" does not, as the community concludes, imply his complicity in the furtherance of black stereotypes. Quite the contrary, Trueblood's position, as Baker argues, exists in a medium of exchange:

In African-American culture, exchanging words for safety and profit is scarcely an alienating act. It is, instead, a defining act in aesthetics. Further, it is an act that lies at the heart of African-American politics conceived in terms of who gets what and when and how. ("To Move Without Moving, 343–44)

While the material implications of Trueblood's actions are clearly manifested, it is also apparent that he has operationalized a system whereby his performance insulates him from communal censorship. In two novels by Ernest Gaines, *Of Love and Dust* and *In My Father's House,* it is censorship that mediates the tasks of the heroes. Like Trueblood, these protagonists adopt the paradigm of giving voice (or at least credence) to the painful aspects of their experience, of "reading" society by using themselves as the starting point for analysis. In a culture so devoted to amnesia, this willingness to use memory as a vehicle of self-critique (and thus self-acceptance) runs counter to the societal impulse either to deflect responsibility or to forget it altogether. It is this antagonistic posture that informs the experiences of James Kelly and Phillip Martin. In their respective fashions, both men are forced to reconfigure their fragmented pasts in order to move into newly defined spaces from which they can reenact new identities. For Jim Kelly, this movement leads to storytelling, a transgressive act of voice. His narrative of departure is a liminal blues narrative that resists the conspiratorial silence hanging over the plantation from which he escapes. For Phillip Martin, the task of remembering calls for an act of transgressive listening. He must use other voices to fill in the silences he willed into being as a way of escaping the past he shared with his son. A reunion with his son ultimately jeopardizes his social position in the community in which he has served as a civil rights leader. Unlike Kelly, whose narrative voice occurs in the midst of a newly evolving self, Martin sees his life as a public figure shattered to the point where he must rejoin the past with the present as a way to reconfigure a transformation which he has only partially completed. The transformation he seeks, then, is one which neither ignores nor obscures personal failure; it eschews the mythic in favor of the coherent. Both these novels articulate the sense that identities are often formulated under duress. They showcase characters who, via evolution or revolution, must utilize the past to establish coherent selves. Though these selves are no longer as resilient as they were before tragedy occurred, neither are they as prone to delusion. As the blues suggest, the narration of tragedy marks the beginning of healing.

2

These issues first come to the fore in Gaines's *Of Love and Dust.* In this, his second novel, Gaines returns to his interest in depicting the conflict between old and new ways of life, the clash between old and new paradigms of identity formation.[8] Within that project, memory serves as a powerful influence in his characters' lives: their lives are mediated by the social blueprint of Jim Crow, whereby violence is privileged in the collective memory because it is used to reinforce the segregation and racial codes that separate black from white. In this respect it is the memory of violence rather than actual force that enforces passivity and thus upholds the status quo.

This helps us to understand Gaines's decision to begin the novel *in medias res,* its narrative machinery already in motion. The effect of this strategy is to make the reader rely on an act of memory fully to ascertain the present. This can only be accomplished by retrieving the details from the past that will make the encounter at the novel's outset meaningful. Thus, when Jim Kelly looks down the quarters and sees the rapidly approaching dust, he lacks the intuitive equipment to discern the dust's ominous potential. But as Gaines himself has pointed out in an interview with John O'Brien, dust functions as a metaphor for death, and so the novel's first image raises the question of survival and what kinds of resources are needed to do so.[9]

As the title intimates, Gaines posits love as the antithesis of death. Though love is regenerative and capable of producing a new social condition, the characters lack the ability to institute love and resistance simultaneously. Dust obscures and negates this possibility, stirring acts of memory that prevent the quarters from seeing beyond it, from gazing forward in spite of the presence of evil and death. That Gaines renders "love" and "dust" as simultaneous events proposes that life on the Hebert plantation is characterized by stasis. He introduces two characters into this scenario of social death: Marcus Payne and Jim Kelly. When Marcus emerges out of the dust looking for Kelly, it represents that moment when the latter's past, present, and future become intertwined with the former. It could be argued that *Of Love and Dust* depicts Marcus's exploits; he represents a figure of resistance, while Jim serves merely as witness to the events surrounding Marcus's arrival. However, a more precise reading would lead us to conclude that the novel is a symbiosis between Marcus and Jim. Marcus needs Jim to tell his story, Jim tells his story because of Marcus's impact on his life. Moreover, there are problems with Marcus telling his own story—the reader would become trapped in the point of view of an outsider who lacks insight into the workings of the plantation and the quarters. Thus Marcus cannot tell his own story because his actions always indicate his distance from the community. As Gaines explains:

> When you get to Marcus, you get a one-sided thing. It's like trying to get Gatsby to tell a story of *The Great Gatsby*. You can't do that. I needed a guy who could communicate with different people. I needed a guy who could communicate with Bonbon, the white overseer, with Aunt Margaret, with Marcus. (O'Brien, *Interviews*)

Gaines's narrative strategy is realized through Jim Kelly; as the novel's overarching voice he serves the function of mediating among the plantation's various spheres. And like Nick Carraway, Jim's credibility as mediator is unobtrusive enough to lead the other characters to fill in the gaps in his narrative without displacing his narrative authority.

The mediation Jim undertakes is performed on the ritual ground of language. We find a clear example of this in his relationship with Sidney Bonbon, the Cajun overseer. Because Jim is well versed in the language of mechanization, the farm machinery provides the circumstances for his relationship with Bonbon. As he recounts:

> It was me when I showed Bonbon I was good with any machine he had there. Maybe if I hadn't showed him how good I was he wouldn't have put so much trust in me. He wouldn't have treated me different from the way he treated all the others. He wouldn't have told me things about himself, things about his family—things he never told nobody else. No I had to show him how good I could handle tractors. And every time I did, he told me a little bit more. And since I knew all about trucks and tractors, I was the person he chose.[10]

Jim's mechanical ability leads Bonbon to cross the boundary of racial difference into the space of sanctioned remembrance. Trucks and tractors provide the means for Bonbon to ignore Jim's inequity of social status, to add flesh, blood, and bone to his authoritarian presence as overseer. What this also suggests, however, is that Gaines equates labor and narration; Jim's status as "good worker" sets him apart from the other blacks on the plantation. This leads, as Keith Byerman has argued, to his medial status on the plantation; his fluency in the mechanical sphere makes him a receptacle of memory.

This is further exemplified by Jim's relationships with the other blacks in the quarters. While he could easily be the object of resentment due to his status, Jim avoids this because the other language he speaks is that of the blues. As guitar-playing blues performer, he gives voice to the rage, hurt, and frustration that characterize black life on the plantation. And because the blues is the cohabitation of pain and experience, Jim is a necessary presence in the community's well-being.[11] Moreover, the musical expression of these feelings is acceptable to the whites on the plantation, who lack the ability to decode the songs' utility as social commentary. In addition, the intimacy Jim occasions in the quarters through his music positions him as both teller and character in the narrative structure of the novel. This allows him to recount Marcus's actions even as he gives voice to his (and thus, the quarters') anxieties about him. As bluesman, he can interpret the behavior issuing from Southern racial conventions, even as he can be openly critical of himself for failing to challenge them, for choosing ease over resistance.

But this points at the other aspect of Jim's character: his disillusionment. Jim's spiritual malaise translates into an inability to engage his environment. This is evidenced at its most basic level when he looks at the toilet in his backyard, "ready to tumble at the first light breeze." Though he promises that he'll fix it "[o]ne of these Saturdays" he knows this will never happen. At a more substantial level, there is Jim's indifference to the plantation store, with its two rooms, one for whites, the other for blacks. This physical manifestation of Jim Crow represents a site maintained, at least in part, by consensus; though the blacks on the plantation may not like being segregated, the store's importance to their sustenance neutralizes their desire to challenge its racial policy. As Jim observes when he enters the store,

> if you were colored you had to go to the little side room—"the nigger room." I kept telling myself, "One of these days I'm going to stop this. I'm going to stop this; I'm a man like any other man and one of these days I'm going to stop this." But I never did. Either I was too tired to do it, or after I had been working in the field all day I was too tired and just didn't care. (*Dust,* 43)

What makes this passage important to my critical purpose is that Gaines uses repetition to demonstrate, on one hand, Jim's frustration and anger. But more important, the fact that he repeats "I'm going to stop this," illustrates Jim's memory at work: he remembers all the times he has promised to resist degradation, projecting his resistance into the future. But this assertion is framed by two sentences in the past tense, indicating the way the future is overwhelmed by the past.

Moreover, the toilet and side room serve as effective representations of Jim's disempowerment: the latter as a place where he is victimized and feels powerless to resist, the former as a site of privacy gone awry. Jim responds to both places with an apathy he cannot overcome; he knows that action is called for but he cannot muster the resolve to act. Despite his relatively comfortable status in the plantation hierarchy, Jim pays a price both publicly and privately.

Jim's disillusionment, we discover, emanates from a deeper wellspring of hurt. This becomes clear during the novel's opening chapters when Jim remembers his former lover, Billie Jean. Drawn by the fast pace and material trappings to be found in the city, Billie Jean abandons the plantation and Jim. We find out that he comes to the Hebert plantation, not because he wants to break from the past, but rather because he wants to sustain it. Hence, when he wakes before work, Jim sits on the bed, and remembers:

> thinking about her and remembering four, five, six years back. Remembering the nights coming in from the field and the big tub of hot water waiting for me; and Billie washing my back, and then us in that old Ford, heading for town. And dancing and dancing until late, and then hurrying back to that bed and loving, loving, loving until morning. Then hitting that field again, half dead, and then back and the tub of hot water and the dancing and the loving. (*Dust,* 22)

"Maybe that's why [Daddy] hangs around here," he reflects, "It reminds him a little of the old place and he figures that one day you might pass by and decide to stop" (*Dust,* 23). In an interesting turn, Jim refers to himself in the third person, as if to suggest a former persona, now lost. In this fragmented state, he is able to see the source of his pain, but incapable of bringing resources to bear to transcend it. Instead of utilizing his ability to play the blues and thus achieve some emotional distance from the past, Jim's hope is that Billie Jean will return to loose him from his self-imposed exile. Hence Jim's present hinges on this faulty paradigm of memory where all therapeutic means are located outside his purview; he cannot exert himself in any gesture oriented toward the future because he is trapped in the past.

This becomes clearer when, after a day of driving the tractor, Jim sits down with his guitar and starts to play:

> I sat on the steps and started playing the guitar. I thought about Billie Jean and played softly at first, then I tried to forget her and played something fast and hard. But I thought about her again and went back to the soft thing, then I tried to forget her and went back on the hard. (47)

Here Jim's inability to sustain a tempo for the duration of a song suggests that he can neither reflect, which would call for a critical attitude toward the past, nor forget, which would lead him to improvise a new, concrete (e.g., "hard") pattern for his life. For all his facility with tools and repair, Jim cannot engage in an act of self-repair, largely because he cannot conceptualize narrative as a form of labor. Though he plays the blues, the passage above demonstrates his inability to use them as a tool to place Billie Jean into a functional perspective. As Sherley Anne Williams has observed:

> The blues deal with a world where the inability to solve a problem does not necessarily mean that one can, or ought to, transcend it. The internal strategy of the blues is action, rather than contemplation, for the song itself is the creation of reflection.[12]

In short, Jim is not yet a blues performer because he fails to yoke performance to the task of reflection. Though he plays in the quarters, he subordinates the importance of interrogating his own experience to using the blues as a way to consume his leisure time. And because of the status that accrues from his work for Bonbon and Marshall Hebert, he sees no need to project the idea of labor into the personal sphere. Thus he does not recognize the blues as a "tool" whose value lies, not in restoring the past, but in shaping that damaged past into a usable resource.

It is important to recognize, then, that memory frames Jim's workday, a variation on his life with Billie Jean where work is subordinate to physical pleasure. Indeed, the act of remembering is as much an act of labor for Jim as working on the tractor. Because of his propensity to position relief outside himself, his crisis of agency can only be relieved by the illusion of an aggregated self provided by work. Further, as a member of a community whose sole purpose on a plantation is labor, Jim has no recourse to power, save that which is offered by religion. His religious faith takes the form of conceptualizing God as an indifferent figure, insensitive to a fault. Though Jim makes the sign of the Cross before he eats, he rarely prays due to his feeling that God "d[oesn't] hear a word," having "quit listening to man a million years ago." In Jim's mind all God does is "play chess by Himself, or sit around playing solitary with old cards." This view of God as a figure of total neutrality, coupled with his own apathy, indicates the level of Jim's self-imposed peripherality. If he is a medial figure, he is likewise a marginal one; while he is far from indifferent about the plight of others, he lacks the self-interest necessary to question his own plight seriously. As such, he represents the communal voice in its most expedient form whereby the needs of the individual are subordinated to the needs of the group. But Gaines's attention to Jim's specific form of hurt suggests that his narrative masks a deeper imperative.

Marcus's arrival in the quarters offers Jim an opportunity to discover a new kind of responsibility. Because the reader discerns the novel's events through Jim's consciousness, *Of Love and Dust* is significant as a work of fiction because it refuses to allow the reader to identify with heroic action of an individual sort. Jim's narrative describes Marcus's actions, but these come to us through the filter of his communal bias. Since Gaines does not present Marcus in romantic contour, we cannot step outside the quarters' point of view to see his actions in terms other than those Jim privileges in his narration. As a result, Marcus is the classic badman from African American folklore. Paradigmatically, Gaines's characterizations of Jim and Marcus evoke convergence and anomaly: the voices of the plantation "converge" in Jim's act of narration, Marcus's actions are anomalous, they resist conventional practice.[13] Indeed, he appears to be incapable of getting along or fitting in anywhere on the plantation.

As I noted above, Jim's status on the plantation grows out of his "bilinguality," his ability to bridge discursive domains. However, this ability to mediate the boundaries between discursive systems works to cement, rather than challenge, the status quo. By contrast, Marcus is a figure of complete resistance, largely because he remains so self-interested. Soon after his arrival at the Hebert plantation, Marcus states, "I ain't cut out for this kind of life." In Jim's narrative authority is such that we interpret this in the simplest terms possible: Marcus is unwilling to take responsibility for the man he killed and, thus, life on a plantation is unacceptable. Further, because Jim recounts Marcus's uncooperative posture in a number of different settings, Marcus appears, through Jim's credible narration, as a threat to communal well-being.

But we need to address the manner in which the reader is prevented from formulating an alternative reading. Though Jim's life is characterized by its conformity and apathy, what shapes his relationship with Marcus is his adherence to the past, to the workings of memory. Marcus, as self-centered anti-hero, focuses his attention on the present and, later, on the future. He may realize the danger of such an attitude, however he values self-determination over group acceptance. In contrast, Jim's notion of self always functions within a system that produces either interdependence or approval. Thus, he tells Marcus, "You can't make it like that. . . . They got the world fixed where you have to work with other people" (*Dust,* 235). While Jim most certainly sees a conspiracy at work, he lacks the imagination necessary to envision an alternative. His statement articulates his desire to participate in an established paradigm. Hence, he believes that community should be preserved at all costs, even if it means that the individual must relinquish claim to the right to rebel.

Ironically, Marcus is victimized, at least partially, by the constraints of oral culture. According to Berndt Ostendorf, oral cultures

> never expand beyond the horizon of the present collective. They are finite and sedentary and, one should add, conservative and nationalistic. Their chauvinism is due to a strong adherence to a policy of withholding choice and stabilizing that balance of controls which has guaranteed survival until now. By way of compensation they will create a sense, however unfree, of togetherness and the means of ritual catharsis. But this will turn into a trap whenever any one member wants to assert his individuality and advance beyond the horizon of the group.[14]

As badman, Marcus is described as "the convict," with a reputation for making trouble for the group. As such, he threatens the quarters' sense of well-being. Jim's narrative, though sympathetic to Marcus's plight, remains fixed upon Marcus's rebelliousness. These acts of resistance, large and small, challenge the rituals that shape and define relationships both within the quarters and without. For example, Marcus refuses to wear khakis out to the field, choosing to wear a silk shirt and dress shoes because he refuses to accept his lot on the plantation. In one of the novel's most humorous moments, he starts a brawl with Murphy Bacheron (another badman), a man "nobody was crazy enough to hit." As the brawl demonstrates, Marcus's rambunctious attitude is infectious to the point that the entire house erupts into violence. After attempting and failing to woo Pauline, Bonbon's black mistress, he succeeds in seducing Bonbon's wife, Louise. As the fence around Bonbon's house symbolizes, Louise is both prisoner and prize. In a setting that has such prohibitive racial and sexual taboos, this is a transgression of the highest order, one that will most certainly have an impact on the collective.

Marcus seizes on this opportunity, despite the fact that it endangers both himself and the quarters. The reason for this, as Ostendorf alludes, is that the quarters are expected to exercise control. As the brawl suggests, anti-social behavior is not problematic until it threatens white control of the plantation. The quarters, and specifically Jim, are responsible for holding Marcus's behavior in check. Because of this imperative, the attitude that informs his actions is interpreted as recklessness instead of resistance. This is so, despite the fact that Marcus is clearly empowered by his liaison with Louise. Jim notices when "Bonbon came out there in the evening he made [Marcus] sweat again. But he didn't seem to mind" (119). And though Jim threatens him, Marcus continues his attempt to get closer to the overseer's wife. Jim concludes, "Sure as hell, that sonofabitch is going to start trouble before all this is over with" (123).

Jim's prediction is correct. Marcus's relationship with Louise becomes a communal threat and as such, inhibits communal activity. This indicates both the excessive nature of Marcus's power and the manner in which that power is simultaneously attractive and repellent. Marshall Hebert, the plantation owner, becomes intrigued with the prospect of using a physical confrontation between Marcus and Bonbon for his own ends. But it is here that we can begin to see the past's impact upon the quarters' sense of possibility. Bishop, who serves as Hebert's butler, refers to Bonbon's brothers and observes, "That boy touch Bonbon, them brothers go'n ride" (122). He knows that the lynching ritual used to enforce the sexual taboo between black men and white women is strictly, and often blindly, administered.[15] The community's need to hold Marcus in check is indicative of the need to sacrifice the future in order to preserve the ritualized present. After they learn that Marcus has been recruited by Hebert to kill Bonbon, the quarters fear the kind of retribution Marcus's actions will precipitate. This is evidenced in Jim's description of the quarters:

> Soon as I crossed the railroad tracks, I could see how dark and quiet the quarters was. There wasn't a light on in any house. There wasn't a child playing anywhere. Nobody sat out on the gallery waiting for supper to be done. Not even a speck of smoke came from any of the kitchen chimleys. The whole place was dark and quiet, it looked like everybody had moved away. But they hadn't moved away, they had locked themselves inside the houses. All of them had heard what Marcus was supposed to do and all of them was afraid (270).

In the face of a paradigm that consists of resourcefulness and resistance, the people in the quarters hold fast to the old ways.

Most certainly, Marcus is an individual to be feared by both the folk and the white plantation owner for he possesses the potential, were it to become collectivized, to topple the plantation system and render social ritual incomprehensible. Because his self-interest takes on such hyperbolic forms, the overt and covert forms of rebellion he enacts breaks the cycle of small skirmishes that hold the status quo in place. Before Marcus arrives, the quarters are satisfied with small victories gained at the system's expense or with status that, like Jim's, is calibrated inward in order to create the illusion of upward mobility. However, the plantation can accommodate this type of resistance because it leaves the larger system of Jim Crow intact. But Marcus's single-mindedness argues that defying convention through open resistance is a viable route toward an integrated self. Thus, his lack of humility, in light of the ways Jim Crow promotes passivity and self-immolation, is at once therapeutic and disruptive. In this light, Marcus challenges Jim to break out of his stasis when he asserts, "stop being old fashioned. . . . Where would people be if they didn't take a chance? You know where? Right here. Right here in this quarter for the rest of they life" (248–49). The problem is that the quarters exercise a collective memory, and thus they equate this form of individual risk-taking with death. Jim's narrating through the collective vehicle renders Marcus's act of signifying completely inert. However Jim's idolatrous relation to the past makes him incapable of switching the valence of Marcus's assertion from negative to positive.

He is prevented from seeing that, as a figure of resistance, Marcus is sufficiently empowered to confront history. Marcus's power is best exemplified when he puts his foot in the door to the Hebert house to keep Bishop from closing it in his face. The plantation's historical continuity with slavery is ruptured, and thus, Bishop tells Jim, "He just pushed his foot in there. . . . The house his great-grandparents built. The house slavery built. He pushed his foot in that door" (215). Bishop, comfortable as a house servant via the status quo, knows that Marcus threatens not only his status but the viability of the system that creates it. Marcus's transgressive act ruptures the plantation's illusion of pastoral tranquillity. But more than this, he reveals the spurious relationship between racial inferiority and history. Though Marcus's actions could empower the quarters, their lack of interpretive equipment leads them to feel only fear and ambivalence: fear because they know that violence is a likely result and ambivalence because Marcus's actions unveil the plantation's illusion of order as unstable. Lacking an alternative paradigm to Jim Crow, they cannot conceptualize a way to emulate Marcus's behavior while turning it toward socially productive ends.

The other aspect of Marcus's resistant posture is his willingness to use Marshall Hebert as a resource to achieve his own ends. He knows Hebert hates Bonbon and wants him to kill the overseer. Because blacks in the quarters are lower in the social hierarchy than either the plantation owners or the Cajuns, Hebert wants to manipulate Marcus by promising him that he will go free. This points at an important thread in Gaines's fiction. Despite the fact that it was self-defense that led Marcus to kill Hotwater, African Americans' lack of standing in the Louisiana legal system nullifies this aspect of the narrative. Since the system does not place high value on black lives, acts of intraracial violence are seen as a drag on the system of due process reserved for whites. The result is that quasi-legal measures have been put in place to contend with intraracial violence: one can be sent to the state penitentiary or bonded out to a plantation and work off the time. Lacking access to the self-defense plea after he kills Hotwater, Marcus must exploit the class conflict between the plantation owners and the Cajuns.[16] While I would stop short of arguing for Marcus as a character possessed with capabilities of revolutionary scope, it is important to note his ability to exploit the rift between Bonbon and Hebert to his own advantage. The value of a man like Marcus is that his resistant posture becomes available to the community as a resource for collective change.

Part of Jim's role as narrator of Marcus's tale is to recontextualize intraracial violence, to give it a new meaning. In this sense, Jim represents the kind of perspectival shift necessary to see the macro-significance of events taking place on the Hebert plantation. Thus, at the end of the novel Jim observes:

> And what had Marcus done that was so wrong? Yes, he had killed—yes, yes—but didn't they give him the right to kill? I had been thinking about this in the field all evening and I had said to myself, "Yes, yes; it's not Marcus, it's them. Marcus was just the tool. Like Hotwater was the tool—put there for Marcus to kill, like Bonbon was the tool—put there to work Marcus. Like Pauline was a tool, like Louise was a tool." (*Dust,* 269)

This marks Jim's realization that the "plantation system" is not a source of steady labor, but an intricately designed drama whose aim is to keep blacks in their place by pitting them against one another. By constructing Marcus, Hotwater, Bonbon, Pauline, and Louise as "tools," Jim redefines the nature of work and recognizes his own complicity in the plantation scheme. The Hebert plantation offers the illusion that black labor resides outside an historical context, but it requires the individual to disconnect memory and narrative. Its numerous episodes of brutality and violence have sufficient repressive force to make physical labor a hindrance to acts of memory. Hence, through labor Jim can indulge his escapist impulse and thus provide the surrogate for a life with Billie Jean, a way of confining his marginality to a personal axis without considering the social axis. He must realize that he, too, is a tool: in assisting, in even a removed way, to break Marcus, he is maintaining both his own illusory status and the plantation's racial hierarchy.

Throughout his stay on the Hebert plantation, Marcus's propensity to satisfy his immediate desires have clashed with Jim's more deliberate, community-minded routine. Jim's status as narrator effectively prevents the reader from making a positive judgment on Marcus's behavior. However, this is due to the fact that the latter's rebelliousness and self-centeredness are seen through the lens of family and community. Within such contexts, these characteristics are injurious, if not potentially destructive.[17] But Marcus's act of manipulating the legal system (and Marshall Hebert) in order to be with Louise requires, as Jim comes to realize, radical vision and the courage necessary to pull it off. Further, seeing Marcus within the framework of the plantation hierarchy as a cog in a larger machine forces Jim to shift his point of view from the quarters as microcosm to the South as macrocosm. This gesture marks Jim's shift in political consciousness and argues that Marcus is the anomaly that prefigures the paradigmatic shift of the civil rights activity of the next decade.

We must also recognize Jim's relationship to machines, the source of his medial status, as a source of illusion. Though it ushers him into a kind of quasi-intimacy with Bonbon, inevitably his status as narrator is compromised because he is forced to remain neutral in plantation matters that would threaten his status as driver. In short, if Jim is to reach a narrative space where his voice can articulate the need to break out of the stasis that entraps him, he needs Marcus's defiance. What this means is that *Of Love and Dust* is, in Patricia Waugh's words, a "self-begetting novel."[18] Hence, after reading the novel, we are forced to consider the tone of Jim's narration because of its abrupt shift. For this "shift" seemingly coincides with Marcus's transition from badman to hero and likewise marks Jim's transformation from mediator to bluesman. I would argue for critical precision here and assert that *Of Love and Dust* has been a story about Jim all along.[19] Thus, we can account for his change in attitude toward Marcus:

> No, I didn't blame Marcus anymore. I admired Marcus. I admired his great courage. And that's why I wanted to hurry up and get to the front. That's why my heart had jumped when the tractor went dead on me—I was afraid I

wouldn't be able to tell him how much I admired what he was doing. I wanted to tell him how brave I thought he was. He was the bravest man I knew, the bravest man I had ever met. (*Dust,* 270)

Jim sees Marcus's attitude of resistance as the correct response to a confined state of being. Though the plantation almost breaks Marcus (and Gaines does suggest that Marcus undergoes a transformation of his own), Jim realizes that Marcus's refusal to let go of his plans to run away is not the sign of irresponsibility. Rather, it is Marcus's refusal to allow a corrupt system to define what he should value and how he should live.

It is clear that Jim's transformation is substantive because it exposes the gap between de jure and de facto legal practices that the civil rights movement, beginning with *Brown v. Board of Education,* would later exploit. I want to suggest, however, that neither Marcus's small (and failed) rebellion, nor Jim's narration for that matter, bring about large-scale, concrete changes on the plantation, for Jim's observation regarding Marshall Hebert is correct: "He was police, he was judge, he was jury" (198). But Jim's story does serve another, albeit abstract, purpose: his voice stands against both the written representation of the event and the quarters' interpretation of Marcus as troublemaker. By disclosing that what we know from Aunt Margaret will become a secret discourse, Jim's voice bursts from the constraints of coded discourse to establish the political element undergirding blues performance.

Further, we can see Jim's narrative as one which abandons disillusionment for faith. Though Marcus is killed before he can escape, what Jim embraces when he decides to see him off is the hidden potential of rebellion, the possibility of its success. Jim's workday is disrupted by Marcus's escape, which points to a more symbolic breakthrough: the memory of Billie Jean (the source of his ruined potential) is preempted as the iconographic force in his life and remade into a cipher. Jim can now assign her any kind of meaning that he wishes, including that of a figure rendered inert by the past.

While Gaines gives no indication of a restoration of Jim's religious faith, it is certain that he has recovered his integrity. This is best evidenced when he goes to see Marshall Hebert after Marcus's death. When Hebert offers Jim a letter of recommendation, he is offering at once the warning that Jim must leave the plantation and a commodity whose price is Jim's silence. However, unlike Ellison's hero in *Invisible Man,* Jim opens the letter, reads it, and tells Hebert, "No, sir, I'll get by. . . . Thanks very much" (278). Jim eschews the blind innocence that sealed the fate of Ellison's hero, choosing instead to read beneath the surface of the text. This kind of active literacy occasions self-determination and thus allows Jim to break out of the cycle of corruption underpinning the plantation's hierarchy.

The necessity of Jim's departure is understood by all the folk in the quarters. Indeed, in his final exchange with Aunt Margaret (a source of Jim's narrative scope) we see how the community's memory is selective, if not repressive. "Yes, you got to leave. . . . You see you won't forget," Aunt Margaret observes. When Jim asks, "You done forgot already, Aunt Margaret?" she responds in the affirmative (279). In a community so committed to oral history and storytelling, one would be hard pressed to believe Aunt Margaret's claim. It does, however, imply several issues. First, she asserts that, on matters of interracial contact, memory and silence are an inseparable compound; to break silence and engage memory in such an instance is to invite punishment, if not death. Second, she knows that Jim's transformation is such that he will create a new amalgamation: he will remember Marcus, what happened to him and why, and (perhaps most importantly) what made him heroic. Because of this, there is no way he can live within the constraints of the Hebert plantation.

The weight of Jim's act is further underscored by the novel's last scene. As Jim departs, Aunt Margaret accompanies him to the road. But after only a short distance, he observes, "When I looked over my shoulder, I saw her going back home" (281). The old woman's return to the plantation signals the solitary nature of Jim's choice, the singularity of liberation here. Moreover, the growing distance between him and Aunt Margaret, when contrasted with the novel's opening scene (where Marcus emerged out of the dust), suggests Jim's break with the past. In this sense, she is a double for Billie Jean, who turned her back on Jim to go elsewhere. Here, however, Jim abandons a fixation on the past in favor of self-interest.

3

Jim Kelly can be characterized as Wayne Booth's "privileged" narrator.[20] He has access to all the people who can give his narrative its fullest shape, but at no point in time does he make the claim that the story he relates is his own. He is therefore a narrator whose act of telling is not supported or corrected in an "implied author" of the text. It is left to the reader to infer that Jim's departure from the plantation and the narration of the events that lead to it are interconnected. It is necessary, then, for the reader to perform an act of "re-vision" on Aunt Margaret's receding form at the end of the novel.[21] Whereas Jim's gaze codifies the growing distance between them as the end of his life in the quarters, the reader must reverse this code and make it synonymous with possibility. Jim Kelly's departure signals the end of his denial because he allows himself to embrace narration as a point of dehiscence rather than occlusion.

Moreover, Jim avoids the complex fate of Ellison's hero by assimilating the innovative posture characterized in Marcus's heroic behavior into his own actions. Jim does not help the reader to reach this conclusion because his telling of the tale is linear (with the exception of the flashbacks he weaves into the tale, which serve to fill out the narrative); it begins with Marcus's arrival on the plantation and ends with his own departure. The telling of the tale takes place shortly after he leaves, sometime in the same year. We know this because of Jim's observation that Julie Rand, Marcus's grandmother, has calendars on the wall that, as he says, "dated from the late thirties up to *this year*—forty-eight" (*Dust,* 10; my emphasis).

Of Love and Dust cannot be considered a framed tale, unless one also points out that the frame must be constructed by the reader of the text. While Jim's narration includes questions and answers to questions from the person he is addressing throughout the novel, at no time does he comment on the possibility his departure represents. Indeed, Jim remains in the performance mode; his act of disclosure remains true to the task of relating Marcus's story. This indicates both the pervasive nature of Marcus's presence and his own ambivalence on leaving the plantation.

This likewise indicates that Jim, on departing, moves into a liminal space from which he narrates his tale. He can offer commentary on the circumstances that lead to Marcus's death because they represent the tools of separation that allow him to break free from the plantation's illusion of comfort. But even as his view of Marcus changes, his view of himself remains largely beyond articulation. Also noteworthy is the fact that every time Jim relates either the thoughts of one of the characters or his own thoughts, these interior monologues are enclosed in quotation marks. There is no need for these thoughts to appear in this fashion unless Jim is giving voice to them, telling his listener what he or someone else was thinking. As the voice of the community (not just as the novel's narrator), Jim has access not only to the events as characters relate them, but to their personal responses to those events as well. As a good listener, skilled in call and response, Jim is adept at weaving these other thoughts into Marcus's narrative, using them to fill out the shape of his oral performance. But liminality also means that he can give voice to thoughts that, due to racial convention on the plantation, must remain private. Jim's ambivalence about himself reflects his inability to assemble a coherent sense of his place in the present. And since memory on the plantation functions in the service of silence and restraint, Jim represents a radical break from plantation convention in his use of memory. His engagement of the mechanisms of remembering sever him from the role of communal voice; the blues he "sings" are his own. His act of narrative disclosure is the sign of a deprivatized consciousness, allowing him to give voice to his tale in its entirety. Thus, when he discloses the events surrounding Marcus's death and the antecedent emotional responses to it, his narrative functions in contrast to written history, placing events on equal footing with the *perception* of those events.[22]

The novel valorizes telling, not just remembering, as a sign of transformation; Jim's movement from innocence to insight is, in the end, as important as Marcus's death. For it must be remembered that Jim does not approve of Marcus's actions for the bulk of his narrative, largely because he sees events in communal terms. The shift into a metahistorical reading of events liberates him from the plantation's constraints, a shift that suggests that Jim's physical journey and the acquisition of a new voice are intricately connected. This would indicate that Gaines's novel is a reworking of the slave narrative: Jim moves from the neoslavery of the plantation to an isolated, but nonetheless freer, narrative space. It is an ambiguous liberation to be sure: the black body here does not function inside the same metonymic space as that of the freedman, whose narrative requires authentication. Jim's "escape" leads him toward a form of solitude that belies the role of mediator: he does not "speak for" those who, like Aunt Margaret, have decided to stay in the quarters. Rather, their voices take up a place within his own voice: he sings the blues they refuse to sing. But only by considering Jim's act of disclosure within the novel's circularity can we see this. He is loosed from the collective suffering in the quarters, but we are left with no way to ascertain what awaits him beyond the plantation. We do not, for example, know with certainty how he will characterize his relationship with Billie Jean in his new life. His departure will allow both her and the Hebert plantation to function metonymically. More, we can infer from the manner in which Marcus inspires respect and admiration in Jim that he internalizes the value of personal rebellion, which includes rebelling against one's own delusions.

3

I have conceived of *Of Love and Dust* as a novel of conversion; Jim's narrative must be seen as a conversion narrative largely because his movement from complicity to voice is likewise a transition from stasis to mobility. In this regard the text argues for a kinship with *In My Father's House,* for there we find an invitation to ponder once again the pervasive force of memory. If we are to believe W. B. Yeats's assertion that "memories are old identities," we must recognize the task of trying to unravel *In My Father's House* as one that poses the question of whether acts of self-transformation can (or should) render the past ineffectual. Moreover, I would argue that Gaines's intention is to show how difficult it can be both to narrate the past and resist static formulations of identity. Unlike *Of Love and Dust,* which deals with the relationship between intimacy and voice, this novel is informed by the relationship between intimacy and change. Certainly this, in part, requires us to read the novel as one that proposes to meditate on the necessities of African American leadership. However, what we find is that Gaines veers from the examination of leadership in terms of its public configurations. Rather, he portrays leadership as an enterprise often fraught with personal demons.

Set in the early 1970s at a time when the civil rights community was struggling to reassert itself after Martin Luther King's death, *In My Father's House* captures a moment of growing entropy. Phillip Martin is a civil rights leader in St. Adrienne, a small Louisiana town. This character represents an inversion of Gaines's usual depictions of the African American clergy, for Phillip Martin is an activist, neither conservative nor conciliatory despite his status as a clergyman.[23] In what is surely an intentional turn, the character of Elijah describes Phillip Martin as "our Martin Luther King." And in the wake of King's death, with activism on the wane, as his name suggests, he "fills" the role of Martin.

But this kind of status is not without its problems, and it is here that we find Gaines investigating the problem of African American leadership. Heeding Ellison, whose own protagonist was generated by the sense that "when the chips were down, Negro leaders did not represent the Negro community,"[24] Gaines offers us a man whose career is marked by his heroic exploits, his seemingly unshakeable commitment to the community. As Gaines relates, what "Phillip Martin is called to do . . . is lead."[25] Hence Phillip's role is to be in the foreground as the unquestioned authority behind civic activism. Phillip has achieved the charisma and public visibility sought by Ellison's hero, and unlike that character, he has internalized the belief that he is indestructible. Though he has successfully constructed himself as the icon for change in St. Adrienne, Phillip's control relies on his propensity to rely on what have become conventional forms of protest. As Keith Byerman points out, Phillip's

> problem is that protest has become so routine that the black middle class has become cynical about its effectiveness and the more radical elements question

the participation of whites. Martin, who established himself a decade earlier, cannot adapt his techniques to the changing circumstances. He still has the power, through his white associates, to compel action but not belief or enthusiasm. He is a man comfortable in the present but about to be bypassed by history.[29]

This marks a significant problem, for, as we will discover, Phillip is a man wholly constituted in the present and near future. As an activist, his actions would seem to be directed toward the future of St. Adrienne. However, he believes it is a future that requires his presence to give it shape and substance. But his reliance upon what has become an outmoded form of protest, his inability to improvise a movement capable of embracing new ideas and voices, speak to a deeper, more fundamental issue: his inability to reconcile the past and the present.

4

Gaines's narrative strategy in *In My Father's House* differs from *Of Love and Dust* in that he chooses an omniscient narrator rather than a first-person narrator. Hence the novel opens, not with Phillip, but rather with a stranger who arrives in St. Adrienne looking for him. The stranger, going by the name of Robert X, is seen and discussed by the entire community. He walks around St. Adrienne and is often seen behind Martin's church or near his street. Though his reason for being in St. Adrienne is unknown, his gaunt face and wandering eyes imply that he is near death. When Robert X meets Elijah, the church pianist who rents a room in Phillip's house, he finds out that there is to be a party at Phillip's the following week. By opening with Robert X, rather than Martin, Gaines implements a gothic tone to frame Phillip's presence. The younger man's mysterious presence is ghost-like, a projection of an irreconcilable past. His fixation upon the physical structures Martin inhabits suggests that they are sites of public status whose private realities hover at the edge of narrative.

Hence, before Phillip Martin appears in the novel, Gaines has provided several instances where he is assessed and evaluated as a public figure. For example, when Elijah meets his friends at a local bar, Phillip's party invites commentary. One of Elijah's friends observes, "That whole thing's over with. . . . He did some good work but's it all over with now."[27] The effect of this is to situate Phillip as a man who creates public discourse; he is a man seen and talked about. The terms used by younger, more disillusioned blacks denote him as a figure of depletion, an icon of a moment just passed. But the time, just two years after the death of King when a leader of epic proportions is so deeply longed for, has allowed Phillip to sustain enough of his public influence that he is perceived by an older constituency as effective.

The curiosity Robert X entertains concerning Phillip Martin indicates a deeper, more substantial drama than that of a civil rights leader whose popularity is on the wane. The novel's title intimates that an encounter of a different sort is at hand. Thus, when Robert X appears at Phillip's party (which we discover is to celebrate the coming demonstration at a white owner's department store), the shock of seeing him knocks the older man to the floor. Referring as it does to Christ's assertion of God's abundance of resources, *In My Father's House* is just as concerned with apportionment and depletion as its predecessor. It also recalls the parable of the prodigal son, a parable Christ relates in response to the Pharisees' notion that men of public status should not convene with men of lesser social worth. Phillip's collapse must be read, then, as the symptom of an abrupt encounter with his forgotten past: a time when he lacked the emotional resources to fulfill the role of father. However, the whites and middle class blacks at the party interpret his fall as the sign of overwork, the result of his public role. This misreading occurs at the novel's conceptual nexus: the public life of men, the transgressions that threaten to rupture that life, and the ability to find resources that can sufficiently incorporate transgression and reflection to create a flexible, but coherent, sense of self.

It is here that we must consider the importance of intimacy. What does intimacy mean for our purposes and how does it square with the terms that we have already set forth? Michael G. Cooke provides what is perhaps the most assiduous definition of intimacy:

> Intimacy . . . signalize[s] a condition in which the African-American protagonist (male or female, pugilist or philosopher, activist or ascetic) is depicted as realistically enjoying a sound and clear orientation toward the self and the world. It denotes a state of mind where one is, in Wordsworth's paradoxical phrase, "free to settle," or, in other words, comely and resolute in one's own being as well as sensitive and effective in dealing with social entities and forces.[28]

As a man who lives a life that is energized by the public sphere, Phillip Martin is a figure for whom intimacy, or at least the search for it, is essential. For as Cooke observes, intimacy represents "a thorough involvement with the world and along with that a degree of immunity and superiority to sociopolitical shibboleths . . . 'a wider recognition of the universe' " (*Afro-American Literature,* x). Moreover, Cooke's distinction between the "intimacy of gesture" in which Phillip has come to be engaged and the "full and unforced communication with the given, the available, and the conceivable in human experience in a particular time and setting," represents the journey he must undertake if he is to acquire a coherent sense of who he is. In many ways, Phillip is the logical result if Marcus Payne were to survive and take up a life devoted to social rather than political resistance, which would explain his preoccupation with transformation. Whereas Marcus, as self-centered youth, could only play out the role of the questing son (hence his relationship with Jim Kelly), Phillip seeks to fulfill the role of father. For him, his public role has familial importance because it attempts to link these two estranged positions.

Hence, the idea of having a party before the demonstration begs the question: what is being celebrated, empowerment in the present or the victories of the past? Objectified by his own hubris, Phillip sees Robert X and the shock of recognition becomes a moment of depletion. Byerman's description of the former as a "ghost" is apt here, for the gothic aspects of Phillip's past take physical shape, rendering the present incoherent.[29] What his presence articulates is that Phillip's apportionment—the physical and material splendor of his present life—is linked to his son's spiritual depletion. Indeed, the gothic overtones of *In My Father's House* intimate Gaines's concern that the public roles African American men assume inevitably diminish their spiritual resources. As I will discuss in Chapter 5, what often concerns Gaines's fictional protagonists most deeply is their desire to maintain or nurture kinship ties. This notion is worth our attention here because Phillip's public status is fueled by the act of truncating memory, where the past is synonymous with his activism. The scene where Robert X stands before him calls for a deeper inquiry: what are the motivations for public life, and are those motivations foregrounded by the need to expunge the past?

The moment when Phillip falls illustrates, therefore, the contingent nature of identity. This is underscored by Gaines's sense that Phillip's single-mindedness leaves his self-concept vulnerable to collapse. His weakness, he notes in his "Conversation" with Marcia Gaudet and Carl Wooten, the reason

> he does not get up, is he let the liberal decide who . . . he is. He let the liberal white decide who he is. They decided he was tired, and he accepted their decision without saying, "No, I'm not. This is my son." That is why he failed.[30]

Phillip's dilemma reminds us of Ellison's protagonist in that he is defined by others. Suddenly, "the Movement" is not enough, for Gaines insists that Phillip's white political allies are

> the sort of help he could go to get something moving like [voting], but they're the same people who kept him on his back when he wanted to get his son.

That's part of the scheme: We can help you to get a drink of water, we can have you sit at the counter, but we cannot help you to understand your son or your son to understand you. Our policies are not written that way. ("Conversation," 59).

This forces us to reassess the question Ellison poses in Chapter 21 in *Invisible Man*: could politics ever be an expression of love?; and to articulate its inverse: can love ever be an expression of one's politics?

Under such terms, Robert X's arrival forces Phillip to reassess the meaning of his labor: is it a genuine desire to bring about change or is he running away from his past? Phillip looks at his house, the symbol of his achievement and observes:

He was proud of this house. He had worked hard for his family, his church, the people, and the movement, and he had been proud of that hard work. He thought he had done a good job, at least both black and white had told him so. But now, after seeing the boy in the house, after falling and not getting up, he had begun to question himself; What really was Phillip Martin, and what if anything had he really done? (*Father's House,* 72)

If we are to ascertain the full nature of Phillip's angst, we must consider here spiritual conversion. Phillip's passage from sin to salvation, his journey from brutality to manhood, acquires such public currency that the personal crisis that produced his transformation assumes a lesser weight. The significance of this, as David O'Rourke insists, is that conversion "allows us to resolve immobilizing crisis in a mobilizing way and deal with potentially destructive forces in a creative way."[31] As an example of his being imbued with a new set of resources, Phillip's civil rights activity is the creative embodiment of his "salvation." But a problem arises when he inhabits a space where his spiritual mandate is a wholly public manifestation. This means that he must always demonstrate his salvation through acts of public display; activism becomes synonymous with spiritual coherence.[32]

But Robert X's presence leads Phillip to renew his conjugal ties and thus to confront the contingency of a public self. As the agent of change in St. Adrienne, the act of embracing his son is synonymous with his embattled past. However, his public status cannot support both initiatives. Thus, when he attempts to bail Robert X out of jail, the sheriff will comply with his request only if Phillip agrees to call off the demonstration. The past and present collide, not only because Gaines poses them as irreconcilable concepts, but also because they demand that Phillip manifest authority in two distinct conceptual spaces at once: one personal, the other public. It is important that it is Sheriff Nolan with whom Phillip must negotiate in order to get Robert X out of jail, for he is the one individual positioned to understand how Phillip possesses the ability to transform his jail from a space of confinement and punishment to a space of resistance and social consciousness.[33] Because Nolan and Phillip have known one another for most of their lives, the discussion between Phillip and Nolan provides us with a sense of the scope of Phillip's conversion:

> As a young deputy Nolan had arrested Phillip several times for fighting. Twice he was picked up as a suspect in killings, but neither time was there enough proof against him. As the sheriff of St. Adrienne, Nolan had arrested him more than once for civil rights demonstrations. The two men had no love for each other; still there was no running hatred for each other either. Each felt the other was doing his work the best way he knew how, and both accepted the fact that there would be conflicts between them. (83)

When Phillip requests his son's release, Nolan sees it as an opportunity to reclaim the jail as a site of white supremacy and control. What was a form of antagonistic cooperation between the two men becomes a barter arrangement through which the sheriff recognizes that he can circumvent legal procedure.

Phillip's request is a necessary (albeit reluctant) move, an attempt to structure a space where he can converse with Robert X as father and not as public figure. Hence he barters for his son using the only commodity at his disposal: his public role (and the scheduled demonstration against the storeowner, Chenal) as civil rights spokesman. What he fails to anticipate, however, is that Robert X—whose real name he cannot remember—has no investment in Phillip's life as an activist. Thus he cannot bring his persuasive skills to bear on their encounter.

When Robert X and Phillip finally get an opportunity to talk, the former accuses his father of "raping" his mother. Though Phillip denies it, citing his love for the younger man's mother, Johanna, he adheres to this interpretation of events. The boy accuses him of trying to pay off the crime when he recounts the three dollars Phillip offers. Phillip's tearful response is crucial to understanding his motivations—political and otherwise:

> I was paralyzed. Paralyzed. Yes, I had a mouth, but I didn't have a voice. I had legs, but I couldn't move. I had arms, but I couldn't lift them up to you. It took a man to do these things, and I wasn't a man. I was just some other brutish animal who could cheat, steal, rob, kill—but not stand. Not be responsible. Not protect you or your mother. They had branded that in us from the time of slavery. That's what kept me on that bed. Not 'cause I didn't want to get up. I wanted to get up more than anything in the world. But I had to break the rules, rules we had lived by for so long, and I wasn't strong enough to break them then. (102)

This statement corresponds with Phillip's recollection of the day Johanna and her children leave the Reno plantation. Before his first encounter with Robert X at his house, he has had a dream:

> He could still see Johanna in the black overcoat and black hat waving her arms and calling to him. But why black? Why black? He had never known her to wear anything but the brightest colors when she was here. Why black now? He could still see the oldest boy at the tailgate of the wagon reaching out his small arms. But the other two children went on playing as if nothing was happening round them. He ran as hard as he could to catch them, but the wagon slowly and steadily moved farther and farther away. (53–54)

This dream of failed paternity must be juxtaposed with what actually transpired twenty-one years previous, but also considered in terms of how Phillip remembers it and the way memory and symbols form an interpretive confluence.

As he sits in his study, remembering the dream, Gaines's narrator calls our attention to a collage with John F. Kennedy, Martin Luther King, and Robert Kennedy on the wall. And hanging "evenly with the first" collage is another one containing pictures of Lincoln, Frederick Douglass, and Booker T. Washington. That Gaines identifies the pictures as "collages" is an important detail, one that has deeper critical implications. Thought of in the most formal of terms, the photos as "collages" would represent a kind of visual dissensus, the "ultimate disaffection [of leaders] whose . . . choices don't fit."[34] The collages fail to achieve this level of complexity; rather they create a consensual myth whose purpose is to truncate politics, protest, and history into a simplistic relation, one whose representational strategy somehow proposes that Douglass and Lincoln, for example, stand in political and social accord.[35] This harmony likewise posits this visual "collaboration" as the means by which the successful enactment of African American citizenship was achieved. If we consider both sets of portraits more closely, we find that the African American leaders are positioned alongside white elected officials. One reading of this arrangement would be that African American leaders, whose authority derives from their ability to manifest a persuasive rhetorical presence, must work in concert with men whose authority is derived by law. But we can also read it as an imbalance of power. As such, it articulates the manner by which this iconographic arrangement of civil rights figures is finally a set of ciphers invested with false meaning. Indeed, if we look more closely at the collage of King and the Kennedys, what we find is that, in actuality, each represents the failure of the dream. Or perhaps, more precisely, each represents the dream rendered incomplete by violence. What this suggests is that, like these men, Phillip is incapable of making the dream real, doomed to be trapped in the realm of a public dream-myth. Moreover, the dream of his failed fatherhood takes place in the midst of a failed public dream. That he remembers the dream in the midst of a veritable "pantheon" of heroes articulates the fact that his public life has inflections that are, at root, deeply personal.

We need, however, to understand the depth of Phillip's disorientation. After remembering the dream, he looks at his Bible, which is turned to the fourteenth chapter of John. He begins to read, but he stops as he begins the third verse. The unread portion reads as follows: " . . . and prepare a place for you, I will come again, and receive you unto myself; that where I am, *there* ye may be also." This statement encompasses a promise of return, a fulfillment of longing. As we see in the next verse, the disciples are skeptical. They require evidence that they are in the presence of the Father, most notably the disciple Philip, who says, "Lord, shew us the Father, and it sufficeth us." As Phillip thinks about why he fell and did not get up, he turns back to the pictures on the wall and realizes, "These great men always gave him encouragement when he was troubled. In his heart he asked them now for guidance." He realizes this before he prays, "quietly to the *picture* of Christ on the cross" (my emphasis). This is a pivotal moment in the novel, one that should help to clarify Phillip Martin's dilemma. Like his biblical counterpart, Phillip relies on physical evidence, on icons, to maintain spiritual contact. Moreover, his first choice is to look to public men for guidance. His prayer is aimed at a representation of Christ's liminal moment, an instance before the Resurrection, as if Gaines wants to suggest that Phillip's "conversion" is one doomed to fail because it relies on idolatry rather than faith. Moreover, he seeks to refute the dream by bringing the force of his transformation to bear; but this is a misinterpretation of the dream. He reads the dream as a slightly revised version of the past, but in fact the dream is the call to interpret events in the present.

What lends such importance to these seemingly innocuous details is that Phillip's entire career as a public figure is predicated on the moment that necessitates his conversion to a more spiritual life. In his interpretation of conversion experience, he links emotional apathy with civic activism. His comments to Robert X reveal that his public life has been devoted to avoiding immobility. While he is correct in his assertion that racial segregation and discrimination divested him, like other black men, of the emotional resources necessary to maintain his family, the course he chooses to overdetermine political activism and thus become a man of action comes at the expense of spiritual growth.

Though his notion that family matters are finally political is a correct assessment, Phillip Martin has inadvertently chosen the wrong path to reconcile social justice and filial responsibility.

5

The remainder of the novel consists of Phillip's quest for reconciliation. This results in an attempt to recreate the conditions which produced his original "conversion." Like Ellison's hero, Phillip must search for a way to conjoin his life into a coherent narrative which will lead him towards the conclusion that he is "nobody but himself." Before he can do this, however, he must journey into the past to reconstruct his past life and connect it with the present in order to integrate these disparate parts into a unified identity. The key figure in this quest is his old friend, Chippo Simon. Chippo lives across the river in Baton Rouge, which Gaines suggests is St. Adrienne's antithesis: a gothic underworld of gambling establishments, juke joints, and tiny cafes. In a manner reminiscent of Orpheus, Phillip must venture into this place to find the lost portions of his past, the self he left behind. Gaines's use of an omniscient narrator suggests, then, that the novel is not concerned with Phillip's ability to tell a story. Rather, it is concerned with the ability to recover an understanding of the importance of listening. As "community spokesman," Phillip cannot be the one to tell his tale, for his voice is that of civil rights leader and preacher. His search is for another voice, one that can articulate his longing for emotional agency and intimacy.[36]

Phillip's search for Chippo leads him through Baton Rouge, where he meets individuals who direct him toward his spiritual goal by helping him confront important issues. He stops in a cafe for coffee and there meets an older man, a preacher like himself. The man is poor and, unlike Phillip, he is a "public figure" only because the cafe owner considers him a nuisance. He differs from Phillip also because he is faith and love personified, even in the face of rejection and poverty. Later, he meets a younger man just returned from Vietnam, who is trying to recruit other men to carry out a violent resistance against capitalist America. He values "bullets and fire" over Phillip's adherence to non-violence. Here Gaines evokes the muddle of agendas that the seventies brought to black leadership after King's death. Thus, Phillip Martin's journey into the past likewise leads him back toward the substance of what gave his life as an activist meaning; he is searching for the renewal of kinship at two levels: with his son and the community. The last figure from his past is Adeline Toussant, a former lover. Though she may be seen as the temptress, what is more important—

and appropriate—is her assertion that she has a very different sense from his of their time together, and thus he finds that historical narrative is neither fixed nor absolute. Though he dismisses her interpretation of what has transpired between them out of a need to maintain a sense of his power with women, her resistance to Phillip's version of their shared history suggests the limitations of Phillip's masculine influence, a fact he refuses to acknowledge outwardly. However, Phillip's quest for his son is motivated by the sense that his patriarchal influence is extremely limited. The invitation Adeline extends to Phillip is a nod to the past and thus it does not offer the resources he needs to resolve his crisis of identity in either the present or the future.

When Chippo finally arrives, Phillip asks to hear about Johanna. Reluctantly, Chippo tells the tale, much of which he has heard from a storekeeper in San Francisco. Phillip is reminded that Robert X's real name is Etienne and that Johanna never stopped loving him. The story also relates the source of Etienne's spiritual malaise. The storekeeper tells him that Etienne has turned his room into a "crypt" after his brother goes to prison for murdering the man who raped their sister. Besieged with guilt that he himself did not kill his sister's attacker, Etienne goes into a state of hibernation. The family lives in an apartment in the basement of a three-story building; thus this hibernation has Faulknerian overtones. Entombed in guilt, the only way for Etienne to "recover his manhood" is by killing Phillip.[37]

Chippo recalls that the root of the problem lies in the tremendous burden placed on Etienne by Johanna:

> He was the man of the house. The man of the house. She told it to him that day he left from here. She told it to him right here in front of me. When you didn't come out of Tut's house that day, she told him that till you did come back to them he was go'n be the man of the house. She took him by the hand, looking straight in his face—a scared, confused little boy. I told her it wasn't right. I told her he wasn't but a chap himself, and it wasn't right. I told there'd be other men, and she oughtn't force this burden on him. But she didn't hear a word I said. (194)

Coherence is at issue here on several levels. When Phillip's and Johanna's "family" disintegrates, she makes Etienne into a surrogate partner, but his manhood is conditional, contingent on Phillip's return. This leads to the annihilation of his masculinity because he can neither protect her nor replace Phillip as a lover. When Etienne comforts his sister after the rape, he compromises his role as "man of the house." His filial response to the crisis is correct but his figurative status as lover and protector make this response inappropriate. Antoine's decision to kill the rapist is an instance of self-apportionment, the elements of which are of greater substance than what Etienne receives from

Johanna. When Etienne visits him in prison, he realizes a shift in power has occurred. "When [Antoine] pulled that trigger," Chippo relates, "then he was the man. His sister, the way she looked at him, let him know that he was the man. Even Johanna. Even Etienne himself let him know he was the man" (198).

When Antoine is released from prison, he and Justine move to New York, pursuing a symbolic journey eastward that erases the familial past. Antoine and Justine choose to be "dead" to the rest of the family, a choice which voices their opposition to the incestual nature of Etienne's and Johanna's relationship. The east represents an opportunity to begin again: for Antoine and Justine as a coherent family unit, and for Etienne to renew his depleted manhood. As a result, however, the family collapses into incoherence. Etienne's search for the father originates as an attempt to "slay the father," but torn between attempting to free himself from Oedipal conflict and recovering his own identity, he is locked in stasis, the anti-hero trapped in an incoherent state. Chippo's story provides the meaning for Phillip's dream: the son who longs to embrace him (if only to kill him) and the two children who ignore his presence altogether. Chippo tells him to forget the past, but Phillip responds:

> I went to religion to forget it. I prayed and prayed and prayed to forget it. I tried to wipe out everything in my past, make my mind blank, start all over. I thought the good work I was doing with the church, with the people, would make up for all the things I had done in the past. Till one day I looked cross my living room. (201)

He realizes that his "fall" in his living room is the rupture of a mythic reality. His ministerial life is called into question because, as the young Vietnam veteran asserts, the civil rights movement has failed to reconcile the differences between fathers and sons.

In My Father's House ends when Alma, Phillip's wife, tells him, "We just go'n have to start again." I want to cite this at the outset in order to begin to isolate the most important aspects of Gaines's authorial intentions. At one level, Phillip's public role is ruptured because he has been stripped of his title as president of the St. Adrienne Civil Rights Committee. However, this negative circumstance is actually the means for Phillip's transcendence. Because he has formulated his entire career as a public figure on notions of the past, indeed, making the past an idol to whom he bows, Phillip uses memory as a guide for his action in the present. Thus Alma's response to Phillip when he announces to her, "I'm lost," is a statement invested solely in things present, a signal for him to follow.

However, we need to consider the substance of Phillip's remark.

Faced with an instance where he must reassess his life as a public figure, Phillip's greatest challenge is to see Etienne, who commits suicide by jumping off a bridge, as an anomaly he can no longer control. Phillip's deep sense of guilt has made his public life devoted to making himself worthy for his son's return. While this is not in itself a transgression, what makes it so is that he engages in a paradigm of leadership that requires him to construct the past as an idol. He chooses to do this rather than adopt a new posture, one that would allow him to articulate the connection between kinship and political activism. The failed paradigm nullifies this relation, and insists instead upon the relationship between civil rights and activism. This means that Phillip works at cross-purposes to his own rhetoric which, after all, is formulated upon notions of endurance. As he relates to Chippo, his memory remains fixed on that time when he lacked the ability to move:

> I was telling my boy today what keep us apart is a paralysis we inherited from slavery. Paralysis kept me on that bed that day he knocked on that door. Paralysis kept me on that floor Saturday when I shoulda got up and told the people who he was. I thought fifteen years ago when I found religion I had overthrown my paralysis. But it's still there, Chippo. How do you get rid of it? How do you shake it off? (202)

Phillip's need for intimacy offers the means for him to construct a more viable public role. His problem has been one of attempting to accumulate the wrong kinds of resources. Thus, Alma's recognition that she and Phillip are the key, as parents, to a new paradigm is likewise her assertion that resources yet exist to accomplish his task. Alma also allows us to reassess Phillip's earlier announcement that

> Love is the only thing. Understanding the only thing. Persistence, the only thing. Getting up tomorrow, trying again, the only thing. Keep on pushing, the only thing. (37)

Phillip begins with love and ends with conflict. Though this rhetorical posture appears to offer the potential for positive results, it actually obscures success because it posits proliferation over process. This rhetorical "stockpiling" serves an emotional purpose, drawing as it does on the sermonic mode. It fails, however, in its political goal of rendering the confrontation with Chenal as the alteration of a community's impulse to act against itself. Thus, the achievement of intimacy is subordinated to political confrontation.

But here we need to return to the idea of conversion, for by doing so we can see that Phillip Martin is an allegorical figure who forces us to reconsider the political climate of the seventies. As David O'Rourke suggests, conversion literally means a kind of turning . . . a turning from the road we are on to another. It is not a minor turning, but one that comes about for reasons that seem to be running us more than we run them and to a new way that affects the whole of our life. ("Experience of Conversion," 9)

O'Rourke insists that conversion is not a singular event. Rather it is an instance of great complexity. Thus, he argues, conversion is "more complex than it is often perceived. The complexity is to be found principally in the fact that conversion occurs in several stages." This observation has special relevance to our inquiry into Phillip Martin, for as both convert and activist he makes the connection between his earlier "paralysis" and his public role as civil rights leader. This conflicts, however, with his role as spiritual leader. As such, he must lead by faith; he must manifest a persona imbued with limitless resources, even when those resources appear to be depleted.

Herein lies the problem. Phillip's misconceptions regarding spiritual conversion intimate the reason for his difficulty. His failure of faith is a failure to grasp the complexity of conversion. O'Rourke outlines three stages of conversion, which he refers to as the "noisy phase," the "quiet phase," and the "integrated phase" (10). Phillip Martin, community activist, the loud voice calling others to action, remains locked in this first mode of conversion, which "begins with the inner conflict in search of resolution and surfaces in the frequently ebullient change that we commonly call a conversion." Consider his statement toward the end of the novel:

I was an animal before I was Reverend Phillip J. Martin. I was an animal. [God] changed me to a man. He straightened my back. He raised my head. He gave me feelings, compassion, made me responsible for my fellow man. My back wasn't straightened before He straightened it. My eyes stayed on the ground. I took everything I could from my fellow man, and I didn't give him nothing back. (211)

And thus, Phillip concludes:

I woulda looked at my son going by the house, and I woulda forgotten him—if it wasn't for Him. But He changed me, and I can't forget my son. I can't forget my son, young lady. I can't ignore my son no more. That's why I say He owed me my son. Once He made me a human being. He owed me my son. (212)

Phillip's problem is that Etienne's departure prevents him from resolving fully the inner conflict O'Rourke describes. His activism is motivated by the desire for penance on the one hand and the notion of earthly reward on the other. Moreover, it relies on public displays of demonstrative energy. Both of these signal Phillip's transition from one form of social visibility to another. After his conversion, his role as leader continues to be grounded in his sense of superiority:

> I've taken my fellow man by the hand and led him the way you lead a small child: led him to that courthouse, led him to the stores, led him to that bus station. . . . But I asked nobody to do a thing till I had done it first. I was ready to get the first blow, what I've received many many times. But I kept going, kept going. (211–12)

But he has failed at the more difficult task of reflecting on his life. He can only accomplish this by moving beyond the public sphere. As O'Rourke notes, the "quiet phase" is a time

> of reflection, of withdrawal, a time for making sense of what has happened. It is a time for interiorization, for moving the choice of a new direction in life from the sphere of emotions and enthusiasm to the center of the person's being. This time of quiet and withdrawal is an integral part of the conversion process. For some, this phase is seen as the loss of conversion, and the attempt to prevent the move from visible enthusiasm to quiet is seen as a religious duty. ("Experience of Conversion," 10)

Clearly, Phillip Martin is entering this phase of his conversion experience. It is a liminal moment, but one that he resists because his religious orientation associates public action with the maintenance of the conversion experience. His confusion as to his future course and his feelings of rejection arise from his failure to see conversion as an ongoing process. Like Ellison's hero, who evolves to a point where he can reflect on his experience and integrate those reflections in the form of a written text, Phillip must make the transition from shouting to solitude. Only then can he move to the final stage, the integrated phase, where, as O'Rourke suggests, the individual

> has integrated the substance of the conversion into the rest of his or her being. The period of retreat and withdrawal has provided the time to make sense of what has happened, to integrate the change of conversion into the person's history and life, and to form that synthesis of all these parts that comes as its result. (10)

And, in what should surely remind us of invisible man's insistence that his hibernation is a "preparation," O'Rourke observes that the convert, upon entering the integrated phase is

> prepared to enter again into the community in a more active way. But, this time the activity comes, not from the overflow of emotional energy that results from the resolution of conflict, but from the convert's convictions. No longer is he insisting that any and all in his circle listen to what has happened to him, but rather he is offering to tell them who he now is and what he believes. (10)

Like Ellison's hero, Phillip Martin's public life is not over. As Beverly Ricord informs him, he still has much to do. However, the novel's conclusion intimates that he will do his work differently; his life as activist may give way to another life, one aimed at leading other people to a new sense of possibility. Though he has been relieved of his duties as president of the St. Adrienne Civil Rights Committee, he still has his church. Like invisible man's hole, Phillip's church offers a space for him to renew his depleted psyche. I want also to return, if only momentarily, to his office. It, too, represents a space of transformation. However, it cannot serve him as shrine. The pictures of Douglass, Washington, Lincoln, King, and the Kennedys are not idols; they represent "images of kin." Like theirs, Phillip's life as an activist is characterized by conflict and failure. But here, he can use them as touchstones of the real, not as mythic figures; they can help him reference his own experience. More important, the African American figures in particular offer him images of self-made men whose lives were devoted to human agency. Lincoln and the Kennedys offer images of public martyrs, which in and of themselves offer little except that they can point him toward the ultimate martyr: Christ. For what differentiates the latter from the images of the former is not His death on the cross, but the resurrection that follows it. Alma's call for Phillip to "start again" is thus her awareness that falls from public grace of the type Phillip has experienced are ultimately tests of faith. In a more integrated state of being, Phillip will learn to collaborate, not only with Alma, but with others who share his concerns. But as O'Rourke suggests, the liminal phase in which we find him at novel's end is a necessary step toward a new way to read—and thus give voice to—his life's concerns.

6

Taken together, *Of Love and Dust* and *In My Father's House* represent Gaines's extended rumination on the role of memory in the individual's transformation. It is necessary, however, to locate these novels within their regional context. For one might argue that those who challenge the status quo in Gaines's Louisiana are either killed like Marcus or stripped of all desire to live like Etienne. Or one might argue further that they end up like Jim Kelly and Phillip Martin, locked in ambiguity. To be sure, Kelly and Martin find themselves at the periphery of their communities, having lost the status they accrued via the conventions of their respective settings. But what makes their experiences of a conceptual piece is their realization that memory has prevented them from constituting fresh space in which to manifest proactive identities. As we have seen, both men find themselves in liminal circumstances. For

Kelly, this requires a physical break from the Hebert plantation that allows him to conjoin memory and voice, but not to locate his narration in a particular place and thus articulate his plans for the future. For Phillip Martin there is the need to embrace solitude, to loose himself from the past even as he integrates it into his experience. Phillip must learn to accept Christ's injunction that "the first shall be last."[38] At novel's end, he can only articulate his inability to site himself.

One way to read this liminality on the part of Gaines's protagonists is to remember that they are Louisianans. Though both endure transformations that leave them with the task of relocating themselves within the community, they represent a more pervasive notion. Both embrace resistance as a vehicle of identity and both undergo conversion experiences that loose them from paralyzing circumstances. However, neither finds his turn of fate a guarantee of either safety or status. Nor can they utilize memory unless they are also willing to tell their stories. To do otherwise is to fall back into a static mode in which their status only appears to be secure. In these instances, the temptation to remember must be staved off, requiring these characters to use labor as a way of blocking access to the past.

What Gaines suggests here is that the Louisiana past, as these characters experience it, can either restrain action or serve as a resource to an integrated state of selfhood. In allegorical terms, Gaines's characters represent the kind of labor necessary for Louisiana to become a more inclusive, democratic space for black and white alike. While both Jim Kelly and Phillip Martin endure soul-destroying losses, they are also literary gestures toward an alternative paradigm for understanding black life in Louisiana. That Gaines chooses to render the future in ambiguous terms for both characters intimates that he eschews the impulse to construct Louisiana as a polemical space where its problems are easily solved or where black and white represent good and evil, respectively. Rather, he depicts it as an evolutionary space; the arrival of integration will not, Gaines suggests, transform Louisianans as much as it will put their lives on a different course. Hence, like Kelly and Martin, Louisiana undergoes a conversion from one form of community to another.

Both these novels posit slavery as the force which continues to effect Southern identity. If slavery is analagous to a Godless circumstance, a road to ruin, then the South's transformation begins with the Civil War. However, as Gaines's rendering of conversion as a complex, multiple-staged event denotes, the violent changes brought on by the war gave way to a phase that ran from Reconstruction till the 1950s, when Jim Crow conventions normalized relations between blacks and whites.[39] A character like Jim Kelly represents the singular need to break out of a repressive circumstance. Set in the 1940s, *Of Love and Dust* works out the beginnings of what would become, in the next decade, the protest against the degradation of Jim Crow.

In chronological terms, Phillip Martin represents the "integrative" phase of Southern conversion. He is successful at transforming the symbolic sites where Jim Crow flourished. However, what his character calls us to recognize is the necessity for transformation to be continuous. His personal movement into the quiet phase of conversion, the need to "start again," proposes that Louisianans, and indeed all Southerners, must embrace their failures as part of a coherent process which, far from insuring utopian outcomes, will merely allow them to create a more collaborative narrative posture. The ambiguity surrounding Phillip Martin at the end of *In My Father's House* represents a kind of catholicity. His gothic past has ruptured the present as he previously understood it; conversely, this is also the exact moment when he can break free from the past, when he stumbles upon the necessary resources to establish relationships oriented toward the future. In this regard, Gaines's depiction of an activist with a tangled past asserts again the need to understand the relationship between freedom and literacy. For what Phillip Martin acquires via the necessity to integrate past and present is a new way to read signs. Like Ellison's hero, who chooses reflection and discovers that it is an act of resistance in and of itself, Phillip's movement into a reflective mode signals a new approach to activism. As preacher, Phillip stands as the bridge between the sacred and secular worlds. Though his status in the latter is diminished, the former offers an instance of infinite resources.

What this means is that these two novels must be seen as a celebration of the *task* of transforming the South. Though his fiction often depicts brutal circumstances, I would argue that, like Ellison, Gaines believes the South (and thus, the nation as a whole) is an undiscovered country. The past is therefore a necessary, albeit precarious, resource and Gaines's fictions argue for an open-endedness as it pertains to the South. As Gaines related in an interview with Charles Rowell:

> Faulkner says something like the past ain't dead; it ain't even passed. . . . I don't know that you can escape the past. If it were possible, I would have escaped it myself, because Louisiana is definitely not only my past but my present also. I believe I, myself, and my writing are good examples to support that observation that you can't escape your past. There is a difference between living in the past and trying to escape it. If you do nothing but worship the past you are quite dead, I believe. But if you start running and trying to get away from the past. . . . It will run you mad, or kill you in some way or the other. So you really don't get away. It's there and you live it.[40]

Hence, neither Jim Kelly nor Phillip Martin is a figure who finds a way to escape the past. Rather, they are characters who discern new ways to use the past. As Gaines's remarks above suggest, the individual is faced with the need to find a way to use the past rather than discard it. Kelly and Martin, though flawed in character, are also the sign that the process of transformation requires acts of memory brought to life via the act of witnessing. Though the story may be one that brings sadness and confusion, it is finally what must be brought to bear to insure that change is everlasting.

Chapter 4

"If It's Going To Be Any Good, It's *Your Story*": Legibility, [Un]speakability, and Historical Performance in McPherson's "A Solo Song: For Doc"

> This was no everyday event:
> reports of madness
> with too much technique
> for the life force,
> the flow tuned in and broken apart.
> —Michael S. Harper, "Solo"

1

In the last chapter, we examined Ernest Gaines's explication of the pitfalls of unsanctioned memory. There we examined Jim Kelly's need to separate himself from the familiar in order to enter a space where the act of remembering and the telling it engenders is unencumbered, loosed from communal restraint. That restraint, we discovered, sprang from the entanglement of race ritual and memory: the violent racial dramas that Jim Crow enacts lead, as the character of Aunt Margaret demonstrates, to what she claims is a mnemonic lapse. Jim Kelly is successful in breaking this "tradition of forgetfulness" to tell his tale, however, and in so doing, restores his damaged faith.

Gaines's hero reestablishes the relationship between acts of remembrance and oral storytelling. As we will see with James Alan McPherson's much-anthologized short story, "A Solo Song: For Doc," history in written form can be as emblematic of erasure or forgetfulness ("invisibility in black and white") as when it is illegible and unrecollected. Like Jim Kelly, McPherson's Youngblood is faced with a plethora of recorded omissions and the responsibility of learning how to tell what he knows. Also like Jim, the youngblood must struggle to come to this realization by loosing himself from the prison of rote learning while he embraces improvisation. Unlike *Of Love and Dust,* though, McPherson's fiction structures a very different relationship between teller and audience, one that, in its turn, forces the reader to reconsider the relationship between oral and written forms of history.

Ellison's novel provides, once again, a useful trope with which to interrogate McPherson's story. Recall that moment in *Invisible Man* when the hero, having been kicked out of college, is instructed by the insidious Dr. Bledsoe to seek his fortune in New York City. This comes on the heels of invisible man's accidental transgression against the college president's cardinal tenet: the power he has accrued and the illusion he has created to maintain it must be protected at all costs. Opportunity, as far as the narrator knows, lies in the seven letters Bledsoe furnishes for him as he leaves the campus. Rendered unreadable by the snowy white envelopes that conceal them, the text of the letters is the symbol, not only of Bledsoe's subterfuge, but of the hero's complicity as well. As far as he knows, the college president has, by committing pen to paper, proposed and seconded a course of action to be followed "to the letter." It is only after Emerson allows the hero to read one of the letters that he realizes Bledsoe's correspondence has entwined punishment and opportunity in a seemingly Gordian relation. Though he does not recognize it as such, the protagonist's expulsion is a liberating moment. The signal for this comes from none other than Bledsoe himself when he declares, "if you make good, perhaps . . . well, perhaps . . . it's up to you."

The "crazed" Vet confirms this assessment during the early stages of the hero's bus ride North. "Be your own father," the Vet tells him as he departs for St. Elizabeth's,[1] "And remember the world is possibility if only you'll discover it. Last of all, leave the Mr. Nortons alone and if you don't know what I mean, think about it" (*Invisible Man,* 156). Though the hero receives an alternative to Bledsoe's letters, one that makes his own self-definition a priority, he adheres to his need to travel under the cover of the college president's dubious protection. The problem here is one of the protagonist having to decide which of these sources of counsel is legitimate: one is credible because of the status that accompanies it, the other is totally lacking in credibility because it issues from an example of lost status; one is intentional in its attempt to be helpful, the other only circumstantially so (and thus, by virtue of this, it is suspect unless the protagonist can decipher, separate, and utilize what is useful while discarding that which is harmful). Unfortunately, as the chapters that follow make clear, Ellison's narrator opts repeatedly for the choice confirmed by written evidence, by textuality. He eschews the counsel embedded in the Vet's oral narration, for the safety to be found in Dr. Bledsoe's letters. But only with great difficulty does he learn that the best counsel often comes from places most lacking in credibility. The narrator could choose to refuse the letters or, accepting them, decide not to open the envelopes. But textuality is such a powerful inducement: the hero accepts, as David Carson has pointed out, six paper talismans that blind and misdirect him, either because he lacks the ability to interpret them correctly or because he is led to incorporate them into a plan which is doomed to fail.

My interest in the dilemma Ellison depicts stems from the realization that this has become a recurrent trope in African American literature: the greenhorn who, through a lack of tribal literacy, manifests agency by valuing signs that issue from a textual field. While it is true that in African American literature the achievement of literacy often has to do with mastering the ability to interpret symbols of a non-textual sort, interpretation is often not enough. Essential in any interpretive strategy is the ability to understand the context in which symbols appear. Thus, it is possible to interpret correctly a set of textual symbols, only to be confused because the context remains a mystery. The innocent, as Ellison's hero demonstrates, ignores the oral information designed to clarify the symbols he encounters. This is by no means a new observation, nor is it meant to offer a static dichotomy between the written and the spoken. For it is likewise the case that the oral mode can, in a complex system of communication, be an incomplete arena in which to display one's tribal literacy; the proverbial man of words can deceive as quickly as the man of letters.[2] Its importance here lies in the fact that African American writers use this collision of discursive sites, as Houston Baker suggests, as an "invitation to inventive play."[3] Numerous African American writers have created protagonists who do not learn the full range of possibilities improvisation offers until they are steeped in crisis. Their failure results, as exemplified by Toni Morrison's Milkman, James Weldon Johnson's Ex-Colored Man, or Charles Johnson's Andrew Hawkins, because they attempt to choose one discursive model over the other (e.g., textual, as opposed to aural or visual, evidence) rather than seeking a more useful synthesis. This means that the task is often one of attempting to create a sensibility that does not obliterate the importance of textuality so much as it successfully resituates and harnesses it to a different purpose.[4]

2

James Alan McPherson's short story, "A Solo Song: For Doc,"[5] embodies an African American fiction where the character's task is one of reconfiguring the impact of reading and listening on his own experience. Or perhaps another way to describe the predicament McPherson enacts is one in which the act of inventive play his protagonist needs to perform is one that mediates audience, authentication, and authorship. Hence the combative relationship between teller and listener dramatizes antagonistic cooperation in its most Ellisonian terms. Like the "cruel contradiction" of jazz performance, McPherson's narrator and narratee create a performative nexus that embodies the same "endless improvisation" one finds in the jam session, where the narrator's "riff" on traditional materials leads him to "lose his identity even as he finds it.[6]

Ellison's observations on jazz resonate powerfully in an examination of this particular fiction because the narrator, like the musician, seeks to assert a voice that is not at odds with tradition. Indeed, the tradition expects assertion and sees it as a normal state of affairs. McPherson's title articulates the importance of this consideration, and it suggests that what happens in the space of this fiction is of a piece with jazz performance.

Because of this quality, it is necessary to contend with the story's multiple layers of address. First, there is Doc, to whom the act of "playing the solo" (in the form of telling his tale) is dedicated. There is a narratee whom the narrator addresses directly throughout the story. There is the reader who, through the act of reading, is figuratively "eavesdropping" on a "conversation" between narrator and narratee. And finally, there is the manner in which this text confronts its context; the way telling resists the authority of writing, the way writing attempts to restore the immediacy of telling. Each of these "conversations" refers to something larger and the concentric circles they form demonstrate their importance as ruminations on ontohistory. What makes this fiction ontohistorical is its interrogation of the manner in which certain forms of textual presentation come to stand as history, while others are not valued as such and are seen, in fact, as transgressive behaviors against the master narrative of Anglo-American history.

By what might seem to be the straightforward nature of McPherson's tale—the story of a waiter on the trains named Doc, told by his best friend to a young man whose reading is interrupted and who listens only half-heartedly—we could easily conclude that this is all the story presents. We could jettison the analytical posture that calls us to examine its structural mechanisms rather than its thematic significance. In light of this decision, then, would we see the title of McPherson's story simply as a gratuitous gesture? Perhaps, but Larry Kart provides us with grounds for an alternative interpretation when he argues that the connection between jazz and literature might be that jazz has more or less spontaneously developed in the course of its life musical parallels to preexisting literary forms. I've always thought of the typical good jazz solo as being more or less a lyric poem. It's a way of stating and elaborating your personal identity, as they say in show business, "in one."[7]

Echoing Ellison's remarks on jazz, Kart articulates the relationship between improvisation and identity:

You're up there, you are you. You don't have a costume on, you're not playing a role. If it's going to be any good, it's *your story.* I mean, it's almost a truism of jazz that when somebody gets up there and plays well, the reaction of a fan who responds in kind is, "He's a good *storyteller.*" The literal storytelling, the personal lyric storytelling, just goes without saying. (134; emphasis mine)

Kart suggests that we can locate the listener as the site of meaning, that the musical solo is a narrative event that calls for the listener to situate him or herself inside the "text." He further observes the fact that soloists "function both as people who are expressing themselves and as actors who have specific roles to play." In other words, it is possible to read McPherson's story as a conversation between a young man and his elder. But to do so, to view this story as an instance where we assign the narrator of the story a singularity of purpose is, as we shall see, problematic. For it is clear that McPherson intends for us to pay heed to the strategies the narrator employs to dramatize the telling. "A Solo Song: For Doc" can be seen as a fiction that enacts what Albert Murray, paraphrasing Kenneth Burke, refers to as "the estimate become maneuver." Murray continues the military metaphor by asserting

In such a frame of reference, style is not only insight but disposition and gesture, not only calculation and estimation become execution (as in engineering) but also motive and estimation become method and occupation. It is a way of sizing up the world, and so, ultimately and beyond all else, a mode and medium of survival.[8]

With its first person narrator, the story evokes the oral tradition, but it also attempts to illuminate the dynamic qualities of that tradition: serving the function of providing the listener/reader with valuable instruction and viable counsel. I agree with Keith Byerman's observation that the story makes use of call and response to accomplish its narrative ends, what he refers to as the narrative's "resistance to itself," a reflection of African American oral performance.[9] However, what I wish to emphasize more forcefully is that the resistance Byerman describes is a stylistic device of both formal and *thematic* import.

To that end, I intend to show how McPherson's story can be read as a fiction whose mimetic structure indicates an epic undercurrent where we can discern the story's deeper thematic intent. The narrative strategies it employs forces the reader to reexamine the story's plot, to discern patterns that recontextualize the heroic portraiture that "Solo Song" enacts. Even more important, however, in order to discern fully McPherson's authorial intent in "Solo Song," we must be mindful of the interplay between speaker and reader that generates Doc's tale.[10] That this story is a "solo song," then, cannot be dismissed as gratuity. Rather, we need to remember that the epic performance is, as Isidore Okpewho and others portray it, primarily a *sung* performance that invokes heroic action to isolate what might be characterized as non-heroic behavior and offer a transformative critique. Thus, the epic *is* a "solo song" that engages in a directed form of cultural work.

3

Like all improvised solos, McPherson's tale functions in close proximity to an audience and to the improvisations that have preceded it. What makes "A Solo Song: For Doc" a fiction that lends itself to misinterpretation (or, at the very least, partial interpretation) is that the epic parameters it attempts to construct are rendered invisible by the story's plot. Before he moves into Doc's tale, McPherson's narrator establishes the audience for the story. Indeed, the reader is privy to a conversation which begins with the narrator addressing a narratee, whom he refers to as "youngblood":

> So you want to know this business, youngblood? So you want to be a Waiter's Waiter? The Commissary gives you a book with all the rules and tells you to learn them. And you do, and think that is all there is to it. A big, thick black book. Poor youngblood. ("Solo Song," 48)

The narrator has interrupted the narratee's reading by offering his own "reading" of the text in question. Here, the young man's purpose comes to him as the paper talisman (the book) before him defines it. However, the speaker also points to the gap between its contents and the desired result. This leads to the tenet of greatest importance: the narrator's intimation that the "big, thick black book" is not the proper instrument to become a Waiter's Waiter, the only kind of waiter one would want to become. The tradition of the Waiter's Waiter references a transcendent state characterized by its ability to transgress surfaces, not the least of which is the "cover" of the black book. Indeed, the narrator reveals it to be a source of misinformation, an instrument of delusion and misdirection that recalls Bledsoe's letters. The old waiter's opening attack argues that the "black book" is a text open to contestation, and a failure to recognize this is the advent of misfortune.

Here, the reader engages the story's contextual mechanisms. "A Solo Song: For Doc" proffers a narrator whose first priority is to subvert the primacy of the printed word by destabilizing the black bible. More, he implies the incongruity between reading and status, a mistake that echoes the blunders made by Ellison's hero. Kart's jazz soloist is manifest in McPherson's story, for we are provided with a narrator who is both teller (soloist) and character (a participant in a larger performance tradition). He is authorized as a teller because the designation "Waiter's Waiter" embodies a tradition. Like the African singer of tales, the narrator's posture in the first paragraph calls attention to the specificity of context necessary to generate the oral epic. That the narration is addressed to "youngblood" and not to the reading audience underscores the fact that the particularities of the context (the younger man reading the "big, thick black book," for example) is what generates the dynamic connection between teller and audience.

In the next paragraph, the narrator moves toward an even clearer delineation of his narrative authority:

> Look at me. *I* am a Waiter's Waiter. I know all the moves, all the pretty, fine moves that big book will never teach you. *I* built this railroad with my moves; and so did Sheik Beasley and Uncle T. Boone and Danny Jackson, and so did Doc Craft. That book they made you learn came from our moves and from our heads. (43)

The narrator challenges the notion of "authorship" as the Commissary would define it. According to him, the "big, black book" the youngblood is reading does not originate from the Commissary at all, as the young man has assumed because of its printed form. Rather, the book is the result of the collectivity of "moves" that emerge from the Old School, from the black men the narrator invokes. In addition, he asserts that not only is the book a result of his (and their) action, the railroad itself is the product of his "pretty, fine moves." The big, black book is therefore a distillation, a deductive text that originates out of unorthodox "authorship." It is the men and not the text that one has to designate as the source of competence and service. Thus to be a Waiter's Waiter is to be the creator of a text, not the recipient. The old waiter establishes a new hierarchy of information that, through the "roll call" of heroes, is historicized. Moreover, the relation of textuality and physical action recalls the manner in which the black male body is associated with pure physicality, incapable of authorial control. Here, however, physicality generates textuality, and it does so using actions associated with elegance ("pretty, fine moves").

The instructions the Commissary sets down, beginning with the one that states that the youngblood must read and learn the rules in order to be a good waiter, are not enough. The task of the older waiter, then, is to unmask the big, black book, to transform it from a legal text that attempts to govern behavior by effacing black authorship into an historical text that signals creativity. In other words, to become useful, the big, black *book* must become the big, *black* book.

The old waiter recognizes that it is the youngblood's act of reading and the conclusions he draws from it, not the text itself, that dislodge him from historical context. Thus, the purpose of the old waiter's reversal of the temporal hierarchy that the text establishes for the youngblood is dualistic: to make him cognizant of the rule book's erasure of black waiters from history and to train him in the intricacies of becoming a Waiter's Waiter. To accomplish this, he must work out the gap between the rule book and the creativity that governs the life of the Waiter's Waiter. He begins to acquaint the youngblood with the subtle differences between blind subservience and veiled resistance when he asks:

> Do you know how to sneak a Blackplate to a nasty cracker? Do you know how to rub asses with five other men in the Pantry getting their orders together and still know that you are a man, just like them? Do you know how to bullshit while you work and keep the paddies in their place with your bullshit? Do you know how to breathe down the back of an old lady's dress to hustle a bigger tip? (43)

Of course, the rule book does not make such strategies available to the youngblood. Indeed, the passage suggests that the rule book omits anything that alludes to the humanity of the waiter. The narrator indicates that it must be won through active participation. Further, the rule book does not define the pantry as an area of combat where it is necessary to "keep the paddies in their place," rather it strips away its significance as the site of race ritual, masking it as a site of labor where the book renders white supremacy unreadable. In this portrayal, the waiter is passive, lacking in self-respect or dignity.

As a revisionist historian, the old waiter illustrates the manner in which a knowledge of history functions as protective device. Moreover, as a member of the Union, the narrator can assert, "I'm sixty-three, but they can't fire me: I'm in the Union. They can't lay me off for fucking up: I know this business too well" (44). It is also possible to see McPherson's speaker as a trickster figure. This is especially so, in light of Robert Pelton's observation that tricksters are

> beings of the beginning, working in some complex relationship with the High God; transformers, helping to bring the present human world into being; performers of heroic acts on behalf of men; yet in their original form or in some later form, foolish, obscene, laughable, yet indomitable.[11]

And the narrator is positioned to offer commentary on the "beginning" when he points to a picture of the railroad company's founder and observes:

> Look at the big picture at the end of the car, youngblood. That's the man who built this road. He's in your history books. He's probably in that big, black bible you read. He was a great man. He hated people. He didn't want to feed them, but the government said he had to. He didn't want to hire me, but he needed me to feed the people. (44)

In forcing the youngblood to examine the portrait as yet another historical text in need of scrutiny, the old waiter reconfigures the origins of the railroad company, stripping away the veil found in conventional forms of history. The founder is not the benevolent captain of industry the books portray; as the narrator describes him, he is characterized by greed and anti-social feelings. More, by making the history an inclusive one the narrator underscores the manner in which the black waiter is responsible for "building" the railroad. Likened to God by virtue of his supposed "authorship" of the black bible, the antagonistic cooperation between the black waiter and the founder (clearly a riff on Ellison's founder) fuels the old waiter's narrative. He transcends his own chronological presence, replacing "them" (the original black waiters hired by the company) with "me." As griotic figure, the waiter has assumed the authorial control necessary to incorporate himself into the tale, despite the fact that he could not have been present during the railroad's early days. But, as a Waiter's Waiter, the initiation into that number allows him to subsume the voices that have told the tale before him.

As a trickster, the old waiter is a transgressive figure. Thus, he tells the youngblood, "I know this, youngblood, and that is why that book is written for you and that is why I have never read it." Like Ananse the spider, he doubles as agent and adversary, modulating between the two poles of provocateur (chaos) and guardian (order).[12] Thus, even as he does his job, he does so for reasons that are his own, which evokes a DuBoisian sense of doubleness. The waiter understands this because of the black book: the company attempts to diminish him, but his self-awareness deflects this assault. He is able to act within the space of his own chronological reality, and thus he says, "That is why I am sitting here when there are tables to be cleaned and linen to be changed and silver to be washed and polished" (47). The old waiter indicates both his grasp of the information the rule book contains and his resistance to its dictates.

This serves to reflect the youngblood's strict adherence to the timetable laid down in the black book. The old waiter's task, however, is to create a space in which he can teach the youngblood "something in the summer about [the] business [he] can't get from [the] big, black book." And to do this, he must disrupt the flow of linear time and along with it, the rule book's primacy. This leads him to observe:

> But wait. It is just 1:30 and the first call for dinner is not until 5:00. You want to kill some time; you want to hear about the Old School and how it was in my day. If you look in black book you would see that you should be polishing silver now. (45)

Here the waiter creates a dramatic tension by juxtaposing the youngblood's desire to hear his story against the duties prescribed by the big, black book. In "killing time," the youngblood is shuttled into a state of antagonistic cooperation; he enters a magic circle where the rigidity of rules is subverted by calling attention to them and then ignoring them. By heightening rather than dismissing the temporal conditions in which the tale is to be told, the old waiter forces the youngblood to acknowledge the shared dangers of violating textual boundaries:

> Look out that window; this is North Dakota, this is Jerry's territory. Jerry, the Unexpected Inspector. Shouldn't you polish the shakers or clean out the Pantry or squeeze oranges, or maybe change the linen on the tables? (45)

It is important to recognize McPherson's strategy here, all of which appears in what is designated as Part 1 of the story. Even though the story of Doc is of a piece with the story's framing machinery, we should not view this as a structural fault in the story. By making note of the fact that the train has entered "Jerry's territory," the older waiter raises the stakes for listening to the story. Listening is transformed into a dangerous act, not merely a frivolous one. The youngblood's initiation has begun but it is conducted by the older waiter, for he is cut off from company policy.[13] Suddenly, this is no minor deviation, as the waiter's next brilliant stroke informs us:

> Jerry Ewald is sly. The train may stop in the middle of this wheat field and Jerry may get on. He *lives by that book.* He knows where to look for dirt and mistakes. Jerry Ewald, the Unexpected Inspector. He knows where to look; he knows how to get you. *He got Doc.* (45; emphasis mine)

The older waiter encloses the youngblood in a complex set of binary oppositions: talking versus reading, order versus chaos, the Old School versus Summer Stuff, and the Old School versus the Company. But all these oppositions are meaningless outside a context that can decipher their importance; they only achieve utility within the space of the confrontation between Doc and Jerry Ewald, the Unexpected Inspector. It is the representative anecdote that gives meaning to all the rest and thus gives rise to the youngblood's need to hear the tale. But further than this, the old waiter establishes interest in the tale because he uses the outcome of the confrontation as the instrument to pique the youngblood's curiosity.

Remembering that the epic form underscores the story's construction identifies the liminal state of the youngblood as of formal importance, for the youngblood is not a passive listener here. Quite the contrary: as the old waiter's narrative strategy suggests, the youngblood's future depends on what he will hear in the Doc/Jerry Ewald narrative. Thus the past has a direct impact on the story's narrative "present." This, in its turn, explains the double consciousness of the old waiter, his status as teller and character in the narrative he relates. As a trickster able to bridge order and chaos, the narrator must be able to pay heed to constraint without being bound by it. However, this linkage relies on the old waiter's awareness of, if not his adherence to, the status quo. In "telling off" the youngblood, then, the old waiter liberates him from the rule book as a behavioral model as he makes him aware of its destructive force. The youngblood fails to realize that he is part of a larger scenario where his ability to listen and pay heed to the old waiter's tale has profound ramifications for his life, long after his work on the trains is over. In this sense, then, it is important to recognize the old waiter's antagonistic posture as a sign of his investment in the youngblood.

While Keith Byerman has dismissed the youngblood as a symbol of youthful innocence and naïveté on the one hand and the loss of tradition and arrogance on the other, I would offer a different reading.[14] Byerman's reading relies on an approach to this narrative that privileges the speaking subject over the listening subject. The act of speaking is contestational because the old waiter has to compete with the black book to get the youngblood's attention. The old waiter discerns this fact and exploits it rather than ignoring it. Thus he observes:

> Now you want to know about him, about the Old School. You have even put aside your book of rules. But see how you keep your finger in the pages as if the book is more important than what I tell you. That's a bad move, and it tells on you. You will be a waiter. But you will never be a Waiter's Waiter. (45–46)

The youngblood's interest in the story is originally mediated by his adherence to a written text (he wants to know how the book "got Doc"). However, his liminality, the fact that he is between old and new forms of awareness, suggests that even as he is separated from the book as a model of behavior, he has not yet been imbued with another choice and so he holds on to what he knows.

But further, if we focus our critical attention on the old waiter—what he says as opposed to what he implies—we see that the youngblood's listening skills leave much to be desired. The result, unfortunately, is that the ability to discern the transformative nature of Doc's tale is compromised because the old waiter (in a second-person narration) is the sole means through which to register the change in the youngblood's behavior. Because McPherson renders the entire narrative performance "to" the youngblood, the story ends without providing evidence that the youngblood has been transformed. Indeed, as the story draws to a close, the old waiter tells the youngblood:

> I couldn't drink with you, youngblood. We have nothing to talk about. And after a while you would get mad at me for talking anyway, and keeping you from your pussy. You are tired already. I can see it in your eyes and in the way you play with the pages of your rule book. (72)

It is possible to read the youngblood's restlessness as a sign that he does not glean the deeper meaning of Doc's tale. But I would assert that we must not draw conclusions about the youngblood based on what the old waiter observes. It is because of this that the intricacies of McPherson's narrative performance must be more closely examined. If we, as readers, "listen" to the individual we perceive to be the narrator of this story, we are left to conclude that the youngblood has failed to understand the tale's message. But if this happens, we, too, have failed to understand the double-edged nature of this fiction. McPherson's story presents us with a problem: that of how to discern what a written text obscures. Thus, it is easy to conclude from the last paragraph that the old waiter has wasted his time in telling his tale:

> And I wonder why I should keep talking to you when you could never see what I see or understand what I understand or know the real difference between my school and yours. . . . You have a good story. But you will never remember it. Because all this time you have had pussy in your mind, and your fingers in the pages of that black bible. (72–73)

If we return to Ellison's discussion of antagonistic cooperation, we recall that the formula for what he refers to as the "true jazz moment" is based on the jazzman's simultaneous *discovery* and *loss* of self. Because he recognizes this, having told a story whose very telling embodies this type of maneuver, the old waiter breaks the narrational link between himself and the youngblood. If the youngblood is to become as skilled in improvisation as he, the old waiter knows this ability is developed in solitude. Indeed, this message lies at the very center of Doc's tale: its main point concerns what happens when an individual fails to discern the value of metaphor. Doc's tale must be understood, then, as a cautionary tale. It masks itself as a story about the Old School, but part of the old waiter's real intent is to warn the youngblood about the dangers of stagnation.

This is clearly reflected in what young jazz musicians, particularly those who are cocky and brash, encounter when they confront their older, more seasoned peers. Coleman Hawkins describes what happens to young players when they arrive in New York City to play jazz: "When they first come *here,* I don't care what they were in their hometowns, when they come *here,* they get cut. . . . They have to come here and learn all over again."[15] This is underscored by Bill Crow, who makes clear in his collection of jazzmen's anecdotes, that some of the most innovative playing arises out of being "cut."[16] In light of this ritual process among jazzmen, the old waiter's act of "telling off" the youngblood is likewise a part of a larger process. Rather than signifying the loss of tradition, the old waiter gives voice to a tradition of signifying: hence the old man, by adopting a posture of dismissal, challenges and demands a response in the form of the younger man's "solo song." Like the youngblood, the old waiter has been "broke in by good men" just like Doc. Part of that process, which the old waiter describes within the space of Doc's tale, involves being tested by one's predecessors and acknowledging the existence of a "professional" hierarchy that functions within a context of apprenticeship and mentoring. What we see on the part of the old waiter is the act of rending (or "reading?") the youngblood in order for him to reconstruct himself. Having been through the process himself, he remembers that his own "education" left him space for self-definition. He knows that the book, as the instrument of the Commissary, has "moves" of its own that offer the illusion of autonomy, but his act of "re-membering" Doc recalls a moment where he and his fellows were "immune" to the contaminating influence of the text. The old waiter demands that the youngblood operate with the same set of possibilities.

Thus, if we take the old waiter's act of "telling off" the youngblood at face value, we are guilty of exactly the same type of dismissal of the written word that Doc's tale has warned us against. Further, to identify with the narrator, as if the narrator of the story and the old waiter are one and the same, increases the possibility for misinterpretation. Let me offer, here, a reading that attempts to bring text and context into a state of functional alignment.

It is true that we read in "A Solo Song: For Doc" a "text" that occurs in the *voice* of an old waiter who "schools" a young man on what life on the trains was like. But what I would like to assert is that it is the *text* of the old waiter's story that we read; the old waiter is not the author (the "real" narrator, if you will) of the text. Rather, it is the youngblood himself who provides us with this text. This evinces two responses:

First he answers the old waiter's challenge and becomes a good listener, so good that he sets the tale down with flawless accuracy. Second, the old waiter's tale is a transformative one indeed. What makes for the strongest proof of this is the fact that the youngblood includes all those instances where the old waiter mocks, admonishes, and dismisses him. If we read "the text" positioned inside the context, we can read this fiction as one where the storyteller relates an instance of blindness rather than insight. But if the old waiter's role is to teach the youngblood the business, to prepare him for symbolic forms of combat, then one has to question the posture he takes at the end of the story. Particularly in light of the great pains he has taken to tell Doc's tale in the first place. For it is not the text of Doc's tale that is most important here; rather, what is most pressing is the interface between text and context.

What this recalls is Ben Sidran's observation that the oral person, rather than embodying information through words, instead *becomes* the information itself. This would explain why the youngblood, as the narrative's effaced author, would not unveil himself in the course of the fiction. For it is a fiction whose narrative course pivots on the act of signifying. And the targets in this instance are the acts of both reading and writing. Knowing that the story is, indeed, a "solo song" dedicated to the memory of Doc, the youngblood must subvert his identity, even as telling the story simultaneously represents its assertion. For what resonates in the old waiter's voice, takes center stage within the space of the written version of the tale, is the manner in which acts of speaking *underscore* acts of writing. Writing becomes synonymous with speaking. The youngblood subsumes the old waiter's voice in the same way that the latter subsumed the voices of those who told him about the early days of the railroads. Thus, even as the story comes to us in the form of writing, it subverts the primacy of writing and continues to validate the oral (and aural) tradition. For the youngblood's voice, as a writer, is made one with the speaking voice of the old waiter.

What this means, in addition, is that we can read the youngblood's "fingers in the pages," as the sign of transformation we have been anticipating for the duration of the story. At the story's outset they might have signaled his adherence to the written word as a behavioral catalyst. However, after hearing Doc's tale, where he knows that Doc has been "beaten . . . by a book," they take on a different aspect. Like the grandfather of Ellison's invisible hero, the narrator of "Doc" becomes "a spy in the enemy's country." That is, his fingers in the pages of the black bible no longer sanction the erasure of black waiters from railroad history, rather, they intervene on this state of affairs because he knows the story the book obscures. What appears to be the waiter's dismissal of the youngblood's potential at the story's end is, in actuality, a call to action. The response in this instance is reflexive: the youngblood creates a narrative that celebrates the voices of his predecessors. Thus, he performs a narrative act that is at once self-immolating and self-affirming.

Though he has chosen to write the tale, rather than tell it, his "solo song" affirms the tradition. As "summer stuff," one can conjecture that the youngblood is a student, working for the summer (see discussion in the next section). What this means, then, is that the lesson offered by the old waiter is one whose value supersedes the material context in which it has been related. It cannot reach beyond itself because the story endorses—by virtue of the fact that the youngblood effaces himself throughout—the voice over the written word. This is a metafiction, then, because it is writing that, as fiction, attempts to write a tradition into being even as it undoes itself as a written record of that tradition. And like Ellison's protagonist, we find a narrator who is truly comfortable with invisibility. He does not need to assert his presence, he finds his voice in the voices of others and in so doing, affirms his own.

4

But if this is not enough to substantiate my case, consider then a structural analysis of the story that reinforces the notion that it has epic intentions. Given the fact that all epics, in the pro forma sense, begin *in medias res*, let me argue that McPherson's narrator—the youngblood—discovers his authorial dilemma within the space of Doc's tale. If we view the epic confrontation solely as Doc's tale, however, we have no way of explaining why McPherson uses the entire first section of the story merely to set up the telling. "A Solo Song: For Doc" can indeed be categorized as a simple framed tale. However, if the story depicts men whose innovative abilities have allowed them to perform acts of resistance on a daily basis, would they not be able to see that the necessity is not one of passing on their particular skills as waiters, but rather the need to pass on a tradition of resistance?

Again, this story's Ellisonian origins need to be made clear. Recall the following passage, found in the Epilogue, where the narrator speaks of "affirm[ing] the principles on which the country was built and not the men." In what serves as the youngblood's guiding blueprint, he continues:

> Or did he mean that we had to take the responsibility for all of it, for the men as well as the principle, because we were the heirs who must use the principles because no other fitted our needs? Not for the power or the vindication, but because we, with the given circumstance of our origin, could only thus find

> transcendence? Was it that we of all, we, most of all, had to affirm the principle, the plan in whose name we had been brutalized and sacrificed—not because we would always be weak nor because we were afraid or opportunistic, but because they had exhausted in us, some—not much, but some—of the human greed and smallness, yes and the fear and superstition that had kept them running. (*Invisible Man,* 574)

I quote Ellison at such great length here because it is important to recognize that the antagonistic cooperation between the old waiter and the youngblood is one which has more to do with the performance of his duties as a citizen than it does with his duties as a waiter. In a profound reversal, the task of the youngblood is to occupy form, to embrace citizenship from a posture of authorship. Because greed and corruption have compromised substance, the challenge the old waiter issues is for the younger man to believe in the spirit and dignity that produced the laws and not the men who write them. Thus, when the old waiter observes that he, like Doc, will be "beaten by [a book]," and tells the youngblood that "it will never get" him, what he reveals is his plan to fortify the younger man with the necessary tools to escape the fate of the Old School. And the "Old School" refers to anyone who believes that an unchallenged legal text offers protection.

But as I demonstrated in the first chapter, Ellison's novel also attempts to assume an ontohistorical posture. "What Did I Do To Be So Black and Blue" is the means by which the invisible narrator "slips into the breaks" and explores the subterranean aspects of American history. Ishmael Reed makes this clear in a poem entitled, "Dualism (in ralph ellison's invisible man)" where he writes:

> i am outside of
> history. i wish
> i had some peanuts, it
> looks hungry there in
> its cage.
>
> i am inside of
> history. its
> hungrier than i
> thot.[17]

What Reed's poem articulates is essential to an understanding of McPherson's "A Solo Song: For Doc." The poem asserts that Ellison's hero, and McPherson's youngblood are both figures who realize their place inside history. In the case of the latter, the youngblood becomes aware that he is always already inside the text. Thus the "fingers in the pages,"

Part I	> > > >	Part II	> > >	Part III
Youngblood reading the "black bible"		Doc's tale		Youngblood dismissed by old waiter as "failure"; end of Old School
*		*		*
beginning		middle		end

Figure 1. Structural components of "A Solo Song: For Doc" as framed tale.

are not, as some might suggest, interventionary in the sense that they bring information to the text that has been excluded. Rather, the youngblood's intervention comes in the form of making his audience aware of how the Old School (into which he is being initiated) omits itself from textuality (their position in narrative space *subsumes* the railroad's exclusive version of history) by privileging orality. Moreover, the old waiter's tale is one that calls for a synthesis of information, for it is Doc's tale, and not Doc, that the youngblood needs to reproduce. Here is where the synthesis between the oral and the written becomes important. The youngblood's self-effacement, his decision not to reveal himself as author of the text, means that we, too, must step into textual space. The old waiter knows that history, as the black bible reflects it, is conditional (e.g., if you follow the rules, you won't be fired). However, it should be noted that, despite the old waiter's distaste for Uncle T. Boone ("T" as in "Tom" perhaps) and his depiction of black inferiority, he includes him as part of the Old School. Though this seems an unimportant detail, the old waiter again provides a model of historical discourse that is inclusive, that structures inclusiveness at the conceptual center. Thus, inclusion in the narrative is not based on an agreement with Uncle T's ideological position (or lack thereof), but on his presence, his participation.

What "Solo Song" works out, then, is an epic pattern that begins with the interplay between the old waiter and the youngblood. It is there that we must turn—and return—if we are to understand McPherson's authorial strategy. Consider the diagrams in Figures 1 and 2. If we remember from Ellison's prologue that "the end is in the beginning and lies far ahead," then the story's epic intentions become clear, in fact doubly so, because the "end" can be viewed either as that moment when the old waiter closes his tale about Doc and the Old School, or the "end" can be viewed as the moment when the youngblood begins the

II > > > > > >	I > > > > > >	III
Part 1 of story: opening (*in medias res*)	Parts 2, 3, (Doc's tale)	Part 4 of story, Youngblood telling story
*	*	*
*	*	*
*	*	*
symbolic "middle"	symbolic "beginning"	symbolic "end"
*	*	*
*	*	*
*	*	*
(where youngblood begins his "written" tale)	opening of "heard" story told by old waiter	close of "heard" story: call and authorial response

Figure 2. Symbolic structure of "A Solo Song: For Doc" as epic tale.

tale, as it appears in "written" form, having been chastened about how to go about the work of telling the tale. In terms of the story as an "epic," the youngblood's "fingers in the pages " coincides with the invisible narrator's decision "to put invisibility down in black and white " and his desire "to make music of invisibility." But they also provide the means for him to revise the story, to put into the narrative that which has been lost or obscured. The youngblood's posture must be one which rests on a sense of himself as contributing author and active reader. He must be able to interpret the black bible as a text which encodes both authority and subalterity and calls for him to interrogate the American Master narrative, which records and recalls a different point of view, one that excludes by reifying the boundaries between "inside" and "outside." What McPherson's story asserts is that this boundary is permeable, diaphanous. This recalls, of course, DuBois's Veil, and if the youngblood's story is important, it is so because his authorship is the sign of his movement into double consciousness.

However, the story also forces the reader to engage a collision of a different sort: the conceptual clash that occurs between acts of writing and acts of telling. As Walter Benjamin observes, the storyteller, the authorial equivalent of Sidran's "oral man," is a figure "who has counsel for his readers."[18] However, what we think we see in "Solo Song" is an instance of failed counsel: the youngblood hears Doc's story, but never alters the hierarchy that places textuality higher than orality. But this reading depends on ignoring the role signifying plays in this fiction. As a signifying text, "Solo Song" works out Benjamin's distinction between the oral table and the novel, namely that the storyteller

> takes what he tells from experience—his own or that reported by others. And he in turn makes it the experience of those who are listening to his tale. The novelist has isolated himself. The birthplace of the novel is the solitary individual, who is no longer able to express himself by giving examples of his most important concerns, is himself uncounseled, and cannot counsel others. ("The Storyteller," 91)[19]

The old waiter of the story, if we are to consider Benjamin's observation carefully, is the perfect narrative vehicle for the youngblood to capture this moment and conserve its imperatives. While it may seem that McPherson's story speaks to the end of an era, and certainly it can be read as such a tale, to read it as a fiction which signifies on the acts of both fiction-making (as the black bible, in its guise as rule book, is a fiction) and reading (in the form of passive, non-interventionary forms of reading) makes this story resonate in productive ways. And like the speaker in Reed's poem, the reader needs to know that s/he is "inside of history," but it takes a synthesized act of reading, writing, and speaking to make this clear.

5

For all the discussion on McPherson's depiction of a young man who learns how to preserve tradition by putting "invisibility down in black and white," there is yet another way to assess this fiction's authorial intent. Examining the first and last paragraphs, it is clear that this fiction signifies on the actual reader, holding the text in his or her hands, trying to substitute the act of reading for experience in the world.[20] What makes this a viable argument is that the term "Waiter's Waiter," is so easily transformed into the term "Writer's Writer." In that respect, I want to posit this fiction as McPherson's act of paying homage to Ralph Ellison (who, after all, often returns to relationship between study and experience[21]). Indeed, we might even consider the conversation between the old waiter and the youngblood to be a conversation between Ellison and McPherson.

This text works out, then, what Gerard Prince has asserted as the relationship of the narratee and the narrator: "whether or not he assumes the role of character, whether or not he is irreplaceable, whether he plays several roles or just one, the narratee can be a listener . . . or a reader."[22] Further, as Prince concludes, only by constituting an act of "sharply delineated reading" can we identify McPherson's use of the narratee in this fiction as a strategy that conjoins style and function to make an argument about the nature of writing. We know from McPherson's comments in "On Becoming an American Writer" that he worked, during his summers off from college, as a waiter on the trains running from Chicago to the Northwest.[23] Hence, we can read the exchange between the old waiter and the youngblood as McPherson's recollection of his own experience. This proposes, then, that "A Solo Song: For Doc" is McPherson's attempt to deconstruct the relation between text and context. While his fiction admonishes the reader for being too invested in reading to consider the warning embedded in Doc's tale (as a writer, failing to read can, in essence, cost you your life), it also bristles at the notion that reading can replace experience as the writer's main resource. But rather than establishing an "either/or" binary, this fiction invests itself in the ideology of "both/and." If we are to have any opportunity to negotiate this fiction, we must pay heed to its constant reminder that the reader must connect text and context. As such, this is an African American fiction that dislodges itself from the strictions of the New Criticism, issuing a call for the reader/critic (or the writer/critic) to utilize more supple strategies of investigation. Hence, when we map race into this discussion, we can see that McPherson calls our attention to the unspoken relationship between race and writing.[24] The reader (in the form of the youngblood) must learn exactly what is at stake in learning his or her craft and resist the impulse to rely solely on what appears on the page. Because the discourse of race plays so powerful a role in the creation of American identity (and McPherson argues, in the erasure of certain aspects of that identity), failure to do so will mean that acts of reading are likewise instances of negation. Only by restoring the relation between text and context does the reader have an opportunity to make reading an active intervention in the tangle of American identity politics. What we find is that both Bledsoe and the Vet are correct: in the struggle to create identity, in order for the reader to "make good," self-reliance is key.

Like Ellison's Trueblood, then, the narrator of "Solo Song" must decide that he is nobody but himself, for his act of telling is one characterized by its solitude. Further, his rendering of the old waiter's "revision" of a book of rules is analogous to a collision between history and law, because the "black bible" is an historical text that *masquerades* as a legal text. But as the *black* bible, the process of telling becomes all important. The manner in which the story is passed down from one generation of participants to another stands as the faith and the hope, the song of praise that looks back in order to look ahead. By extracting the unspeakable from the legible, McPherson's youngblood is a musician par excellence, a singer of tales who possesses a keen ear, a deft hand, and a mean embouchure.[25]

Part III
The Lower Frequencies

Chapter 5
Voices from the Underground: Conspiracy, Intimacy, and Voice in Gaines's Fictions

what is lost is his voice in your voice; gained in what you say and do.
—Michael S. Harper, "Gains"

1

Southern writing often fuses communal memory and storytelling with resonant force. In Eudora Welty's short story, "The Wide Net," for example, a community of men gather to drag the river for William Wallace Jamieson's wife after she leaves a note informing him she has gone to drown herself. Though such news should cause great urgency, if not total despair, the crisis soon turns into a celebratory moment, complete with a fishfry and a long nap after the meal. In William Faulkner's story, "Spotted Horses," a herd of wild horses wreak havoc in a town when they break out of their corral. Afterward, the men gather on the porch of Will Varner's general store to swap tales about their respective attempts to capture the beasts. In Zora Neale Hurston's *Their Eyes Were Watching God,* men and women on the muck gather after a hard day's work in the fields to "tell lies." And back in Eatonville the men of the community hold a "funeral," complete with a eulogy, for a dead mule.

Examples like this abound, and they can be found in the fictions of black and white authors alike. As implements of "everyday use," stories are sites of an intimacy that articulate the South's complexity. But they can just as easily speak to the manner in which secrecy, manipulation and deceit are all to be found in Southern fiction. Thus Southern communities often combine the intimate and the conspiratorial into an often indistinguishable relation. In Welty's story, William Wallace

Jamieson finds that his wife has been hiding all day to teach him a lesson about the responsibilities of fatherhood. In Faulkner's story, Flem Snopes manipulates the men in Frenchman's Bend to buy horses that men like Henry Armstid can neither afford nor control. The conspiracy Snopes initiates demonstrates the New South's collapse into the empty consumerism and mass arousal Faulkner associated with a region doomed to live out the legacy of "glorious failure."[1] And finally, Hurston's Janie realizes, after a bout of domestic violence, that she has "an inside and an outside," and she concludes, on one hand, that men like her husband Jody use violence and coercion to force women into silence and submission, and on the other that her value to Jody is largely ornamental. Thus, while the depiction of communal energy is a common motif in Southern writing, let me propose that community evokes terrain that is complex, not necessarily common. Because what finally binds Southern communities cannot be attributed merely to shared geography. The aforementioned acts of telling and celebration have a great deal to do with the manner in which storytelling is the only way to use communal resources to move from the conspiracy of silence that characterizes life in the South to a more intimate, open relationship where a new social contract can be negotiated.

The writers of both races also share, perhaps especially in creating images of community in the South, the inherent struggle of writing in the shadow of William Faulkner. This struggle takes on a particular charge for the African American writer who often seeks to join Faulkner in imaging community at the same time that she or he seeks to undo the seemingly "indestructible racial myths" Faulkner has promulgated, sometimes in the name of defining community.[2] For Faulkner's writing often explores how lives characterized by ruin and distortion or shame and reluctance are managed in public space. Of course, race plays a major role in such an enterprise and Faulkner's explication of the South as a defeated "nation within a nation" likewise means that he explores aspects of African American citizenship. But this also marks Faulkner's ambivalence about racial justice and African American humanity. For while his propensity toward nostalgia (as we see in a story like "Was") made it possible for him to demonstrate the flexibility of race relations, it also rendered it impossible for him to imagine a character who, upon recognizing the limitations of white supremacy, could say "no" to racial injustice in overt ways. Clearly, Faulkner's black characters specialize in stiff-lipped negotiation rather than confrontation.

Ralph Ellison offers us a means to understand the pervasive impact of Faulkner's fiction. In "Twentieth Century Fiction and the Black Mask of Humanity," Ellison remarks:

Faulkner's attitude is mixed. Taking his cue from the Southern mentality in which the Negro is often dissociated into a malignant stereotype (the bad nigger) on the one hand and a benign stereotype (the good nigger) on the other, most often Faulkner presents characters embodying both. The dual function of this dissociation seems to be that of avoiding moral pain and thus to justify the South's racial code.[3]

The "moral pain" to which Ellison refers intimates that Faulkner's fiction ultimately evades the deprivation that segregation and discrimination in the South imposes on whites no less than blacks. Dilsey's "endurance" in *The Sound and the Fury* should offer some comfort, particularly in light of the fact that she escapes the destruction visited upon the Compson family. But Faulkner's decision not to provide her a section of her own in the novel, while it marks off her moral strength, likewise swears her to secrecy. The prayers and exultation during the church service Faulkner depicts notwithstanding, Dilsey's "narrative," if there is to be one, will take place in the world beyond. Ellison concludes, then, that for Faulkner and other white, Southern artists, "the Negro becomes a symbol of his personal rebellion, his guilt, and his repression of it."

In short, the African American novelist (and especially those born in the South) is invariably locked in an "engaging disengagement" with Faulkner; attracted to his power of description and mastery of language, but repelled by his perpetuation of racial myth. One finds that this is most certainly the case for Ernest Gaines, especially since he has alluded to Faulkner's influence over "every Southern writer" who has followed him. But despite this, his task as a writer remains one of attempting to manifest an artistic vision of the South which is uniquely his own. This project takes on major dimensions when we consider the weight under which all African American writers labor in confronting the South as a site of fictional exploration. For African American Southern writing seems to move between two poles: the documentary and the transcendent. The former describes the degrading circumstances of Southern life, depicting the terror and violence, the political disenfranchisement and peonage, embodied in a segregated society. The latter attempts to situate African American folk culture as a resistant, coherent force out of which characters are able to manifest some semblance of either self-consciousness or self-recovery. Thus, the South crystallized in African American literature as a site of folk imagination, a space where, prior to the Civil Rights movement, agency often assumes covert forms. But, as the documentary impulse suggests, it is also a space of national shame and contradiction.[4] The South, then, is a site of exhaustion and potential, and the contiguity between these two sites makes them nearly indistinguishable. Hence, called for are characters able to manifest what Robert Stepto refers to as "tribal literacy," even as they seek to make the South a freer, more democratic space.

What all this proposes is that Black Southern writing speaks implicitly to issues of African American citizenship: marking off its limitations, chronicling breaches of the social contract, but also giving voice to the ancestral past where individuals have resisted racial brutality, even at the cost of their lives. This makes it necessary to examine the mysterious nature of African American citizenship as it takes place in the South. The dilemma this presents for African American writers who come after Faulkner is one which calls them to emulate his ability "to start with the stereotype [of African Americans] . . . and then seek out the human truth it hides." That is, the stereotype is a resource that must be processed into a form that allows for heightened awareness or reflection. For example, one can use satire to lampoon the stereotype until it collapses under the weight of its own absurdity, as writers like Ishmael Reed and Douglas Turner Ward have done in *Yellow Back Radio Broke Down* and *Day of Absence,* respectively. Or one can delineate the nature of white, Southern oppression and the various forms of personal rebellion needed to supersede racial stereotypes, as Richard Wright did in *Black Boy* and *Uncle Tom's Children.* Inevitably, this task of challenging racial stereotype leads the African American writer to trace the enterprise to its source: the South's tangled racial history.

Faulkner's depiction of Mississippi, as Craig Werner argues, centers on the notion that the South—the land and the people who inhabit it—is cursed by the legacy of slavery.[5] However, when Gaines confronts Faulkner's construction of history, the past serves as an important resource, not as a curse but as a necessity in the task of demystifying the surroundings.[6] Thus, Gaines underscores the importance of history and place:

> After [my first] two books had been published as well as the collection of stories, *Bloodline,* I realized that I was writing in a definite pattern. One, I was writing about a definite area; and, two, I was going farther and farther back into the past. I was trying to go back, back, back into our experiences in this country to find some kind of meaning to our present lives.[7]

Gaines's observation echoes what we know of Faulkner's best fiction: it engages history and geography as a symbolic nexus and his writing seeks a way to lend meaning to what is finally a *national* experience.[8] All this is to say that Gaines shares Faulkner's desire to demystify the South, even as he works to investigate both the nature of regional sin and the folks' attempt to preserve their dignity and power. But, as Craig Werner observes, Gaines "takes [the] ritual ground . . . [of Faulkner's] endurance narrative and reclaims it for the African American tradition." Werner additionally points out, "Faulkner's narrative of endurance focuses on the 'enduring [black] saint,' who is physically enslaved but spiritually free. This figure's primary commitment is to the salvation of both blacks and whites in the next world." ("Tell Old Pharaoh," 714). Gaines's characters, by contrast, attempt to navigate a course toward meaning and order while their attention is focused on acquiring a viable set of symbolic and spiritual resources for themselves and their community in the world at hand. Here, one finds that Gaines's admiration of Ernest Hemingway's fiction serves him well, for Gaines's characters often exemplify "grace under pressure."[9] And with good reason, for as Michel Fabre has observed of Gaines's world:

> This world is enclosed by gates, barbed wire, hedges between fields. Curtains of trees between kingdom-like plantations, territory marked by the seal of one man or another; sinuous streams and dusty roads; guidepost trees, guardians and symbols of permanence; fields of corn and sugar cane whose last rows are never reached. . . . In short, a rough place for hardened men. The sensuous presence of nature is both witness and protagonist; rays of light that are so icy or gleaming hot that they force their way through the screens of the masters' houses whose gloomy libraries filled with trophies cannot protect them from sunlight or twists of fate. ("Bayonne," 112)

Out of these conditions come Gaines's protagonists, whose struggles for humanity take shape most times in the form of first person narratives. In a region so heavily dominated by silence, what is left unsaid forces Gaines's narrators to utilize their community's oral resources to reach the truth, if not by hard-fought deductive skill, then by inference.

The result of this approach to character is a hybridized version of the two questing figures Robert Stepto describes as the articulate survivor and the articulate kinsman,[10] and which I categorize as the "articulate witness." The articulate witness is loosed from the static condition of Faulkner's endurance narrative and set on a journey toward literacy (e.g., eloquent narration) in a symbolically free space *in the South.* These characters function simultaneously as both kinsmen and survivors in a narrative type I refer to as the narrative of emergence. In relating the sometimes horrific tales of love and death in the South, Gaines's narrators exist in a space where they break from convention to conjoin memory and voice. Jim Kelly, Miss Jane Pittman, and the old men in *A Gathering of Old Men* continue to live in the South, but the act of telling their stories, in the face of conditions not conducive to storytelling, makes them witnesses. And what they bear witness to is simultaneously the burden of navigating the hostile confines of Southern race ritual, where a misspoken word or a random glance can lead to death and the desire to undertake behavior that signals a new order. The prefigurement of this character is, among others, the narrator's grandfather in *Invisible Man.* As the narrator relates, the old man is "an odd old guy" who "never made trouble." However, consider his familiar "deathbed speech":

> Son, after I'm gone I want you to keep up the good fight. I never told you, but our life has been a war and I have been a traitor all my born days, a spy in the enemy's country ever since I give up my gun back in the Reconstruction. Live with your head in the lion's mouth. I want you to overcome 'em with yeses, undermine 'em with grins, agree 'em to death and destruction, let 'em swoller you till they vomit or bust wide open. . . . Learn it to the younguns." (*Invisible Man,* 16)

What makes this such a necessary consideration is the manner in which the old man insists upon the importance of resistance as a legacy to be passed on from one generation to the next. Further, not only does he use the opportunity to unmask himself as a "traitor," and thus a figure of agency and stealth, he also suggests that meekness is a form of treachery, which suggests that form and function do not always follow. The effect of this, of course, is best realized in the hero, who sees the old man's words as a "curse." However, as the novel unfolds, this "curse" is in reality a counterspell, one that undoes the curse dramatized in Faulkner's writing and, I would argue, creates the space in which we find Gaines's protagonists. Indeed, as I will demonstrate in this chapter, Gaines's characters struggle to maintain, if not renew, kinship ties. And so that space is one that centers on public acts of voice.

Community is realized in Gaines's work through his characters' collective struggle to discover new ways to bring human energies to bear on a region where past sins linger and people continue to rely on outmoded social conventions. As a result, his characters are faced with the problem of extricating themselves from constricting mythologies. The predicaments these protagonists face are shaped by a tightly controlled racial hierarchy that restrains mobility. In the face of this, numerous survival strategies crystallize, and one finds these characters ignoring the paradigmatic relationships of vision and silence, amnesia and resignation that shape the quality of human interaction. As Fabre notes, Gaines's fiction often portrays the frustration that accompanies his characters' difficult search for integrity in the face of growing social disintegration.[11] They begin, then, as figures of liminality, whose aggregation is achieved through the vehicle of narration.

In a world so tightly delineated by codes, Gaines's characters are in a state of constant negotiation. Keith Byerman observes that the most successful of Gaines's characters are those

> who negotiate their way amid the forces of racist repression; folk parochialism that is in fact an acceptance of that repression; and open resistance, which often leads to death. These characters survive by accommodating themselves to the existing system without sacrificing their dignity and by living on the psychological edge of the folk community, near enough to absorb the genuine wisdom of that experience but not so close as to fear change and resistance.[12]

As storytellers, Gaines's narrators take responsibility for presenting the prohibitive nature of black life in the South. Like Ellison's hero, they achieve coherence by using the resources that will help them survive.[13]

However, the acts of negotiation Byerman describes also point to an ever-present dilemma: unable to conform to Jim Crow conventions, and opting against the life-threatening aspects of open rebellion, Gaines's characters often fall into a state of social or emotional disorientation. This is often prompted by a serious disruption of the social routine. At the narrative's outset, the reader enters Gaines's fictional world to find events set in motion by these disruptions. This implies a larger sense of design. Far from suggesting lack of originality or inventiveness, the repeated use of disruption to initiate a narrative space points toward more compelling circumstances which lead, not only to an excavation of the past, but toward a new form of eloquence that will reorder the present. In each of his fictions, the disruptive moment signals the transgressive, serving as the point of contact between the spoken and the unspoken, the precursor to the rupture of illusion and conspiracy. Because the reader enters Gaines's fictional world to find disruption imminent, the novel's opening can be contextualized only if the reader understands the normative conventions that have been disturbed. The storytellers among Gaines's characters give utterance to the unspoken dangers that have constrained the community and in so doing, break the relationship between silence and an acceptance of social conventions (Fabre, "Bayonne," 115). Gaines opts for call and response rather than what Werner describes as the Faulknerian pattern of repetition and revenge. While Faulkner's protagonists engage in an excavation of their past, it is finally a journey from which they can never return (Werner, "Tell Old Pharaoh, 725). In traversing the symbolic ground between the Civil War and Civil Rights, Gaines's characters encounter private forms of upheaval. But by bringing it into the public space of utterance, they find themselves empowered rather than entrapped, and they exert the will to live in the world on their own terms. As we will see, voice and the achievement of coherence usher in the sense that life will never be the same after hidden transgressions enter the field of spoken language.

2

An individual's attempts to recodify his relationship to a community, pondering the resistance to change, is at issue in Gaines's first novel, *Catherine Carmier.*[14] A cursory reading of the text reveals a bildungs-roman, where an angry and confused young man returns home to Louisiana. But the novel's deeper impulses tend toward the gothic: the hero's perplexity is generated by the private horrors intruding upon his need to configure a public life. Indeed, given the direction of Gaines's later fiction, the question arises as to what he is attempting to accomplish in this novel. Its characters call attention to racial polarities that none wish to challenge. The physical environment itself offers a deadly fusion of desolation and fertility. In short, this is a world distin-guished by its narrowness and its adherence to a perverse sense of order. However, what Gaines suggests as "order" exacts costs from the black folk who inhabit this plantation community, requiring someone who is both inside and outside to shatter the stalemate.

Hence Jackson Bradley, the novel's hero—a young man driven to make a difference, but completely unaware of how to do so. He is incapable of merging successfully the influences of his Southern up-bringing and his education in the North. As Jackson exemplifies, the acquisition of literacy, like notions of the North, is bound up in myth. Configured as such, education is a source of agency, where study is the key to discovering a voice and the tool that carves the niche in which to exert that voice. Robert Stepto has argued, however, that African American literature "has developed as much because of the culture's distrust of literacy as because of its abiding faith in it."[15] His observation is useful because it implies that literacy (and the citizenship it enables) is not an instance of simple procurement. Its relationship to the quest for freedom involves a great deal of risk: acquiring the means to decipher the codes of the dominant culture is an enterprise fraught with danger and complexity. What interests me here is that African American literature abounds with personas who embody the manner in which literacy not only thwarts the communal impulse, but also places the individual in either physical or emotional jeopardy.[16] That jeopardy results from both the individual's ability to decipher codes and the ideology locking them into place. Reality becomes tainted by the conspiritorial; the benign mask of the familiar becomes unrecog-nizable, and thus the hero is threatened at every turn, largely because she or he cannot discern the source of the danger.

Under these circumstances, Gaines's Jackson represents yet another revision of DuBois's "The Coming of John." Like John, Jackson leaves the South a boy and returns an adult poised to accept the responsibility of a public role. Moreover, he evokes the motif of the returning hero, expected to rejuvenate the surroundings. The world to which he returns, however, is a post-feudal space where there are old people who remember a time before they were banished from the land, and young people who have no choice but to move to the city because the land offers no opportunity. Jackson's return signals an opportunity for the people in the quarters to resist this decline and be renewed. In looking at this novel's trajectory, however, Jackson Bradley is perhaps the most unsuccessful of Gaines's characters. As the first of Gaines's "middle characters," he must demonstrate the ability to balance his individual needs against those of the community, and he differs from those due to follow because he remains so focused on his own needs. Jackson's inability to reconcile the community's needs with his own points at an important distinction: *Catherine Carmier* is the only Gaines novel that utilizes a protagonist whose alienation speaks to the incapacity of American society in its entirety. Like DuBois's John he, too, encounters the Veil in its multiple incarnations.

Within the space of its plot, *Catherine Carmier* has much to do with the dilemma of the hero returning to redeem a fallen space. But what distinguishes Jackson is that he does not wish to occupy such a role. Indeed, this novel utilizes the tools of the immersion narrative to accomplish its ends.[17] Jackson's return is his opportunity to reconnect himself to his folk origins, and thus to be renewed. His responsibility, as the folk see it, is to render the world manageable and familiar. His Aunt Charlotte articulates this when she states, "You everything, Jackson" and continues:

> They ain't never been nobody in the whole family to go far's you done gone; to get your kind o' learning, to travel like you done traveled. Nobody. . . . In ever' family they ought to be somebody to do something . . . you all they is left, Jackson. You all us can count on. If you fail, that's all for us. (*Catherine Carmier,* 98)

Her observations are shaped by her sense that Jackson is both apex and terminus of his family's history, its ultimate achievement. This places Jackson in a precarious state: he is the arbiter of either redemption or apocalypse. But herein lies the dilemma: Jackson's life in Louisiana led him to construct the North as a site of both liberation and empowerment. However, the North turns out to be a space where racial barriers exist, though they are not enforced by the quasi-legal codes he finds in the South. The North, as Jackson soon discovers, is geographically distant from the South but, because of the way racism and discrimination are rendered invisible by the illusion of free access, it is conceptually adjacent. He learns that integration and acceptance are not synonymous:

> It had happened suddenly. It had sneaked up on him. No, no, it had not. It had only come less directly than it had in the South. He was not told that he could not come into the restaurant to eat. But when he did come inside, he was not served as promptly and with the same courtesy as were the others. When he went into a store to buy a pair of pants or a pair of socks, he was treated in the same manner as he had been in the restaurant. . . . These incidents were not big. They were extremely small when you thought of them individually. But there were so many of them that they soon began to mount into something big, something black, something awful. (*Catherine Carmier,* 92–93)

Like DuBois's John who looks "sharply about him," discovers the Veil, and decides to return South anyway, Jackson's return is a grudging and temporary one at best.

Jackson's return—especially as Charlotte responds to it—evokes its Christocentric nature. As Christ-figure, he has the power to redeem, validate, reward, and regenerate. For the Cajuns, he signals a new order. When two Cajuns see Jackson's friend, Brother, waiting for him, one asks, "You think he one of them people? . . . Them demonstrate people there," referring to civil rights workers organizing in other parts of the South. But because he has neither the will nor the resources, Jackson is in no position to serve this function. Herein lies the importance of the novel, not only in the Gaines canon, but also in terms of Gaines's relationship to Faulkner and Southern literary history. While Jackson's likely return to the North means that he does not fit my definition of an articulate witness, he does set the stage for the Gaines characters who later fill this role. His importance lies in rupturing the myth of endurance, encountering the fetishization of land situated in Southern literature,[18] and deconstructing the plantation romance.

To this end, Gaines employs two types of narrative vehicles: Faulkner's narrative of endurance and the Southern plantation romance. He sets these two narratives in motion toward one another, knowing that their collision will create fresh space for a new kind of Southern narrative. To understand this we need to examine the characters Jackson encounters and how he interacts with them. There are the black peasants, who live in the quarters, and the Carmier family, who live nearby. Their relationship unfolds from a distance, mostly through the stories the peasants tell.

Raoul is a Creole farmer, the last farmer working the land on the Grover plantation who communes with neither black nor white. From one generation to the next, he and his family have kept themselves separate. This includes his wife, Della. However, as we find out, Della has not always conformed to the Creole disdain for neighborly contact. Gaines's Madame Bayonne, Jackson's former teacher, makes use of her position on the periphery of both the black and Creole communities by employing a dispassionate historical gauge, a role she is able to perform because she is poised to observe without judgment. As Madame Bayonne relates,

> Della was happy when she first came up to that house. She was happy in the way that only a few people can be happy. There was no fear of anything; she had a decent word to say to anyone who went by that house. Not only a few people, but many, many have stood in front of that gate talking to her. She could lean on that gate talking for hours on end. (*Catherine Carmier,* 115)

But Madame Bayonne concludes, "Then it all stopped. It stopped without warning. One day she was talking to you, the other day she was not. Everyone knew what had caused the change—Raoul; and everyone accepted it. Only she could not" (115). Della's refusal to conform to Creole racial codes leads to her decision to have an affair with a black man, by whom she has a child, and later, after the child's racial identity is discovered, to Della's censure. The next child she bears, a girl, is taken away and sent to the city to be raised by Raoul's relatives. Raoul's fierce patriarchalism is a reversal on Ike McCaslin, who is "father to no one," and who has, because of his father's incestuous relations, given away all claim to his family's property. But Gaines uses Raoul and Della to illuminate the larger issue—that endurance, as Raoul and Della enact it, can just as easily signal dysfunctionality as dignity and as such requires a complicity of grand scale to maintain it. Thus, unlike Ike who uses his skill as a woodsman (as opposed to hunting, as we find out in "The Bear") as the means by which to displace desire and the impulse for control that ownership requires, Raoul repudiates Della to embrace husbandry, ownership, and property with ever-increasing fervor. The land as fetish wards off the evil to be found in Southern racial convention. Hence, the Carmier attitude toward the land is at once resistant and retrograde. As Madame Bayonne points out:

> Why the land, you ask? Why the land? It happened long before Raoul was born. Probably his great-grandfather was the first one to find out that though he was as white as any white man, he still had a drop of Negro blood in him, and because of that single drop of blood, it would be impossible to ever compete side by side with the white man. So he went to the land—away from the white man, away from the black man as well. The white man refused to let him compete with him, and he in turn refused to lower himself to the black man's level. So it was to the land where he would not have to compete—at least side by side—with either. He was taught to get everything from the land, which he did, and which he, through necessity, was taught to love and to depend upon. (116)

Raoul's singularity of purpose is likewise an exercise in self-hatred. For while his stand against the Cajun incursion is heroic, what finally sustains him is his unwillingness to be categorized within the conventional racial matrix. The land becomes a text on which Raoul can inscribe the illusion of racelessness, since he can farm "as well as the next man." However, as Della exemplifies, those who choose community over familial separatism are nullified in Raoul's world.

Conspiracy, in the form of Della's infidelity and Raoul's guilt and self-loathing, is ever-present in the memories of their dead son, Mark. His is an apt name, for he literally "marks" the combined sin of adultery and pride Della and Raoul enact. When he is killed by a falling tree, it is ruled an accident, but in truth, Raoul is responsible for the boy's murder. Thus his love for Catherine, his first daughter, is driven by guilt and fear. As Madame Bayonne observes:

> So he went to Catherine. She was to be victim now, cross-carrier now, as long as he was alive. If she goes for a visit, she must hurry back or he goes after her. When he's sick, it must be her hand which puts the medicine in his mouth. . . . They have put her in this position—behind those trees—and nothing . . . outside those trees is allowed in that yard. (118)

Catherine is both savior and prisoner. And the gothic energy pertaining to the Carmier house—with the trees in the yard acting as the veil hiding the family's secret—attracts Jackson, who, as disillusioned savior, is likewise imprisoned. Madame Bayonne knows that Jackson's return rekindles his feelings for Catherine. However, I submit that Gaines's Catherine symbolizes more than just a forbidden love interest here. As "cross-carrier" she stands at the interstices of the plantation romance and the endurance narrative. She represents the nature of the plantation romance: simultaneously alluring and restrictive in its adherence to nostalgia and avoidance. She also dramatizes the entrapment of the endurance narrative: she becomes a symbol of deference, placing the needs of the patriarch before her own. Hence the roles of lover and daughter become tangled, suggesting that the two narrative impulses, as they regard African American identity, have what amounts to an incestuous, and thus self-destructive, relationship. If Catherine seems categorized as temptress, it is because the plantation romance is so clearly driven by a restorative impulse that attempts to seduce all who would write about the South.[19] If she is victim, what makes her so is the denial endemic to the endurance narrative; thus, she is not saint, but martyr.

As one both inside and outside this dying community, Jackson is the narrative figure for whom Faulkner's endurance narrative is a cross too heavy to bear. Unlike Lucas Beauchamp, Jackson must give voice to this entrapment. But Gaines uses the romance with Catherine as a way of calling our attention to the manner in which the plantation romance paradigm, driven by the desire for consummation (as the sign of patriarchal longevity), truncates possibility. When Madame Bayonne gives voice to why Jackson should stay away from Catherine (she tells Jackson that Catherine "cannot leave that house ") Gaines reveals the danger embodied in the implicit link between the plantation romance and the endurance narrative: their configuration is nothing short of a prison house of silence. Jackson's confusion, the emptiness and spiritual bankruptcy he exhibits, signifies the tenuous nature of such narrative hybridity.

Moreover, Jackson's inability to find community in the South, coupled with his nearly singular pursuit of a life with Catherine, argues for a reading of the novel as a text steeped in irony. In short, we must read *against* all the characters in the novel; none can be considered to be the ultimate source of narrative truth because each functions with information so heavily mediated by ritual that they can only function within a discourse of secrecy. And they do so to the exclusion of everything else. One could note, for example, that Gaines describes Jackson's visits to Madame Bayonne, which he undertakes in order to avoid his aunt's invitation to attend church. Consider Gaines's description of their discussions:

> Madame Bayonne was always glad to see him, and as soon as he came in, she offered him something to eat or a glass of her homemade wine. Jackson would accept the wine, and he and Madame Bayonne would sit at the table drinking and talking. Madame Bayonne wanted to hear his opinion of the Freedom Riders and the sit-in demonstrations by the Negro students in the South. He would sit there talking with her until he was sure that Charlotte had left, then he would leave for home. (107)

This passage alludes to the fact that, though events in the novel take place contemporaneously with the Civil Rights Movement, very little of the characters' energy is directed toward its concerns. Hence Gaines does not include Jackson's "opinions" regarding the Movement; the reader never finds out his position because he has no designs on participation. This is further evidenced when he goes to the plantation store. Jackson refuses to drink beer in the sideroom reserved for blacks, but this marks the extent of his resistance to race ritual. While he may see the manner in which race confines him, Jackson's concerns never shift from their egocentric path. Though he knows he generates the ill-feeling of black and white alike, Jackson makes no attempt to bridge his experiences with those of his community. Unlike other protagonists from African American fiction who must return to the folk community for self-renewal, Jackson makes no such gesture. Rather, he is positioned exactly between the hostile whites and the increasingly hostile blacks:

> He knew that the people on the porch were looking at him. But what did he care? It gave him a sense of importance to know they were concerned about him. He turned his head to the side. The Cajuns quickly looked away. He almost laughed. What fools. Just because he did not clown in front of them and drink in the sideroom with the other Negroes, they were suspicious of him. Already he had heard that they were asking whether or not he were a Freedom Rider. What a joke. He a Freedom Rider? And what would he try to integrate, this stupid grocery store? He felt like laughing in their stupid faces. . . .
>
> The Negroes were also looking at him. He could tell without turning around. No, they were no better than the Cajuns. Just as bad. Behind his back they called him "Mr. Stuck-Up." He was not "Mr. Stuck-Up"; he could not think of anything to talk with them about, and drinking in that sideroom was out of the question. He would never go in there. Let them call him what they wanted. (174–75)

Jackson acts out, in this fictional instance, the limitations of both the endurance narrative and the plantation romance. He does not wish to take on any of the hagiographical tasks of Faulkner's "enduring saint," who serves the purpose of moral standard bearer. Nor does Jackson want to perform the purification rites (in the form of social activism) associated with the redemptive saint whose purpose, after all, is to restore the past, not to initiate the future. What he seeks, however, is the personal regeneration necessary to assume a life that eschews the mythic in favor of belonging, inclusion. But this is itself a myth. Thus, when he and Catherine finally consummate their romance, the prospect of a life together can only be formulated as a question. "My life," Jackson asks, "Are you my life?" (148). His desire is to find a source of power he can harness to create a sense of coherence. Like the invisible man, Jackson knows that he needs light to manifest form. Catherine, despite the fact that she cannot grasp the complexity of his angst (though she informs him that she can), becomes, in the throes of his hibernation, what he needs to achieve personhood. Thus, he concludes, "You're like the light. Your hair, your face; your smile, your body. You're light. You're life" (149).

In contrast to Ellison's hero, who comes to realize in his hole that "there's the mind," Jackson fails to embrace this position because he refuses to assume responsibility for his own life. And this is so despite the fact that he wants to resist confinement:

> I don't want to give up, do you understand? I don't want to ever give up! There are so many people who have gone up there—who have come from all over the world up there—and not being able to find what was promised them, they've given up. I don't want to be one of those people. (149)

Jackson voices his unwillingness to abandon the promise of American democracy, despite the fact that he has come to know the "master narrative" as a narrative of failure. However he is just as unwilling to embrace antagonistic cooperation, choosing escapism and avoidance over a more syncretic, activist posture:

> I saw the wall rising, but I fought it. But it kept rising, kept rising, and still I fought it. So many times, I almost gave up. So many times. But I kept fighting it. That's why I left, that's why I came here. I had to get away—at least for a while. I don't believe in being walled in. I don't believe in it. I'd rather die than to live in hatred and fear. (149)

Jackson articulates the difficulties of the endurance narrative as he also suggests Gaines's authorial intention, which is to cause its collapse by ironizing it. Interestingly, Catherine responds to this diatribe, not with words, but with tears. Though her reasons are narrated they are never vocalized, demonstrating her inattention to Jackson's concerns. Indeed, Catherine is characterized almost completely by an unwillingness to speak, a resistance to change, and her almost blind sense of loyalty. But Jackson interprets her silence as complicity, the necessary ingredient for domestic safety. It is this illusion of stability that attracts him. The reader is informed by the omniscient narrator that Catherine plans to break off their romance. But as a character loosed from the narrative of endurance, engaged in the early stages of hibernation where his awareness of what he left is clear, Jackson cannot conceive of Catherine's ambivalence. But it is that ambivalence, her desire to cling to Jackson and push him away, that symbolizes the shortcomings of the plantation romance. For within its confines black characters' attempts to satisfy their own needs require at the very least a cursory nod to segregation. The ability to manifest them in tangible form is restricted to small skirmishes that leave the status quo intact because negotiation is chosen over open demonstration.

It is here where Gaines's fiction breaks rank with Faulkner's to create fresh narrative space. For while the latter was willing to assert the plantation's corruption, he was unwilling to create a space where his black characters were reviled by life in the defeated South, not only because it offended their moral sensibilities, but because that corruption diminished their humanity. Gaines is willing to agree with Faulkner's reading of the plantation to a small extent. Bud Grover, the owner of the plantation where the Cajuns and Raoul struggle for dominance, is described by Madame Bayonne as "lazy," and she observes, "I doubt if he knows where he is half of the times." As such, we can discern a concealed comment about the way Faulkner's nostalgia masks his racial ambivalence and the inability to locate himself in a

South rendered unfamiliar by the infusion of protest and governmental concern.[20] Hence Grover gives the Cajuns the best land because "white still sticks with white." And because it is his land, he retains, through subtle and often coercive means, his position atop the Louisiana racial hierarchy.[21]

Raoul's determination, therefore, has much to do with his recognition that he too must acknowledge the racial hierarchy by fighting to maintain his position above the blacks on the plantation. As the vehicle for the narrative of endurance, however, the enduring saint must make his or her way alone. It is this characteristic which leads Jackson to admire Raoul:

> He had all the reasons in the world to hate him. . . . But he did not hate Raoul. Instead, he admired him. There was something about the man, different from all the others around there. What was it? Yes, he knew. He was still trying to stand when all the odds were against him. That was it, that was the only thing. He liked that in people, he liked that in anyone. (176)

Raoul anticipates what Gaines does much later with Mathu in *A Gathering of Old Men*. Unlike Mathu, Raoul is the father rendered incomplete by the act of violence he commits against his son. Jackson, on the other hand, is the son in search of the father. It is this aspect of *Catherine Carmier,* though, that leads the novel's narrative machinery toward self-immolation. The plantation romance and the narrative of endurance are forms that utilize the patriarch as the conceptual pivot. However, the former suggests that the role of the patriarch is incontestable (hence Catherine's unwillingness to break from Raoul). The latter results in some form of self-abnegation or stasis. Thus Gaines's novel revises Rider from Faulkner's "Pantaloon in Black," who acts out his grief at his wife's death by killing a white man and thus fails to endure because he chooses resistance (albeit of a misdirected sort) over negotiation.[22] But Gaines's narrative strategy attempts to focus those limits within a circumstance peopled by blacks. While Rider's longing for his wife can only be fulfilled in the afterlife, Jackson's desire to have Catherine does not lead him to an act of random violence. His fight with Raoul at novel's end serves a very different purpose. It can be argued that the novel uses the Oedipal conflict to achieve closure; Jackson defeats Raoul, and thus the silence surrounding the murder of his son is broken. And as Della points out, Jackson serves as doppelganger, doubling for the son Raoul has killed:

> She'll go. He'll see to that. And I'll make her come to you. Not a reward for what you did, Jackson. If you was anybody else, you wouldn't'a lived to walk out of this yard. But you Jackson. Marky. You been Marky ever since he—since he died. He died by accident, you understand what I'm saying? . . . Out there

tonight, my husband and Marky was fighting. Whose side I was supposed to take? No side . . . not after living like this all this time. No, tonight it had to be settled. (247–48)

The fight between Raoul and Jackson restores domestic convention to the Carmier household; Catherine is freed from the dual roles of wife and daughter, and Della can resume taking care of Raoul.[23] However, Gaines is not content with the idea that the fight resolves everything. We must remember that this is a novel steeped in misreadings; thus the fight's importance is overstated—it works out the dynamics of father and son and creates the possibility for an alternate domestic reality, but it does not resolve Jackson's inner turmoil. Though Della tells him to wait for Catherine to come to him, even "[i]f it takes twenty years," the last words of the novel are perhaps the most telling: "He watched her go into the house. He stood there, hoping Catherine would come back outside. But she never did" (248).

Gaines has commented on the fact that he does not believe that Catherine could leave the South.[24] If this is so, if he has written this kind of inflexibility into Catherine's character, then we must attempt to understand the novel's ending in different ways. I want to read Jackson's solitude and immobility as Gaines's attempt to illustrate the resulting null space when the machinery powering the plantation romance and the narrative of endurance is disabled. The implication of this is that Jackson must avail himself of another narrative vehicle, one that situates his loss within the space of a new awareness of the world around him. Jackson remains a liminal character, but he has moved closer to the transgressive posture necessary to meet the challenges of the narrative of emergence. For this reason, Gaines leaves the romance between Jackson and Catherine incomplete because neither character is capable of bearing the burden of the paradigmatic shift required to meet the demands of another narrative form outside the South.

Though it seems out of place—especially if one wants to essentialize the African American Southern hero—*Catherine Carmier,* like Ellison's "Flying Home," or DuBois's "The Coming of John," speaks to the manner in which certain forms of community are preceded by both solitude and the willingness to break out of stasis. Jackson is left in the uncertain territory between social death and renewal. And when viewed alongside the other fictions in Gaines's canon, *Catherine Carmier* is a novel that creates space for the fictions that come after it. By writing a novel chronicling, if only by implication, "lost love," Gaines deconstructs and ultimately shuns both the denial of the narrative of endurance and the blind loyalty of the plantation romance. And by leaving that romance unresolved, Gaines plots a new set of narrative coordinates.

If anything, this particular Gaines fiction is probably closer in intent to Hemingway than to Faulkner. For while the latter portrayed the South as a place embodying "frustration, failure, and defeat," and thus sought to "overhaul standard American history," Craig Werner points out that Gaines's fiction attests to the fact that "the black writer coming to Faulkner finds both a fellow in bondage and a new incarnation of Pharaoh" ("Tell Old Pharaoh," 716–17). Indeed, Jackson Bradley may be a closer relative to Jake Barnes (note the similarity of their names) than to any of Faulkner's tortured scions. Jackson's solitude at the end of the novel is of a piece with Jake's realization at the end of *The Sun Also Rises* that he, too, will be alone, that his relationship with Brett Ashley is illusory. While Jackson has not yet reached this state of awareness, what I want to suggest is that he prefigures Gaines's next hero, Jim Kelly, who sings the blues. In his state of pre-hibernation, Jackson Bradley is prepared to work out the exigencies of "love and hate and impossible circumstances which to the courageous and dedicated [can] be turned into benefits and victories."[25] If we think here about Jackson Bradley as the proto-blues-hero, one poised to discover the value of his humanity by realizing the need to sing about his troubles, then *Catherine Carmier* sets the stage for what is to come in the Gaines canon.

3

As Gaines moves from *Catherine Carmier* to *The Autobiography of Miss Jane Pittman*,[26] his fiction focuses on characters who must acquire communal dexterity in order to bring it to bear on the conspiracy of silence that maintains race ritual in Louisiana. I want to begin my discussion of *The Autobiography of Miss Jane Pittman* by acknowledging the shift in perspective embodied in its narrative frame. Recognizing the long history of the slave narrative—both those authored during the nineteenth century and those collected in the 1930s during the Federal Writers Project—Gaines provides the reader with a fictional "editor" whose purpose, it would seem, is to authenticate Miss Jane's story. Gaines recognizes the nineteenth-century slave narrative's use of authenticating documents and intimates that this novel's task is to identify the anomalies that ensue from this format. So the novel uses storytelling as a corrective device, with community, not written documents, providing the force necessary for narrative authority to cohere.

Since we find that Miss Jane is one hundred ten years old, she is the perfect narrator in a corrective history. But, as the novel's "preface" informs us, Miss Jane resists constructing herself (or allowing herself to be constructed) as the sole historical source. She is not about to allow her story to be limited to the confines of her perceptions. The history teacher who wishes to record her story has other ideas:

> I had been trying to get Miss Jane Pittman to tell me the story of her life for several years now, but each time I asked her she told me there was no story to tell. I told her she was over a hundred years old, she had been a slave in this country, so there had to be a story. When school closed for the summer in 1962 I went back to the plantation where she lived. I told her I wanted her story before school opened in September, and I would not take no for an answer. (*Miss Jane,* v)

The history teacher attempts to force Miss Jane to collectivize her life, to distill it into narrative. His request is based on the notion that one can distill a life spanning more than a century into a summer's worth of information. Further, when he is asked why he wants to know Miss Jane's story, he replies, "I teach history . . . I'm sure her life's story can help me explain things to my students" (*Miss Jane,* v). The historical resonances embedded in Gaines's narrative strategy become apparent here. As a rhetorical device, an instrument of abolitionist propaganda, the nineteenth-century slave narrative gave voice to the horrors of slavery, but it often did so at the expense of authorial control (unless one considers the narratives of Douglass or Harriet Jacobs as examples of resistant narratives that create authorial control). The "editor," as Gaines employs him, serves the purpose of bringing the historical process itself into question. His desire to use Miss Jane as an "explanation," while admirable, proceeds from a false assumption. Mary, Miss Jane's companion, challenges this assumption when she asks, "What's wrong with them books you already got?" This is a pivotal question because it addresses the dichotomy between written and spoken history. While it appears that Mary's question accepts the inadequacy of written history, she is actually voicing the foundations for her distrust of literacy. Because the editor is making the same mistake as the books he wants to revise—that history is one voice and that adding one more voice, Miss Jane's, will correct its omissions—Mary calls into question his desire to create a historical text which displays a new paradigm. Hence the teacher's reply, "Miss Jane is not in them," illustrates his failure to understand that his historical method (along with the brusque nature of his approach) must be overhauled before he can revise the product. Moreover, when Mary tells Miss Jane that "You don't have to say nothing less you want," she asserts the fact that Miss Jane's "story" is not public domain. This connotes something even more fundamental: that Miss Jane's "right" to speak also includes the implicit choice of *not speaking*.

This points at what I find a necessary consideration in the novel: *The*

Autobiography of Miss Jane Pittman implicitly addresses the issue of community. Miss Jane's life, which the teacher/editor sees as serving so neat a purpose, is finally the symbol of much more. But he must learn how to configure antagonistic cooperation into historical practice. Thus, he finds that despite the fact it is Miss Jane's story he came seeking, in practice

> others carried the story for her. When she was tired, or when she just did not feel like talking anymore, or when she had forgotten certain things, someone else would always pick up the narration. Miss Jane would sit there listening until she got ready to talk again. If she agreed with what the other person was saying she might let him go on for quite a while. But if she did not agree, she would shake her head and say: "No, no, no, no, no." The other person would not contradict her, because, after all, *this was her story.* (*Miss Jane,* vii)

Though it is Miss Jane's voice that "narrates" her story, what the teacher/editor reveals is that she participates in an historical chorus embodying numerous points of view, including an old man named Pap who often serves as her "main source." They create a scenario where Miss Jane's and the teacher/editor's narrative collaboration exists in a communal matrix that essentially "saves" information from being lost. History, as *The Autobiography* demonstrates, is participatory and inclusive. Because the teacher/editor insists upon making historical presence and American citizenship synonymous, he must amend his "method" accordingly. This entails the act of discarding the metaphorical construction of history as a "flowing," linear narrative. As Miss Jane and the other voices perform it, history is random, chaotic, a fact that escapes the teacher/editor's grasp:

> There were times when I thought the narrative was taking ridiculous directions. Miss Jane would talk about one thing one day and the next day she would talk about something else totally different. If I were bold enough to ask, "But what about such and such a thing?" she would look at me incredulously and say: "Well, what about it?" And Mary would back her up with: "What's wrong with that? You don't like that part?" (vii)

Once again, the teacher/editor fails to recognize that his desire for chronological unity merely replicates the principle of exclusivity that characterizes the history he wants to revise. Clearly, it is pertinent to mention Ellison's notion of history as a randomly configured and often repetitious construction here. For the novel's "preface" articulates the manner in which the teacher/editor, as one who has assumed the task of challenging a faulty paradigm, must stumble onto the paradigm meant to replace it. His attempt to force conceptual unity on Miss Jane's speech demonstrates that "what happened " to Miss Jane is what he refers to as "history." Thus, he wants her to structure her telling to accommodate his authorial purpose. However, Miss Jane reminds him that "history" is a selective discourse; it discards that which does not suit its imperatives. And since her experience is grounded in communal activity, she does not wish to organize it into neatly formulated narrative units. Rather, the context that her fellow narrators provide is more of a catalyst than the teacher/editor's task. Hence Miss Jane's tale is not a result of whimsicality, but of call and response. Though we are often prone to construct the idea of storytelling as a purely textual event, one that structures very rigid formulations of teller and audience, Gaines's "preface" forces us to restore the jagged-edged nature of oral performance where teller and audience straddle the conceptual boundaries that separate them. Thus, when the teacher/editor says, "I just want to tie up all the loose ends," Mary responds, "Well, you don't tie up all the loose ends all the time. And if you go to change her way of telling it, you tell it yourself. Or maybe you done heard enough already? . . . Take what she say and be satisfied" (vii). Mary's admonition reminds us that history is a construct and as such can afford the elegance of neatly orchestrated endings. If the teacher/editor is attempting to create a history of African American citizenship as an inclusive, ever-revisionary construct, he must loose himself from the reflex desire for closure. Indeed, Miss Jane's story is clearly one that demonstrates coherence rather than closure. Though both Mary and Miss Jane know that the teacher/editor's task involves both excavation and interpretation (cf. McPherson's scarred woman), they resist the call for order. By refusing to be bound by a hierarchy of narrative labor, in which the act of ordering disparate events into a linear narrative is privileged, Miss Jane refutes the truncation of her life into a set-piece or a folktale.[27]

It is also important to note that the teacher/editor begins interviewing Miss Jane in the summer of 1962, a time when Civil Rights activity in the South is beginning to gather momentum. This means that Miss Jane's narrative subsumes two major historical signposts: the Civil War and the Civil Rights Movement. The implication, of course, is that her narrative offers a commentary on the nature of African American community and citizenship. Thus, the story, as "organized" by the teacher/editor, comes to us in four books: The War Years, Reconstruction, The Plantation, and The Quarters. This structure is distinguished by its movement from dispersion to intimacy, a journey from the disconnectedness of the post-slavery moment to the transformation of the quarters into a community displaying agency. Miss Jane's voice in the four books captures, on the one hand, various forms of African American mobility, and on the other, the form of Southern impenetrability. What constitutes the impregnability of Jim Crow society, as Miss Jane relates, is the conspiratorial nature of signs. Hence, signs that should clarify meaning are either ignored or shrouded in secrecy, and black and white alike engage in a vow of silence coerced by violence and denial.

Thus, one of the interior messages of Miss Jane's tale is that old age is a site of great complexity.[28] But this makes old age a site of both respite and complicity; the system yields benefits for those whose age allows them to withdraw from plantation labor but it demands loyalty to the status quo.[29] Gaines uses Miss Jane as the vehicle to deconstruct this relation. As Miss Jane enacts it, old age represents the ability to decipher signs and to determine when one should and should not ignore them. And, as her one hundred ten years suggest, this is a skill that one acquires only gradually. This is alluded to at several points in the novel; Miss Jane's life is shaped not only by her ability to "read signs," but her failure to read them as well.

This is first evidenced when the young Jane and Ned pause during their journey to Ohio at the old man's cabin, where he pinpoints their position on a map. Here Jane discovers that she must amend her sense of how chronological time and geographical distance relate. The old man shows her that three days' worth of walking is not enough traveling to get to Ohio. Further, his knowledge of latitude and longitude is important because he makes Jane aware for the first time that her life is characterized by the intersection of geography and power. Jane's inability to decipher symbols also means that she lacks the ability to understand that their power is maintained by ideological force. When she asks the old man how long it will take her to get to Ohio, the old man responds, "The boy'll never make it. You? I figure it'll take you thirty years. Give or take a couple." He comes to this conclusion after relating a narrative that includes Jane's and Ned's capture and reenslavement by Confederate veterans in Arkansas and her marriage to a black man whose self-hatred leads him to treat her brutally until Ned kills him. After their escape to Tennessee, where Ned is killed, Jane finds her way to Kentucky, where she cooks and cleans for a white family till she can trick another man to take her to Ohio. But once there she discovers there are "a hundred Browns" in Cincinnati and twice as many in Cleveland, where "the only white Brown people can remember that ever went to [Louisiana] to fight in the war died of whiskey ten years [before]." While this "flash-forward" narrative never unfolds in the novel, the point is that Jane's desire to find Brown has to be mediated by its placement in cultural time and space. Though the story does not dissuade her from continuing the journey, Jane realizes "how wrong [she has] been for not listening to people," and after four more days of travel she and Ned land on the Bone plantation that ends Book I of the novel.

While there is strong evidence that Miss Jane's story centers on the men who have an impact on her life, beginning with Corporal Brown, I submit that the deeper resonances of her story lie in the talismans she acquires through her contact with them. To view Jane's autobiography solely in terms of its male characters is likewise to suggest that her primary role is that of an onlooker to historical events. But this is true only if one ignores the manner in which her narrative conflates the issues of community and citizenship. Her role as articulate witness portends a more active role and one sees Gaines using natural events like floods, personal events such as her spiritual conversion, and political figures like Huey Long to locate her narrative in time and space and to remind us of the epic nature of Jane's story.

The first talisman Jane acquires, of course, is her name. Though the manner in which she moves from Ticey to Jane Brown is clearly problematic (Brown names her after his wife), I would argue that the journey Jane undertakes to find Brown—where she discovers the futility of finding him—serves as a mediating force (we can note that she no longer uses Brown's name as her own). Hence, the journey, with all its decisions and setbacks, becomes synonymous with nomenclature because of the trials which test Jane's endurance. And indeed, it is Jane's failed endurance that sets her on a journey characterized by its concern with signs.

It begins when Miss Jane dreams of Joe Pittman's death; she sees him thrown against a fence and killed by a black stallion. When the black stallion of her dream is brought to the plantation, Jane is horrified by the stories the men tell about the horse: he is a ghost, a "devil horse" that can run for days without tiring. She goes to a conjure woman to determine Joe's fate and there she finds that Joe will die after he falls three times. She misinterprets the prophecy and concludes that the moment is imminent, though the conjure woman does not specify whether it is this particular black stallion that kills Joe or one he will encounter much later. She attempts to supersede the signs by getting a powder from the conjure woman that will make Joe too sick to ride the black stallion. As she leaves the conjure woman's house, Jane feels secure in the knowledge that she can save Joe's life. But the next day, her uncertainty returns:

> I felt shaky. How did I know that powder was go'n work? Maybe she had just gived it to me because I was worrying her so much. She didn't take time to pick a bottle, she just grabbed the first one she came to. Matter of fact I wanted some powder out of that little green bottle, not that red one. I got more and more shaky. (96)

Jane's desire to control fate anticipates the editor's attempt to control her story. Lacking faith in the conjure woman's ability, she cannot understand the substance of the prophecy. Rather than using the powder to stop Joe from riding the horse, she goes into the corral the night before the men are to break the horses and frees the black stallion. While trying to bring the horse back to the plantation, Joe is killed when the stallion jerks him from his horse and drags him through the swamps. Joe Pittman's premature death is the result of Jane's failure to heed correctly the signs that foretell it. But more than this, Jane is guilty of engaging in a conspiracy against history. He does not die, as in her dream, from being thrown against a fence, he is dragged to death because she intrudes on the flow of history. Her unwillingness to accept the relationship between life and death is itself an evasion of signs. (Joe Pittman tells her that "man come here to die," and the conjure woman tells her "Nothing can stop death.") Freeing the horse is her attempt to prevent the inevitable. Jane's error rests in her failure to recognize the conjure woman as someone who does not acknowledge boundaries between the present and the future or between the living and the dead. She fails to see her as a reliable intermediary. Jane keeps Joe Pittman's name, to acknowledge the fact that "no man would ever take his place," and, as I would argue, to mark the necessity of leaving history to follow its chaotic path.

This lesson occurs in Jane's personal space, but as her relationship to Ned Douglass suggests, it has ramifications that extend into the community. After twenty years, Ned returns from the Spanish-American war and begins teaching. He has assumed the surname "Douglass" because he believes in the teachings of Frederick Douglass who held the belief that "everybody ought to work together." What makes this important is that Ned has chosen Douglass's philosophy over the more conciliatory politics of Booker T. Washington.[30] This also means, of course, that his life is endangered. But perhaps of greatest importance is the fact that Ned chooses to engage a paradigm of citizenship characterized by coherence rather than denial. Moreover, Ned continues to wear his U.S. Army uniform, a sign that he understands the process of citizenship to be a contestational one.

Ned gives what Gaines refers to as a "sermon at the river." What is significant is that Ned articulates a model of citizenship characterized by its inclusiveness and its unwillingness to embrace cultural chauvinism. Indeed, one has to read this passage, given the time period in which it was published, as being aimed at black cultural nationalists and white supremacists alike:

You got some black men . . . that'll tell you the white man is the worst thing on earth. Nothing horrible he wouldn't do. But let me tell you this. . . . If it wasn't for some white men, none of us would be alive here today. I myself'll probably be killed by a white man. . . . But even when he raise the gun or the axe or anything else he might use I won't blame all white men. I'll blame ignorance. Because it was ignorance that put us here in the first place. Ignorance on the part of the black man and the white man. (108)

Ned's "sermon" fixes a reading of the American polity in place as a site created as much by violence and the failure of insight as by successful labor. Indeed, he continues his remarks by citing African complicity with the slave trade, the fact that "our people fought each other, and the white man bought the captives for a barrel of rum and a string of beads. I'm tellin y'all this . . . to show y'all that the only way you can be strong is to stand together" (109). Gaines's inclusion of this chapter, which precedes Ned's death, is important because it demonstrates his adherence to a coherent model of democratic practice particularly when Ned states, "America is for all of us . . . and all of America is for all of us." This recapitulates Ellison ("All of it is part of me"), veering from the separatism of cultural nationalists of that moment and those who were Gaines's contemporaries. Though Ned does not relish violence, neither does he relinquish the notion that racial conflict is a possibility and so it is an important, though not necessarily desired, element of democratic struggle, a part of a larger process of transculturation.

When Ned finishes his sermon, Jane looks in his eyes and reads that he knows his death is imminent. While Jane attempts to prevent Ned's death by trying to convince him to leave, his refusal ends in his death. But before she narrates this portion of her tale, Jane breaks the chronological flow of the narrative to inform us that Ned's death, like Joe Pittman's, has resulted in another talisman, another sign that connotes the presence of a counter-narrative to that signified by the plantation romance. By identifying Ned's burial place, along with the land on which his school was built after his death, Jane distinguishes symbolic territory whose significance lies in narrative space. After Joe Pittman's death, Jane learns the lesson of maintaining contact with the dead, as this passage suggests:

we kept the place where his school was and where he was buried. It will never be sold. We collect from people to pay the taxes and keep up the land, but it is ours. It is for the children of this parish and this State. Black and white. We don't care. We want them to know a black man died many many years ago for them. He died at the end of the other century and the beginning of this century. He shed his precious blood for them. (113)

While this passage seems to run counter to Faulkner's admonition that the curse on the South stems from the fallacy that land is a commodity to be owned, Gaines suggests that a middle ground exists. Though Jane refers to ownership, it is an ownership of inclusion and sharing that crosses racial boundaries. It represents, therefore, the anomalous and stands as a break from convention, as Jane further testifies:

> I remember my old mistress, when she saw the young Secesh soldiers, saying, "The precious blood of the South, the precious blood of the South." Well, there on that river bank is the precious dust of this South. And he is there for all to see. We have a marker for people to stop by and see if they want to. (113–14)

Of course what enables seeing here is the willingness to loose oneself from the denial that foregrounds Southern historical myth. Jane's decision to use "dust," rather than "blood," means that Ned's gravesite is both memorial and blueprint. Hence, Gaines subsumes the plantation romance in a more comprehensive narrative. The act of reading signs, then, serves the larger task of creating coherent community. But that coherence must accrue out of individual choice. The marker, which represents an alternative model of American citizenship, is visible only if the individual wishes to see it as such. To that end, Gaines employs several small arias designed to illustrate the relationship between signs and action. The first of these is found in Book 3, when Jane "finds religion." While this chapter seems to be a digression, I would assert its importance inheres when juxtaposed against Jane's attempt to reach Ohio. Whereas that journey was completely mediated by the material world, Jane's spiritual journey covers her whole life. Indeed, Ned and Joe Pittman, the two most important figures in her life, appear in her vision where she carries a heavy load of bricks across a river. When they ask her to let them carry the load, Jane refuses to relinquish the burden. The symbolic importance of this is two-fold: first, it establishes Jane's act of narration as a form of labor in and of itself, and second, it marks her ascent to a position of mastery in the task of reading signs. That she denies the two figures who best represent "the fire and the hearth" suggests that her role is one that eschews comfort and safety. Moreover, unlike Dilsey, who hears Reverend Shegog's sermon but does not narrate the story of her spiritual awakening, Jane assumes an authority necessary for the remainder of the book.

The reason for this becomes clear in the next chapter, "Two Brothers of the South." There we find that Robert Samson, the owner of the plantation, has two sons, Tee Bob and Timmy. The former is his son by his wife, Amma Dean, the latter is the result of his sexual liaison with a black woman in the quarters. They are both his sons: Jane informs us that "Robert never tried to hide it, and couldn't even if he wanted to because Timmy was more like him than Tee Bob ever would be" (139).

But it is Tee Bob who turns the novel toward closure. After Timmy is forced to leave the plantation, Tee Bob fails to understand the reasons for his departure. And since his father has lived by the code of silence encircling white Southern manhood, he never explains, because for him, the code is so firmly entwined with everything else. As Jane points out:

> Robert thought he didn't have to tell Tee Bob about these things. They was part of life, like the sun and the rain was part of life, and Tee Bob would learn them for himself when he got older. But Tee Bob never did. He killed himself before he learned how he was supposed to live in this world. (147)

Tee Bob's death foreshadows the collapse of the wall of silence synonymous with white supremacy on the plantation. Like Ike McCaslin, Tee Bob is a liminal figure, caught between the conventions of white male privilege and his desire to relinquish that privilege. When he falls in love with Mary Agnes, a Creole schoolteacher, he tries to persuade her to run away with him but she refuses. He goes into the family study, where he writes a note to his mother and then kills himself. Earlier, in a conversation with Jane, Mary Agnes had commented on her relationship with Tee Bob, saying, "Robert is more human being than he is white man." Of course, race ritual will not allow Tee Bob to exert his humanity in this way. And because of this, Gaines is able to illustrate the way all are diminished by the adherence to such dehumanizing conventions.

Further, we can see the way Faulkner's *Go Down, Moses* resonates here. Unlike Ike McCaslin, who repudiates his birthright when he discovers his father's act of incest, Tee Bob can find no way to reconcile his love for Mary Agnes with his role as plantation scion. Though it is his "right" to have Mary Agnes in a clandestine fashion, Tee Bob's transgression comes from his unwillingness to accept this convention. Moreover, before he kills himself, he expresses his despair in writing. This revision of Faulkner posits that the written word is not enough; it must be accompanied by an interpretive energy that resists conventionality.[31] Hence, it is Tee Bob who articulates a paradigmatic shift away from the gothic impulse of concealment toward a more open expression of care.

This bold reversal is enabled by the letter Tee Bob writes before taking his life. The lynching ritual rests, in part, on the failure to acknowledge responsibility. As a surrogate for legal activity, lynching means the African American body, when burned or hanged, is incontrovertibly shrouded in guilt. Under the circumstances, Tee Bob's dead body cannot be "read" unless it is placed in this container. His act of self-sacrifice is denied intentionality. Anticipating this, the only way Tee Bob can assume authority over his actions is to write the note explaining his actions.

Again, we see how Gaines sets an alternative narrative form on a collision course with the plantation romance. Tee Bob's attachment to Mary Agnes inverts, and indeed, mimics, Joel Chandler Harris's relationship between Uncle Remus and the little white boy. However, where the latter never attempts to displace pastoral nostalgia, Tee Bob's letter articulates desire of a different sort. Though we are never told the contents of the letter directly, what distinguishes Tee Bob's act is that, even in suicide, he chooses textuality and legibility over self-erasure.

This is underscored in the exchange between Jules Raynard and Jane, after Tee Bob's body is found in the library along with the note.

> Somewhere in the past, Jane. . . . Way, way back, men like Robert could love women like Mary Agnes. But somewhere along the way somebody wrote a new set of rules condemning all that. I had to live by them, Robert at that house now had to live by them, and Clarence Caya had to live by them. Clarence Caya told Jimmy to live by them, and Jimmy obeyed. But Tee Bob couldn't obey. That's why we got rid of him. All us. Me, you, the girl—all us. (193)

Jane expresses her incredulity at the idea that she is implicated in Tee Bob's death, by responding, "All right, let's say I'm in there. . . . Where I fit in, I don't know, but let's say I'm in there" (193). This is an important move because Jules and Jane reconstruct the "text" of Southern race ritual as one involving a *collaboration* between black and white. Consider, then, this further exchange between Jane and Jules.

> "But ain't this specalatin?" I said.
> "It would be specalatin if two white people was sitting here talking," Jules Raynard said. . . .
> "But it's us?" I said.
> "And that makes it gospel truth." (194–95)

Jules's narration of the events leading up to the suicide is anti-climactic. What is important is that the exchange cannot take place, cannot assume any narrative authority, without Jane's presence. Moreover, as "gospel truth" and not speculation, which would undermine any attempt at an assembly of Southern rituals surrounding interracial union, the "text" Jules Raynard relates recovers Tee Bob's story from the realm of indecipherability. It also refers to an alternative history, one lost in the wake of the codes presently mooring social relations.

Further, it makes implicit the notion that Tee Bob envisioned an alternative paradigm of racial interaction; because his actions are anomalous, however, with no one (Raynard, Jane, Mary Agnes, etc.) to validate them in public space, he bears the brunt of a collective violent act.

This anomaly, in the form of an alternative historical interpretation, becomes the talisman essential to the novel's concluding section. Indeed, when one considers Jane's discussion of Jimmy Aaron as "the One," its relationship to the "Plantation" section has much to do with issues of intimacy. For if the Tee Bob/Mary Agnes liaison signals the codes that prevent certain forms of intimacy, it also references the mythogenesis necessary to efface their intentionality as codes created by human beings. Jim Crow conventions are, of course, about power relations. If Jane is implicated in the Tee Bob/Mary Agnes scenario, it is because she, like the other blacks on the plantation, has chosen to avoid interpretive agency in favor of safety. For to interpret in ways that bring together disparate forms of information, as Ned Douglass's death illustrates, is to transgress—to call attention to the artificiality of racial hierarchy. Because the threat of death is always present in the South (and often death of a random sort, as the massacre at the novel's beginning suggests), the individual dares not attempt to call attention to the contradiction inherent in Southern conspiracies of race. To do so, Jim Crow conventions assert, would bring retaliation down on the black community in collective terms. What is needed, then, is an individual who is willing to sacrifice him/herself as a way of suggesting that actual death is preferable to social death. Clearly, there is a sacred thread to be discerned here: Jimmy Aaron, as "the One," is most certainly a figure of resurrection, a trope Jane validates historically:

> People's always looking for somebody to come lead them. Go to the Old Testament; go to the New. They did it in slavery; after the war they did it; they did it in the hard times that people want call Reconstruction; they did it in the Depression. . . . They have always done it—and the Lord has always obliged in some way or another. (199)

If Jimmy Aaron is "special" in any way it is because he is seen almost from birth as a break from convention. But this "break" is also the point of contiguity between old and new paradigms. Jane explains the reasons for this when she talks about Jimmy's family heritage:

> I don't need to tell you who his daddy was. That don't matter—and, yes, it do. Because if his daddy had been there the cross wouldn't 'a' been nearly so heavy. Oh, heavy it would 'a' been—it had to be—because we needed him to carry part our cross; but the daddy, if he had been there would 'a' been able to give him some help. But he didn't have a daddy to help him. The daddy had done what they told him a hundred years before to do, and he had forgot it just like a

hundred years ago had told him to forget. So it don't matter who his daddy was, because you got some out there right now who will tell you his daddy was somebody else. Oh, sure, they all know who he was, but still they'll argue and say he was someone else. (199–200)

Without the previous exchange between Jane and Jules Raynard we could not discern the weight of this transgressive act of voice here. And further, what makes this passage important is that it begins by invoking the Christ narrative: the Son sent to do the Father's work alone. But then it shifts back to the secular zone, where Jane infers that Jimmy's father is a white man who denies all claim to Jimmy. The passage ends with the sacred and secular in a state of conceptual overlap: Jimmy Aaron is a product of mysterious circumstances—in sacred terms (the Savior personified) and in social/secular terms (the product of an interracial union).[32] Understanding this and the novel's use of heroic figures who engage in various forms of self-sacrifice (Joe Pittman, Ned Douglass, Huey Long, and Tee Bob), we know that Jimmy Aaron, as "the One," is destined to die.

Ultimately, however, it is not the "crucifixion" that should draw our attention. Rather, the life as usable trope is stressed. The key is that his actions are witnessed and narrated; his story is told by Miss Jane, who at the time of the telling is 110 years old. As Gaines suggests, it is not enough to act. His fiction returns repeatedly to the necessity of telling. Jimmy's importance lies in what he catalyzes; he is not a force unto himself. Jane underscores this by talking about how Jimmy was "chosen":

Lena [Jimmy's great aunt] was the first one to ask him if he was the One, then we all started wondering if he was the One. That was long before he had any idea what we wanted out of him. Because, you see we started wondering about him when he was five or six. I ought to say everybody except Lena. Lena started wondering about him soon as she saw him that first morning. . . . We all did later. When he was five or six we all did. Why did we pick him? Well, why do you pick anybody? We picked him because we needed somebody. (200)

The importance of all this, which Jane informs us is never spoken, is that Jimmy and Jane have an affinity for recognizing communal needs. The combination of Jimmy (whose actual death renders unacceptable the social death that characterizes life under Jim Crow) and Jane (who, by virtue of her age, has resisted death and thus become able to resist social death) is important, because they replicate the same configuration we found in "Just Like a Tree." Both of them are sources of intimacy in the quarters. Thus, *The Autobiography of Miss Jane Pittman* establishes the link between narrative and intimacy. It is precisely because of Miss Jane's age that we can accept the manner in which her narrative gaze travels outward to capture historical events and place them in bold relief to much smaller events. In this light Jimmy Aaron's being born right before World War II serves to place him in the web of global transformation. History, as Miss Jane performs it, is inevitably a set of concentric circles that move inward, until we find that one's relationship to historical narrative is generated through the intimate affiliations of community.

But despite this, *The Autobiography* does not entertain notions of either leadership or talismans without problematizing them. We find that Jimmy Aaron, upon reaching adulthood, is expected, as "the One," to enter the ministry. Here, Miss Jane's struggles with spirituality (which she talks about at the beginning of Book 3) help us to understand Gaines's attempt to dismantle the correlation between religiosity and leadership. Like Emmanuel in "Just Like a Tree," Jimmy indicates a paradigm shift. And like Aunt Fe, Jane is designated as his spiritual precursor. But if Miss Jane represents an awareness of the way spirituality affects the secular world, she is likewise imbued with the ability to see the latter's effect on the spiritual life of the community. Indeed, Gaines's use of African American sports heroes like Joe Louis and Jackie Robinson asserts the important role both men play in Miss Jane's attempt to formulate a democratic vision of times to come. Ironically, baseball is the reason Miss Jane is stripped of the title of "church mother." But because both Miss Jane and Jimmy represent figures of innovation, heroic figures like Louis and Robinson articulate not only African American competitive spirit but also how that spirit is the fuel to future struggles.

However, the more important relationship to be discerned here is that which exists between Jimmy and the teacher/editor. As "the One," Jimmy takes on the task of reading the newspapers and writing letters for people in the quarters. Like his Biblical namesake, Aaron, Jimmy's role is to speak for the people. Miss Jane talks about how Jimmy is so "interested in the people" that his speaking voice results from his ability to listen to them. This is reflected, Miss Jane realizes, in Jimmy's ability to "say just what you wanted to say. All you had to do was get him started and he could write the best two-page letter you ever read. He would write about your garden, about the church, the people, the weather. *And he would get it down just like you felt it inside*" (204–5; emphasis mine). And by a brilliant stroke Miss Jane decides to tell the teacher/editor about the boy who takes over the reading and writing after Jimmy leaves the quarters to attend school in New Orleans. Unlike Jimmy, the other boy is "something else":

> What was in the paper, that's what he read. He didn't care how bad you felt. He came to your house to read what was in the paper, he didn't come there to

> uplift your spirits. If Jackie stole a base, he read that. If Jackie didn't steal a base, he read that too. . . . Same when it came to writing your letters. Wrote what you told him and nothing else. When you stopped talking, he stopped writing. "I don't know your business if you don't know it," he used to say. "I come here to write your letter, not think myself crazy." (205)

This is an important contrast—not the digression it would appear to be—because Miss Jane is addressing the manner in which she hopes the teacher/editor will approach the project at hand. This suggests that throughout the *Autobiography* Miss Jane gives voice to her distrust of the teacher/editor's listening skills. Jimmy's gift is his ability to utilize his intimate relationship with the people in the quarters to construct both a communal voice and the voices of individuals within that community. These are dually important considerations, not only because Miss Jane wants to guide the teacher/editor toward a non-intrusive posture, but also because she wants to point at the inherent wrongheadedness of collecting history merely to "explain things." Jimmy's ability to adopt both a transgressive posture as it relates to reading (he "reads" Miss Jane's mood and adjusts the news to fit her emotional state) and an interpretive posture as a writer are important cues for the teacher/editor to recognize. For Miss Jane is articulating the importance, on some level, of challenging the sanctity of written texts. As the site of either exclusion or truncation, the newspaper Jimmy reads requires him to assume an interventionist posture, one that imagines a black reader. While it could be argued that his alteration of Jackie Robinson's game statistics is mere deception, what is more plausible is Jimmy's awareness that "news" communicates not only what happens in the world but also people's place in that world. By becoming a reader of texts who ignores what's there in favor of what *needs to be there*, Jimmy suggests that "the One" 's task is to address issues of social position.

In contrast, the other boy's unwillingness to read more than what appears in print suggests the clearest sign of hopelessness. His inability to transgress the written word means that he will likewise not challenge the sanctity of law, even if that law is defective. His distance from the community is further signaled by his inability to write what the people feel. Because he is unable to write unless he is dictated to, the other boy lacks the ability to speak for others. While it seems that Miss Jane is being unnecessarily cruel when she describes the boy as "Monkey boy," what she really gives voice to is his inability to combat—as either a reader or a writer—the negative stereotypes used to portray African Americans.

Here we can address the novel's final turn in productive ways. First, Gaines's novel demonstrates the significance of the Civil Rights Movement's impulse to make the preacher into the vehicle of social justice.

As "the One," Jimmy is conceptualized by the folk in the quarters as a preacher. His lack of desire to preach is misinterpreted by the people as the wane of his religious zeal. Only Miss Jane understands Jimmy's different role. Like Aunt Fe in "Just Like a Tree," she too is indicative of an earlier paradigm, one that makes Jimmy her spiritual kin and she his spiritual helper.

When Jimmy returns to the quarters, Robert Samson has threatened the folk with eviction should they decide to engage in Civil Rights activity. In Samson's view, the fact that none of his "tenants" pay him rent is the sign that theirs is an equitable relationship. The relationship is inequitable, of course, but the conspiratorial nature of Southern race relations is foregrounded by the act of rendering inequity unrecognizable as such. It is Jimmy's task, given his ability to engage in transgressive acts of reading and writing, to name the conspiracy and marshal the resources necessary to render it ineffectual. To do this, he must eschew his role as voice of the people in order to embrace a different role: as the source of coherence, Jimmy's value lies in his status as vessel, not voice. When Jimmy goes to the church to issue a "call," the church members are ambivalent, if not hostile. However, he knows that his life will be endangered if he attempts to lead a demonstration and he also knows that his role as "the One" is to bind the people into a coherent body. Thus, he tells them:

> I don't feel worthy because I'm so weak. And I'm here because you are strong. I need you because my body is not strong enough to stand out there all by myself. . . . We have just the strength of our people, our Christian people. That's why I'm here. I left the church, but that don't mean I left my people. (224–25)

He not only draws a distinction between Christian ritual and the quest for equality, he also suggests that his role is to render the people, not himself, visible. As the guide into the secular world of law, he knows he will fall into a state of incoherence without the support of the folk who continue to embrace the spiritual world. But, like Jane, Jimmy has come to understand the working of the sacred within the secular world. The folk have too often deferred their freedom to the hereafter, but Jimmy suggests that they can bring their spiritual energies to bear on the world of their everyday experience.

The outcome is almost anticlimactic: Jimmy is killed the morning of the march to Bayonne and thus realizes the fate of all those characters in Gaines's novels who attempt to enact abrupt challenges to the status quo. The novel ends, however, with Miss Jane saying, "Just a little piece of [Jimmy] is dead, the rest of him is waiting for us in Bayonne" (245). Miss Jane's importance to the demonstration lies in the fact that, like

Jimmy, she is an adept reader of signs. As such, she alone possesses the ability to construct a coherent model of resistance. Moreover, this is an instance when the influence held by the conservative elements in both communities is nullified. Miss Jane's age represents the "pass" that enables her to participate in the demonstration and to return to Samson to live after it is over. But along with this, the look she and Robert exchange is of great importance. "Me and Robert looked at each other there a long time, then I went by him" (246). The "look" has a multiple function: first, it encapsulates the entire history of the South; second, it brings the conspiracy (and immobility) of silence to a state of closure; and last, the anomalous notion of a 108-year-old black woman (the icon of immobility) walking past the plantation patriarch (the icon of license) signals the paradigm shift taking place.

If *Catherine Carmier* was Gaines's attempt to create fresh narrative space, then *The Autobiography of Miss Jane Pittman* gives voice to what is required to make that space viable. Its Ellisonian overtones notwithstanding, *Autobiography* bears a strong kinship to McPherson's "A Solo Song: For Doc," discussed in the previous chapter. As in that story, Gaines's novel posits a self-effacing narrator (despite the fact that he reveals himself at the start of the text). Like McPherson's "youngblood," Gaines's narrator must enact an historical practice that effaces his presence as it foregrounds the presence (and the present) of the community. To ignore the teacher/editor, then, is a severe critical oversight. For though Miss Jane's voice renders the narrative, we know that it has been the teacher/editor's task to organize Miss Jane's (and the community's) stories into a coherent narrative. This task, we know, includes the act of omission.

Jimmy's role anticipates that of the teacher/editor, who is also most comfortable serving as vessel rather than voice. His original intent, to "explain things to [his] students," was misguided largely because it placed him in the role of narrator, a task for which he is ill-suited. The novel's title, *The Autobiography of Miss Jane Pittman,* is the sign that he has arrived at a new state of awareness. The best indication of this is found in the next-to-last sentence of the teacher/editor's preface, "This is what both Mary and Miss Jane meant when they said you could not tie all the ends together in one neat direction." Here we find an interesting construction, for the sentence suggests that the original intent of the teacher/editor's project was to explain the past. But what Miss Jane makes clear is that one's life as a reader of signs establishes nothing more than a *usable present* in which invisibility plays an important role. This novel, like "Solo Song," is about the symbiosis of traditions: the teacher/editor is rendered invisible by Miss Jane's narrative, the conclusion of which occurs, not on the novel's last page, but within the space of his "preface." The teacher/editor is the ultimate articulate witness; he finds community, and he gives voice to that community's collective experiences. In the process, he discovers that history is not a static phenomenon in which one intervenes in order to bring it to a favorable state of closure. If anything, Jimmy's death—his "failure" to lead—speaks to the manner in which the transgressive figure in Gaines's work is the doorway to process. That process may be one of self-recovery or one of discovering community, but like Ellison's narrator and Tod Clifton, like McPherson's self-effaced narrator and Doc, Gaines posits a narrator who looks for the truth only to lose himself among kin.

4

The theme of losing oneself among kin transfers itself into two other works in the Gaines canon: *Bloodline,* a collection of novellas, and *A Gathering of Old Men.* Though there is a twenty-year gap between the two books, nonetheless they share a very strong formal and thematic relationship. Both texts exhibit strongly delineated communal voices. The stories offer a variety of voices, ranging from that of a six-year-old boy to those of a group gathered at a family event. Along with this formal trajectory, the two texts offer several overlapping themes. First, they display a gothic impulse in the form of tension between public and private forms of disclosure. Second, both texts focus attention on African American approaches to the law. Third, both texts utilize the trope of Ellisonian hibernation as a sign of self-recovery. The fourth characteristic these texts share is that the narration occurs in the first person. This final aspect suggests that the literary project in these texts differs from that in texts where Gaines uses a third-person omniscient narrator. In those texts, as I discussed earlier, the protagonist's search for coherence is located within the attempt to find the missing pieces of a narrative in order to construct an integrated self. Thus, they are not tellers, they are listeners whose search for coherence rests on a unified narrative.

Because I have already discussed several of the stories from the collection, let me focus on the first story in *Bloodline* as an example of what I have described above. It offers a glimpse of domestic convention on the plantation and how the rupture of convention affects the community. In "A Long Day in November," the story's narrator is a six-year-old boy named Sonny, and the story concerns the conflict between his parents over his father's car. As a child, unskilled in the conventions of adulthood, Sonny does not "edit" his narration; he gives voice to all he sees and feels. So when his mother, Amy, leaves his father and takes him to his grandmother's house, and he hears the old woman encouraging his mother to leave, he says, "Ah, but I don't like Gran'mon too much, she's always talking bad about Daddy" ("Long Day," 78). Adult convention would prohibit this thought, but Sonny, as the channel through which we receive the narrative, makes no distinction between public and private. Because he can understand disruption in his life in only the most basic terms, he cannot rationalize his actions. He goes to school, but because of the parental dispute, he has not had time to learn his lesson. His anxiety translates itself into a physical response:

> I don't know my lesson. I don't know my lesson. I don't know my lesson. I feel warm. I'm wet. I hear the wee-wee dripping on the floor. I'm crying. I'm crying because I wee-wee on myself. My clothes wet. Lucy and them go'n laugh at me. Billy Joe Martin and them go'n tease me. I don't know my lesson. I don't know my lesson. I don't know my lesson. ("Long Day," 24)

The symmetrical shape of this passage, with Sonny's realization that he is wet being enclosed by the fact that he does not know his lesson, suggests that he mirrors the state of affairs at home. The prepared lesson is the public expression of domestic harmony (which includes the "lesson" of when and where to use the bathroom, a point Gaines makes by emphasizing that Sonny uses a pot for this purpose). When his teacher, Miss Hebert, asks him why he does not know his lesson, Sonny tells her that he and his mother have left home. She correctly assesses that Sonny is responding to the conflict and writes a note for him to deliver to his parents.

Amy has left Eddie, her husband, because he spends more time with his car than with the family. After begging her to return home and asking advice from folk in the quarters, Eddie goes to see Madame Toussaint, the plantation conjure woman. When he arrives, she already knows that he is there to see her about Amy, wanting advice as to how to bring her home. She asks for three dollars, but Eddie only has seventy-five cents. She takes it, looks into her fire, and tells him to "Give it up." This is as much advice as the money will buy. As a woman who specializes in "reading" events and interpreting how people can alter their fortunes, the character of Madame Toussaint suggests that, for both Eddie and Sonny, there is a lesson that has not been learned. This is a story about acts of interrelated misreading: Sonny cannot read his lesson, Amy's mother thinks Amy should be married to Freddy Jackson, and Eddie cannot understand Madame Toussaint's advice. The task for Eddie is to unravel the mystery of Madame Toussaint's reading or get the resources necessary to get more information (which means he needs another $2.25). He initially eschews this solution and attempts to work from what he knows.

At this point, the boundary between public and private is irreconcilable; the whole community knows that there is marital strife between Amy and Eddie; the whole class knows that Sonny has wet on himself. Eddie can return the household to its conventional status if he correctly interprets the advice, but this calls for him to listen and it is his inability to hear which prevents him from acting on the reading:

> "Give it up." Give up what? I don't even know what she's talking about. I don't even know what she's talking 'bout. I hope she don't mean give . . . Amy up. She ain't that crazy. I don't know nothing else she can be talking 'bout. (51)

To avoid the responsibility of finding out, he attempts to use other men's advice from Madame Toussaint. But none of this information is useful; it has no bearing on the "lesson" he has failed to learn. He must return to Madame Toussaint for a more thorough reading of his situation. After taking the money, the conjure woman tells Eddie that Amy wants to come home and that the way to get her there is for him to burn his car. Eddie resists the idea, saying that Madame Toussaint has misread the flames and given him someone else's advice. When he asks Amy, however, she agrees to come home if he follows through. The car burning assumes the significance of a manhood ritual, one which the whole community comes out to witness. As the car burns, Rachel, Amy's mother, says, "I just do declare. . . . He's a man after all" (71).

After the car has been burned completely, Amy and Sonny return to their cabin. Amy attempts to restore the house to its conventional status within the community by having Eddie beat her so that his masculine status will be restored along with it. But this is an illusion.[33] Amy has deeply internalized the conventions of a patriarchal household, where white women are imprisoned within the domestic sphere; her demand for a beating is designed to create the illusion that Eddie is the "man of the house." Clearly, the act of burning the car raises Eddie to a new understanding of familial responsibility and his role within the matrix of kinship. Though the story's outcome could be read without acknowledging its context, it must be remembered that the entire scenario occurs on a plantation where the white man is the unquestioned symbol of power. Thus Amy adheres to the domestic paradigm white supremacy creates and perpetuates. Madame Toussaint alludes to the cult of domesticity when she tells Eddie:

> Women like to be in their own house. That's their world. You men done messed up the outside world so bad that they feel lost and out of place in it. Her house is her world. Only there can she do what she want. She can't do that in anybody else house—momma or nobody else. But you men don't know any of this. (61)

Amy's call for domestic violence is, inevitably, a call for domestic convention. She eschews her mother's solution of taking up with another man, and when Eddie protests the need to beat her, she threatens to leave again. She coerces him, then, because she concludes that the public act of beating her will restore their household's private status, remove it from scrutiny by situating the familiar communal drama of a man exerting authority over the domestic space through violence. Eddie's unwillingness to beat her, the fact that he cries, and his elation at Amy's return home signals his desire to loose himself from more conventional expressions of manhood. However, Amy's adherence to patriarchal convention leads to the compromise of Eddie's transformation. Because Amy fails to realize that the act of burning the car has restored his integrity, she can only assign positive meaning to Eddie if he beats her.[34] The story offers an ironic twist on the notion of immersing oneself within the space of kin, for it is here that we can also see where Gaines sets up the conditions from which his characters, both later in the collection and in his canon, will have to loose themselves.[35] For, in essence, Amy's manipulation of Eddie (and by implication, Sonny) continues their entrapment within a masculine code formulated outside the black community, a code whose adoption necessitates a new, resistant posture.

5

We see the beginnings of such a posture in Gaines's fourth novel, *A Gathering of Old Men*,[36] where the relationship between intimacy and voice is worked out yet again, though this time in a communal rather than a personal way. While this novel's use of multiple narrators gives it a formal similarity to Faulkner's *As I Lay Dying*, thematically this fiction is more aptly contrasted with Eudora Welty's short story, "The Wide Net." Though they are structurally dissimilar, *A Gathering of Old Men* and "The Wide Net" are both thematically centered around the attempt to balance communal and familial forms of intimacy. In the process, both fictions investigate the issue of maturation and its impact on community. Welty's short story concerns William Wallace Jamieson's maturation from irresponsible manchild to husband and father. Gaines depicts maturation from the point of view of old men, whose status as "uncle" (in the best of situations) belies their rank as elders.[37] We see here the racial inflection of maturation: men prevented from occupying symbolic territory, characters struggling to move from a state of perpetual boyhood to manhood.

The plot of *A Gathering of Old Men* centers on the murder of Beau Boutan, a Cajun sharecropper working on the Marshall plantation.

When he is found shot near the quarters, with old Mathu standing near the body holding a shotgun that has just been fired, Candy Marshall, the plantation owner's niece, comes up with a plan requiring the old men in the surrounding parish to arrive on the plantation carrying fired shot guns and spent shells. Mathu has worked for the Marshalls most of his life, but now he is old and ailing. He is the closest thing to a father Candy has known after the death of her parents and the only one among the black men in the parish who has stood his ground against Fix Boutan, Beau's father, and the Cajuns. Because of this, he is the prime suspect in Beau's murder. Fix Boutan has a long history of terrorizing the blacks in the parish. As the leader of the vigilante violence that sustains segregation and racism, his power reaches such mythic proportions that, as Sterling Brown's poem, "Old Lem," suggests, when he rides, he and his men do not "come by ones . . . they come by tens." Hence much of the novel takes place between Beau's murder, the likely prospect of Fix's revenge, and the quarters' preparation for his arrival.

This forms the backdrop for a more substantial event: the deterioration of the machinery driving the racial drama in which blacks and whites play circumscribed roles. Because that drama functions in what are very nearly contractual terms, both communities have come to accept the notion that surface appearances should not be breached. White supremacy is so pervasive, the law cannot (or will not) settle disputes between black and white with any consistency. As far as the space of negotiation is concerned, the two communities have very little room in which to maneuver.

Given this, what makes the comparison between the two fictions of such utility here is their depiction of events, best characterized as carnivalesque. Anthropologist Victor Turner points out that the carnival moment is characterized by "a place which is no place and a time which is no time."[38] The characters experience "the reverse of their daily selves," assuming roles that are unfamiliar, moving into spaces which are likewise mysterious and beyond explanation. What results is an instance whose predictability is nullified. The people in the quarters (*Gathering*) and the men who accompany William Wallace on the river-dragging ("Net") move from what Turner would describe as an indicative state, where they are bound by a system of rational thought, to a subjunctive mood, where they assume a more willful, emotional posture leading them to challenge its dictates. Thus, William Wallace looks down at the river "as if it were still a mystery to him." And Mat, one of Gaines's old men, observes on his way to Candy's plantation that he feels good, knowing that he "and all the rest [of the old men are] doing something different, for the first time" (*Gathering*, 40).

Further, both fictions utilize strong evocations of place, the river and the quarters, but these give way to scenarios whose collapsed time and space create the conditions for new forms of intimacy. This new intimacy is marked by the dissipation of urgency, which is replaced by gestures more improvisatory than exigent: the search for Hazel Jamieson's ostensibly drowned body gives way to a celebratory ritual of food and male playfulness; the likelihood of Fix's arrival generates a reflectiveness which supercedes notions of personal security. What this suggests is that the carnivalesque moment provides the conduit for a society to pass from one paradigm of behavior to another. Thus Gaines's novel portrays a drastic change in the valence of black communal energy.

This is signaled by the manner in which the journey to Marshall plantation takes on a ceremonial air. As they are heading down to the plantation, Chimley, Mat, Billy, Jacob, Dirty Red, Cherry, and Yank are all "feeling proud." When they arrive at a graveyard, just above the plantation, where each man has a family member buried, they find their respective family plots and remember the forgotten stories of their ancestors. For example, when Jacob kneels next to the grave of his sister, Tessie, Cherry remembers how she died: the victim of white men who drowned her in the river on Mardi Gras in 1947. Jacob's French Creole family refused to take her body, leaving it to be buried with the darker skinned blacks she moved among. Cherry looks at Jacob clearing weeds from the grave and realizes that Jacob's presence is perhaps to "make up for what he had done to his sister over thirty years ago." This gesture leads each of the men to find his family's gravesite, to see the confrontation with Fix as a moment of redemption. When the other men arrive, Clatoo tells them to fire their guns and adds, "Let them down there hear you" (*Gathering*, 48). This is not only because Candy has instructed them to do so; it also denotes a more important gesture: the reclamation of an ancestral voice. The gunfire is obligatory, but that obligation, the old men each come to understand, belongs to their kin; it serves as a symbolic gesture meant to "avenge" the deaths of folk who have been brutalized by racial violence and degradation. The ritual has a transmogrifying effect: changing them from "tramps" into "soldiers," marking their emergence from hibernation and commemorating the first time in their lives that they have attempted to play socially responsible roles.

What makes this such a powerful moment is that Gaines uses subtle indicators to articulate the divisions among blacks in the parish. Gaines has talked about Louisiana's problematic racial politics, especially when complexion is at issue. For example, Cherry looks at Dirty Red and remembers, "We had never mixed too well with his people. We thought they was too trifling, never doing anything for themself." But the urgency of the moment leads him to look at his companion through different eyes, and thus he concludes, "Dirty Red was the last one. Maybe that's why he was here today, to do something for all the others" (*Gathering*, 46). As we will see over the course of the novel, each of these men has reasons to be ashamed about his life. But the carnivalesque allows each of them to adopt new postures. What is essential to an understanding of this moment, then, is a recognition of these men as performers. Remembering Hymes's definition of performance, they take responsibility for presentation to an audience, an audience consisting of kin both living and dead.

Storytelling abounds in *A Gathering of Old Men*. It destabilizes the regulatory machinery that has shaped their sense of possibility and becomes the vehicle that carries the old men into transgressive space. The negations that have shaped their lives become sites of affirmation because they enter the realm of narration. And in each instance, the old men use narrative to give voice to the past. This project is enhanced by the presence of Sheriff Mapes, who serves, on the one hand, as the initial audience for the old men's stories. On the other, he is a narrative foil. Trying to get the old men to confess that they did not kill Beau so he can arrest Mathu, he uses slaps and threats to attain this goal. His other tool, however, is to remind the old men of their past reputations, to explain why they could not possibly have committed the murder. Each man persists in claiming responsibility for the murder. Each of the stories centers on the brutality of race ritual and its impact on the lives of the old men and their kin.

In effect, they are guilty; though each lacked the courage to perform it in the past, by telling their stories they bring the repressed violence into utterance. The stories often have to do with events where they or their kin have been deeply injured. "We had all done the same thing some time or another," Rufe observes, "we had seen our brother, sister, mama, daddy insulted once and didn't do a thing about it" (97). Each man's story voices his motives for killing Beau. When Mapes asks Uncle Billy why he killed Beau, he cites revenge as a motive:

> What they did my boy. . . . The way they beat him. They beat him till they beat him crazy and we had to send him to Jackson (the state mental facility). He don't even know me and his mama no more. We take him candy, we take him cake, he eat it like a hog eating corn. . . . That's no way to be. It hurts his mama every time she see that. (80)

As rumor would have it, Fix and his men are responsible for the beating, just after his son returns home from World War II. Another man, Tucker, relates a tale reminiscent of John Henry when he tells of his brother beating the Cajun tractors with only a team of mules. After this heroic feat, the Cajuns beat him to death. The story recapitulates the John Henry folktale, but this time it is not the effort of beating the machine that kills John Henry but the men who own the machines. Gable tells how his son is executed after being falsely accused of rape by a white woman. Coot talks about fighting in France with the 369th. When he returns to Louisiana, he is threatened after whites see him wearing his decorated uniform. Yank talks about his life as horse-breaker. "Anybody needed a horse broke, they called on Yank," he says, "cause they knowed I knowed my stuff" (98). Perhaps the most serious indictment comes when Johnny Paul and Corrine speak up. Their speeches do not speak to violence, but instead about the way the Cajuns have irrevocably changed the way of life in the parish by taking over the land and destroying it with their machines. Johnny Paul claims responsibility for killing Beau because there are no more flowers:

> That's why I kilt him, that's why. . . . To protect them little flowers. But they ain't here no more. And how come? 'Cause Jack ain't here no more. He's back there under them trees with all the rest. With Mama and Papa, Aunt Thread, Aunt Spoodle, Aunt Clara, Unc Moon, Unc Jerry—all the rest of them. . . . Thirty, forty of us going out in the field with cane knives, hoes, plows—name it. Sunup to sundown, hard, miserable work, but we managed to get it done. We stuck together, shared what we had, and loved and respected each other. (91–92)

His narrative recalls a time when labor in the fields was synonymous with community. But it also reconstitutes the credibility of the inhabitants. When he asks Rufe, Clatoo, Glo, Corrine, Rooster, and Beulah, "What y'all don't see?" he strips Mapes of the ability to dismiss the quarters as a site of desolation and death. Rather, the quarters was a place where flowers represented a sign of resistance, and as Johnny Paul makes clear, it also represents a love for the land. Johnny Paul's "violence" against Beau is a gesture toward preserving both the land and the community that respects it. Corrine echoes this sentiment when she observes:

> That river. . . . Where the people went all these years. Where they fished, where they washed they clothes, where they was baptized. St. Charles River. Done gived us food, done cleaned us clothes, done cleaned us soul. St. Charles River—no more, though. No more. They took it. Can't go there no more. (107)

Against this exhaustion of natural and emotional resources, Gaines posits a force that has the potential to renew the territory. The football team at Louisiana State University becomes a sign of the collision of public and private sensibilities. Gil Boutan, Fix's youngest son, is a star fullback on the team, alongside Cal Harrison, a black halfback. Together they are known as "Salt and Pepper." The significance of their pairing goes beyond the football field, as Sully, a quarterback on the team, makes clear:

> It would be the first time this had ever happened, black and white in the same backfield—and in the Deep South, besides. LSU was fully aware of this, the black and white communities in Baton Rouge were aware of this, and so was the rest of the country. (112)

While this aspect of the novel appears to be a digression, its presence in the novel alludes to the epic scale of the old men's resistance. The endurance narrative, with its enduring black saints, encodes that which has been lost and is longed for in conjunction with black silence and passivity. We need to consider the pastoral here as well. As the folk invoked it, the land offered a refuge, a site where they could at least tender a scrap of dignity in the face of racist assault and exclusion. Losing the land is about losing community; thus the Cajuns become scapegoats from the exhaustion of possibility. Gaines's novel proposes, however, that their placement on the land occurs within a larger set of economic factors. Hence Gil and Cal renew the land; their status as complimentary elements ("salt and pepper") restores the lost resources of the land and initiates the terms upon which a newly constituted community can cohere. By using football, Gaines works out the manner in which the pastoral site of community is renewed by a site where the bodily labor expended upon the land is rechanneled to formulate an inclusive community where talent is the key to participation and which allows regional anxiety to be displaced. As *A Gathering of Old Men* intimates, sports is the new site of endurance, and African American participation is synonymous with African American citizenship.[39]

When Gil hears of his brother's death, he goes to Marshall to learn the details surrounding the murder. After Candy tells him that she murdered Beau, Gil expresses disbelief, and then offers another perspective of the event:

> You never did like Beau. . . . You never liked any of us. Looking at us as if we're a breed below you. But we're not, Candy. We're all made of the same bone, the same blood, the same skin. Your folks had a break, mine didn't that's all. (122)

Gil is part of a new generation and he gives voice to the class conflict that characterizes the confinement of the Cajuns, their entrapment within the working class. Candy, as part of the landowning class, views them from her higher position in the hierarchy. Thus, the novel brings into focus the changes taking place in the realm of class as well as within the racial sphere. But Gil suggests that class is the fulcrum upon which all other issues rest.[40] He represents integration on several fronts: not only is he the teammate of a black player, he represents a new form of upward mobility for his working class family. In this regard, his struggle is no less important than that of the old men. Indeed, he and Cal represent a New South, one that will use football as a way of redefining its regional identity. Thus Gil's agenda is very different from his father's, with its orientation toward the maintenance of racial hierarchy. In recognizing the benefits of a new order, Gil asks the question, "Won't it ever stop? I do all I can to stop it. Every day of my life, I do all I can to stop it. Won't it ever stop?" (122). Gil calls for an end to both race and class conflict because each of these limits his possibilities.

Gil is a football player who wants to be "All-American." Clearly, this is another instance of Ellisonian doubling: "All-American" pertains to football and to the larger project of embodying the entire culture, acknowledging its constitutive impact on American citizenship. When he confronts his father, Gil tells him that "People died—people we knew—died to change" the racial situation. He identifies with the African American struggle for justice, and thus he eschews violence as an avenue of retribution. Moreover, he brings into the family narrative the voices of people from whom his father would hold himself socially apart, for their actions have, in effect, created the conditions for his collegiate career. For this, however, he is repudiated by both father and family.[41] Again, we find an instance of ancestral rupture as the means to coherence at the dual levels of self and nation. Russ, one of Mapes's deputies, articulates the substance of what Gil has done and what course of action he must follow when he tells him to play in the game against Ole Miss the next day:

> Sometimes you got to hurt something to help something. Sometimes you have to plow under one thing in order for something else to grow. . . . *You can help this country tomorrow.* You can help yourself. (151; emphasis mine)

Russ's use of the agricultural metaphor underscores the renewal of pastoral space, linking agency and cultural vitality with a contemporary sensibility. The football game between Ole Miss and LSU is thus a symbolic confrontation between the future and the past.[42] In going against his family, Gil chooses the future and like so many of Gaines's black protagonists, he, too, hovers between an individual resistance to racial convention and his family's adherence to conventional racial identity. Gil therefore is an important figure because he engages in the type of negotiation which leads him to choose symbolic action as the middle course between violence and passivity. Moreover, he signals the new societal paradigm, where the carnivalesque can find expression through sanctioned acts of symbolic violence (in this instance, football) rather than in socially directed forms which emphasize racial superiority. Implicit in this story, as Gil demonstrates, are the narratives of those whose efforts made it possible for "Salt and Pepper" to exist. A living metaphor, Gil and Cal are the visible result of desegregation and the political struggle necessary to make it manifest.

The novel repeatedly calls for the carnivalesque impulse to invert its closures, to make them into possibilities. The character of Mathu offers an excellent example, for it is he who is perhaps most transformed by the entire event. Indeed, just as Gil chooses to stand alone, Mathu discovers community. The latter has held himself apart from the other men in the quarters because of their cowardice. He has referred to himself as an "African" because he knows the whites "won't let [him] be a citizen in this country." But Mathu is transformed from being a "mean-hearted old man" into a member of the community:

> I been changed. . . . I been changed. Not by that white man's God. I don't believe in that white man's God. I been changed by y'all. Rooster, Clabber, Dirty Red, Coot—you changed this hardhearted old man. (182)

Mathu enters a space in which he simultaneously discovers individual citizenship and communal ties, a space that turns on participation rather than avoidance. As he voices his new-found respect for the old men who have told their stories, his posture moves out of a zone of resistance and stasis, where he expresses his unwillingness to connect because he eschews conciliation, to a much more transcendant state which allows him to see himself in the stories of others.

But here the novel takes another twist. Charlie, Mathu's son, appears to turn himself in for Beau's murder. He returns from hiding in the swamp, where he has escaped to after killing Beau. He tells his own story, and the telling marks his transformation, his achievement of manhood:

> Something like a wall, a wall I couldn't see, but it stopped me every time. I fell on the ground and screamed and screamed. I bit in the ground. I got a handful of dirt and stuffed it in my mouth, trying to kill myself. Then I just laid there, laid there, laid there. Sometime round sundown—no 'fore sundown, I heard a voice calling my name. I laid there listening, listening, listening, but I didn't hear it no more. But I knowed that voice was calling me back here. (193)

Like Bigger Thomas and Cross Damon, two of Richard Wright's protagonists created by acts of violence, Charlie lashes out at the degradation Jim Crow has inflicted on his entire life. But killing Beau is not an act of creation in itself, as is often the case in Wright's novels. Rather, Charlie assumes the status of "Mr. Biggs " (a play on Wright's Bigger perhaps) when he returns to take responsibility for his actions. Thus, retaliation and the willingness to be accountable combine to transform Charlie from "boy" to man. When Mapes calls Charlie "Mr. Biggs," it is the sign that his manhood is acknowledged by all.

The novel offers a somewhat anti-climactic gun battle between what is left of Boutan's mob and the old men, after which Charlie and Luke Will, the leader of the whites, lie dead. Gaines's real intent here is to suggest that racial conflict inflicts serious wounds on black and white, particularly in an environment where equality of treatment under the law exists. More, it allows the old men to follow through on their promise to stand with Mathu, to fight in the event of a confrontation. In a highly symbolic and integrating ritual, the people—including the women, children, and Candy—touch Charlie's dead body in hopes that "some of that stuff he found in the swamps might rub off on [them]." The community coheres around this final act. Candy's participation in the ritual is symbolic in a different way. She has tried to uphold the plantation tradition begun by her grandfather and father. Her desire to protect "her people" originates within a patriarchal and white supremacist matrix. But Charlie's killing of Beau likewise destroys the Marshalls' paternalistic hold on the blacks who live in the quarters. Though Candy's view of the blacks in the quarters is benign, inevitably it relies on a set of outmoded conventions and assumptions. The ritual frees Candy from her imprisonment within patriarchal myth.

The scene has other implications besides its use as a means of closure. By using old men who have found their voices and have chosen resistance over conciliation, this fiction challenges the plantation romance and its pervasive effects on Southern fiction. Remembering a figure like Uncle Remus, who functions in the service of sustaining both white supremacy and the longing for a lost way of life, these old men challenge this marginalization of African American agency. Furthermore, as the product of Cajun working men rather than plantation aristocrat, Gil releases us from Joel Chandler Harris's "little boy" who feeds on Remus's stories in order to reinvigorate the pastoral space as a site of aristocratic dominance. The coupling of folk narrative with weapons speaks powerfully to the issue of democratic enterprise. For what it suggests is that human loss is no less important in the quest for American citizenship than human advance. Indeed, innovation in a democracy relies on the willingness to accept the prospect of failure.

This helps us to understand Gaines's decision to use Lou Dimes, the white newspaper reporter, as the novel's final voice. While this act could be interpreted as further capitulation to racial hierarchy, I interpret it first as Gaines's suggestion that the end of the story's importance lies in the fact that the conflict ends in a court of law. Second, Dimes as a reporter suggests the merging of oral history and journalistic enterprise. His description of the trial, while offering a comic turn, demonstrates perhaps what democratic encounters in the future might look like: Fix Boutan attends the trial accompanied by the Klan and the Nazis, while the blacks are supported by the NAACP and a group of "black militants." Dimes describes the trial as "something astonishing but not serious." What is perhaps so amazing to Dimes is the presence of groups with such divergent views within the legal arena. But this demonstrates the novel's commitment to a carnivalesque vision: the legal hearing offers an instance of racial stalemate, a reversal of Southern legal convention where whites are protected. Moreover, the collective guilt of all the defendants likewise proposes that black and white alike bear responsibility for transforming the South. Thus Dimes's narration measures the distance from Faulkner's paternalism to this newer tone, which is at once intimate and transient. Dimes makes no attempt to explain history, to apologize for it; rather, he reports events in such a way as to suggest that each of the principles is a performer in need of an audience, and thus there are likely to be many versions of the forthcoming tale. The end of the novel, then, deconstructs the primacy of the white male voice, because the novel's narrative format has argued that voices are contingent on other voices whether they are discordant or not. *A Gathering of Old Men* signals a regional narrative whose inclusiveness eschews Western forms of dualism, "either/or," in favor of Michael Harper's liberating modality of "both/and." And as in "The Wide Net," the both/and relationship is situated between the carnivalesque reversals and societal renewal. Just as William Wallace Jamieson has fiercely embraced his responsibilities as a husband and father by story's end, the old men likewise enter a space where they eschew their fear and embrace resistance. Like Miss Jane, they are "protected" by old age, but the gun battle suggests that they move into a space where they choose risk over safety. This choice moves them into a coherent space where they experience newness, because, ironically, they throw off the limitations of innocence. The "guilt" under which they end the novel is a site out of which a new narrative can be written.

6

That new narrative is begun, ironically, through an act of authorial flashback. Gaines's latest novel, *A Lesson Before Dying*,[43] rather than moving forward in time to explore the contemporary South, moves backward in time, using allegory to make a commentary on the African American odyssey in the South. Characters like Jefferson and Charlie Biggs submit themselves to legal authority, and by doing so choose death, thereby calling our attention to the dignity with which they meet it. But they also make us aware of the societal breach that creates the circumstances leading them to their demise. For Jefferson, the legal system's flaws are made evident, not only through the inequitable verdict that sentences him to death, but also because the only rationale that can be offered in his defense relies on his exclusion from the category of humanity. When Jefferson accepts his impending death, signified by the diary he keeps, he embraces his humanity by asserting a reflectiveness previously thought to be beyond his grasp. As he dies, the children in school praying for him have written evidence that argues his value, and theirs, as a human being. For Charlie Biggs, violence prefigures his break from convention and heralds the coming of a new kind of community. The defense of his humanity falls outside the legal arena; his act of violence inaugurates a space where a stature of his own choosing, one where he acts responsibly, comes to the fore. However, it is his death that galvanizes the community. Like Jefferson, his dead body serves as rhetorical implement: all the inhabitants of the Marshall plantation touch his body, now a magic site of power, rendering the community coherent and new.

Storytelling plays an important role in all the communities Gaines depicts through first-person narration; it gives voice to the intimacy that lies within the comprehension (but outside the realm of propriety) for black and white alike. More than this, however, the partially realized communities Gaines portrays lie just at the edge of the secular space of law; interaction between black and white is guaranteed by rituals not sanctioned by the social contract. Given this contradiction, *A Gathering of Old Men* and *A Lesson Before Dying* persuade us of the necessity of recognizing the role that guilt and redemption play in the enactment of a new social order. Reliance on ritual needs to be understood as an act of collective persuasion.

But what is perhaps more important, as we bring this discussion to a close, is that Gaines's fiction uses metonymy as a rhetorical tool to a set of issues necessary to confront. He establishes the importance of this moment when, in *A Lesson Before Dying,* Jefferson's lawyer attempts to assert his innocence. In many ways, Jefferson's lawyer is as lacking in imagination as Robert Charles's attorney in McPherson's "A Sense of Story." Consider here his speech, which, oddly, asserts a "liberal" position to an all-white, all-male jury:

> Gentleman of the jury look at this—this—this boy. I almost said man, but I can't say man. Oh sure, he has reached the age of twenty-one, when we, civilized men, consider the male species has reached manhood, but would you call this—this—this a man? No, not I. I would call this a boy and a fool. A fool is not aware of right and wrong. A fool does what others tell him to do. (*Lesson,* 7)

The defense attorney continues:

> Gentlemen of the jury, look at him—look at him—look at this. Do you see a man sitting here? Do you see a man sitting here? I ask you, I implore, look carefully—do you see a man sitting here? Look at the shape of the skull, this face as flat as the palm of my hand—look deeply into those eyes. Do you see a modicum of intelligence? Do you see anyone here who could plan a murder, a robbery, can plan—can plan—can plan anything? A cornered animal to strike quickly out of fear, a trait inherited from his ancestors in the deepest jungle of blackest Africa—yes, yes, that he can do—but to plan? To plan, gentlemen of the jury? No, gentleman, this skull here holds no plans. What you see here is a thing that acts on command. A thing to hold the handle of a plow, a thing to load your bales of cotton, a thing to dig your ditches, to chop your wood, to pull your corn. That is what you see here, but you do not see anything capable of planning a robbery or a murder. He does not even know the size of clothes or his shoes. (*Lesson,* 8)

The lawyer's closing argument is distinguished by its attempt to persuade the jury to implement a new social gaze through which to ascertain Jefferson's story. In order to establish Jefferson's innocence, the lawyer strips him of all intentionality. But to accomplish this, he has to use the South's metonymic system, where black men occupy an antinomian space vis-à-vis white men. In order to establish Jefferson's innocence the lawyer must rely on twelve white men acquiring a new form of literacy. Collectively, they must view Jefferson with new eyes. What makes this move viable is the lawyer's ability to maintain racial hierarchy (by drawing, in part, from the pseudo-scientific rhetoric of African American inferiority) alongside what I believe is his fervent and serious attempt to save Jefferson's life. But fervor notwithstanding, working in a social paradigm that relies on African American degradation ultimately nullifies its force. The lawyer's narrative becomes incoherent, largely because it neither argues for a new social order, nor challenges the present one; indeed, his most grievous error is his failure fully to conceptualize his audience, to cross racial lines to tell a new kind of story.

But after the guilty verdict is handed down by the white jury, it is striking that Jefferson's godmother does not wish to refute the verdict, only the lawyer's characterization of her godson. Thus she tells Grant, "Called him a hog. . . . I don't want them to kill no hog. . . . I want a man to go to that chair, on his own two feet" (*Lesson,* 13). When she asks Grant to go to the prison to see Jefferson, she is asking him to intervene on a narrative fallacy. Her request is nothing short of asking him to free Jefferson from metonymic confinement: to transform him from "hog" to man.

Hence Gaines's decision to include Jefferson's diary is key to an understanding of the novel's signifying energy. For this novel's intention, in part, is to situate the quest for literacy alongside the necessity of recognizing one's audience. While the reader has to struggle to navigate through Jefferson's poor spelling and lack of punctuation, this difficulty is intended to challenge the reader to elevate substance over form. Further, Jefferson's diary operates within a context of call and response. Grant challenges Jefferson to explore his deepest thoughts, Jefferson responds by using the diary to construct a narrative chain extending back into his childhood, to situate himself within a history. From this vantage point, he is able to achieve coherence, where memory, reflection and sensation come together within the act of writing to assert that he has the resources necessary to meet death. Thus one of the last entries in Jefferson's diary states, "i aint had no bisnes goin ther wit brother an bear cause they aint no good an im gon be meetin them soon" (233). Here Jefferson takes responsibility for his actions, for his decision to ride with Brother and Bear to the liquor store. But this passage's force issues from his conflation of right and wrong with the concept of the hereafter. Whether it be heaven or hell is a moot point. The fact that Brother and Bear are present suggests that he sees their transgression in the proper social context; however difficult the circumstances, they made an inappropriate choice, one Jefferson should have recognized as such. What is important is Jefferson's movement into a space where he assumes a philosophical posture, where he ponders the meaning of his death.

This novel highlights issues of metonymy (what does it *mean* to be African American?) by examining the manner in which Grant and Jefferson must form an alliance to reverse the antinomianism that distorts their ability to generate useful dialogue. In short, Grant must come to the realization that it is he who is the greenhorn; in his innocence, he has bled valuable resources out of the community and, in wanting to leave, made no commitment to replace them. This is evidenced in an exchange between him and Reverend Ambrose in which Grant tells the older man, "I don't owe anybody anything." The minister responds:

> You think you educated, but you not. You think you the only ever had to lie? You think I never had to lie? . . . That's why you look down on me, because you know I lie. At wakes, at funerals, at weddings—yes, I lie. I lie at wakes and funerals to relieve pain. 'Cause reading, writing, and 'rithmetic is not enough. You think that's all they sent you to school for? They sent you to school to relieve pain, to relieve hurt—and if you have to lie to do it, then you lie. . . . You lie and you lie and you lie. She been lying every day of her life, your aunt in there. That's how you got through that university—cheating herself here, cheating herself there, but always telling you she's all right. . . . You ever looked at the scabs on her knees, boy? Course you never. 'Cause she never wanted you

to see it. And that's the difference between me and you, boy; that make me the educated one, and you the gump. I know my people. (217—18)

To make his point, Reverend Ambrose equates his work with lying, but his argument more accurately references faith. Because his task is to serve as faith personified, Ambrose suggests that faith is indeed a form of lying, for it proposes that lives characterized by despair and degradation hinge upon the ability to imagine and articulate better circumstances, even in the very midst of trouble. To have faith, then, is to engage in performance; Ambrose's successful enactment of tribal literacy rests on his ability to link imagination and performance. His task is wholly audience-oriented: in articulating his faith, he likewise imagines both himself and his flock in a redemptive space. Unlike McPherson's John Butler, whose faith collapses in on itself to become hubris, Gaines's Ambrose sees himself as a communal resource whose function is not therapeutic, but analgesic.

But Gaines's characteristic distrust of religion is evidenced by Grant's unwillingness to assume this same function for Jefferson, for he is completely incapable of utilizing folk religion as a personal resource. Grant's posture needs to be understood in light of his growing awareness that Jefferson does, indeed, have something to say. When he refuses to "lie" to Jefferson about heaven, what he asserts is his unwillingness to do what Gaines might suggest is Ambrose's (and other religious men's) blind spot. In asking Grant to lead Jefferson to religion, Ambrose is also asking him to fill the role of surrogate father. This is a role he is unequipped to perform, although his name "Grant" suggests that it is his role to create the space for Jefferson to achieve his own sense of an afterlife. Similarly, Gaines's decision to give the character the name "Jefferson " signals the manner in which another Jefferson (Thomas Jefferson) co-authored a text which configured a body politic. Jefferson's task, as Gaines's intimates, is to use the diary to reconfigure his body, to use imagination and writing to move from nullification to awareness. In directing his writing toward Grant, Jefferson acknowledges an audience and the fact that the dictates of call and response demand that he respond to Grant's call for him to explore his life. As such, the diary is a co-authored text, one which never relinquishes or diminishes the importance of audience collaboration.

But Gaines's unwillingness to resolve clearly the novel's religious conflicts points to his ambivalence regarding Faulkner's enduring saints. That Jefferson does not imagine a conventional afterlife suggests Gaines's awareness that it is finally the living who must find new resources. If Jefferson's life has value, then, it is because there will be men and women, perhaps those sitting in Grant's classroom, who will use that life as the cornerstone of a new society, one which eschews the conventions of the status quo. The achievement of literacy, and here a literacy which combines Reverend Ambrose's faith with Grant's pragmatism, must be attuned to the presence of anomaly, finding it and improvising upon it.

This helps us to understand the ending of the novel, which occurs in a space very similar to *A Gathering of Old Men*. On the day that Jefferson is executed, Grant is at his school. Paul, one of the sheriff's deputies at the jail, arrives and gives Grant Jefferson's diary. Their exchange is important and it asserts the manner in which Gaines's articulate witness has developed over the course of his canon. Paul tells Grant that Jefferson "was the strongest man in [the] crowded room" where the execution took place. He reports Jefferson's last words, directed to Reverend Ambrose, "Tell Nannan I walked." Paul looks at Grant and says, "Allow me to be your friend, Grant Wiggins. I don't ever want to forget this day. I don't ever want to forget him" (255). However, in the most important aspect of their exchange, Paul says, "I'm a witness, Grant Wiggins." Not only does Paul forge a kinship with Grant (one that in the 1940s was a perilous one indeed), he likewise asserts his willingness to tell a coherent story, one that speaks to the transformative force of Jefferson's death. When Grant invites Paul to speak to his class, at that moment we see the collaboration which could not save Jefferson's life, but which in the present provides the resources for others to achieve a different outcome. Gaines's decision to make Paul the novel's most articulate witness (since he was present at Jefferson's execution) is a poignant one indeed; it is a white man who asserts the strength of a black man, and thus it suggests that the ability to testify is not racially inflected. The novel's conclusion provides us with a secular redemption: Wright's Max hears Bigger's story but can find no way to act on the message; Grant and Paul represent cultural renewal in ways that reverse this exhaustion of resources. They achieve a reversal of the negative valence attached to African American identity, and so create the possibility of a new metonymy and as such a coherent sense of place.

7

Gaines's fiction offers us numerous instances to observe the articulate witness and hence his/her relationship to Ellison's hero. Gaines's "witnesses," particularly in the novels rendered in the first person, tell the tale of their break from convention. This requires them to find a balance between the communal voice and their individual voice. Thus, Jim Kelly relates events in *Of Love and Dust* which other narrators relate to him in order to fill out his narrative. Miss Jane defers to other members of the community when her memory fails. Felix, in the story "Bloodline," allows us to hear all the voices in the story. These narrators combine aspects of Stepto's narratives of ascent and immersion. They carve out a free space where they can tell their tales, but this movement is enabled through an engagement of community. In other words, they cannot relate the particulars of their "ascent" without a simultaneous "immersion" in the community. Furthermore, these narrators remain in the South. Thus, their ascent is figurative, not geographical. They are credible commentators on change in the South because they have witnessed the substance of that change—either directly or vicariously—and by choosing to endure it move from Faulkner's "enduring saint," to participating sinner.

The last scene in *Of Love and Dust* offers an example. The last image Jim sees is Aunt Margaret walking back to the plantation. The growing distance between Jim and the old woman dramatizes her retreat into silence, as his departure signals his movement toward narration, whereby he can fuse remembrance and utterance. This act of "re-membering" anticipates his reconstruction of the past. In a moment that recalls and then revises Lena Burch at the beginning of Faulkner's *Light in August,* Jim has indeed "come a far piece." He chooses to break from the plantation's illusion of order to enter a space where he recovers his integrity. Integrity symbolizes the need to unify history and place and leaves him no choice but to leave the Hebert plantation. Gaines's use of gothic convention is oriented toward the liberation of his characters. They emerge from the "ruined house" to articulate a new ordering of materials that form a more cohesive unity. This unity rests on a new set of narrative conventions where the articulate witness breaks the silence that accompanies being "buried alive" in the symbolic crypt of Jim Crow and engages in acts of disclosure that finally "speak for" a habitable South.

We can also see the progression from the incoherence of exclusion toward the coherence of the communal voice, where Gaines's characters loose themselves from the horrific silence Jim Crow imposes and discover their potential as agents of change. Gaines's fiction works out the creative tension existing between the spoken and the written word. Characters like Ned Douglass, Jimmy Aaron, Miss Jane, Charlie, Aunt Fe, Jefferson, and Grant suggest that the boundary between these two forms of discourse is permeable. In this sense, it reflects the African American notion of the boundary which exists between the living and the dead.[44] The dead live on in the voices of the folk and in the succeeding generations who listen to these voices. In valorizing the communal voice, Gaines and his characters engage in the search for a voice that leads to a new sense of personal worth and integrity and thus reverse the South's social exhaustion. It is this revitalized story that becomes a crucible in which we confront all the things we are and do not turn away.

Chapter 6

"The Life of the Law Is Thus a Life of Art": Antagonism and Persuasion in McPherson's Legal Fiction Trilogy

> the broken heart and the broken
> tongue are the theme of the evening; betrayals
> in pictures, offered in court, the racist judge,
> friends and colleagues, raised on literature,
> unable to see the crown of thorns, the landscape,
> a woman who'd been saved unafraid to testify.
>
> —Michael S. Harper, "Certainties,"

> "What is to be done? I propose we do the wise thing, the law-abiding thing."
>
> —Ralph Ellison, *Invisible Man*

1

As we turn in this chapter to an assessment of James Alan McPherson's fiction, perhaps there is a way to ascertain the ramifications of literacy, storytelling, and rhetoric as they pertain to legal matters. Perhaps it is a matter of seeing the mundane in new ways or choosing faith rather than disbelief. In an essay entitled "Perspective of Literature," Ralph Ellison tells the story of how, as a boy living in Oklahoma City, he worked for Mr. J. D. Randolph, the janitor of the State Law Library. Though the workings of the governmental process fascinated and mystified the young Ellison, his memories of that time and place were stimulated by a recurrent experience:

> while I was never able to observe the legislature in session, it was not at all unusual for me to look up from pushing a broom or dusting a desk to see one of the legislators dash into the library to ask Jeff—Mr. Randolph was always

addressed by his first name—his opinion regarding some point of law. In fact, I soon came to look forward to such moments because I was amazed by the frequency with which Mr. Randolph managed to come up with satisfactory answers, even without consulting the heavy volumes which ranged the walls.[1]

This moment, with those like it in other fields of endeavor, is part of African American lore: an African American intelligent enough to hold a higher station whose rise to prominence is checked by the discriminatory policies of Jim Crow. However, as Ellison takes care to inform us, J. D. Randolph's role as janitor was doubly belied: first, by the fact that he was one of the first black schoolteachers in the state of Oklahoma, and second, by the large number of books he owned and read. In the context of the fact that many of this nation's greatest legal minds acquired their skills by "reading the law," Mr. Randolph is a symbol of the African American presence in the lawmaking process, not only because he knows the law but also because his literacy allows him to negotiate a role within the legislative act itself. Considering the segregation that characterized life in Oklahoma in the twenties, this is a powerful notion. For despite Mr. Randolph's exclusion on racial grounds from participation in Oklahoma state government as a legislator, Ellison suggests that he was nonetheless a participant in the tangled process of American democracy. It is not my intention here to diminish Mr. Randolph's exploitation. But I do wish to emphasize the fact that, for the briefest of moments, J. D. Randolph and the inquiring legislator were part of a community that broadly acknowledged the common language of jurisprudence. The scenario above alludes to Ellison's awareness of the complexity and mystery involved in the formulation of American citizenship. That complexity issues from the fact that Mr. Randolph must be "read into" the legislative process; his physical absence in the State Legislature is balanced against his knowledge of law, which the white lawmakers make use of with great regularity. In other words, Mr. Randolph is a resource of which the legislative process avails itself.

Jeff Randolph's story serves as a powerful trope for the relationship between American law, African American participation in the "democratic experiment," and American literature. As John Callahan instructs us, Ellison sees the formation of government and the creation of a national literature as part of the same intellectual territory, a territory where acts of governance are likewise acts of imagination, calling for such bold acts of improvisation.[2] Jeff Randolph is a powerful figuration; he evokes the necessity, again, of looking beneath the law's surface reality to find instances of human agency overshadowed by a reductive image of law. As one who appears to be an outsider, Randolph forces us to reassess notions of audience. For here to be a member of the audience is simultaneously to be an active part of a process. Randolph's know-how makes him a valuable resource. His ability to provide counsel without consulting the shelves suggests he embodies democracy so thoroughly that his grasp of law supersedes the texts that contain it. The importance of Ellison's rhetorical gesture lies in its challenge of the boundaries between participation and spectatorship.

I want to weigh the depth and scope of Ellison's insights against James Boyd White's remarks in his *Heracles' Bow.*[3] There he argues that law is not "a set of rules or institutions or structures . . . but a kind of rhetorical and literary activity." This leads him to conclude that "the activity of the law is at heart a literary one." (*Heracles' Bow,* x–xi). The law White envisions is a literary/rhetorical project. In his view, the law's societal function is to create community. And the basis of community is

> a set of terms, texts, and understandings that give to certain speakers a range of things to say to each other. Two lawyers on opposite sides of a case, for example, look at the same statutes, the same judicial opinions, the same general conventions of discourse in the law, and this set of common terms—this common language—is what enables them to articulate to themselves and to each other (or to a third party, such as a judge) what it is they agree and disagree about. And the very fact that the lawyer speaks a legal language means that he or she inhabits a legal culture and is a member of a legal community, made up of people who speak the same way. (*Heracles' Bow,* xi)

The law can therefore be constituted within the field of the humanities (xii). Like its literary sibling, the law is "the art of making meaning in language . . . the integration into meaningful wholes of the largest and most contradictory truths." Thus the lawyer

> must know what the literary person knows, that he or she is always a person speaking to others in a language that is contingent and imperfect. And the excellence of mind required of the lawyer, like the excellence of the composition the lawyer makes, *is integrative: a putting to work in the same text of as many of one's resources and capacities as possible, organized in a meaningful way.* (*Heracles' Bow,* xii; my emphasis)

White's redefinition of the legal enterprise recalls Ellison's construction of American identity as a set of "perplexing questions." Moreover, he also refers to the necessity for the lawyer to utilize resources effectively. Indeed, to participate in the legal community is to master the ability to bring disparate strands of information into coherent alignment. Further, both men locate their respective enterprises within the context of intellectual and moral struggle: Ellison refers to the classic American novels of the nineteenth century and their concern for the "moral predicament" of the nation, while White discusses the legal confrontation as one where there is "a real disturbance in real lives."

Disturbance. Moral predicament. What role do these play in the formulation of a democratic community? For help in addressing these issues, let me turn to White's work in *Heracles' Bow.* The book's first chapter, "Persuasion and Community in Sophocles' *Philoctetes*" argues that the play establishes a fundamental contrast "between treating another person as an object [or an instrument] of manipulation—as a 'means' to an end—and treating him [or her] as one who has claims to autonomy and respect that are equal to one's own: that is an "end" in himself" (*Heracles' Bow,* 3).

What makes White's examination of the play relevant to the work of this chapter is his concern with the persuasive communities that develop and the way those communities symbolize the rhetorical positions that help us to ponder how a society should treat its citizens.[4] The central question the play asks is

> who we become, individually and collectively—who we can become—in our conversations with one another. What kinds of selves, what kind of communities do we establish with each other in our speech, especially in our persuasive speech? (4)

As White observes, Philoctetes will only comply with a rendering of the story that is inclusive, that redefines his exclusion by creating a "common language." In this sense, Ellison's J. D. Randolph story forms the perfect analogue for *Philoctetes,* where the task of creating a coherent community requires that

> a speaker would have to find a way of talking about what has happened, and what will happen, that Philoctetes and the Achaeans could both accept, and which could thus serve as the ground of a newly constituted community between them. . . . "way of talking" [means] a whole language: a shared set of terms for telling the story of what has happened and what will happen, for the expression of motive and value. (6)

As Moses Hadas points out, "Philoctetes has been badly, and in his judgment unfairly, used by his society and is determined never to cooperate with it again."[5] Unlike Philoctetes, whose wound is physical, J. D. Randolph is a victim of the conceptual wound of racial stigmatization. Like Philoctetes, however, he is abandoned, excluded from the formal communal dialogue of legislation. Both Philoctetes and Jeff Randolph endure assaults on their personhood that should preclude cooperation of any sort. What constitutes the conceptual bridge between Ellison's and Sophocles's respective viewpoints is the manner by which both call for the individual to eschew personal suffering and embrace a participatory mode. Further, this calls for revisionary acts of storytelling that can correct the flaws in the communal process. This corrective posture includes relating—and acknowledging as such—instances of self-delusion as a fundamental part of the collective narrative.[6] This forces the society to examine its rationale for mistreating its citizens; what may seem to be a matter of expedience may turn out to be mere caprice. For example, Odysseus, having used Neoptolemus to trick Philoctetes out of Heracle's bow, informs him "we have no further need of you, now that these arms are ours. . . . Perhaps your treasure will bring me the honor which ought to have been your own" (*Philoctetes,*). Though Odysseus's purpose is one of helping the Greeks to win the Trojan War, he is willing to use guile and deceit to acquire the bow which compromises the integrity of his cause. A similar instance is to be found in Thomas Jefferson's indictment of King George III for the disgrace of slavery. As Ellison argues, Jefferson's rhetorical strategy in the Declaration of Independence "announced a new corporate purpose," and did so by providing "his pro-slavery colleagues an escape" via rhetorical means from any serious assessment of the contradiction of slavery.[7]

Hence we need to understand the essential role Neoptolemus plays in *Philoctetes.* It is he who abandons Odysseus's strategy of achieving the bow "by any means necessary," in favor of persuading Philoctetes to rejoin the Greeks. What he does, of course, is to affirm the principles, despite the tremendous pressure he feels to conform to Odysseus's dictates. But in resisting this posture and adopting a stance rejecting exploitation in favor of inclusion, Neoptolemus's actions are reminiscent of Ellison's rationale for African American citizenship: failure to affirm the principles endangers the collective's purpose. Moreover, note the comment Neoptolemus makes to Philoctetes, after the latter expresses the desire to kill Odysseus: "Men must needs bear the fortunes given by the gods; but when they cling to self-inflicted miseries as you do, no one can justly excuse or pity them. You have become intractable. You can tolerate no counselor. If anyone advises you, speaking with good will, you hate him, deeming him a foe who wishes you ill." Philoctetes's illness, though it has alienated him from his fellows, must become, as Neoptolemus suggests, the crux on which he bases his participation in the sacking of Troy. In short, his wound must become the sign of his heroic response, not an excuse for withdrawal. As the comradeship between Neoptolemus and Philoctetes suggests, Ellison's notion of "speaking for" the Other, articulating shared stories, is the foundation of an inclusive community. In looking at *Philoctetes,* White concludes, "persuasion is not the art of manipulating others to adopt one's position, but the art of *stating fully* and sincerely the grounds upon which one thinks common action can and should rest" (*Heracles' Bow,* 17).

For Neoptolemus and Philoctetes, and for Ellison and J. D. Randolph as well, the struggle for coherence, for reintegration, is always manifest.[8] Thus, the symbolic importance of an act must check the impulse to allow ends to justify the means. Hence, the call for Philoctetes to reintegrate himself into Greek society, to give up his "love for his own illness," needs to be understood in light of Ellison's observations regarding the "serpentlike malignancy" that came to characterize American democracy during the Revolutionary period. But like Philoctetes, who has become accustomed to suffering, Ellison suggests that the "split in America's moral identity . . . fog[s] the American's perception of himself, distort[s] his national image, and blind[s] him to the true nature of his cultural complexity ("Perspective of Literature," 33). It becomes clear why Ellison's vision of American identity is so heavily steeped in the blues: the individual must reconfigure misery as the necessary resource for insight; indeed, misery is an occasion for reflection, an action in itself. But where does this leave the individual who has chosen to return? White concludes:

> To one who learns to see things and to think about them as Neoptolemus does . . . it is not only immoral but unrealistic to think that all that is required here is the physical acquisition of an instrument, an inert bow and its arrows. What is required—and this is after all what the soothsayer saw—is that the breach in the community created by Philoctetes' abandonment must be healed, and it can only be healed by his free and voluntary return. He must become a member of the community once more. (*Heracles' Bow,* 19–20)

I want to use White's assessment as a kind of pivot, one that allows me to situate James McPherson within this discussion. Ellison's and White's ruminations are essential in formulating the terms for this chapter's examination of what I refer to as McPherson's "legal fictions." Though Ellison uses the term more broadly, I use it to refer to those McPherson short stories set in or near the legal arena. Though it is possible for us to read these fictions as signals that the legal system is both inept and corrupt, I would propose that we need to understand this fictional project as part of a tradition of American writing whose goal is irreverence. This conclusion issues both from Ellison's question, "Why . . . has the lawyer or the judge seldom appeared in our literature, serious or popular, in heroic roles?" and from his answer:

> One answer is that the presentation of the law in an unfavorable light allows for the formal expression and sharing of attitudes which are impious and irreverent, and that given such attitudes, they must be socially controlled, made

visible, and socialized; otherwise they might be a force for the destruction of social order. ("Perspective of Literature," 326)

Ellison's notes Twain's depiction of lawyers and judges in *The Adventures of Huckleberry Finn* and *Pudd'nhead Wilson,* Herman Melville's use of the *Amistad* case in "Benito Cereno," and his lawyer in "Bartleby the Scrivener" (who cries "Ah humanity!" at story's end) to illustrate that the depiction of the law in literature has not shied away from either the tragic or the comic. Though McPherson's stories most certainly call for serious reflection about the law, they are, in the tradition of Twain, just as easily moments for Americans to "laugh at the courts and perhaps at the Constitution itself" (327).

The significance of this, as the following remarks by Ellison make clear, lies in the symbolic arena of language, for

> it is through the symbolic action, the symbolic capabilities of language, that we seek simultaneously to maintain and evade our commitments as social beings. Human society in this regard is fictitious, and it might well be that at this point the legal fictions through which we seek to impose order upon society meet with, coincide with, the fictions of literature. Perhaps law and literature operate or cooperate . . . in their respective ways these two symbolic systems work in the interest of social order. (329)

What makes Ellison's remarks of such importance here is his insistence on a perspective that embraces fluidity, that allows space for the experimental by its acknowledgment of a ritualistic thread underscoring society's quest for order. Like White's lawyer/rhetorician, Ellison's writer is equally engaged in the formulation of statecraft. And so, when he refers to "legal fictions," issues of national identity that call for such deep reverence are actually dealt with over a wide field of ritual inquiry. Dramatizing the manner in which the legal process mirrors the dynamics of American culture, McPherson's legal fictions not only demonstrate his legal training (Harvard, class of 1968), they also allow him to tap the ritualistic possibilities of the legal confrontation. Thus we find an important confluence: acts of reading (and thus also acts of misreading) issue from the resources (and the misapplication of resources) we bring to bear on the judicial circumstance and vice versa.

McPherson's fictions examine the synergy formed by race, gender and geography, their function in the words, "We, the people . . ." If it is true, as Albion Tourgee's brief asserted (as quoted in Chapter 1) that the Fourteenth Amendment ushered in a new paradigm of American citizenship, one which called for new rhetorical strategies upon which to base community, then these fictions explore their characters' unwillingness to relinquish outmoded paradigms of reading in order to utilize the legal apparatus in an innovative manner.

2

Sophocles's play offers us an individual, in the form of Neoptolemus, who begins the play as part of a community whose main resource is guile and deceit. Because he chooses rhetoric and persuasion over subterfuge, his original goal is supplanted, leaving him in a different community whose imperatives insist on integrity. What he recognizes is that to act without integrity, to use rhetoric as a tool of deceit, ultimately jeopardizes everything he holds sacred. Thus, when he persuades Philoctetes to join him, to rejoin his fellow Greeks, it results from his newfound ability to make connections between the present and the past, between events at hand and those that have yet to be realized.

The significance of constructing coherent models, as Sophocles insists, lies in their ability, as conceptual bridges between past, present, and future, to create new sources of self-reflection. Indeed, on encountering Neoptolemus (and after Hercules's call to rejoin the war) Philoctetes moves from a self-reflection foregrounded in victimization to one based on an anomalous experience. This drive toward the portrayal of anomalous experience informs African American literary tradition; it argues that an injurious experience (slavery) authorizes acts of storytelling that not only challenge the validity of previous (racially exclusive) narratives, but also authenticate one's place as participant in the ongoing project of formulating a coherent community. McPherson's impulse to "practice law" in his fiction leads me to trace the concern with storytelling found in his legal fictions back to Ellison's *Invisible Man*. The kinship between Ellison and McPherson make *Philoctetes* a useful critical tool, largely because it raises issues that pertain to the whole of Ellison's novel, and in particular to Chapter 13 (the pivotal eviction scene) where the hero discovers his public voice. My decision to link this scene with McPherson's fiction stems from my realization that both the novel and the stories display a concern with new paradigms of literacy that underscore rhetorical gestures whose goal is the creation of persuasive communities.

Ellison's eviction scene employs an important rhetorical vehicle to accomplish its ends: sermonic performance. Not only does the sermon bring into focus the relationship between rhetorical expression and community, but it helps us to understand the African American practice of redefining the parameters of "legal" behavior so that acts of protest and resistance are valorized for community use. With its deployment of rhetoric that "state[s] fully . . . the grounds upon which one thinks common action can and should rest," the sermon collectivizes effort and serves as an important resource in the formation of a usable present. Thus we must consider the manner in which the eviction scene moves, on two levels, from incoherence to coherence: first, the invisible narrator's discovery of his public voice; he moves from an inarticulate state to eloquence where he can articulate the substance of the event in terms of its metonymic value. Second, the crowd gathered to witness the eviction encounters the narrator's newly adopted rhetorical posture and moves from disorganization to unity.[10] What becomes clear is the sermon's importance as an instrument of persuasion; through call and response, the sermon exhorts both speaker and listener toward a symbiosis whose first goal is self-scrutiny, and whose ultimate goal is the formation of a spiritually constituted community of action.

The African American sermonic performance is constructed around a schematic unity exemplified by its ability to bridge themes.[11] The sermon bridges the gap between uncertainty and faith, galvanizing that faith into action. Further, it demystifies—through its use of metaphor and analogy—the relatively intangible idea of "the right thing to do." What is implicit within the sermon, then, is a sense that the community of faith it attempts to create is in accordance with the "law" embodied in the Scripture (often read beforehand) and to which it may make repeated references. The sermon accomplishes its desired ends because it achieves a response in the listener whereby the shout or the chant evidencing attention and agreement is, in actuality, the beginning of the positive action that the sermon is designed to elicit. Thus, the congregation's ability to manifest its faith in the secular world often hinges on the preacher's ability to confront the world's obstacles in whatever form they may assume inside the church. The first obstacle within the sermon performance then is silence, for it may signify detachment, disbelief or disunity. These can be located in either the preacher or the congregation, or both. As Gerald Davis points out, the preacher must be successful at "lining up" the congregation before she or he can realize the sermonic form. And this phrase, he suggests,

> should not be taken to mean that African-American congregations can be browbeaten into predictable response patterns by a black-robed preacher-general. Rather, the term is intended to identify that portion of a congregation's energies that are voluntarily yielded to the preacher for the duration of the sermon. It is the preacher's task and duty to charge the preaching environment with dynamic energies and in so doing to induce the congregation to focus oral and aural mechanisms on the content and structure of the sermon performance. . . . An African-American congregation listens attentively and critically to a sermon and can instantly withhold assent and response if a preacher fails to speak acceptably. ("*I got the Word in me,*" 17)

Thus the relationship between preacher and his or her congregation is a dynamic one. When a preacher fails to "prepare" the congregation for the message, time must be devoted in the sermon to "raising the spirit of [a] dead church" rather than to the sermon's message. (17)

It may be helpful to think of the sermonic performance as dramatic potential transformed into action. The sermon intimates that overcoming impediments of faith signifies God's power as a creator of texts. The events taking place within the individual's life are ciphers to be read. Hence, the sermon is the way toward a new form of literacy, creating an interpretive space where the life becomes configured as text. This leads to action foregrounded by faith. The unity signified by a chorus of "Amens" represents an intertextual moment, an instance where the listener hears the preacher's words and locates meaning within the space of his or her own life.[12] This is the task of Ellison's hero: to use the constitutive rhetoric found in sermonic discourse to create an intertextual response and thus unified action. Like the African American preacher, he must become "locked into a dynamic exchange" with the crowd.

Ellison's eviction scene begins by dramatizing the narrator's rootlessness, his propensity to view his surroundings as a collection of totally randomized signs that elude his ability to order or interpret. "Extremely agitated," the narrator leaves Mary's house, only to discover that the "whole of Harlem seemed to fall apart in the swirl of snow" (*Invisible Man,* 261). The attack of whiteness on the "black" space that is Harlem notwithstanding, what is also clear is the manner in which the snow renders the surroundings meaningless, incoherent. But this state mirrors the "hot inner argument" taking place within the narrator. As he walks past "the endless succession of barber shops, beauty parlors, confectioneries, luncheonettes, fish houses, and hog maw joints," he gazes upon what is most certainly "a curtain, a veil" to be stripped aside. Ellison's DuBoisian allusion and subsequent inversion (the disposal of the Veil) accompanies the narrator's passage into an iconographically ambiguous space where he encounters a window "filled with religious articles." There he finds

> two brashly painted plaster images of Mary and Jesus surrounded by dream books, love powders, God-is-Love signs, money-drawing oil and plastic dice. A black statue of a nude Nubian slave grinned out at me beneath a turban of gold. I passed on to a window decorated with switches of wiry false hair, ointments guaranteed to produce the miracle of whitening black skin. "You too can be truly beautiful," a sign proclaimed. "Win greater happiness with whiter complexion. Be outstanding in your social set." (*Invisible Man,* 262)

This symbolically charged space is so important because each of the objects described is indicative of talismans that, in the narrator's view, are failed protections ranging from the spiritual to the superstitious. But the purpose of each, the narrator realizes, is to provide the Harlemite with material power in the white world. This tumultuous string of icons continues until it reaches a conclusion via the ointment that portends to offer passage into the white world. In truth, it serves as the catalyst for deeper divisions with in the black community, foregrounded by the intraracial politics of caste distinction.

When the hero meets a man selling baked yams, he retreats into nostalgia. Rescued from the metonymic assault he has just encountered, believing that he has entered a space where signs, meaning, and intentionality are in alignment, the invisible narrator eats one yam, returns to buy two more, and asserts, "I can look at it and see it's good." However, as he has done so many times previously, the narrator has been seduced by the rhetoric of surfaces. The old man selling the yams issues a warning, "everything what looks good ain't necessarily good," but the narrator concludes that the yams are his birthmark, the symbol of a new self devoted to the equivocation of pleasure and identity.[13] But this singularity of consciousness and purpose gives way when he bites one of the yams and, finding it frostbitten, throws it into the street. Interestingly, this act signals the collapse of his "new" self, returning him to his original state, in the midst of an overwhelming indecipherability.

Ellison's use of the sermon here must be understood in light of its power to invert—as opposed to avert—failure. If we look at the pattern his hero follows in the chapter we find that he moves from uncertainty to clarity and, on arriving at the scene of the eviction, back to uncertainty again. This trajectory is significant because the sermon, as the preacher performs it, is not the symbol of moral superiority. If a sermon is to be successful, the preacher must take care not to imply that he or she stands in judgment of the congregation. Thus the preacher must be able to reference personal experience, to use him or herself as a laboratory where uncertainty and faith comingle to create the necessity for spiritual intervention. What the preacher demonstrates, though, is the willingness to submit once spirit intervenes. The sermon works out the movement from conflict to accord, from the conformity of secular blindness to the ecstasy and insight indicative of spiritual community.

Sermons often begin by articulating solitude as a place of peril, an instance where one is susceptible to temptation, disobedience, or disillusionment. When the narrator sees the eviction taking place, he is embarrassed, first because he discerns the grief it causes, but then he is embarrassed because he realizes he has never seen an eviction before. He finds himself apart from the crowd gathered to watch the eviction, sees the crowd as a community that excludes him. He grasps the eviction's impact when he recognizes a "self-consciousness" about those watching,

> as though they, we, were ashamed to witness the eviction, as though we were all unwilling intruders upon some shameful event; and thus we were careful not to touch or stare too hard at the effects that lined the curb; for we were witnesses of what we did not wish to see though curious, fascinated, despite our shame, and through it all the old female, mind-plunging crying. (270)

Note the beginning of the passage where the narrator begins by placing himself outside, then abruptly resituates himself by changing the pronoun from "they" to "we." It is only when the narrator stops to look at the "clutter of household objects" piled on the sidewalk that, when linked, they begin to provide a map. He catalogues the objects, which consist, among other things, of a pair of "knocking bones" used by blackface minstrels, plants, a straightening comb, false hair, a curling iron, a tintype of Abraham Lincoln, a magazine picture of a Hollywood star, and a plate commemorating the St. Louis World's Fair. Also among the clutter are High John the Conqueror, a card that says, "God Bless Our Home," and an Ethiopian flag. The narrator cannot yet give order to this jumble of icons. He finds protection against the incursion of white hostility, amid objects suggesting either racist iconography (the minstrel's knocking bones) or implements (false hair, straightening combs, and curling irons) of self-distortion.

As the narrator looks further, he finds that the old people's belongings begin to yield images of kinship and belonging—an emblem from the Masons, a card saying "Grandma, I love you," and an old baby shoe. These are contextualized, however, by the three voided insurance policies and a picture with the headline "MARCUS GARVEY DEPORTED." Here we find symbols of kinship and security giving way to symbols of dislocation, jeopardized kin.

But it is only when the hero picks up the old man's manumission papers that he can position himself to "read" the objects piled on the curb. Note that Ellison's narrator finds the document in "a frozen footstep," and tells himself, "It has been longer than that, further removed in time." However, this collision with the materiality of history, and his subsequent denial of it, give way to a conversion experience of such magnitude that empathy transports him across the boundary separating him from the couple. He experiences a conceptual shift where their possessions move from an incoherent "jumble" on the sidewalk to a collection of signs loaded with meaning:

> I turned and stared again at the jumble, no longer looking at what was before my eyes, but inwardly-outwardly, around a corner into the dark, far-away-and-

long-ago, not so much of my own memory as of remembered words, of linked verbal echoes, images, heard even when not listening at home. And it was as though I myself was being dispossessed of some painful yet precious thing which I could not bear to lose. . . . And with this sense of dispossession came a pang of vague recognition: this junk, these shabby chairs, these heavy, old-fashioned pressing irons, zinc wash tubs with dented bottoms—all throbbed within me with more meaning than there should have been. (273)

The transformation of his gaze significantly evokes other texts within the invisible narrator's sense of self; they suggest shared stories, a common history and cultural background.[14]

It is this "text" from which the hero will "preach." Unlike the narrator, who had never before seen an eviction in the North, the crowd has an intimate knowledge of what they are viewing. However, theirs is a purely spectatorial energy. This is evidenced when one of the men in the crowd observes that the crowd should take matters into its own hands, "but ain't that much nerve in the whole bunch." Another responds, "There's plenty of nerve . . . all they need is a leader" (268). Though he does not yet realize it, the narrator has encountered a "flock" in need of the rhetorical tools that will make them a community.

But it is only when the situation threatens to dissolve into violence, when the flock is poised to become a mob, that the narrator finds a voice. He begins "lining up" his sermon, begins the process of call and response. Thus his "sermon" consists of the narrative units that Davis observes within the African American sermon. The first unit comes when the hero asserts that black folk are a "law-abiding and slow-to-anger-people." In this particular unit, the invisible narrator cites the need for leadership and organization. He attempts to describe the actions of "that wise leader in Alabama" (ostensibly Booker T. Washington) as the model the crowd should adopt. However, this approach fails because he attempts to accomplish by vague reference what he needs to accomplish with rhetoric. It fails to persuade the crowd because he asks them to imitate the "wise leader," whose actions, after all, belie racial solidarity. The narrator must correct his course to avoid the perception that he wants them to be "handkerchief headed" rats. As "shepherd" he wants them to be sheep, but he must convince them that this need not be a sign of passivity or resignation.

His failure forces him to regroup, to move on to the next thematic unit of his speech: "What are we to do?" This breaks off the initial rhetorical attack, which called for the crowd to restrain its anger, defer to its "law-abiding" sensibility, and allow the eviction to continue. The next move is for the narrator to focus the crowd's gaze on the old man, to respecify their attention from cathartic anger to acting on behalf of the powerless. By turning the crowd's attention to the old man and his possessions in the snow, Ellison's hero circles back to recover the earlier performance unit that failed:

> He's eighty-seven. Eighty-seven and look at all he's accumulated in eighty-seven years strewn in the snow like chicken guts, and we're a law-abiding, slow-to-anger bunch of folks turning the other cheek every day in the week. What are we going to do? What would you, what would I, what would he have done? What is to be done? I propose we do the wise thing, the law-abiding thing. (277)

The narrator attempts to bind the crowd into a persuasive community by calling attention to the old people's possessions. To do this, he has to use his rhetorical skill to evoke the process by which he came to see the value of those possessions. He must pull the crowd into the same interpretive space, where they, too, can "read" the objects as elements of a coherent text. By doing this, he posits the act of recognition as a conversion experience. If the possessions throb inside the hero "with more meaning than there should [be]" the crowd, too, experience a way to turn their propensity to violence to other ends. And if they are likewise "slow-to-anger" they must find a way to answer the question the narrator poses at the end of the passage I cited above.

His next move is to invoke the notion of kinship as a way of displacing the boundaries between the crowd and the old couple. "Look at that old woman, somebody's mother, somebody's grandmother, maybe. We call them 'Big Mama' and they spoil us and—you know, you remember." This reference to African American familial convention allows him to refer to the old man as "Father," and to reinforce the idea that the crowd and the old couple are part of the same persuasive community. At this point, the hero moves to his next unit:

> Look at them, they look like my mama and my papa and my grandma and grandpa, and I look like you and you look like me. Look at them but remember that we're a wise, law-abiding group of people. And remember it when you look up there in the doorway at that law standing there with his forty-five. Look at him, standing with his blue steel pistol and his blue serge suit, or one forty-five, you see ten for every one of us, ten guns and ten warm suits and ten fat bellies and ten million laws. *Laws*, that's what we call them down South! Laws! And we're wise, and law-abiding. And look at this old woman with her dog-eared Bible. What's she trying to bring off here? She's let religion go to her head, but we all know that religion is for the heart, not for the head. (278)

By invoking a self-reflexive gesture, whereby the old couple become a double icon (the crowd's familial past and adherence to law legitimated by sacred force), the hero diminishes the authority of the policeman blocking the crowd's path into the building. A unit is called for that begins to link the crowd's realization that it is their ancestral past strewn on the sidewalk with the old woman's emotional request for prayer. A conceptual tie is made between the endangered past and the uncertain future, leaving the hero with the task of inserting a sense of a viable present, in which the crowd can act responsibly.

This portion of the eviction speech is distinguished from the beginning by the hero's use of call and response as the resource fueling the "sermon"'s narrative units. When an angry man yells that the old couple have been "dispossessed," the narrator seizes this word to turn the sermon toward its denouement. Thus the narrator is able to shift from the previous narrative unit (where he describes the presence of the police) to connect the act of prayer with breaking the law. The shift bridges the space between the sacred and the secular and it likewise suggests that the act of giving voice to one's concerns is an act of resistance. Having established that the old couple's desire to pray and read the Bible is the sign that they want "to break the law," the narrator is able to posit the crowd's anger as a response characterized by their propensity not for illegality but justice.

> "Dispossessed?" I cried, holding up my hand and allowing the word to whistle from my throat. "That's a good word, 'Dispossessed'! 'Dispossessed,' eighty-seven years and dispossessed of what? They ain't *got* nothing, they cain't *get* nothing, they never *had* nothing. So who was dispossessed?" I growled. "We're law abiding. So who's being dispossessed? Can it be us? These old ones are out in the snow, but we're here with them. Look at their stuff, not a pit to hiss in, nor a window to shout the news and us right with them. Look at them, not a shack to pray in or an alley to sing the blues! They're facing a gun and we're facing it with them. They don't want the world, but only Jesus. They only want Jesus, just fifteen minutes of Jesus on the rug-bare floor. . . . How about it, Mr. Law? Do we get our fifteen minutes worth of Jesus? You got the world, can we have our Jesus?" (279)

Here the narrator moves into a new narrative unit: he equates the eviction with the power of the law to deprive the old people of their inalienable right to pray. Having begun his speech with the idea that the folk are "law-abiding and slow-to-anger," the narrator replaces the conventional notion of law with the folk notion of a "higher" law, a sacred law that validates African American oral expression. His rhetorical style shifts from the formal mode to the vernacular, which not only communicates his connection to his audience, but also makes a distinction between secular and sacred forms of law. Moreover, the passage contains the narrator's suggestion that sacred power, coupled with prayer, is a legal site which does not require the proliferation of codes to enforce behavior. Thus the "fifteen minutes of Jesus," the narrator calls for is preferable to the "ten million Laws" of the secular world where one's destiny is still uncertain.

By turning the crowd's gaze toward an act of reading that is self-identifying and collective, the hero creates the energy necessary for them to posit for themselves a "higher law" against the legal authority of the policeman. The narrator brings the crowd to the realization that they, too, are being evicted, uprooted from their heritage. By using the term, "Mr. Law," to describe the policeman, the narrator makes him the symbol of the secular world where the crowd lacks power and voice. The request for the policeman to give the audience their Jesus, is, in sermonic terms, the narrator's rhetorical conflation of sacred space (the next world) and action. The observation that the old couple "ain't got nothin," "cain't get nothin," and "never had nothin," is useful because it deflects attention from the objects on the sidewalk as purely material artifacts and renders them as symbolic implements which serve the purpose of amplifying the collective voice in its attempt to contact the spiritual world. As such, they assume the role which the objects the narrator viewed in the storefront could not: they become protections.

Having accomplished the difficult move of making a "they" into a "we"; the narrator enacts the sermon's final unit. Citing the old couple's possession of a dream book (a sign of their belief in the relationship between dreaming and progress) whose "pages went blank and . . . failed to give them the number," the narrator equates the dream book with the icon of the "Seeing Eye" hovering above the pyramid on the United States dollar bill. When he refers to the "Great Constitutional Dream Book," he suggests that the old couple's status as U.S. citizens should justify their faith in the power of dreams. Further, because that text refers to Africa, the eye, described by the hero as "blind," lacking "luster," and "cataracted like a cross-eyed carpenter," the dollar, as icon, cannot serve as a means of self-valuation. The significance of this is that the hero rejects the connection between the lack of material resources and illegality. However, this is the beginning of the sermon's collapse: the narrator has made a move whose parameters extend beyond the purview of the crowd's interests. Their impulse is to deal with matters at hand; they seek to redress not democracy's failings as a whole—an act that would require them to create new icons—but merely the old couple's plight as dispossessed citizens whose possessions are out on the street due to the legal authority they see before them. The narrator's speech breaks down because he comes to overemphasize the symbolic over the concrete.

Hence the crowd's attention becomes transitory, evidence of the narrator's ambivalence about where and how to direct their energy. When the crowd begin their attack on the policeman, they break the dynamic relationship with the narrator and act on their own. When the crowd surges forward to attack the policeman, all the narrator can do is redirect their energy, which he does by getting the people to take the old people's possessions back into the apartment building. He creates a persuasive community but it is transient, incapable of sustaining the energy that binds it together.

This scene leads, of course, to the invisible narrator's encounter with the Brotherhood, where he is robbed of his voice and falls into the same patterns that precede the eviction scene. He breaks ranks with the Brotherhood after his eulogy for Tod Clifton (another moment when he utilizes the sermonic performance mode to create a persuasive community) and falls into the hole where he discovers his voice as a writer rather than as an orator. It is here that he brings the act of writing and "the principles" (ostensibly, the ideas behind the Constitution and Declaration of Independence) into the same conceptual space: the "hole" where he contemplates a new interpretation of history. By affirming these, the invisible narrator assumes a rhetorical and persuasive stance from which he attempts to disclose the multi-racial nature of American reality, to "speak for" a new vision of community.

3

If White and Ellison explore the nature of injury, there is likewise an implicit discussion regarding the nature of protections. In the last chapter, we saw how a character like Miss Jane Pittman acquired and became skilled in the use of talismans, in lieu of access to legal redress. As I turn to McPherson's stories, it is important to keep in mind these stories' placement in the legal arena. Though a story like "A Solo Song: For Doc" could be described as a legal fiction, dealing as it does with issues of protection and injury within the context of a waiter's rule book, the fact that it does not take place in or near the legal arena forces me to exclude it from discussion here. What distinguishes this group of stories is their attempt to deal with the characters' proximity to legal resources. And if Ellison's narrator dealt with the notion of "failed protections," we see McPherson answering this call by attempting to discern why the protections to be found in the law are faulty and require constant maintenance.

I want to begin my discussion with a story from *Hue and Cry,* "An Act of Prostitution." This story is distinctive in its depiction of the misuse of legal authority. It begins, significantly, in the meeting room of a municipal courthouse. It is a private, preparatory space. In the literal sense, it is where lawyer and client can gather to plot a collective strategy by finding a common language to implement during trial. In the figurative sense, as we will see, it suggests the privatized, closed nature of law, by evoking the "backroom," the seamy side of the legal community. Two of the main characters, Jimmy Mulligan, a court-appointed attorney, and his client, Philomena Brown, are locked in serious verbal combat. The woman is charged with street walking and public nuisance. The issue is whether the woman should plead innocent or guilty. For Mulligan's part, she is guilty and he advises her to "get some sense and take a few days on the city." It is striking that the story's omniscient narrator refers to Philomena as "the whore." However, the story makes no mention as to what charges she faces.

The disagreement on matters of strategy, then, lacks a context for the reader to invest allegiance to the characters. Moreover, the apparent dislike Philomena and Mulligan have for one another makes them unable to collaborate in order to produce positive results. Indeed, the dismissive look Mulligan aims at Philomena when she enters the room, coupled with his question, "How do you want to play it?" suggests the antithetical nature of their relationship and that he is there, not as her advocate, but as her point of entry into the penal system. Indeed, the fact that he puts down his pencil and legal pad, refusing to write anything and thus render her innocence, in a rudimentary legible form, argues his unwillingness to align himself with her. And so, the initial requirement for the relationship between Mulligan and Philomena to continue is for her to acknowledge her guilt. Mulligan demands, "cop a plea or I don't take the case."[15]

The soundest possibility, as Mulligan sees it, is to present a case which does not stray very far from the state's original assertion. By refusing to accept Philomena's request (which includes a rationale for her request) for him to help her avoid a return to the city lockup, Mulligan's "defense" is non-existent. This explains in part why McPherson does not use the term "public defender," choosing the title, "lawyer," instead. Though we know Mulligan is a court-appointed public defender (Philomena tells him, "The judge told you to be my lawyer and you got to do it"), his unwillingness to assist her represents the unnavigable distance between attorney and client. By law he is required to present her wishes before the court, but Mulligan's insistence that Philomena's case has "a snowball's chance in hell" of success alludes to the legal system's real intention here: to abolish all those it would deem untouchables.

In light of this, we need to pay attention to the manner in which McPherson manages the reader's emotional response. The story's language inhibits the reader's sympathy toward Philomena. For example, McPherson's descriptions of her, filtered through Mulligan's consciousness, are at once comic and degrading:

a huge woman, pathetically blonde, big-boned and absurd in a skirt sloppily crafted to be mini. Her knees were ruddy and the flesh below them was thick and white and flabby. There was no indication of age about her. Like most whores, she looked at the same time young but then old, possibly as old as her profession. ("Act," 156)

Philomena's race (despite the "blackness" her name implies) is established as white; the narrator describes her in terms far from flattering:

She sat across the room, near the door in a straight chair, her flesh oozing over its sides. He watched her pull her miniskirt down over the upper part of her thigh, modestly, but with the same hard, cold look she had when she came into the room. (156)

What this description proposes, when we view it as part of the exchange between lawyer and client, is that matters of race only appear to be present. Though the story's opening does not make this clear at the outset, when the narrator fixes into place a physical description of the whore, it is class, not race, which seems to explain the high level of enmity between Jimmy Mulligan and Philomena Brown. McPherson's use of the word "lawyer" further solidifies this story's predicament as one which issues from class difference. However, Jimmy's Irish surname, his role as court-appointed attorney, and the fact that he does not represent a higher class of client all reveal his immigrant background and an upward mobility of limited altitude.

His unwillingness to cooperate with Philomena, in spite of their racial sameness, leads her to read him out—or rather, misread him—by calling him a Jew. Her insistence that he is Jewish, and thus excluded from the exalted category of Anglo American whiteness, is her attempt to remind him of his outsider status. Thus, when she tells him, "You ain't got no choice," she challenges his dismissal of her case by arguing that like her, he is characterized by limited options. Their respective postures demonstrate alternative responses to a hostile environment. Collectively, however, they could achieve ends that would magnify their possibilities. But Mulligan opts for irony rather than solidarity. His response to Philomena's coercive gesture is thus designed to deflect her gibes: "You're a real smarty. That's why you're out on the streets in all that snow and ice. You're a real smarty all right" (156). Mulligan not only challenges Philomena's reading of his ethnic identity, he counterattacks on the class front by asserting the differences between them: he is an insider, and she is just as surely an outsider since she works in "snow and ice." Implicit in this attack is a fundamental assumption that the differences between them crystallize around a mind/body dichotomy that is intended to reinforce his position within the category of whiteness (and of course maleness) and remind her that, after all, she makes a living by selling her body. Though

Philomena is in no position to refute Mulligan's barbs, she does remind him of his low status in the legal profession by cursing him:

> Screw you, Yid! . . . Screw your fat mama and your chubby sister with hair under her arms. Screw your brother and your father and I hope they should go crazy playing with themselves in pay toilets. (156)

Clearly, Philomena is Mulligan's superior in the area of familial debate (otherwise known as the dozens). And she also understands that Mulligan's attempt to establish a chasm of class difference between them is strategically faulty. The insider/outsider dichotomy he attempts to establish has no currency, Philomena suggests, because it in no way insures moral superiority. Philomena resists the lawyer's attempt to diminish her by constructing a false past for him, one that is Jewish and masturbatory, and by calling his attention to the conceptual slippage of class difference: what takes place inside can be just as immoral as what takes place outside.

While it may seem that I place more significance than is merited on what is only a two-page exchange, let me offer the reminder that McPherson, in writing a short story, has chosen a literary genre that often eschews character development in favor of the more difficult task of collapsing rigid social positions. As such, "An Act of Prostitution" proffers a meditation on the legal arena by providing us with characters of "low moral energy" engaged in what turns out to be a morally charged circumstance. However, the moral valence of the story is obscured by its turns, the most significant of which occurs when Ralph, another lawyer, interrupts Philomena's and Mulligan's exchange. We need to understand the importance of Ralph's entrance, especially in light of the "curse" Philomena has placed on Mulligan. Because this story situates the concept of persuasive communities in opposition to the necessity of utilizing protections to ward off evil, Ralph's entry is, as we will see, fortuitous. In a gesture that demonstrates the negotiative aspect of the legal profession, Ralph tells Mulligan, "I got a problem here." He has an Italian youth accused of stealing a car. Ralph tells Mulligan that the youth has only stolen a car "twice before," and he thinks the "Judge might go easy" if events put him in a good mood before his client's trial ("Act," 157). When Mulligan asks what value this arrangement holds for him, Ralph motions toward Philomena and outlines his plan:

> So I was thinking. The Judge knows Philomena over there. She's here almost every month and she's always good for a laugh. So I was thinking, this being Monday morning and all and with a cage-load of nigger drunks out there, why not put her on first, give the old man a good laugh and then put my I-talian boy on. I know he'd get a better deal that way. (147)

Ralph's plan is mutually beneficial: Mulligan's "sacrifice" provides the Italian youth with vital protection (in the form of a lenient sentence) against an ill-tempered judge and Mulligan can eradicate Philomena's curse. Moreover, the exchange unravels the notion that the courtroom is a space designated for public discourse; Ralph's and Mulligan's scheme unmasks the "trial" as a format mediated by private design. This suggests that the "common language" characterizing White's notion of law rests on an adherence to well-worn myths and concepts that exist as a reified, and impenetrable, text. Hence, when Jimmy Mulligan raises the objection that the Judge will "throw the book" at Philomena after he gets his "good laugh," Ralph offers a persuasive rationale for the sacrifice:

> Look, buddy . . . you know who that is? Fatso Philomena Brown. She's up here almost every month. Old Bloom knows her. I tell you she's good for laugh. That's all. Besides, she's married to a nigger anyway. (158)

Here the story acquires its racial dynamic: Philomena is "racialized" because of her marriage to an African American man. This is the opening Mulligan exploits in order to lift the "curse" placed on him by the prostitute. "She's a real smarty," Jimmy tells Ralph, "She thinks I'm a Jew," which in the latter's mind is justification enough for exploiting Philomena. For this story pivots on the reification of categories and the ability to "read" those categories while translating them into advantage. However, the characters manifest power and influence because they use the act of misreading to create self-realization. The challenge, as McPherson demonstrates, is for the characters to find ways to hold their categorical identity in place. Hence, Jimmy asks Ralph, "Isn't she I-talian?" to which Ralph responds, "Yeah. But she's married to a nigger" (158). Philomena's "ethnicity" is transmogrified into a racial designation because she lacks the resources necessary to withstand this deformation of categories.

This produces another important result. Philomena as "black" is stripped of narrative agency, and so Mulligan tells her, "If you got a story, you better tell me quick because we're going out there soon and I want you to know I ain't telling no lies for you" (158). A responsible attorney would know, of course, that lying is but one option and an undesirable one at that. However, because Mulligan chooses racial solidarity over professional solidarity with his "client," he can likewise adhere to the conventional script that accompanies racial encounters in the legal arena: the "black" body as a site of illegality and narrative ineptitude which is best utilized as an example of guilt personified. Thus Mulligan reduces Philomena to a visual surface by telling her, "Forget the story. . . . Just pull your dress down some and wipe some of that shit off your eyes. You look like hell" (158). By deciding Philomena is best presented "as is," with no narrative to accompany her physical presence, she is stripped of her most important protection in the legal arena: the fundamental notion that no matter how guilty she *looks,* she is innocent until *proven* guilty.

Ralph, Mulligan, and the Italian youth exist as a persuasive community. The Italian youth has more value in the legal structure than Philomena because ethnicity and race produce a different set of signs for the judge to read; they do not exist on the same conceptual plane. Though Jimmy points out that Philomena is Italian, her ethnicity is nullified by her decision to cross the color line. Further, "the cage-load of nigger drunks" coupled with the fact that it is Monday morning means that the Judge's angry mood must be leavened before he can display leniency. The African American men on trial and Philomena (who is married to a black man) are assigned positive value only insofar as they represent a resource to entertain the Judge and thus maintain the status quo.

This is not necessarily the case as the story shifts, in Part II, to the courtroom, where we find the Judge "in his Monday morning mood." Though the story's narrator describes the jurist's mood in terms that belie a friendly scene, what gives this setting the potential for justice is that the Judge is "very ready to be angry at almost anyone." All categories, racial or otherwise, are sources of annoyance for the Judge and therefore just as likely to achieve the same negative result. "There would be no mercy this Monday morning," the narrator relates, "and the prisoners all knew it" (159).

But this spectacle is not without an audience. The proceedings are peopled by a group of men who fill

> up the second row of benches, directly behind those reserved for court-appointed lawyers. There were at least twelve of these old men, looking almost semi-professional in faded gray or blue or black suits with shiny knees and elbows. They liked to come and watch the fun. (160)

This "jury" has the effect of recapitulating the conventional Southern jury, notorious for subjecting the black defendant to the most hostile of judgments. Knowing that Philomena is to be the object of a male gaze of this sort and that her appearance parodies that of the "respectable woman," Mulligan's elevation of the image over the word is designed to take full advantage of the courtroom as a performance space. The Judge is likewise aware of this fact, which is demonstrated when one of the old men tells Jimmy shortly before the first case, "Watch old Bloom give it to this nigger." And when Bloom examines the black man standing before him, the latter having forfeited his right to counsel, he assumes the role of prosecutor rather than arbiter. In a fit of humor and disgust, he states that if the drunk's wife "has one more kid, she'll be making more than me" (161). Though Bloom gives them a quick, threatening glance, the old men know that the Judge is performing for them.

Because of the relationship between race and spectacle, Jimmy Mulligan's task is not only to shift Judge Bloom's mood, but also to create a space where Bloom can perform. In seeking to influence Bloom's decision on the Italian youth's case, Jimmy recognizes that Judge Bloom's "bad moods" take the form of abuse and ridicule thinly veiled as humor. His decisions on the cases he hears become opportunities for him to assume responsibility to his audience (the twelve old men in the gallery) and reconstruct each defendant's "story" into comedy. Mulligan seeks to make the courtroom into a space where laughter and performance conjoin in such a way that Philomena Brown, rather than the Italian youth, will be the object of the Judge's anger. The success of this enterprise, then, relies on the defendant's obvious guilt. When this contextual condition is met, the Judge is free to narrate the circumstances of the offenders guilt before he renders his sentence. His posture shifts from a position in legal discursive space where he arbitrates disputes toward a mode of address that acknowledges (and indeed, upholds) interior and exterior features of the social structure. Of course, the law is an interior space that, in this story, constructs race as a sign of exteriority. As "An Act of Prostitution" captures it, then, the legal arena is a performance space where whiteness and maleness are the preconditions for persuasive status.

This is further evidenced by the next case. Irving Williams, a black soldier, enters the court room accused of the assault and battery of a white policeman. The prosecuting and the defense attorneys are both black; the former is a police detective described as being "tough but very nervous" and the latter is merely described as a "plump, greasy black man in his fifties." The case proceeds in normal fashion, with the detective examining the police officer allegedly attacked by the soldier. The police officer testifies that he and his partner were called in to help subdue a crowd of blacks who he says were "running up and down the street and making noise and carrying on" (163). On seeing the defendant, who was returning from a costume party wearing a red costume, complete with cape and red turban, "carrying a big black shield right outta Tarzan," the officers went in "to grab [the soldier] before he [can] start something big." He felt justified because it appeared to him "that the crowd was getting mean. They looked like they was gonna try something big pretty soon" (163).

We need to consider the officer's use of interpretive tools here. From the vantage point of an authority figure, the "jumble" of black people on the street constitutes a riot, simply because they have gathered. Unlike Ellison's hero, however, the officer does not cross the figurative boundary that separates him from "them." Encountering a "crowd of colored people running up and down the street and making noise and carrying on," the officer never makes the more important leap, as we saw in the Tod Clifton eulogy scene, where the narrator sees "not a crowd but the set faces of individual men and women." This roiling mass of humanity never achieves a measure of individuality sufficient to become coherent as a community. Hence Williams, located at the front of the crowd in exotic costume, is "read" as the leader. His shield which is "right outta Tarzan" suggests that he has moved from the subservience that blacks portray in those films to defiance. In a reworking of Ellison's riot scene at the end of *Invisible Man,* this "black warrior" seems to be leading a mass of angry black folk. The only way the officer can read the situation as a coherent text is to constitute it as riot, as a threat to white authority. It also suggests that anger is the only force that can bind blacks into a persuasive community. The officers feel justified, then, in hitting the defendant with their nightsticks and taking him down to the station. Before he can be cross-examined by the "oily lawyer," the court room's attention shifts to take in a new dilemma:

> Standing against the back walls and along the left side of the room were twenty-five or so sternfaced, cold-eyed black men, all in African dashikies, all wearing brightly colored hats, and all staring at the Judge and at the black detective. (164–65)

The black men, "all bearded and tight-lipped," lock hands and form a "solid wall of flesh around almost three quarters of the courtroom" (165). When the defense attorney begins to cross-examine the police officer, his testimony begins to unravel. The black detective rises to object and is showered with threats and epithets, muting any opposition he might offer. The soldier explains that he was returning from a costume party and was actually trying to "break up the crowd with [his] shield" when he was attacked by the police officers. It is at this point, however, that the Judge intervenes and says, "That's enough. . . . That's all I want to hear. . . . This case isn't for my court. Take it upstairs" (168). This is an important turning point in the story, and it illustrates the closed nature of the legal arena—its inability to expand its parameters to include "new stories." The scene is characterized by its reversals. The black men who come into the courtroom and enclose it in a "wall of flesh" transform the courtroom from a performance space oriented toward the exercise of white male privilege into one recognizing blackness as an authoritative, historical posture. Further, the soldier's innocence, demonstrated by his more credibly rendered testimony (coupled with the fact that the defense attorney breaks the credibility of the officer's testimony (166–67), negates Judge Bloom's power to perform. Enclosed in a wall of blackness, the "interiority" of the courtroom is recalibrated to respond to an alternative form of spectatorship. This marks another reversal: the law, as it attempts to perform its task of maintaining social structure, is itself subsumed by a force that calls attention to the inadequacy of that structure. Thus the black police detective's presence in the courtroom is "reread." Within this revision, he serves the interests of a racist legal system and thus the charges of "Uncle Tom" and "handkerchiefhead flunky" characterize his complicity. Inside the "wall" his presence can only be read in negative fashion; shifting his status from officer to offender.

When Judge Bloom recognizes that the reconfiguration of legal accountability makes him the object of a black spectatorship imbued with its own imperatives and thus forcing him to listen rather than speak, his only recourse is to regain control by refusing to "hear" the case. Because the case is characterized by African American assertions of innocence, Bloom concludes that the case "isn't for [his] court," because his court assumes the guilt of its defendants. However, the problem the Williams case presents needs to be understood as a matter of judicial expertise, not jurisdiction. This suggests the difference between recognition and reading: Judge Bloom's skills lie in the area of recognizing signs and acting on them; he lacks the ability (or the desire) to realign his lexicon to accommodate new and different kinds of stories. His unwillingness to hear other stories signals his inability to ascertain those stories, not as performance sites, but as interpretative sites.

The racial nature of the encounter also affects the spectatorial aspects of the courtroom, which is described as "tense and quiet." And the twelve old men stare "stiff and erect," at Irving Williams. The playful language McPherson uses here implies that the fulfillment of desire that accompanies Bloom's mistreatment of defendants is negated. The white men in the courtroom are aroused by the events surrounding the Williams trial, but the arousal is truncated, and they are forced to "exchange glances with each other up and down the row" (165). In short, they can only turn their gaze on one another as a way to interpret "the solid wall of flesh" surrounding them. But this represents an unveiling: the white, male gaze as it is "contained" is likewise historicized. In the presence of an alternative view of history (the language of which is signified by the black men's derisive posture towards the black policeman), one that indicts them and challenges their privilege, the white men can only look to one another as a way to reestablish convention. McPherson's language is intended, then, to register the masturbatory nature of spectatorship, the culmination of which comes in the form of Jimmy Mulligan's twice-uttered, "Oh, hell."

We need to remember Ellison's observation that judges and lawyers have not "appeared in our literature . . . in heroic roles," for the story's turn toward closure reasserts this notion. Thus, when Philomena Brown's case is called, Ralph tells Jimmy: "Do a good job, Jimmy, please. . . . Old Bloom is gonna be awful mean now" (169). Interestingly, Philomena smiles in response to the black men in the courtroom. She does not set herself apart from the men because they are black; rather, she is empowered by their act of resistance. Her smile alludes to the potentially positive impact their presence may have on her own case; Judge Bloom's "bad mood" is checked, rendering him powerless to intrude in the legal process. However, their departure returns the status quo to the fore.

This is evidenced as Jimmy gets ready to begin. When one of the old men asks, "Ain't that the one that's married to the nigger?" (159), which Mulligan affirms, he tells him to "make sure they give her hell." The white men in the courtroom view the intrusion by the black men as an affront to their power. Because of her marriage to a black man, Philomena becomes the object of their rage. This scenario offers what *Philoctetes* manages to avert at its close: the use of an individual as the "means" to an end. Thus Mulligan gives up his right to cross-examine the arresting officer and puts Philomena Brown on the stand. By calling Philomena to the stand, he makes her a witness against herself. He knows that "success," deferred until the Italian youth receives his sentence, rests on the persuasive community he can create, the constitutive rhetoric he can bring to bear on the situation. That rhetoric is located in the realm of comedy and his examination of Philomena is designed to restore the spectatorial convention displaced during the Williams trial and thus nullify Philomena's curse. Hence he asks her a series of disjointed questions that culminate with Philomena telling the court her husband's name. His name, "Rudolph Leroy Brown, Jr.," brings muffled laughter, and it is at this point that Mulligan's strategy begins to create a persuasive community bound by laughter rather than legal rhetoric. This line of questioning destroys any possibility for Philomena's testimony to achieve credibility, largely because she is denied narrative agency. The fact that the policeman testifies to her conversation with two black men in a car prompts a reading that refutes her claim that she was looking for a job as a file clerk. Though this might indeed be the case, especially since the possibility exists that information of this sort is exchanged via less formal channels than in the white community, Mulligan never takes the opportunity to argue for Philomena's innocence from the standpoint of cultural difference. Furthermore, we are prevented from formulating an alternative reading by virtue of the fact that the search for "work" takes place on "Beaver avenue" at two o'clock in the morning.

When Judge Bloom intercedes, his act of usurping responsibility for presentation from both Jimmy Mulligan and Philomena Brown shatters any "persuasive community" Mulligan and the prostitute represent, the creation of which has been the lawyer's intention from the outset of the trial. Of course, the gap that allows Bloom to interrupt the testimony and insert himself as its rhetorical center has been present throughout the story. However, it marks a moment when he delights in the reappropriation of his courtroom's performance function, which he acknowledges with a "broad grin." When he sentences Philomena Brown to "six months on the State," he reasserts his power and fulfills his "contract" with the other white men in the courtroom: the maintainance of a legal system that empowers those who are white and male.

It is not my position here to suggest that "An Act of Prostitution" is not designed to elicit a humorous response in the reader. However, we must not overlook the ramifications. The reader, no less than the "twelve angry men" who form the "jury," participates in the "act of prostitution" this title describes. McPherson's language leads the reader to marginalize Philomena, even though it is she who is victimized by a corrupt legal system. He describes her as "the whore" and "the fat whore," using words like "heavily" or "ooze" that color our perceptions of her actions. Inevitably, this story replicates the classic legal scenario: our act of reading is shaped by the same types of stereotypes to be found in Jimmy Mulligan's defense. The laughter in this story evokes the manner in which race and law lack the cultural equipment to deconstruct stereotypes as highly contingent categories.

More, by directing the reader away from indignation and anger at Philomena's exploitation, McPherson suggests that only through a more active form of reading can we avoid being complicit in the exploitation of the accused. This suggests that Philomena's presence in the courtroom must achieve a new level of complexity that allows for more than one "reading" of her body: not as a source of humor, but as a site of male exploitation. McPherson's description of the Italian youth as a "pretty boy with clean, blue eyes" (172) suggests that racism and sexism converge at a site where whiteness and maleness are categories inherently more attractive than the racial Other. Thus, when Angelico Carbone comes into court, his presence marks the climax of a masturbatory act, the valorization of white, male narcissism. Ralph alludes to this when he tells Jimmy, "The kid's name is Angelico. Ain't that a beautiful name? He ain't a bad kid" (169). Though he, too, is a repeat offender, what makes Angelico "beautiful" is his ability to sustain his status within the categorical field of whiteness.

"An Act of Prostitution " is significant as an American fiction, then, because it interrogates the manner in which the legal arena is a site whose power issues from the illusory category of whiteness and its ability to sustain its legitimacy. Judge Bloom's asserted intention to "throw the book" at Philomena Brown (whose name implies that she is a "lover of brown men") suggests that any attempts to supersede racial categories will be met with violent (e.g., textual) force. Angelico, Judge Bloom, Ralph, Jimmy, and the twelve old men are a persuasive community whose most important task is to resist assault on their categorical identity. Failure to do this, as the opening of the story proposes, is to risk falling into a zone of categorical slippage, where identity can be established along lines that eradicate whiteness and maleness as preeminent sites. The law, as McPherson portrays it here, is constructed as a protection against the curse of all Philomena Browns; for she signals both the arbitrary nature of white, male power and the fact that white women are a "resource" that must be controlled at all costs. As her experience indicates, the legal arena is characterized by a brand of exchange where narcissism calls for the denigration of the Other. As an end in itself, the inherent danger here lies in failing to transgress surfaces.[16] McPherson suggests that oppression is located within the act of misreading, which achieves contractual status when individuals agree to lock a particular set of misreadings (such as racism and sexism) in place, valorizing an interpretive space energized by self-delusion of the worst sort.[17]

4

A similar state of affairs exists in McPherson's story, "Problems of Art." This tale, however, takes a different narrative course than the story discussed above. In this story, Corliss Milford, an attorney retained to represent Mrs. Mary Farragot as she faces a drunk driving charge, is forced to contend with his faulty "reading" of African American culture. Unlike "An Act of Prostitution," where McPherson suggests that powerlessness accompanies Otherness in a courtroom, "Problems of Art" offers a more optimistic assessment of African American engagement with the legal process. The story begins with Milford sitting in Mary Farragot's apartment, waiting for her to return from an errand. As he waits, he realizes that he is uncomfortable. But as he looks around, he cannot understand why, for what he observes offers no apparent clues:

The living room itself, as far as he could see around, reflected the imprint of a mind as meticulous as his own. Every item seemed in place; every detail meshed into an overriding suggestion of order.[18]

Milford's examination of Mrs. Farragot's apartment, the fact that he confers the positive notion of order on it, is based on his own concept of what constitutes "order." Because he can see in the room signs of his own intellectual meticulousness, he cannot understand why the room does not welcome him, does not make him comfortable in a situation that so obviously reflects his own imperatives. He thinks back to Mrs. Farragot to see if he can find an inconsistency, but he realizes that the "neatness [does] no damage to the image he [has] assembled even before visiting her at home." What this suggests is that Milford has come to Mrs. Farragot's apartment with a "reading" in place: his socially constructed version of "Mrs. Farragot" leads him to conclude that her personal life argues "neatness and restraint," which he includes in his written profile of the woman. Thus, the apartment should reinforce this reading. When it doesn't, Milford is made uneasy. He feels that the details in the apartment, though they "[mesh] into an overriding sense of order," imply contrivance. The apartment is analogous to "a sound stage on a movie lot." Milford suspects an "undisclosed reality," as if closer scrutiny would not yield meaning, but a blank text that would render the issue of meaning completely moot.

However, Milford cannot help but feel there are images in the apartment that hint at the possibility of a contradiction in the orderly presentation of Mrs. Farragot's home. The first is a painting of Jesus on the wall. Milford regards it as "cheap," suggesting an impoverished artistic imagination. The second is a picture of a man Milford believes is Mrs. Farragot's husband Willie, in his army uniform, saluting. However, on second examination of the picture, Milford discerns the subject's significance. He notices "a bugle stood upright on its mouth just at the soldier's feet; in fact, the man's left brogan was pointing slyly at the bugle. This was why the man was grinning" ("Problems," 98). McPherson's photograph of "Sweet Willie" offers tropes on several aspects of Ellison's novel. First, the bugle evokes Armstrong's horn in the Prologue, where the trumpet is described as a "military instrument" that Armstrong bends "into a beam of lyrical sound." In addition, Sweet Willie's grin alludes to the Ellison narrator's grandfather and his call to "undermine 'em with grins." These allusions combine to suggest that the photograph captures an image of a "yes-saying trickster" even as it alludes to a self-interest that neither the uniform nor the American flag can contain. Sweet Willie's "salute," which Milford characterizes as "majestic," parodies an allegiance to the flag. Milford's paradigm of reading leads him to misread the photograph. He remembers that Mrs. Farragot is a "grass widow," a woman who has been deserted by her husband. He perceives Sweet Willie as an irresponsible husband who has driven Miss Mary to frustration. Since Sweet Willie is a man who "reeks of irresponsibility," Milford assumes that this accounts "completely for the bitterness that had compelled her to request specifically the services of a white lawyer" ("Problems," 98). Milford extends this reading and conjectures that perhaps "all the men Mrs. Farragot knew were like" Sweet Willie. His appraisal of Sweet Willie's photograph and the assumptions that hold it in place, in spite of his liberalism, suggest that the space where Mrs. Farragot "fits" best is in a narrative where black men are marked by their irresponsibility.

Furthermore, Milford is so confident in his ability to read images that he reconstructs his presence as the room's conceptual center. He evaluates the orderliness of Miss Mary's living room and places it in the space of his rhetorical posture. Thus he concludes that he has "reentered the living room at another level" and is now capable of sympathy. What this implies is not Milford's ability to read Mrs. Farragot's apartment from her point of view, but instead Milford's shift from reading to interpretation, to a reification of his surroundings that makes his perceptions synonymous with reality. When Milford turns his attention back to the painting of Jesus, he realizes that the picture does not "draw one into it." He goes on to observe:

> Its total effect did no more than suggest that the image, at the complete mercy of a commercial artist, had resigned itself to being painted. The face reflected a nonchalant resignation to this fate. If the mouth was a little sad it was not from the weight of this world's sins, but rather from an inability to comprehend the nature of sin itself. (99)

Milford's assessment of the portrait is grounded in the classic portrayals of Jesus in Western Art and Biblical narrative. Because these images portray Jesus as a white man, Milford is repulsed by an image that seems to parody these "standard" representations. His decision to categorize the painting as parodic belies his ability either to identify with Mrs. Farragot or to reenter "the living room on another level," for he fails to recognize the fact that the portrait might intend to lampoon Christianity rather than celebrate it. Indeed, its "inability to comprehend the nature of sin itself," demonstrates Milford's fixed position within the conventional master narrative. Mrs. Farragot's decision to hang the portrait may be a greater statement of her distrust of and distance from a white Jesus. As a lawyer working at "Project Gratis," Milford fails to recognize that Mrs. Farragot's inability to pay for a lawyer in no way suggests that she lacks resistant zeal.

Mrs. Farragot returns to the apartment with Clarence Winfield, who launches into a version of the tale. But before he does so, Mrs. Farragot offers this admonishment:

> Speak good English now, Clarence, for the Lord's sakes . . . We got to go downtown. And there's one thing I learnt about white people: if they don't understand what you saying, they just ain't gonna hear it. (100)

Realizing that Clarence's story is not for a black audience, she knows his "performance" of the tale must be tailored for a different context, one where Winfield begins as object rather than subject. Hence her observation that whites' inability to comprehend black speech carries an implicit analysis of the power relationship in the venues ("downtown") where whites are in authority. Her conclusion that they "just ain't gonna hear it" asserts the notion that otherness is the equivalent of erasure. Further, the idiom of Winfield's story, because of its variance from "proper" English, is indeed "not heard" by white authorities (consider Judge Bloom here) because it represents a resistance to the hegemony of the "master tongue." Mrs. Farragot's attempt to "shape" Winfield's narrative and the fact that she looks "conspiratorially" at Milford lead him to conclude that her testimony has been substantiated. Milford records notes from the rambling narrative Winfield relates. When he reaches the end of the story, Mrs. Farragot responds, "What I wanted me in the first place . . . was a white boy that could make some logic of all that," which affirms Milford's posture (108). As they wait for the hearing to begin, Milford replays the drive to the Department of Motor Vehicles office. He looks at Mrs. Farragot with

> new appreciation of her *relative* sophistication. In the car she had disclosed that she did domestic work for a suburban stockbroker; from listening in on conversations between the broker and his wife, she would have discerned how a bureaucracy, and the people who made it function, must of necessity be restricted to the facts. (108; emphasis mine)

Milford is led to conclude that he must edit and curtail Clarence Winfield's narration, which he regrets because he admires the man's "rough style." He tells him to "restrict your statement to the last part of your story, the part about [Mrs. Farragot] not being drunk when she was arrested." The conclusions Milford draws about both people say less about them than they do about where his perceptual apparatus is positioned in cultural space. Mrs. Farragot's sophistication is "relative" to his (or indeed, any white man's) sense of how the world functions. So impressed is Milford with the "narrative" that he creates (Mrs. Farragot's assimilation of "how government works"), that the "logic" he applies to the situation leads him to conclude that he cannot "use" the improvisational quality of Winfield's speech. Thus Winfield's story shifts from an act of testifying, where he provides the tale's narrative unity, into the realm of testimony where Milford is empowered to give shape to Miss Mary's tale.[19]

Winfield's rendering of the evening of Miss Mary's arrest is a communal tale; it is inclusive. Not only does he include the bare facts of how Mrs. Farragot has come to be in court, but he lends color and flesh to the narrative by including the voices of all the parties involved, from Big Boy, the owner of the car Mrs. Farragot damages, to Buster Williams, her next-door neighbor. In Milford's version of the tale, this quality of the narrative is lost. It becomes an exclusive narrative that rests on Milford's assessment of what is relevant to his biased concept of narration. If we consider "Problems of Art" alongside "An Act of Prostitution," what becomes clear is that McPherson asserts that voice, the ability to render one's own voice, is a necessity in a courtroom.

The story turns when Mrs. Farragot sees that the officer presiding over the hearing is a woman and not a man. On recognizing this, she reassesses the possibilities at hand and suggests a change of strategy, saying, "Actually, Clarence don't do too bad when he talk. Maybe you ought to let him tell his story after all" (111). Mrs. Farragot's desire to change strategy coincides with her realization that she has encountered an unexpected context in which to ply her narrative powers. The hearing officer's gender eliminates what she sees as one of her largest obstacles: the ability of men to truncate women's narrative agency. This fortuitous circumstance leads Mrs. Farragot to decide that it is in her best interest to assume authorial control over her situation.[20] Milford notices the change in Mrs. Farragot; her resolve has been bolstered and she is "smiling openly."

After Milford questions Otis Smothers, the arresting officer (in an ironic turn, he too is black and from the South), Mrs. Farragot takes control of the hearing. Instead of allowing Milford to question her, she tells her story. The story leaves Hearing Officer Wilson "deeply moved." Thus, when Milford returns his focus to Smothers, he is able to show that the officer failed to give Mrs. Farragot a legally specified sobriety test. When Mrs. Farragot is asked if she received any test, she responds on the verge of tears, "No suh. . . . They didn't offer me nothing in front of my house and they didn't offer me nothing down to the jail. They just taken me in a cell in my pajamas" (115). At this point, Hearing Officer Wilson ends the hearing and informs Milford, Mrs. Farragot, and Winfield that she can retain her license. Milford is pleased with himself, proud of the fact that "He had taken command of a chaotic situation and forced it to a logical outcome. He had imposed order" (116). Thus he is not completely prepared when Winfield responds, "Many's the time I told Miss Mary about that drinkin." Milford sees Mrs. Farragot coming down the hall, notices her "blue dress [swishing] gaily" and the fact that she appears to be strutting in triumph with a smile reminiscent of Sweet Willie on her face.

This scene integrates all the story's disparate elements into a coherent unity. Further, it illustrates several concepts that are critical to an understanding of the McPherson *oeuvre*. First, it dramatizes the power of performance—the fusion of text and context as well as the conscious manipulation of an audience. Second, it offers an example of the way race and gender are sites of negotiation, discursive practices that impact on institutional functions. Finally, the story takes a commonplace event—a license revocation hearing—and transforms it into a trickster tale.

Milford, "perceptive" and self-important, is clearly the object of Mrs. Farragot's manipulative skill. Ironically, though, it is exactly this combination of characteristics, when framed by Miss Mary's ability to create a persuasive community, that leads to the case's positive results. Thus, one can conclude that this is a fiction that tropes Ellison's concern with reversals; it is a classic representation of his call to "change the joke and slip the yoke" through its demonstration of the manipulative power of illusion. And indeed, Milford's inability to read, his reliance on faulty interpretation, allows Mrs. Farragot, a skillful reader of textual convention, to triumph. Further, the story suggests that American cultural production relies on the kinds of distortion Miss Mary enacts. Recognizing her drinking problem, Miss Mary knows she need only represent herself as a teetotaler to be vindicated. Thus she manipulates images, first by arranging her living room in a manner that represents, for her, a place where the presence of alcohol is unlikely. Second, having anticipated the structure of the courtroom as a place where white men are in authority, she "represents" herself with a white lawyer who can provide the illusion of order. She must create an illusion that will bridge the truth and her story in order for Milford to give voice to her story with the legal arena. If Milford internalizes her story, his presence as her lawyer will bring together all the disparate strands into a coherent whole. Thus, she knows that she needs to allow Milford to write her into a state of being, to create a narrative whose origins he locates within the space of his own consciousness.

Miss Mary's astute realization that courtrooms are the domain of men is not so rigidly adhered to that she cannot improvise when she sees that a woman is the presiding officer of her case. The authorial control that testifying represents rests on Miss Mary's ability to realize that the courtroom, a space where difference is often negated, is a potential performance space that allows for improvisation. Because she and Officer Wilson are women, gender as a means of erasure is eliminated. Further, because Officer Smothers is black, race is likewise negated as a site of contestation. By telling her own story, Miss Mary uses a rhetorical strategy that binds her, Officer Wilson, and Milford into a persuasive community against Smothers. This is made clear by Wilson's admonishment of the officer, where she begins "Otis, tell the boys that in the future . . ." Miss Mary's rhetorical approach subverts the misogyny of the legal arena (evidenced by Smothers's "hostile glare," 116) and empowers her act of resistance. As a persuasive community, Wilson and Farragot combine to resist this "misreading (which, in truth, is the correct reading)." The politics of concealment is turned on its head to work for, rather than against, African Americans. By manipulating images of sobriety and respectability, Miss Mary's act of self-representation produces a mythic surface that diverts attention away from her drinking problem.

"Problems of Art," is a story which, like *Philoctetes,* and *Invisible Man,* offers the reader a variety of persuasive communities, the final one being made up of Milford and Winfield, who are left with the task of trying to "straighten [Miss Mary] out." Milford, the naive innocent, is tricked into a new state of awareness where he realizes that his world-view, which moments before had been a source of order, is, in fact, a sign of blindness. Winfield, who knows all about Miss Mary's drinking problems, nudges Milford and causes the water from the drinking fountain to splash into his eyes. The symbolic meaning of this "nudge" is that Winfield recognizes that he and Milford constitute a new community. It is an act of affirmation. Further, this act initiates the rejuvenation of Milford's eyes; Winfield assumes responsibility for teaching him a new way to "read" cultural signs. Thus, this last scene revises Brother Jack's removal of his eye in Ellison's novel. Jack removes his eye and places it in a glass of water, thus refusing to recognize cultural difference. Contained in a glass, the water suggests the ideological containment of Jack's vision. Milford retains his eyes and sees newly, restored by the water in its fluid state. Milford's transformation (however unwitting it may be) suggests that he has been moved to a space where he can read signs from an altered point of view. Whereas earlier in the story he descended to "read" the objects in Mrs. Farragot's apartment, the license revocation hearing teaches him that it is not altitude, but perspective that was, and is, at issue.

However, we must also confront this fiction's presentation of two forms of authorship. As Milford enacts it, authorship is foregrounded by facts, data, and the ability to derandomize signs. Mary Farragot, conversely, establishes an authorial presence whose goal is to overcome disbelief by overwhelming the "reader" with familiar signs. Though these signs are characterized by an instability that makes them vulnerable to an act of close reading; they are effective because they hold attention long enough to deflect scrutiny away from the system at work to organize them. As the portrait of Jesus demonstrates, Mary Farragot recognizes the difference between form and substance. But instead of privileging substance over form, Miss Mary reverses their importance: she knows that a legal confrontation that is seemingly a narrative event is, in fact, a drama whose circumstances can be manipulated in her favor largely because she recognizes the efficacy of improvisation (as opposed to adhering to a script) as a viable dramatic mode. As a fiction, "Problems of Art" is aptly named largely because it forces an interrogation of artistic production as a phenomenon driven by strategies that transform the ornamental into the meaningful. As McPherson suggests, part of the "problem" is that meaning is often achieved via an arrogance foregrounded by the reification of categories. We can conclude from this fiction, at least, that in the hands of the trickster, art is a malleable discursive site.

5

The third part of McPherson's cultural critique is realized in the last story in the trilogy "A Sense of Story." If the two aforementioned fictions are literary acts of thesis and antithesis, then this story serves as the synthesis that culminates the trilogy. Once again, "A Sense of Story" presents a scenario where chaos and order compete within the same conceptual space. The story opens at the trial of one Mr. Robert Charles, a defendant in a murder trial. Having been accused of murdering his employer, Charles sits passively through four days of testimony. Finally, during his attorney's summation speech, he rises, out of order, to speak to the courtroom where he announces, "It wasn't no accident . . . I had me nine bullets and a no-good gun. Gentlemens, the onliest thing I regret is the gun broke before I could pump more than six slugs into the sonofabitch."[21] Charles's outburst comes at the point in the trial when his lawyer is attempting to "tie together" the disparate strands of testimony that will explain his client's motive for killing his employer. The issue is not Charles's guilt, for we find that he has pleaded *nolo contendere* in the trial. The defense attorney's task is to "plead mitigating circumstances" that will lead the jury to conclude that "manslaughter, with life imprisonment, [is all that is] due the state."

The response to the defendant's attempt to testify in his own behalf is silence; we are told that the "entire courtroom was hushed." In the language of courtroom procedure, Charles has spoken "out of order."

That is, he has refused to conform to the convention that allows him the opportunity only to respond to questions posed to him, to speak when spoken to. The reversal here should be clear; when there is a disturbance in a legal proceeding, the judge's call for "order in the court" is a call to return to convention. In this story there is no evidence that any such rebuke is offered by the judge. Thus the silence he offers is ironic, for what it suggests is that Charles, in fact, *restores* order, eradicates the chaos that enshrouds his story and his life. The fictional predicament McPherson presents, then, is how the story's protagonist, the judge presiding over the case, attempts to restore order, to return Robert Charles to conventional parameters of behavior. After dismissing the jury and conferring with the attorneys, the judge retires to his chambers to consider the situation:

> The judge was in a quandary. There was no rule covering such an outburst. There was no way it could be erased from the jurors' minds. There was no point in going on with the trial. The two lawyers and the judge agreed finally that, since the outburst had occurred during the defense counsel's summation, the record of prior proceedings should be examined. In this way it could be determined whether a preponderance of the evidence had already tipped the scales of justice against the defendant, making his confession of insignificant weight. This unfortunate decision was to be left with the judge. ("Sense," 232)

Not only does this passage work to outline the story's central predicament, but it also serves to preface the shift in format about to occur. Thus we cannot ignore the form this story assumes, for "A Sense of Story" posits a new and difficult form of labor for the reader. The story's title signifies on the shape-shifting characteristics of this fiction: the shift from conventional narrative, where the reader is immersed in a fictional world, to an instance where the reader must rely on a character's act of reading to enter the "comfortable" world of plot and action. To achieve "a sense of story," the reader is placed in the uncomfortable position of having to rely on the judge's reconstruction of the trial.

This proposes that one must be clear on what questions this fiction attempts to address. First, there is the question of Robert Charles's innocence. Second, the story gives voice to the forces that shape a legal preceeding. Third, the story critiques the inequities of the legal system. But most important, "A Sense of Story" confronts, like McPherson's other legal fictions, the act of reading, its ability to shape the way we engage the world and, as an act of deciphering the Word, its potential, as Ellison has pointed out, to "blind, imprison, and destroy."[22]

On being supplied with the records, the judge is said to be "scanning" the testimony of the arresting officer. McPherson's choice of words here is important: according to the *Oxford English Dictionary*, two definitions of the word "scan" are relevant here. One is "to look closely, to scrutinize," the other is "to glance quickly, to consider hastily." These definitions, depending on which one is used, determine the depth and nature of the judge's act of reading, and likewise illuminate the "plot" of this fiction. The testimony the judge reads first is that which originates from the questions posed by the assistant district attorney, Paul Lindenberry. Further, of the six witnesses the story presents, the assistant district attorney examines four. The judge's reading is therefore subtly biased toward the prosecution's case. He reads only the cross-examination of one witness by the defense and the examination of one defense witness. The story presents only two instances where the judge reads the defense counsel's attempt to produce testimony on the defendant's behalf.

So how is the act of "scanning" a text employed here? McPherson presents a bifurcated reading of the legal transcripts. More, it asserts the fact that the latter definition of the word "scan" is in play here, for we find that the judge reads "hurriedly through the record." We are made aware of the passage of time because the narrator notes that the judge has a conference at 3:00 p.m., and it is slightly after twelve noon when he finishes reading the testimonies of the arresting officer and one of Charles's co-workers. Thus the reconstruction of the trial does not occur in a temporal vacuum. Because McPherson makes us aware of the time lapse, we know that the reading occurs in a temporal context made more difficult by the press of other events that precede, coincide with, and follow it. Here is another sense of the way the story indicts the legal system: the judge is hurried by the press of other engagements, which forces him to read selectively through the transcript. Certainly, this is a fictional technique meant to create tension, but we can also see this moment as a play on Justice Warren's phrase, "with all deliberate speed." In a comic reversal, the speed of deliberation, as the Judge's act of reading indicates, is likewise the sign of the imprecision of justice.

Moreover, if we consider the judge's reconstruction, through reading, of the events leading up to Charles's outburst in a poetic sense, then the word "scan" takes on another aspect. In poetry, to scan is "to analyze . . . [in order to determine] its rhythmic components." This alludes to the critic's approach to poetic exegesis which relies on breaking the poem into its most basic elements. The judge's act of "scanning the text" serves this same function. He reads in order to determine whether a discernible pattern has developed within the testimony that will negate Charles's outburst. To accomplish this, the judge must engage in an act of narrative reassembly by breaking the testimony into its constitutive parts. The need to go back over the trial testimony after Charles's courtroom speech leads the judge to read up until the point where the speech renders the process incoherent. The judge's act of reading must restore order and thus the illusion of coherence that "due process" presents.

What may not be clear to Robert Charles is that the courtroom, as I have observed above, is a space where representation is realized through the act of manipulating the jury's ability to discern the most coherent narrative. The lawyer's task is to construct a narrative. It is the role of the judge to see that this enterprise follows a set of conventions. Thus what is illuminating in examining the transcripts are the exchanges between the judge and the lawyers. We can conclude that the three men constitute a persuasive community. They speak a common language and work in close relation to one another (as the judge's act of referring to the lawyers by their first names, a real "break" in convention, would suggest). At one point in his reading, for example, the judge underlines a moment in the trial that he deems crucial to the narrative—his exchange with the defense attorney, Franklin Grant, at a point when he allows the prosecution to continue examination of a witness. He observes, "It goes against my better judgment, and perhaps I am wrong, but my intuition tells me there is a sense of story here. I am going to let the testimony in" ("Sense," 239). The role of the judge is to set the boundaries within which attorneys can construct their respective narratives. These boundaries allude to the patterns which Anglo American legal tradition has established. For a case to have a "sense of story" it must somehow suggest a coherent plot. Hence, McPherson implies that legal confrontation here is not intended as a search for truth, rather it is a subjective enterprise that must conform to the judge's sense of narrative as a temporal sequence.[23]

Consider the judge's attempt to articulate what is occurring and his role within the scenario:

> Ladies and gentlemen, I feel I must apologize to you for these lengthy excursions. I have attempted to grant leeway to counsel for both sides, because it seemed to me that my own decisions, based solely on the rules of evidence as I know them, would prevent your hearing the cross-light of competing views, which I consider essential to the adversary process. But it seems now that this trial has lost its direction. *Still, in my mind, law is an art, and my function here should ideally be no different from that of a literary critic.* (250; emphasis mine)

What the judge asserts is what I have tried to suggest in this entire chapter, namely, that the law is a subjective process, one whose domain is artistic and institutional. As an art form, the legal confrontation is subject to the critical evaluation of an arbitrary force. If we examine the racist views of the prosecution's witnesses, we find that the prosecution's narrative agenda rests on the illusion of white paternalism and Robert Charles's ungrateful response. The defense, on the other hand, attempts to portray Charles as a poor, illiterate black who works for a less than model employer, as a man crippled by his Southern background. Neither of these representations of Robert Charles is correct. Indeed, what both narratives suggest is the metonymic slippage inherent within the legal process.[24] Within the courtroom's synecdochical parameters, Robert Charles's "outburst" is in actuality an attempt to resist fragmentation. His act of asserting his guilt is meant to retotalize his life, to restore its integrity and thus its legibility as a readable "text." The American legal community practices its craft in a space where the cipher is rendered meaningful by the most devastating argument.

The story's last pages are magnificent examples of McPherson's ability to mask events of serious cultural import within the familiar and banal. Hurrying to finish his work in order to attend the judges' conference, the judge pauses to look out his picture window, first down at the cars in the parking lot, which from that height look like "toys." And then up through the "specially treated glass," which makes "the sky seem more bright and blue than it really [is]." He prepares to walk out of his office, having left a note for his clerk to enter a verdict of "guilty as charged," but suddenly, impulsively he returns to his desk to read the defense attorney's summation. That moment in the trial is distinguished by its lack of resourcefulness, demonstrating the lawyer's inability to create a coherent story. He presents an "illiterate black man" whose joy at seeing his son graduate from high school is punctuated by the act of firing a gun which, in a state of drunkenness, he takes to work. Through a "lapse of logic," Charles ostensibly confuses celebration with violence, killing his employer when he had only meant to share his good news. The story's last two sentences are most telling: "At this point the defendant interrupted. The judge placed the page neatly, face down, on the top of the pile" (255). In effect, this seemingly nonchalant act is an instance where the restoration of the text to its "original" order is an illusion. The reappearance of the "end in the beginning" trope suggests that Charles's guilt *preceded* his outburst; the judge's decision that he is "guilty as charged" proposes that, had he been innocent of the crime, it would have made no difference. Indeed, his guilt is a moot issue. What is at issue, and what is never addressed in the trial's pages, is the racism that precipitated Charles's action. The picture window provides a useful metaphor, for its distortion of reality allows us to locate the judge at the political and cultural intersection from which he performs his duties as "critic." Moreover, consider the fact that the cars down in the parking lot look like "multicolored animals," and "toys."

They recall Charles's life as an automobile mechanic and represent the artistic domain in which he practices his craft, where his personal value accrues. That the cars appear to the judge as animals and toys is likewise indication that Charles's life never achieves coherent shape within the judge's critical gaze. Though the automobile represents an important symbol, largely because it invokes American industrial know-how, that aspect of the story is understood as a "white" contribution to American history; thus, attempts to intervene and rewrite such a history are viewed in threatening terms. His inability to locate Charles within the necessary artistic and historical context, one in which automobiles are not toys but valuable resource, means that the resources he brings to the "critical" act he performs are meager indeed.

Thus, when the judge returns to turn over and read the transcript's last page, the first words resonate with violent force: "worth very little to the ideal of justice." McPherson's truncation of this sentence not only voids its true meaning but it insinuates the "ideal of justice" as an arbitrary circumstance whose validity is reliant upon the men and women of the jury being able to "envision in [their] minds, and find room in [their] hearts, for an illiterate black." The lawyer places narrative organization and spaciality in conceptual relation. Hence he asks that the jury insert Charles's violent act within the container of illiteracy. As such, the intentionality of his act is nullified and thus becomes so pliable as a narrative that it can be squeezed into the narrowest of spaces without offering resistance to those ideas surrounding it.

But what results, and what Charles's "outburst" is intended to stave off, is the reconfiguration of the black working body into a fragmented object. Though Charles's court-appointed attorney should perform the function of making the best case, which is embedded in the story of the employer Johnson's exploitation of Charles's labor, we see here how acts of misreading lead to acts of faulty telling. The result is that Charles's life is broken into units and then incorrectly reassembled, making what could be a coherent *whole* into a black *hole* that absorbs the critical light turned upon it.

The American legal confrontation offers a double bind, for there exists a text that is "appended" to any other text at hand. The judge's act of reading is shaped by his own racial biases, because he has taken it on himself to decide Robert Charles's fate. Thus, he does not read the inferences of racism that are apparent in the prosecutor's examination of witnesses. Rather, his blindness leads him to rule on the more *coherent* narrative, the one which displays the best "sense of story." Not only does he retaliate violently against the power of Jim Crow racism—the ability of white men to invalidate his dreams and aspirations—but upon being brought to trial, he threatens the power of the legal process itself. By "speaking out of order" he reaffirms his own sense of self-worth and integrity; his speech makes him a coherent figure even as it ruptures the smooth surface of the legal illusion.

Clearly, Robert Charles is a "dangerous" criminal. For like Ellison's hero he is a "thinker-tinker." As a mechanic who invents a new lubricant, who has anticipated the influx of Japanese automobiles onto the American scene, Charles is anomaly personified. This is further evidenced by his co-worker, who remembers Charles's claim that he has "put together a lube mixture that was going to add years to the valves and pistons of them new models [and that] the formula was going to grease his way to a desk job over in the main office" (236). Consider this testimony alongside that of a black co-worker, who observes:

> Me, myself, I felt that I was as good as Mr. Johnson or anybody else. But Bobby Lee, look like he thought he was better than Mr. Johnson. It wasn't like he thought black was better than white. He act like he thought they was something better than black and white, and he already had it in a jug with the stopper in his back pocket. (245)

Ellison's hero recognized technology as a site where democratic possibility and resistance could come into contact. Charles's "story" as it is reconstructed through testimony (and the judge's act of scanning the text) is one of innovation and aspiration. Unlike Lucius Brockway who believes power accrues by embracing the role of "the machine inside the machine," Charles recognizes that the machine is prone to malfunction. As one who has had no problem easing "right into [the] newer models," Charles recognizes that the problem is not one of form but rather one of preventing its fall into dysfunctionality. As both witnesses suggest, his formula for a better lubricant is one which eschews racial categories. The "sense of story" the judge misses, then, is allegorically one having to do with the invention of a new cultural paradigm that eschews race as a social lubricant (which, after all, serves to perpetuate white supremacy). We need to understand Charles as a failed visionary, one whose aspirations for upward mobility are informed by his desire to revivify a malfunctioning democracy.

However, the story's drive toward reassembly leads us away from this aspect of Charles's character. Like Fred Daniels in Wright's "Man Who Lived Underground," Robert Lee Charles envisions a new paradigm of societal management, one that eschews race as an organizing principle.[25] The loss in this story, as in Wright's story, is not an individual one, but a loss which needs to be calculated across the whole of American culture. Looking through specially treated glass, which makes "the sky seem more bright and blue than it really [is]," the judge is a figure who refers to a deeper cultural malaise than that which results from racial strife. For if he is a literary critic, then he is a critic of the "old school," a proponent of New Critical perspectives, which means that he sees the text as a "pure" event. The symbolic terrain the judge fails to acknowledge is not Robert Charles's innocence (which, after all, is not at issue) but his real story, namely, his failure to refashion the American dream.

This narrative suggests that perhaps McPherson is attempting to rewrite Book 3 of Wright's *Native Son.* Where that novel attempts to illuminate the effects of racism from the point of view of an African American man, this fiction, its point of view reversed, suggests that Charles's act of killing someone (and thus by implication Bigger's) argues the need for restraint. Wright's novel suggests that the "text" imposed on Bigger is that of the black man as animal, as rapist crazed by desire. McPherson's tale suggests that Robert Charles's act of violence is initiated by the destruction of his ambitions, which is misread by those who inhabit the story's persuasive community. The prosecutor misreads it as the actions of an ungrateful nigger; the defense misreads it as the act of man who is drunk and acting out his cultural background in the wrong context; and the judge misreads it as the best, most viable ending of a story, the end that proves most resilient to his critical scrutiny.

6

In order to assess the collective impact of McPherson's legal trilogy, I think it best to return to where this discussion began: Mr. J. D. Randolph. As Ellison utilizes him, Randolph serves as a multifaceted trope. In one sense, he signals the presence of an African American idiom, obscured by the myth that the law, as both idea and institution, is synonymous with whiteness. Invoking him is a way of referring to unspoken acts made audible. But Randolph's demonstration of literacy means that his counsel takes legible form, and thus he becomes a figure representing the participation of African Americans in a deeply flawed democratic process. Randolph's facility with the law, the fact that he does not need to "consult the text" when it comes to the law, suggests that his act of reading projects him across the color line as it corrects the failures of literacy on the parts of the white legislators who seek his assistance. He represents the ability to improvise in the face of canonical knowledge, and thus serves as a cautionary trope, warning us against the propensity to read only as far as what attractive surfaces reveal or to rely solely on one-dimensional interpretations of the "sacred texts."

Randolph helps us to return once more to the issue of freedom and literacy. While it is indisputable that the quest for literacy and freedom "is found in every major African American text," McPherson's trilogy asserts that the refinement of literacy is no less important to those who have successfully completed the conventional aspects of the quest. Said another way, McPherson's fictions force us to examine the ramifications of faulty interpretive skills. As McPherson's stories represent the legal arena, we find it to be fraught with blind spots and distortions of epic proportions.

The collective predicament of these three stories mirrors debate taking place in legal theory around the issue of interpretation. For example, consider Ronald Dworkin's assertion that legal practice is "an exercise in interpretation."[26] Thus, he concludes, the law "is deeply and thoroughly political":

> Law is a political enterprise, whose general point, if it has one, lies in coordinating social and individual effort, or resolving social and individual disputes, or securing justice between them and their government, or some combination of these. ("Law as Interpretation," 263)

As Dworkin sees it, the law is not a site of artistic endeavor where issues of aesthetic value come into play. Rather, he argues, a "judge's duty is to interpret the legal history he finds, not to invent a better history." Dworkin envisions the judge as a political actor and thus his task is one of ensuring the smooth operation of governmental machinery by interpreting legal history and applying that interpretation to the instance at hand. In this view, the adoption of an interventionist posture toward legal history is not only inappropriate, it proposes that an authorial posture can displace what is conventionally an interpretive one.

However, as Richard Delgado reminds us, it is not just a matter of interpretation, it is additionally a matter of telling. If, as he suggests, the "stories or narratives told by the in-group remind it of its identity in relation to outgroups," then it is also important to recognize that

> The stories of outgroups aim to subvert that ingroup reality. In civil rights, for example, many in the majority hold that any inequality between blacks and whites is due either to cultural lag, or inadequate enforcement of currently existing beneficial laws—both of which are easily correctable. For many minority persons, the principal instrument of their subordination is neither of these. Rather, it is the prevailing *mindset* by means of which members of the dominant group justify the world as it is, that is, with whites on top and browns and blacks at the bottom.[27]

This assertion intimates that the concept of audience is formulated as much by exclusion as by inclusion or arranged in hierarchical terms while offering the illusion of inclusiveness. Hence Delgado's argument suggests that the *story* surrounding the creation of the laws has been inadequately rendered, and that thus there is a need to correct the narrative of legal history upon which legal activity is based in the present. Indeed, the notion of the law as a place where storytelling occurs is useful because it does not fail to recognize the concept of "history" as one which is mediated by power relations between groups. Such an approach is mindful of audience and the fact that the eclectic nature of audience leads one to see narrative as a problematic instance. The act of interpretation, then, needs to consider the kinds of stories issuing from emerging audiences, their respective "spin" on the master narrative. As Delgado envisions them, members of the legal community are not only storytellers, but storylisteners as well.[28]

Given this dichotomy, McPherson's stories are not arbitrary instances of fiction-making; they are not intended as reflections upon the ineptitude of lawyers and judges. Rather, these stories recapitulate the last sentence in *Invisible Man* ("Who knows but that, on the lower frequencies, I speak for you?") and attune that question to the issue of representation. Hence the legal actors in McPherson's fiction return us to the figure whom Robert Stepto describes as the articulate hero. The trilogy asserts that to engage in the act of "speaking for" someone suggests the manner in which acts of language are likewise acts of representation. McPherson dramatizes the manner in which language is always mediated within a contextual frame that must be rendered visible. As meditations upon the issue of representation and interpretation, McPherson's fictions allow us to see their relationship to such nineteenth-century American texts as *Pudd'nhead Wilson* and "Benito Cereno."[29] For there, too, we find that issues of representation inform textual events in ways that, as Ellison suggests, offer strong commentary upon the nature of American democracy.

Representation is firmly bound up with participation in the democratic experiment and issues of citizenship. For it is at the nexus formed by representation and citizenship that African Americans help to clarify issues of national identity. As John Callahan observes,

> From the beginning, the inferior official status imposed on African Americans in American life complicated the dynamics of audience. Often, African Americans spoke and wrote expressly as agents of change. They sought to persuade a white audience that theirs was a sufficiently compelling story in American terms to warrant the nation's compliance with its values and first principles.[30]

But representation also proposes a more intimate question, one that channels issues of audience through the dilemma of responsibility. As John Callahan would have it, these stories submit the question, "Who you for?" And in doing so, they call for responses to the questions, "Who are your people, your family, your community? What are your traditions, your history, your values?" Mulligan, Milford, and Charles's court-appointed attorney each demonstrates the difficulty of representation. Each brings to the encounters with their respective clients confused allegiances and outmoded interpretive strategies.

However, what is equally essential to this discussion is how the reader reacts to these characters. The issue of "who you for?" becomes paramount when we consider our propensity as readers to identify with the protagonist, to see them as the engines of plot. That relation is problematized in these fictions. In *Reading for the Plot,* Peter Brooks observes that plot is the "outline or armature of the story, that which supports and organizes the rest."[31] What makes Brooks's definition so prescient is his insistence on plot's utility in the formation of meaning. But, as Brooks takes care to point out, central to the original definition of "plot" is the "idea of boundedness, demarcation, the drawing of lines to mark off and order." If, as Charles Johnson asserts, "plots are arguments," then McPherson's stories would seem to offer a comic portrayal of the legal arena and nothing more. However, such an interpretation can only hold if we ignore the irony embedded in these stories. Read ironically, these stories' overdetermination of plot become intentional devices meant to caution the reader against passive acts of reading while moving them toward a posture which embraces reading against the plot.

Without a doubt, each of these fictions is indicative of the inadequacy of the legal arena's handling of racial matters. However, their racial issues notwithstanding, I would suggest that McPherson's trilogy is finally not a racial critique, but rather a *cultural* one. As a commentary on legal practice, each story foregrounds the modern dilemma of the individual versus the system.[32] Moreover, migration and upward mobility (i.e., middle class status) are threads common to each story, not only because they power African Americans into a state of modernity but also because the quest for freedom and literacy is an implicit aspect of both.[33] What this suggests is that McPherson's fictions depict what could be read as "modern" encounters; they examine instances where the body politic adheres to strategies that privilege surfaces and individual encounters with social machinery without considering how those encounters are in fact references to the fate of the collective.

If the lawyer as articulate hero is inherently a figure whose sense of "who [he is] for," is incontrovertible, then these fictions offer protagonists who disrupt this notion. The key to this is McPherson's improvisation upon short story characterization.[34] For what characterizes Mulligan, the judge and lawyers in "A Sense of Story," and to a lesser extent,

Milford, is their immobility, their inability to enact transformation because they so thoroughly embody stasis. This translates into unwillingness to bring their representational skills to bear for their clients because each buys into myths of white superiority that will be compromised if they unloose themselves. This recalls Amasa Delano and the dilemma he faces at the close of "Benito Cereno." When he confronts Cereno and exclaims, "You are saved!" he fails to consider the symbolic import of the event and its transformative effect on the Spanish captain. Delano's unwillingness to see the mutiny in historical terms and thus revise his view of the black slaves as property lacking the historical and aesthetic agency necessary to create an illusion of normalcy (white control of their bodies), is an instance where he considers plot over meaning. Allegorically speaking, Delano concludes that the failure of the insurrection on the San Dominick is likewise the "end" of the distorting effects of black resistance upon the master narrative of white supremacy. However, Cereno's response to Delano's inquiry, "What has brought this shadow upon you?" is simply, "The Negro," and proposes a narrative that eschews the strategy of simple interpretative closure in favor of what is finally a debilitating narrative complexity. Cereno's death at story's end suggests the violent manner in which the boundary between black and white is disrupted. As a figuration whose ideology rests on the assumption that "black" is a metonym for codelessness, a lack of rhetorical (and thus, representational) agency, white supremacy is distinguished by its unwillingness to accept the validity of narratives which resist the "master narrative."

Melville's novella makes us aware of the way irony could be utilized to locate another audience, one devoted to an anti-racist formulation of identity politics, one whose interpretation of history would lead to a revisionist version. This becomes the trope McPherson uses to call the reader to "read against" the plots of these stories, to create an instance of literary insurrection. Hence they call for new configurations of persuasive community that can assert new stories and thus begin to refashion democratic practice. McPherson's stories ultimately challenge our propensity to "plot out" strategies of literary practice that privilege the protagonist. As allegories of narrative desire, McPherson's trilogy of legal fictions recuperates the antagonist, that figure who disrupts narrative pleasure. Thus, the acts of political or legal resistance they enact become moments when the individual "antagonizes" the master narrative, especially if that narrative has excluded him or her. The narrative pleasure to be found in the "sacred documents" can only be discerned, therefore, within the space of a counter-reading which reveals exclusionary acts as instances where the collective is endangered because resources are not adequately deployed.[35] If Mulligan, Milford, and the judge present a problem for readers, then, it is because McPherson uses point of view to give them narrative authority that is difficult to displace, since the fulfillment of narrative desire is so powerful.

As I observed in the previous chapter, storytelling functions in Ernest Gaines's fiction as the act of giving voice to the conspiratorial, the unspoken. McPherson's legal fictions reverse this move by furnishing us with antagonists who have stories to tell and who are, for the most part, not allowed (Mrs. Farragot being the exception) to tell them. Though the law should provide some redress for their injuries, in each instance we come away wondering if this ostensibly therapeutic site is not itself a space whose resources are so exhausted that it can present only the illusion of depth. Hence, we must look at McPherson's stories in terms of what they do not articulate, what the reader must discern when left to his or her own resources.[36] This is especially so when we consider them as fictions that address themselves to the state of American democracy. While they do not offer instances that should necessarily offer optimism, their portrayal of the ineptitude to be found in the legal profession is, in their fashion, the "start of seriousness." And it is only by acknowledging that which we desire but finally cannot possess (as both Neoptolemus and the invisible man demonstrate), that we come to eschew surfaces and embrace what Wolfgang Iser refers to as the "dynamic text." As McPherson would have it, readers and writers, lawyers and judges are all the recipients of a virtual text. The failures of resourcefulness we find in his legal fictions are not, I suggest, intended to lead us to disgust or despair, but rather to a deeper realization of the necessities of imagination as it relates to democracy. If the processes which produced the "sacred texts" are, as Ellison observes, flawed, then depicting the law as the ultimate comedy of errors could well be an exercise of faith that "sets the work in motion and so sets [the American] in motion too" (Iser, "Interaction").

Ellison and McPherson issue together, then, a clarion call to Americans to look again at the "incoherent jumble" that we call American culture and to begin to discern the "new stories" to be found within this tangle of intersecting narratives. Further, as Americans negotiate the journey from status to contract, both writers suggest that their rhetorical stance resides in what Michael S. Harper has defined as the "high mode," a space where the "higher frequency" stands for a kinship that resonates across the web of race, class or gender, because it shuns a mythic representation of kinship and embraces the act of "owning" our collective responsibility. In Ellisonian fashion, atrocity and audacity suggest a double meaning: that even as our past shocks us, we are likewise led to search for ways to better the American cultural enterprise. The nexus of law, literature and race may finally demonstrate that "all of it is part of [us]." Thus, even when we speak in error, we speak for each other and the complex fate we share.

Conclusion

1

Though I would like to argue that *A Lesson Before Dying* is Gaines's attempt to revise Book 3 of Wright's *Native Son* (indeed, the texts share important features), what seems to me to be more precise is to argue for the allegorical significance of Gaines's novel as it pertains to the present. What makes this a viable reading is that the replacement of Max with Grant suggests, through their very names, that Gaines's novel is most concerned with issues of audience and apportionment than with issues of cultural exhaustion. Thus we need to understand Grant's opening words in the novel: "I was not there, yet I was there. No, I did not go to the trial, I did not hear the verdict, because I knew all the time what it would be. Still, I was there" (*Lesson,* 3). Grant represents that allegorical figure meant to denote the propensity to distance himself from men like Jefferson. Gaines's decision to set the novel in the 1940s rather than the 1990s is a move that alludes to the prosperity and mobility that flowered during the post-World War II moment. It also refers to the kind of prosperity that, in the 80s, accompanied the dismantling of the social machinery that saw racial solidarity cross class lines. Though Grant is still a victim of discrimination and segregation, his education nonetheless represents the sacrifices of a community. But he sees it as the opportunity to break from that community and claim sole responsibility for his achievement. His desire to leave Bayonne coupled with his resistance to the idea of helping Jefferson, suggests the dangers inherent in the assertion of a fierce individualism that attempts to achieve its ends at the community's expense.

Gaines's novel enacts a difficult moment, one that perhaps leaves us numb. But when Grant cries at the novel's conclusion, we are left with the question, "Who is he crying for?" Himself? The children in his class? Jefferson? Are his tears indicative of loss? Joy? Relief? Adulation? It is important to ask these questions, largely because they point to what seems to me to be a larger question. Throughout this study I have discussed both Gaines's and McPherson's fictions as arguments for a coherent vision of American citizenship, one which eschews racial boundaries and argues for a collective plight. But despite this optimistic outlook, there is yet the squalor in American cities. There is yet racial exclusivity, which has continued in an unbroken line from decades past, and acts of racial violence which demonstrate the continued pervasiveness of racial chauvinism. How is one to explain these contradictions? And in explaining them, how are we to resolve them?

Here I want to bring McPherson back into the discussion and cite an essay recently published in a volume of essays on race and assimilation. In "Junior and John Doe," McPherson talks about the collapse of the African American "value sense," a phenomenon which he traces back to the 1970s:

> It was during the early 1970's that I first began to get a new and curious message from black people. It was then that I first began to hear the word "they" being used in an unfamiliar, self-preempting way, a way that suggested that the pressure of the racial reaction had penetrated and was undermining the value sense, or the private idiom, of black Americans.[1]

McPherson refers to this as the "integration of outside essence into personal idiom," which takes interesting forms, of which he provides examples, first

> from a friend who had achieved early access to a private club habituated by the white upper class. He gave me some advice he had picked up during his rounds: "*They* say it ain't go'n be the way it *was*. *They* say all this bullshit is *over!*" I next heard . . . a black colleague [respond] to my description of the homeless black people whom I had seen on the streets of New York. "Poor devils," this professor of religious studies said. "Well, *they* won't get *me!*" . . . Then there was the black woman who stepped out of the crowd at a reading I gave at the Library of Congress. "They've rewarded you," she whispered to me. "Now why don't you make yourself useful?" ("Junior," 178; emphasis in original)

McPherson's essay attempts to chronicle the collapse of African American irony. As such, he speaks to the loss of a vital resource, that "minefield of ironies" that allowed African Americans to grasp the "cruel joke at the center of the problematic American identity." As Ellison had argued in the 1970s, African Americans called attention, in a manner reminiscent of Twain, to "the distance between asserted ideals and daily practices." The challenge was one of using irony as a way to contain the contradictions so as not to become overwhelmed by them, to retain a handle upon what McPherson referred to as "the provisional nature of American reality [where] at almost any time "black" could be in reality "white" and "white" could be in reality "black."

However, the 1980s and '90s have brought what, in McPherson's view, are radical changes in the African American idiom, and those changes signaled a deeper loss.

> The fundamental challenge of the 1960's and 1970's was to redefine this special quality of relatedness. . . . What was needed during and after the 1960's was a creative synthesis, one that would lift the whole issue of black American and therefore American identity to a higher level of meaning based on commonly shared valued defined by the experiences of *both* groups. What was needed was a revolutionary model of American identity, an imaginative aesthetic and moral foothold established in the future, with little attention paid to race, toward which all Americans might aspire. ("Junior," 179; emphasis in original)

But as McPherson emphatically points out, this did not happen, and because this imaginative aesthetic failed, the "minefield of ironies was very suddenly exhausted." What are we to make of this? And how do McPherson and Gaines represent responses to this condition? Indeed, what are the characteristics of this condition? As McPherson would have it, this condition is marked by the isolation of the black middle class from the masses. Without irony as a resource, there was no way to assert a counter offensive against this by providing "self-affirming communal gestures."[2]

What this demonstrates is the black middle class's abandonment of the vernacular, the act of embracing a sense of commonality with the white world while throwing off ancestral influences. Certainly, some of McPherson's *Elbow Room,* written in the 1970s, anticipated this, which is perhaps best depicted in the story, "A Loaf of Bread." In that story, the author distinguishes between participation and exploitation. When the store owner, Harold Green, opens his store and gives away all the merchandise to the inhabitants of the surrounding black community, he asserts that the solution to the exploitation he has visited upon them (by charging higher prices for goods in that store than in the stores he owns in white neighborhoods) can most easily be redressed by allowing the community to take what they will from the store for free.

The resulting frenzy leaves the store completely depleted of merchandise and in total disarray. However, Nelson Reed, the leader of a community protest against Green, returns to the store and gives the storeowner a dollar for the bread his wife took from the store earlier that morning. Reed's gesture argues for participatory rather than exploitative status. But the clear mandate falls on the side of consumerism and Reed's call for equitable treatment, which would signal his belonging as an American citizen, is nullified by Green's decision to create a transitive opportunity that presents the illusion of equality but not its substance.

In many ways, it seems to me that McPherson is suggesting that the lure of participation in the marketplace as consumers has displaced the communal impulse to achieve coherent citizenship. Hence the we/they dichotomy running through African American civic discourse represents a stalemate of sorts, a move from the ability to select which aspects of the dominant culture were to be assimilated into the African American idiom to a wholesale embrace of consumption which cuts across class lines. Certainly, the strategies for relieving the desire to consume may differ, but what McPherson suggests is that the middle class use of "they" is as dangerous as the weapons attributed to life on the street.

What has concerned me in the years that passed between 1983, when McPherson received the MacArthur Prize Fellowship, and the publication of "Junior and John Doe" in 1993, has been the fact that he published very little in this ten-year period (ironically, Gaines received a MacArthur in 1993). "Junior and John Doe" has value as an essay, then, not only because it treats us to McPherson's special skill in cultural analysis, but also because it explains, at least partially, the reasons for the nearly deafening authorial silence which marks his presence within African American letters. In the last twelve years, McPherson writes, he has put "great distance" between his family and friends, characterizing Iowa as a site of personal exile. The reasons for that exile lay in the fact that, as he saw it in the 1980s, "black Americans had become a thoroughly "integrated" group. The trends of public life had successfully invaded, and had often suppressed, the remnants of our group ethic" ("Junior," 188). Without this group ethic to draw upon as an artistic resource, McPherson has been unable to find that space from which to fashion fictional narrators who can enact the drive toward the cultural synthesis his previous work has demonstrated.

But we must contrast McPherson's personal exile with Gaines's continued participation. Though more than a decade has passed since *A Gathering of Old Men,* Gaines has steadily continued his career as a fiction writer and teacher. What I find most intriguing, however, is that his novel confronts some of the same issues which mark McPherson's silence. This is surely the case when we compare Reverend Ambrose's notion of "lying" with the following assertion from McPherson:

> Our slave ancestors were familiar with this distinction [between integrity and its lack]. Their very lives depended on the ability to distinguish between moral fashions and meaningful actions. They survived by having sufficient vitality of imagination to pass over the present scene, if its currents were not moving in their direction, and identify their meaning with an age that was yet to come. In

> this way, they kept alive the hope of eventually being able to continue moving towards their own goals. In this way a defeated people kept alive a sense of integrity, a sense of self, even if their bodies were bought and sold. During the worst of material times they provided a standard for the best of material times. ("Junior," 190)

Again, what McPherson references is faith, the ability to direct imagination aggressively into the symbolic sphere. And it could well be that McPherson's authorial silence (at least as far as fiction is concerned) has to do with the loss of faith. His kinship with Ernest Gaines springs, it seems to me, from their choice in the 1970s and '80s to embrace the kind of identity politics he attributed to Ellison above. When we juxtapose McPherson's silence against Gaines's return to the literary scene, the results suggest that Gaines has been able to find ways to renew his artistic resources while McPherson has failed to do so or has chosen not to do so.

But this may explain less than it appears to. It would be a mistake to interpret McPherson's essay as an announcement of his disillusionment with Ellisonian ideals. If anything, McPherson's essay memorializes the conditions in which Ellison's ideas flourished and laments that the cultural soil is no longer fertile enough to nourish them. Certainly, more could be made of Gaines's decision to set his novel in the past and not the present. It could well be the case that he can no more see a way to achieve cultural transformation in the present than can McPherson. That said, let me assert my belief that Gaines and McPherson continue to represent an artistic dialogue, if only because Gaines, an older writer, issues a call for the younger McPherson to return, cultural malaise notwithstanding, to the world of letters, to go back to recording our citizenship in black and white. "Junior and John Doe" represents a gesture, albeit a small one, in the direction that Ellison stated in "Perspective of Literature," which is that the writer's function is to yell "Fire!" as loudly as he or she can. Let us hope that such a gesture insures the promise of an increasing volume of work.

But I do think one could safely conjecture that Grant Wiggins, in the 1990s, would be that figure who would rationalize with ease the abandonment of a figure like Jefferson. Grant's behavior most certainly makes a distinction between "I" and "they," but, set in the 1940s, the novel suggests that redemption is possible, the potential for the renewal of one's communal sensibility exists. For Jefferson's diary speaks loudly at novel's end and, in recognizing his own voice inside Jefferson's writing, Grant moves from being the provider of resources to recipient. Viewed allegorically, Gaines's novel forces us to confront the necessity of revitalizing those sites of memory which will, in their turn, renew our sense of community. For it is Grant's wish, also, to enter a state of self-imposed exile where he can indulge his individual whims. That he chooses not to leave Bayonne speaks volumes about the personal sacrifices necessary to achieve a coherent democracy. Part of the sacrifice could be those acts of remembering which can invest the everyday with symbolic import. It is here, perhaps, where we can interpret Grant's tears; they represent an inversion, that moment when loss is simultaneously gain. And this inversion points to what may be the best way to end this discussion. Perhaps Gaines's novel proposes that Ellison's question, "Who knows but that on the lower frequencies I speak for you?" is best considered from a fresh perspective. Perhaps it does not matter at this time whether the question has been asked, but whether the question, when spoken, is heard.

Notes

Preface

1. Genesis 32:24–32.
2. Kenneth L. Karst, *Belonging to America,* 4.
3. James Alan McPherson, "On Becoming an American Writer," 54.
4. Eve Kosofsky Sedgwick, *The Coherence of Gothic Conventions.* Sedgwick makes use of these terms to describe how plot unfolds in gothic fiction. I use them here to characterize the respective forms of hibernation and voicelessness Gaines's protagonists experience. Several terms, such as "live burial" and "unspeakability," have been taken from Sedgwick's study.

Introduction

1. Quoted in James Alan McPherson's essay, "Junior and John Doe," in *Lure and Loathing: Essays on Race, Identity, and the Ambivalence of Assimilation,* 175–76. The interview to which McPherson refers may be part of what became "Indivisible Man," which appeared in the *Atlantic Monthly* in December 1970. Ellison's quote does not appear in that interview, but he makes comments that have a similar ring to those quoted here.
2. James Alan McPherson, interview with Ralph Ellison, "Indivisible Man."
3. Warren's comments are part of Albert Murray's incisive memoir on growing up in the South, *South to a Very Old Place,* 1971; rpt. 32.
4. Ralph Ellison, "What America Would Be Like Without Blacks," *Going to the Territory,* 110–11, 1985.
5. Ellison, "Twentieth Century Fiction and the Black Mask of Humanity," *Shadow and Act,* 26.
6. Werner Sollors, *Beyond Ethnicity,* 6.
7. Ellison, "On Initiation Rites and Power," *Going to the Territory,* 42.
8. Ellison, "Perspective of Literature," *Going to the Territory,* 333.
9. Ibid., 336.
10. Ellison, "The Novel as a Function of American Democracy," *Going to the Territory,* 316.
11. This reading of the novel is so prevalent as to be nearly a cliché; however, what interests me about this reading (one, by the way, I agree with) is its implication that the hero's failure is the result, in part, of his ambition and his

failure to utilize resources adequately. In thinking about the greenhorn, one needs to consider that the original trope of the African American arrivant is driven by that figure's quest for freedom and literacy. Hence, the escaped slave and later the migrant become figures, who desire to "blend in" to their surroundings by mastering the cultural codes of the new culture and doffing the codes of the previous culture. For Frederick Douglass, it meant changing his name from "Bailey" to "Douglass" in order to elude the Fugitive Slave Act. Or, we can think of a figure like Jake in Abraham Cahan's *Yekl,* alongside Charles Johnson's Andrew Hawkins in *Oxherding Tale.* Both characters, albeit for different reasons, want to fit into contingent identities which will allow them to shed old identities. Johnson's novel provides us with a character named Horace Bannon who asserts the underlying premise of the escaped slave which applies equally to the greenhorn:

> In his bones he wants to be able to walk down the street and be unnoticed—not ignored, which means you seen him and looked away, but unnoticed like people who have a right to be somewheres. He wants what them poets hate: mediocrity. A tame, teacup-passin', uneventful lie among the Many. . . . You look for the man who's policin hisself, tryin his level best to be average. (115)

12. Lucius Outlaw, "Language and Consciousness: Toward a Hermeneutic of Black Culture," 403–13.

13. Ibid.

14. Ellison, "The Charlie Christian Story," *Shadow and Act,* 234.

15. Keith Byerman, *Fingering the Jagged Grain,* 1. Byerman's study has usefully informed my efforts to design a conceptual niche for this study. His demonstration of the uses of a "folk aesthetic," in the works of African American writers provides the foundation on which I build toward my own conclusions. As Byerman suggests, Gaines and McPherson clearly write fictions which negotiate a conceptual "middle ground" between the protest arising out of writers who embraced the "Black Aesthetic" and fiction which eschews racial subjects. Certainly, this circumstance has sparked vigorous exchange. Gaines describes, in an interview with Charles Rowell in 1978, the criticisms he endured from other black writers in the 1960s while recapitulating his own position. We have Ellison's response to the Black Aesthetic, which he asserted in his review of McPherson's first collection of stories, *Hue and Cry,* and in an interview with Michael S. Harper and Robert Stepto in 1979 in *Chant of Saints.* Ellison's comments in the former are worth quoting:

> With this collection of stories, McPherson promises to move right past those talented but misguided writers of Negro American background who take being black as a privilege for being obscenely second-rate and who regard their social predicament as Negroes as exempting them from the necessity of mastering the craft and forms of fiction. . . . McPherson's stories are in themselves a hue and cry against the dead, publicity-sustained writing which has come increasingly to stand for what is called "black writing" . . . McPherson is a writer of insight, sympathy, and humor and one of the most gifted young Americans I have had the privilege to read" (*Hue and Cry,* jacket)

And, of course, to go along with all of this we have McPherson's send-up of black nationalism in stories such as "The Silver Bullet" and "Of Cabbages and

Kings." My decision to study Gaines's and McPherson's fictions comes in part from my fascination with their decision to follow in Ellison's path, despite the fact that the artistic tide had moved away from Ellison in the 1960s. By the late 1970s, however, it seems that the critical tide had swung powerfully back in Ellison's direction, as evidenced in both critical and literary production in the 80s and 90s. To understand the positions attributed to the Black Arts Movement, see Abraham Chapman's essay, "Concepts of the Black Aesthetic," in *The Black Writer in Africa and the Americas,* ed. Lloyd W. Brown or Leroi Jones and Larry Neal's groundbreaking anthology, *Black Fire.* The December 1969 issue of *Black World* provides a useful tool for examining the attacks Ellison endured from proponents of the Black Arts Movement (to which he responds in his interview with Harper and Stepto). Worthy of special note in that volume is Larry Neal's brilliant essay, "Ellison's Zoot Suit," which situates Ellison as the most effective of cultural nationalists.

Chapter 1: Relative Politics: The Literary Triumvirate

1. Lucius Outlaw, "Language and Consciousness: Toward a Hermeneutic of Black Culture."

2. Daniel Boorstin makes the point, for example, that Edison was a "social inventor." This means that his skill as an inventor was based, at least in part, on his ability to gauge public need and to provide a marketable product to meet that need. Ellison's choice of Edison, Ford, and Franklin is based on each man's ability to "democratize" material goods and services. On Edison and Ford, see Boorstin, *The Americans: The Democratic Experience.*

3. Boorstin, *The Americans.* This is particularly the case with Edison and Ford, who were not responsible for originating the idea of the light bulb or the automobile. In both instances, they were successful, as Boorstin suggests, at harnessing the power that animates these products so cheaply and efficiently as to allow a large number of people to benefit.

4. Boorstin 528–29.

5. John Wright makes the point, in his very fine essay, "Dedicated Dreamer, Consecrated Acts: Shadowing Ellison," that Ellison's novel functioned "as a laudable counterpoint to the literature of Black Power and Negritude," allowing white literary critics to embrace the novel's "universality," ignoring Ellison's conceptual machinery in order to blunt the "novel's specific angers into an Abstract statement about Man, and at the same time confining the book to the traditional literary ghetto." While there is strong evidence that the novel has wider implications than those afforded by race, what Wright suggests is that Ellison's task was both to portray African American experience and to highlight his concern with American democratic practice. See in particular pp. 144–46.

6. These characters are important because they represent Ellison's adherence to the symbol of the Renaissance man. As Wright asserts, Ellison's "ragtime version [of the Renaissance man] presented a thoroughly modern and palpably black distillation of an enduring human ideal—adaptive, humane, creative, moral, refined, and heroic." Each of the characters embodies this profile. Wright, "Dedicated Dreamer," 164.

7. Wright, "Dedicated Dreamer," 155.

8. Valerie Smith makes this observation in the chapter devoted to Ellison in her book, *Self-Discovery and Authority in African-American Narrative,* 88.

9. The critical approach I implement in this chapter is generated in part by the work of Thomas Kuhn, who asserts that scientific paradigms (and the shifts that produce them) display two characteristics. First, the achievement as sufficiently unprecedented to attract an enduring group of adherents away from competing modes of scientific activity. Simultaneously, it is sufficiently open-ended to leave all sorts of problems for the redefined group of practitioners to resolve. *The Structure of Scientific Revolutions,* 10.

10. Michael S. Harper and Robert B. Stepto, "Study and Experience: An Interview with Ralph Ellison," 461–62.

11. Ellison, "That Same Pain, That Same Pleasure: An Interview," *Shadow and Act,* 16–17.

12. John Henrik Clarke, "The Visible Dimensions of *Invisible Man,*" 30.

13. Wright, "Dedicated Dreamer," 148.

14. Albert Murray, "James Baldwin, Protest Fiction, and the Blues Tradition," *The Omni-Americans,* 148.

15. Ralph Ellison. "The Art of Fiction: An Interview," *Shadow and Act,* 170.

16. While this seems to reenact the old argument about African American writing, namely that it is too parochial for whites to be able to discern "the human odyssey," or that it lacks "universality," consider Henry-Louis Gates's remarks in an essay entitled "Integrating the American Mind." There, Gates uses a highly Ellisonian formulation to assert, "The study of the humanities is the study of the possibilities of human life in culture. It thrives on diversity. And when you get down to cases, it's hard to deny that what you would call the new scholarship has invigorated the traditional disciplines." What makes Gates's argument so compelling is that he calls for a symbiosis that harks back to Ellison's notion of "speaking for" the Other. Gates's essay is found in his volume of essays, *Loose Canons.*

17. Robert B. Stepto, *From Behind the Veil,* 74–75.

18. Murray, "James Baldwin," 151.

19. Ellison, *Invisible Man,* 581.

20. Ellison, "The Novel as a Function of American Democracy," *Going to the Territory,* 318.

21. Ellison, "The Novel," 318.

22. Ellison, "Brave Words for a Startling Occasion," *Shadow and Act,* 104.

23. Robert G. O'Meally. "The Rules of Magic: Hemingway as Ellison's "Ancestor." O'Meally points to Ellison's wranglings with Hemingway as a way of understanding Ellison's "morality of technique," which issues from his sense that writing is a form of symbolic action that "creates reality."

24. Scott Donaldson, *By Force of Will,* 247. Hemingway, as paraphrased by Donaldson, believed that Twain "reclaimed common language and reoriented American writing from the rhetorical to the colloquial."

25. Toni Morrison, *Playing in the Dark,* 84.

26. Ernest Hemingway, "The Battler," *The Short Stories of Ernest Hemingway,* 83.

27. Ellison, "Twentieth Century Fiction and the Black Mask of Humanity," *Shadow and Act* 34–41.

28. For an excellent analysis of the genesis of African American characters, see Sterling A. Brown's ground-breaking essay, "Negro Characters as Seen by White Authors."

29. Ellison. "Society, Morality, and the Novel," *Going to the Territory,* 254.

30. Albert Murray, *Stomping the Blues,* 31.
31. Boorstin, *The Americans,* 527–37, 548–51.
32. Murray, *Stompin the Blues,* 31.
33. Murray, *The Omni-Americans,* 59.
34. Murray, *The Omni-Americans,* 59.
35. Robert B. Stepto, "I Thought I Knew These People: Richard Wright and the Afro-American Literary Tradition," 195.
36. Ellison, "Society, Morality, and the Novel," *Going to the Territory,* 248.
37. Marcia Gaudet and Carl Wooton, *Porch Talk with Ernest Gaines,* 8.
38. This story offers the same catalyst for a plot as the novel *Of Love and Dust.* Both stories originate in Gaines's personal experience, where he remembers:

> an incident where a friend . . . got in a fight . . . and killed a guy. Three guys jumped on him, and he killed one of them. He was sent to prison. He had been working for a white man, and this man could have gotten him out if he wanted to come out, but he said, "I'd rather spend my time because I killed this guy." So, he went to jail; he went to Angola, the state prison of Louisiana, and he spent five years. (Roger Hofheins and Dan Tooker, *Fiction! Interviews with Northern California Novelists,* 89)

39. Even Munford articulates Gaines's awareness of the inadequacy of Faulkner's model of African American endurance which constructs African American humanity in objective terms, and which is acted upon by forces outside it. Faulkner offers black characters who accept endurance as a viable means of confronting the boundaries of racial convention (Lucas Beauchamp is an example); inevitably they exist in stasis, and meaning is conferred on their existence by whites.
40. As I will discuss in Chapter 6, the legal community has been instrumental in codifying this state of affairs. Here it will suffice to assert that Gaines's concern with surfaces anticipates James Alan McPherson's examination of the nexus of legal discourse, race, and reading.
41. Murray, *The Omni-Americans,* 59.
42. Hattie is intended, in part, to represent the manner in which African American men can be totally emasculated. While Munford's view seems to be ascendant, I have chosen to read Hattie's "femininity" as another form of masculinity. Moreover, Munford, by virtue of the "proposition" he extends to Hattie, is by no means himself the symbol of a "conventional" form of masculinity. I would assert that Gaines avoids the creation of fixed categories here, choosing instead to create looser, more fluid ones.
43. Though Munford makes disparaging references to Hattie, it is clear that Procter incorporates aspects of the latter's masculinity into his own sensibility. My thanks to Jeanine DeLombard, whose graduate seminar essay on Gaines's homosexual characters brought this aspect of the story to my attention.
44. Hofheins and Tooker, *Fiction!* 97.
45. James Alan McPherson, "On Becoming an American Writer," 56.
46. The Tourgee brief is essential to acquire a sense of how McPherson's fictional enterprise was shaped by his Harvard Law School experience. Indeed, McPherson describes it as "a beautiful piece of literature." This is an important detail, for it suggests that McPherson viewed his legal training as a means by

which to develop the appropriate level of seriousness necessary to carry out his authorial vision. The law is a conceptual site, then, not a professional one. Consider Tourgee's brief in this regard:

> This provision of Section I of the Fourteenth Amendment *creates a new* citizenship of the United States embracing *new* rights, privileges and immunities derivable in a *new* manner, controlled by *new* authority, having a *new* scope and extent, depending on national authority for its existence and looking to national power for its preservation (emphasis in original)

What McPherson proposes, as his selection from the Tourgee brief implies, is that the Fourteenth Amendment remade American citizenship, not only for African Americans, but white Americans as well. In his view, the derivative quality of American culture moves from its quasi-legal status to one that is foregrounded in the Constitution itself. What such a moment represents is a paradigm shift of the first order (57).

47. Reading, as McPherson conceives it, has as much to do with "telling off" the reader who would adhere to a conventional notion of American culture as it does with assertions of a conventional literacy. In an essay entitled "Distrust of the Reader in Afro-American Narratives," Robert Stepto observes that "Afro-American literature has developed as much because of the culture's distrust of literacy as because of its abiding faith in it." What this suggests is that McPherson's fiction often attempts to trap its readers in a place of such low narrator reliability that they get ensnared inside the text, and only by enacting a counter-reading to the narrator's "reading" of events can they get out again.

48. Irving Howe, "Mass Society and Postmodern Fiction," 30.

49. James Alan McPherson, "Widows and Orphans," *Elbow Room,* 162.

50. McPherson, "On Becoming an American Writer," 55.

51. Ellison, "The Novel," 318.

52. Dell Hymes, *"In vain I tried to tell you."*

Chapter 2: The Possible in Things Unwritten

1. Marcia Gaudet and Carl D. Wooten. "Conversation with Ernest J. Gaines."

2. James Alan McPherson, "On Becoming an American Writer," 56.

3. Keith Byerman, *Fingering the Jagged Grain,* 41. I would narrow Byerman's assertion here to insist that each generation of African American *male* writers exhibits this need to "deny the father." Indeed, after the resurrection of Zora Neale Hurston's work in the late 1960s, one finds many African American women writers, like Alice Walker, Toni Morrison, Gloria Naylor, and Jamaica Kincaid, claiming a literary ancestry to other African American woman writers. The literary criticism on African American women's literature further traces these linkages. For example, Marjorie Pryse's and Hortense Spillers's fine collection of essays, *Conjuring,* works out many of the ancestral connections between African American women writers.

4. We could refer here to Kuhn's notion of "normal science." Within this concept Kuhn asserts that the task of illuminating the still-dark corridors of a new paradigm falls on the women and men who follow in the footsteps of innovation. Gaines's and McPherson's literary practice, their attempts to move

forward from Ellison, calls for them to signal the parameters of their literary enterprise by reenacting the "break" which enables Ellison's literary inquiry.

5. Ralph Ellison, *Invisible Man,* 156.

6. Gaudet and Wooten, "Conversation," 231.

7. What is particularly striking is that Gaines cites immigrant groups who, like him, are coming to voice as "new" Americans. Their exchange not only occurs across boundaries of nationality, but also dramatizes the cultural exchanges that render America as an ever-evolving instance.

8. Ralph Ellison, "The World and the Jug," *Shadow and Act,* 137.

9. Of the three, McPherson's evocation of the folk community is closest to that of Zora Neale Hurston, who grew up in all-black Eatonville, Florida. Like Hurston's town, McPherson's folk community does not suffer from the ill effects of segregation. Indeed, that aspect of folk experience is "edited" out of folk utterance. Thus, like Hurston's *Mules and Men,* McPherson's essay dismantles the South as a horrific space and reconstructs it as a preparatory one, where he is nurtured into a state of eloquence.

10. Hayden White, "The Literary Form of History," 41.

11. I offer a fuller treatment of that scene in Chapter 4.

12. See my essay entitled, "I Yam What You Is and You Is What I Yam: Rhetorical Invisibility in James A. McPherson's 'The Story of a Dead Man.'"

13. James H. Kavanaugh, "Benito Cereno and the Liberal Hero," 357. Kavanaugh uses Althusser's definition of internal distanciation with regard to Melville's novella, arguing that it "require[s] us, through its principal character, 'to perceive' . . . from the inside, by an internal distance, the ideology in which it is held." This observation is a useful description of the technique McPherson uses to create narrative tension in his stories, and it likewise argues that Melville's story offers a technical innovation he deploys in many of his stories.

14. Ellison, Interview with Steve Cannon, Ralph Ellison, Lennox Raphael, and James Thompson, "A Very Stern Discipline," *Going to the Territory.* This quote is drawn from an interview Ellison revised from the original tapes. The point he makes is an important one: he articulates intra-racial tension around notions of cultural identity that are informed by one (Northern) geographical experience. This experience encodes "culture" as the product, not of the interaction of groups, but of certain forms of exposure and mobility, unavailable, given the prohibitive nature of Jim Crow racism, to Southern blacks.

15. John Wright. "Shadowing Ellison," *Speaking for You,* 79. This essay is an abridged version of Wright's longer essay, which appeared in *Carleton Miscellany* under the title, "Dedicated Dreamer, Consecrated Acts: Shadowing Ellison."

Chapter 3: Tilling the Soil to Find Ourselves

1. Some of the fictions that fall into this category would be Ann Petry's *The Street,* David Bradley's *The Chaneysville Incident,* Alice Walker's *The Color Purple,* Paule Marshall's *Praisesong for the Widow,* and various short stories by James Alan McPherson.

2. This essay builds on the work done by Craig Werner in a 1982 essay entitled "Tell Old Pharaoh: The Afro-American Response to Faulkner." It

seems to me that my discussion of Gaines's protagonist pursues a pattern which Faulkner's protagonists (one thinks here of Quentin Compson and Ike McCaslin), through gestures that privilege the past in their lives, elect not to follow.

3. This is a point Keith Byerman makes in the chapter he devotes to Gaines's fiction in his fine study, *Fingering the Jagged Grain,* 67. As Byerman suggests, African American protagonists must often balance the impulse to pursue individual ends against those of the community in what he terms a "negotiation."

4. Michael S. Harper coins the term "collective-I" in his liner notes for the album John Coltrane. Ellison's remarks can be found in his essay, "The Charlie Christian Story," in *Shadow and Act.*

5. In that respect, we might consider how "bad man" tales function. On one hand, they articulate the outrageous as a way of suggesting the necessity of resistance; on the other, they mark off what is acceptable behavior.

6. Houston Baker, "To Move Without Moving: Creativity and Commerce in Ralph Ellison's Trueblood Episode," 342.

7. African American literature often presents the dilemma that arises when protagonists want to discard necessary parts of their pasts in order to move more "efficiently" into or within the mainstream. What becomes the problem, however, is that the "flotsam" they wish to jettison is exactly that equipment they need to survive. While some protagonists spend the duration of the narrative searching for that which is lost in order to replace it, others, like many of McPherson's characters, display the behavior resulting from the process of discarding necessary personal resources.

8. Sherley Anne Williams, *Give Birth to Brightness,* 169.

9. John O'Brien, *Interviews with Black Writers.*

10. Ernest J. Gaines, *Of Love and Dust.*

11. Ralph Ellison, "Richard Wright's Blues," *Shadow and Act* (1972), 78.

12. Sherley Anne Williams, "The Blues Roots of Contemporary Afro-American Poetry," 125.

13. The language I use here is consciously drawn from Thomas Kuhn.

14. Berndt Ostendorf, *Black Literature in White America.* While I find Ostendorf's analysis to be one which clarifies the nature of Marcus's plight, it is also important to note how closely Marcus resembles the "badman" examined in Chapter 5 of John Roberts's fine study of the folk hero in African American expressive culture, *From Trickster to Badman.* In the instance of Marcus, I would argue that the novel's plot revolves around the way that Marcus moves, at least in Jim's estimation, from "bad nigger" to "badman." Marcus's actions are perceived as being self-serving at the community's expense, but in fact, his actions (set in the 1940s) are the paradigm for the kinds of resistance that will later characterize the Civil Rights (and later, Black Nationalist) movement in the 1960s. In this regard, we can consider characters like Marcus and Toni Morrison's Sula as figures who articulate a new design for African American identity. Their problem is that there is no place for them because the social conditions do not yet exist to absorb their uniqueness.

15. As Keith Byerman has observed, open resistance in Gaines's fiction is often punished by death. *Fingering the Jagged Grain,* 67.

16. This is a theme that Gaines first explored in his collection of stories entitled *Bloodline.* In the story "Three Men," as I discussed in the previous chapter, Gaines creates a character named Procter Lewis who chooses to remain in jail rather than being bonded out after killing a man. Gaines noted in

an interview with John O'Brien that, "I should point out that Procter Lewis and Marcus Payne are the same character; I wanted to show what would have happened to Procter Lewis had he gotten out of prison, the chances he would have taken to attain his freedom" (O'Brien, *Interviews with Black Writers,* 81). What this suggests is that Gaines is interested in the forces acting on black manhood as well as the forms black resistance assumes "when young blacks stand up against the establishment."

17. In this regard, Marcus is literary kin to Morrison's Sula, whom Morrison describes as having an "experimental life," and who "lacking an art form," becomes dangerous to the Bottom because there is nothing to engage her rebellious individualism. Like Sula, Marcus represents a revolutionary figure whose premature arrival makes him useful as a martyr, but not as a leader. Lacking Jim's communal-mindedness, Marcus's behavior is self-oriented and so he is incapable of assuming the leadership necessary to topple the plantation system as a whole.

18. Patricia Waugh, *Metafiction.* Waugh defines the self-begetting novel as "an account, usually first-person, of the development of a character to a point at which he is able to take up and compose the novel we have just finished reading." From this perspective, Jim is "invisible" and his narrative is a sign of his burgeoning self-awareness.

19. I make this assertion largely because Gaines's observation about Nick Carraway intimates that his novel, like *The Great Gatsby,* is finally about Jim's utility as a gauge of the other characters' moral landscapes. Moreover, both characters "narrate" their tales from a distance: Carraway ostensibly "writes" his memoirs, Jim's comes in the form of an oral narrative.

20. Wayne Booth, *The Rhetoric of Fiction,* 159–60.

21. Credit for the word "re-vision" goes, of course, to Adrienne Rich.

22. It could be argued that Hebert's letter of recommendation is a form of written history, one that severely truncates an articulation of the events surrounding Marcus's death. Jim's refusal to accept the letter is, then, a refusal to accept this version of history. Not only does the letter replace veracity with silence, but its function recapitulates the tripartite relationship among work, memory, and voicelessness. To use the letter would mean that Jim's ability to work was tied to his agreement not to talk about what happened. In short, Gaines suggests, the commitment to written forms of history often means that one makes a contractual arrangement to mute the reverberation of the past.

23. One thinks here of Reverend Jameson in *A Gathering of Old Men,* and the preacher in the story "The Sky Is Grey." In both characters, we can see that Gaines's intent is to suggest that it is not spirituality, as Miss Jane displays it, that is problematic, but rather, organized religion. For it is there that the individual conforms to codes that often inhibit the necessity to assume a confrontational posture. Thus the idea of "turning the other cheek" is meaningless until it is situated within a confrontational posture, which is signaled, first, by the young man in "The Sky Is Grey" and later in Phillip Martin.

24. Ralph Ellison, "That Same Pain, That Same Pleasure" (interview with Richard G. Stern), *Shadow and Act,* 18.

25. Gaudet and Wooten, "Conversation with Ernest J. Gaines," 59.

26. Byerman, *Fingering the Jagged Grain,* 95.

27. Ernest J. Gaines, *In My Father's House* 72.

28. Michael G. Cooke, *Afro-American Literature in the Twentieth Century,* x.

29. Byerman, *Fingering the Jagged Grain,* 95.

30. Gaudet and Wooten, "Conversation," 59.

31. David O'Rourke, O.P., "The Experience of Conversion," 8–9.

32. The paradigm that informs African American political struggle in the United States seems to be one which constructs leadership around the metonymic construct of the Hebrews' flight from Egypt. This calls for African American leaders to cast themselves in the role of Moses. Though Moses is indeed flawed—symbolized by the fact that he is a stutterer—his authority issues from the fact that he sees and talks to God. This translates, in secular terms, into a man beyond reproach, who stands as law-giver. However, I submit that African Americans like Martin Luther King, despite any rhetoric to the contrary, are much more in keeping with the figure of David, whose special status is mediated against the turmoil in his house and his inability to control his passions. Unlike Moses, who is clearly a liminal figure, David rules but not without adversity. Though my conversations with Crystal Jones Lucky have recently illuminated Moses, as a figure of passion, I adhere to David, largely because the latter succumbs to erotic passion, working out his emotions within an intimate, as opposed to public, sphere.

33. This is assuming, of course, that Phillip has used the same strategies of non-violent resistance in Louisiana that King used in Alabama.

34. Here, I am drawing on Mary Schmidt Campbell's comments in her introductory essay on Romare Bearden's work, collected in the retrospective *Memory and Metaphor: The Art of Romare Bearden, 1940–1970.* Schmidt's comments as well as those by Sharon F. Patton have helped me to chart a critical course in this portion of my analysis.

35. One need only examine William McFeeley's Pulitzer Prize-winning biography of Douglass to see that he "retained . . . wariness" where President Lincoln was concerned. Though the two were able to forge a working relationship, Douglass was clearly intent on supporting "a man of more decided antislavery conviction" than Lincoln during the latter's re-election bid, and McFeeley also points out that Lincoln "sought almost no counsel from his black constituents" as it pertained to post-Civil-War issues facing freedmen. William S. McFeeley, *Frederick Douglass,* 229–30, 234, 235.

36. While Gaines would claim that he is a better writer in the first person, where the character "takes over," I submit that in those novels where he uses the third person omniscient narrator, the protagonists' quest is to improve their aural skills rather than their oral skills. Neither Jackson Bradley nor Phillip Martin experiences a loss of voice in the literal sense. But because they fail to exercise their voices within the context of a larger design, their search for identity is characterized by violent scenarios that create space for the act of listening. Jackson's violent confrontation with Raoul Carmier in *Catherine Carmier* (which I discuss in Chapter 5) would bear this notion out; he cannot join the disparate elements of his own story until he realizes that his story is part of other stories as well. He is incapable of rendering his own story, partly due to the novel's form: it is a chronologically rendered narrative that utilizes flashbacks sparingly. Were the novel a framed tale, where flashback comprised the bulk of the action, Phillip could tell the tale because he would understand the past's impact on the present. That Phillip must find Chippo to tell him the missing parts of his own story points to Gaines's growth as a writer, his greater facility in the use of storytelling as a dramatic tool. It also suggests an instance when we see a man who is self-reliant eschew such a posture in order to rely on the resources of someone else.

37. This is often a subtext in Gaines's work: the attempt to discover one's manhood by violent means is often the height of folly. While his male protagonists do not shrink from violent confrontation, inevitably they must find other means (in a region where violence and order are so closely related) to sustain their manhood. Women are often martyred (at least symbolically) in what is, finally, a male search for dignity and freedom. While there is the assumption that women are lacking in neither wisdom nor dignity, inevitably their desires are sacrificed for the benefit of men.

38. In this we find him to be literary kin to Richard Wright's Dan Taylor in the short story, "Fire and Cloud." Indeed this novel and Wright's story bear strong affinities. Wright's "Fire and Cloud" can be summarized as a tale concerned with the protagonists' resurrection from social death into the realm of communal agency. Thus the anxiety of influence generated by Wright's story has to be considered here. For the story's conclusion posits a paradigm of leadership that had not been seen in African American literature, namely, a self-effacing leadership that stands as a metaphor for community. The role of leaders, the story suggests, is secondary; it is the people who must form the apex of resistance. At the end of "Fire and Cloud," Dan Taylor's location at the back of the demonstration is an important motif: he represents Wright's sense that if leadership manifests a public persona at all that persona must be generated, not in solitude, but in a collectivity. The story has perhaps its most apparent affinity to Gaines's novel in that both propose that leadership must be flexible, able to adjust to the needs of the people rather than adhering to old tactics.

39. What I am suggesting here is that the implementation of Jim Crow laws, coming as they did out of the notion of white supremacy, represented the South's need to depict itself as a geographical site that honored the past, even as it attempted to modernize its workings. Indeed, as numerous commentators have argued, the South's policy of racial segregation issued from its attempt to ape Northern racial patterns. The fervor that accompanied the desire to preserve Jim Crow is analogous to O'Rourke's observation of a simplistic view of conversion, which finds the convert locked into an attempt to preserve the experience in binary terms (e.g., one is either "saved" or not saved) rather than as an evolving process that is on-going.

40. Charles H. Rowell, "This Louisiana Thing That Drives Me: An Interview with Ernest J. Gaines."

Chapter 4: "If It's Going To Be Any Good"

1. This is the mental institution where Ezra Pound was treated, a fact that Elizabeth Bishop explores in her poem, "Visit to St. Elizabeth's."

2. As Ralph Ellison has asserted in numerous instances, writing exemplifies the mastery of experience through art. The term "tribal literacy" is borrowed from Robert Stepto, who uses it to describe a communal energy that "ameliorate[s] . . . the conditions imposed by solitude." See Stepto, *From Behind the Veil,* 167.

3. Houston Baker, *Blues, Ideology, and Afro-American Literature.*

4. As numerous commentators on the African American sermon have argued, the sermon represents an instance in expressive culture where textuality and orality operate in a creative symbiosis; the African American preacher can

meld a "text" (drawn from the Scriptures) with acts of storytelling that lead to the "message."

5. James Alan McPherson, "A Solo Song: For Doc," *Hue and Cry.*

6. Ralph Ellison, "The Charlie Christian Story," *Shadow and Act,* 234.

7. Michael S. Harper, Larry Kart, and Al Young, "Jazz and Letters: A Colloquy," 133.

8. Kenneth Burke, *The Omni-Americans,* 55.

9. Keith Byerman, *Fingering the Jagged Grain,* 48.

10. Isidore Okpewho, *The Epic in Africa: Toward a Poetics of the Oral Performance,* 32–33. While Okpewho's scholarly concern is with African oral performance as it crystallizes into the epic form, his comments are useful here in a consideration of the fact that, in examining the manner in which McPherson's narrator tells Doc's story, we can discern that the story has been told and retold, a point emphasized in the story on several occasions. Thus, in keeping with Okpewho's point, we need to do more than "admire the [story's representation of] verbal excellence but indeed . . . glean the circumstances that [lead] to its being repeated so many times."

11. Robert Pelton, *The Trickster in West Africa,* 15.

12. By this I mean that the waiter exhibits a form of doubleness that relies, as with all tricksters, on the status quo. See Pelton, *The Trickster in West Africa,* 35.

13. The youngblood has entered into what Victor Turner would refer to as liminality. Within the ritual process, the individual undergoes three distinct phases: separation, liminality, and aggregation. By invalidating the authority of the big, black book, the old waiter has separated the youngblood from all he knows. And by enticing him toward his story of the Old School, the old waiter has brought the youngblood into the realm of liminality, where he is marginal, between ignorance and knowing, law and lawlessness. The waiter pushes the youngblood into the narrative, even as the book pulls against him.

14. See Byerman's reading of "A Solo Song: For Doc," *Fingering the Jagged Grain* 47–51.

15. Hawkins's observation can be found in Nat Hentoff's book, *The Jazz Life,* 46–47.

16. Bill Crow, *Jazz Anecdotes,* 97–98. Crow includes anecdotes by trumpeter Roy Eldridge, who relates an instance where fellow trumpeter, Rex Stewart cut him. . . . "he jumped in and caught my ass. Hit a B-flat, and I ain't never heard a B-flat that high and that loud and that big, in my life! . . . I took my horn and put it in the case. I told the cats, 'You can't play as high as him. Might as well give it up!' I had tears in my eyes." Eldridge's response to Stewart's "call" was to go home and figure out a technique for making B-flat part of his "natural range." What is interesting is that Eldridge begins his story with the fact that he wanted to be like Stewart, and that the older trumpeter had "showed [him] some of [his] first riffs."

17. Ishmael Reed, *Conjure: Selected Poems, 1963–1970,* 50.

18. Walter Benjamin, "The Storyteller," *Illuminations,* 91.

19. Ibid.

20. The poststructuralist revolution might consider such a notion specious, given the fact that what we refer to as "history" or even "experience" is a socially constructed concept. But I would argue that this fiction is invested in the idea of maintaining, if only for a moment, a dichotomy between the world of fiction and the material world.

21. Consider the contents of Ellison's preface to the Thirtieth Anniversary edition of *Invisible Man,* where he mentions the various occupations he held to support his attempt to write fiction. What comes through very clearly is Ellison's ability to transform "everyday" events into the stuff of fiction. Hence, as his interview with Harper and Stepto in *Chant of Saints* suggests, one cannot become a writer through reading alone, one also needs other resources that can only be found in the world. I would argue that McPherson's story attempts to operationalize that notion.

22. Gerard Prince, "Introduction to the Study of the Narratee," 23.

23. McPherson, "On Becoming an American Writer," 55.

24. In many ways, this fiction anticipates Toni Morrison's excellent *Playing in the Dark: Whiteness and the Literary Imagination.*

25. The autobiographical resonances of this fiction likewise underscore McPherson's epic intent. In "On Becoming an American Writer," he talks about his experiences as a waiter working on the trains running from Chicago to the Pacific Northwest, the same route that the train in the story follows. Moreover, that McPherson has a law degree from Harvard also argues that he did, indeed, evolve into someone who heeds the old waiter's charge: that of knowing the difference between law and history.

Chapter 5: Voices from the Underground

1. As Richard Gray points out in *The Literature of Memory,* as part of the "Southern renaissance," writers like Faulkner, Robert Penn Warren, and Thomas Wolfe sought to "examine their regional environment, the American South, [as a way] of acknowledging the death of its traditional way of life, based on the small farm and the great plantation, and recognizing its absorption into the strange new world of industrialism and advanced capitalism" (5).

2. On this point, Michel Fabre observes:

> Faulkner's shadow more than ever since his death hovers over every American writer who writes about the South. This is perhaps more true for the black novelist because Faulkner spoke of his people with so much depth at times and often with so much compassion that his racial myths are the most indestructible ("Bayonne, or the Toknapatawpha of Ernest Gaines," 110).

3. Ralph Ellison, "Twentieth Century Fiction and the Black Mask of Humanity," *Shadow and Act,* 42.

4. One thinks here of numerous examples in African American writing, where the brutality of Southern life comes to the fore: Arna Bontemps's "A Summer Tragedy," James Baldwin's "Going to Meet the Man," Jean Toomer's "Blood Burning Moon" (in *Cane*), and Alice Walker's "The Flowers" (in *In Love and Trouble*) and her novel *Meridian.* And as Jerry Ward asserts in his foreword to the anthology, *Black Southern Writing,* the brutality of the South, as a bastion of white supremacy, led to the crystallization of literary genres via the force of folklore. The historical agency exerted by African American slaves and their descendants comes to us through the storytelling medium (Killens and Ward, *Black Southern Voices* 5–9).

5. Craig Werner, "Tell Old Pharoah: The Afro-American Response to Faulkner."

6. As I observed in Chapter 3, Gaines notes Faulkner's observation that "past ain't dead, it ain't even passed."

7. Ernest J. Gaines, "Miss Jane and I," 34.

8. What this reflects is the impulse one sees running through a great deal of writing and rhetoric by Southerners both black and white. One finds it at the end of Wright's *Black Boy,* in the polemical stance adopted by the Agrarians in the 1920s and in Martin Luther King's posture as a Civil Rights leader. That impulse posits the South as that space most essential in the formulation of a viable form of American citizenship. If it is a region so heavily marked by contradiction, then it is also that space where redemption and healing will have the most resonant effect. The South is that place where, for better or worse, national guilt (regarding slavery) is located and so it is there we look to see if the South has "progressed" to a point where that guilt can be expiated. It is also important to point out that Gaines's admiration for the Russian masters—Turgenev, Chekhov, and Dostoevsky—stems from their ability to create a national literature by depicting the folk. See Marcia Gaudet and Carl Wooten, *Porch Talk with Ernest Gaines,* 79.

9. Gaudet and Wooten, *Porch Talk with Ernest Gaines,* 15.

10. Robert B. Stepto, *From Behind the Veil: A Study of Afro-American Narrative,* 167.

11. Fabre, "Bayonne," 115–16. By "integrity" I mean not only moral soundness, but the ability to constitute a coherent sense of self; to avoid the fragmentation of being, by virtue of one's ability to acquire and utilize adequate resources.

12. Keith Byerman, *Fingering the Jagged Grain,* 67.

13. John F. Callahan, *In the African-American Grain,* 194.

14. Ernest J. Gaines, *Catherine Carmier.*

15. Robert B. Stepto, "Distrust of the Reader in Afro-American Narrative," 301.

16. Consider the examples we find, for instance, in Frederick Douglass's *Narrative of the Life of Frederick Douglass, An American Slave,* where he writes, "I would at times feel that learning to read had been a curse rather than a blessing. It had given me a view of my wretched condition without the remedy. . . . In moments of agony, I envied my fellow slaves their stupidity." W. E. B. DuBois's *The Souls of Black Folk* offers us "The Coming of John." Here the hero acquires literacy at the same time as he confronts the limitations generated by the Veil. John returns to the South, to the town he grew up in, but his newly acquired knowledge makes him uncomfortable there because he "notices the oppression that had not seemed oppression before." Black and white alike see him as an outsider—either as enigma or threat.

17. Stepto first describes the immersion narrative in Chapter 3 of *From Behind the Veil.*

18. Consider, for example, the manner in which the fetishization of land comes through in a book like Twelve Southerners, *I'll Take My Stand,* which offers the agrarian lifestyle as the paradigmatic form of civilization. Moreover, consider Faulkner's "The Bear": its construction of land as an inviolable resource that, when commodified, situates repudiation and nullification as the only viable options in a world cursed by the illusion of ownership. Also, one has to see the Snopes clan as an anti-heroic force, largely because the havoc they wreak stems from their manipulation of land and law.

19. In that its literary origins coincide with the need to restore Southern

male potency after the defeat in the Civil War, the plantation romance, even in the distorted, corrupted form Faulkner presents, has negative implications for the African American characters who inhabit that world.

20. Oates's biography does, in fact, portray Faulkner's decision to "condemn the curse of segregation," however that attitude is tempered by his fear of governmental intervention and the possibility of another Civil War—and thus the South's destruction. His attitudes toward "forced integration" intimated more than a little paternalism and nostalgia for his "native land." Though he felt "southern whites were wrong, their position unsupportable," ultimately his larger concern was one of not wanting to see the South "invaded." See Stephen B. Oates, *Faulkner: The Man and the Artist,* 288–93.

21. Though Grover does not make an appearance in this novel, I would strongly contend that his presence is always taken into account by the characters. Moreover, if one wants to understand how plantation owners function, see Marshall Hebert in Gaines's *Of Love and Dust* (discussed in Chapter 3) or Frank Laurent in Gaines's short story, "Bloodline." In both these fictions, Gaines depicts the plantation in the context of the decline of the plantation system as a whole. Their ill-health and drunkenness symbolize the corruption inherent in the system—as well as its imminent collapse.

22. As Craig Werner points out, Rider is the focal point for "the limits of white perception of and sympathy for blacks." The narrative the deputy relates is meant ironically: to calculate the gulf between white and black and also to dramatize the necessity to read more deeply into human motivation. Werner, "Tell Old Pharaoh," 718.

23. It is not my purpose here to suggest that *Catherine Carmier* ends happily. Rather, what I propose is that this illusion of functionality, coupled with the "defeated patriarch," anticipates the work Gaines does with Phillip Martin in *In My Father's House,* where the defeat opens an avenue toward self-recovery.

24. John O'Brien, *Interviews with Black Writers,* 88.

25. Ralph Ellison, "The World and the Jug," *Shadow and Act,* 140. Ellison's characterization of Hemingway's fiction is a useful way to understand the blues' efficacy in the quest for a syncretic posture. "Because all that he wrote . . . was imbued with a spirit beyond the tragic with which I could feel at home, for it was very close to the feeling of the blues, which are, perhaps, as close as Americans can come to expressing the spirit of tragedy." Ellison appropriates Hemingway into a blues matrix that allows him to supersede the criticisms that he levels at Hemingway in "Twentieth Century Fiction and the Black Mask of Humanity" (*Shadow and Act*). Here, Hemingway becomes a viable source upon which Black writers can draw. As such, Gaines is able to comment that Hemingway is an important role model. Thus, he observes in an interview with Roger Hofheins, "I admire Hemingway because of this grace under pressure thing [in his fiction] which, I think, is more accurate of the black man in this country than the white man. Hemingway, without knowing it, without a lot of younger blacks realizing it, was writing as much about Joe Louis or Jackie Robinson as he was about any white man." Roger Hofheins and Dan Tooker, *Fiction! Interviews with Northern California Novelists,* 97.

26. Ernest J. Gaines, *The Autobiography of Miss Jane Pittman.*

27. Gaines's "preface" is a structural device that forces any literary interventions into the novel's plot to acknowledge, if only by implication, the fact that a "folktale" is always already situated in a very different cultural context from literature. African American folklore theory suggests that stories are often

generated with pedagogical intent, which means that stories are not told for telling's sake. As the "preface" relates, Miss Jane (and the other voices that narrate her tale) eschews both linearity and circularity to tell her story. Hence, Gaines's novel signifies on the necessity to order and shape narrative into neatly formulated products.

28. In the Pre-Civil Rights Movement epoch, old age was the closest that African Americans could get to a sense of belonging and recognition. This came, of course, in the form of the title, "uncle" or "auntie." These would seem to be the signs of entitlement, an instance where African American women and men are granted control over their lives by Southern patriarchs (who have often been raised by them), who nonetheless expect them to adhere to the norms established by Jim Crow.

29. Certainly Faulkner's Lucas Beauchamp and Eudora Welty's Phoenix Jackson represent characters who have skills in negotiation and who also represent courage and endurance. But their talents accrue within the system of Jim Crow, which they are often able to manipulate to their own ends but which finally occludes their humanity. Miss Jane represents a paradigmatic shift in this regard.

30. This choice is also made significant because Douglass's autobiography represents an Urtext around the issue of African American literacy and participation in the body politic.

31. For though Ike relinquishes his claim to all property, he never moves beyond a static configuration of black and white. Thus he cannot conceptualize another reality, he merely abdicates participation in the present. When Roth Edmonds's black mistress appears with her son, Ike's response reflects Faulkner's ambiguous attitude, "We will have to wait," he tells her. And what this suggests is Ike's inability to substantialize the future; for all his purported moral agency, he wants to hold the question of black humanity at bay. It possesses limited material substance.

32. Both Joseph Campbell in *The Hero with a Thousand Faces* and Lord Raglan in *The Hero* would suggest that Jimmy's birth, its mysterious circumstances, is the beginning of the heroic cycle. Moreover, as the one "who helped him into this world" (*Miss Jane,* 200), Jane is his spiritual guide, which Campbell suggests is an important role to play in the life of the hero.

33. I agree with Byerman's assertion, *Fingering the Jagged Grain,* 75–76, that Amy manipulates Eddie and confers her idea of manhood on him, rather than allowing him to be autonomous.

34. While this may have the tone of "blaming the victim," what I am trying to assert is that the end of "A Long Day in November" is ironic at best. To read this story as a tale of domestic bliss achieved is likewise to endorse domestic violence as a sign of order and patriarchal culture as the norm. Thus Madame Toussaint's observation that the house is Amy's "world" is questionable, particularly when one considers that Gaines offers numerous examples of women who work in the fields. Amy and her mother, having internalized the conventions of a racist patriarchy, view upward mobility as how closely the black domestic space can mirror its white counterpart. Because this story is so strongly oriented toward the issue of achieving manhood, Amy's beating suggests, finally, that the plantation renders the issue moot.

35. We might also think of Toni Morrison's *Sula* here, where an African American woman creates a narrative where the "return to the womb" is deconstructed as a male prerogative. Eva's act of burning her own son, Plum,

revises this moment and suggests that hibernation, as a site of exhaustion, is finally limiting for women. Morrison's novel can be seen as her act of loosing African American women's stories from this narrative impulse.

36. Ernest J. Gaines, *A Gathering of Old Men*, 48.

37. This is significant, largely because African American men throughout the South were denied this status: they could move from "boy" to "uncle" in the social hierarchy, but this was often the case when they did not challenge the status quo.

38. Victor Turner, "Carnaval in Rio: Dionysian Drama in an Industrializing Society," *Anthropology of Performance,* 123.

39. While this obviously should not be pushed too far, Gaines suggests that sports at least offers a symbolic arena in which African American citizenship in the South is made viable.

40. Again, this could be a "riff" on Gaines's part. As an aristocrat, Faulkner's ambivalence towards blacks was evidenced by his unwillingness to support integration, even as he created characters like Lucas Beauchamp. Mathu's courage and stoicism recall Beauchamp, but the novel's class issues suggest he is a victim of Candy's class bias.

41. This constitutes a revision of Faulkner: unlike Ike McCaslin who repudiates his inheritance, Gil's unwillingness to participate in mob violence leads to a "break" in the family where he is rendered invisible against his wishes.

42. This is also indicative of the symbolic confrontation between Faulkner and Gaines, due to the fact that the former resided in Oxford, Mississippi where the university is located.

43. Ernest J. Gaines, *A Lesson Before Dying,* 7.

44. For a full explication of this notion see John S. Mbiti, *African Religions and Philosophy.*

Chapter 6: "The Life of the Law"

1. Ralph Ellison, "Perspective of Literature," *Going to the Territory,* 321.

2. On this matter Ellison asserts that in "our time the most articulate art form for defining ourselves and for asserting our humanity is the novel." Cf. "Society, Morality, and the Novel," *Going to the Territory,* 248.

3. James Boyd White, *Heracles' Bow: Essays on the Rhetoric and Poetics of the Law,* x–xi.

4. The play deals with the attempt by Odysseus and Neoptolemus, the son of Achilles, to obtain Heracles's bow from Philoctetes. The oracle has informed them that the Greeks will not defeat the Trojans without Philoctetes and his bow. However, a snake bite has left Philoctetes with a wound whose stench leads his fellow Greeks to maroon him on the island of Lemnos. Odysseus comes up with a plan for Neoptolemus to deceive Philoctetes and rob him of the bow, while leaving him marooned.

5. This is so because of the wound he receives when he is bitten by a snake while directing his "fellow chieftains to a particular altar on the voyage to Troy." See Moses Hadas's introduction to the play in *The Complete Plays of Sophocles,* 181.

6. In Ellison's view, the American revolutionary project was endangered almost from its inception, due to the unwillingness of the Framers to accept responsibility for slavery. "Perspective of Literature," 332.

7. *Philoctetes,* 332. Ellison quotes Katherine Drinker Bowen's observation of Jefferson's earlier drafts of the Declaration, that "in Jefferson's indictment of the King he nowhere states that slavery is a disgrace to Americans. Instead, he turns his anger on the wrong culprit, twists a shameful fact of American life into an instrument of propaganda against George III, condemns the slave trade, then draws the sting by putting the blame and responsibility on the King of England."

8. "Coherence" here means the individual's attempt to see him- or herself as part of a collective. Moses Hadas suggests that *Philoctetes* enacts the individual's need to belong as the play's driving tension, casting the bow as "a symbol of responsibility which goes with special capacities." *The Complete Plays of Sophocles,* 181.

9. White, *Heracles' Bow,* 18. This recognition leads Neoptolemus to create a persuasive community that is driven by self-recovery rather than revenge. He learns that he need not "read" his responsibility to society in such literal fashion.

10. Thus performance plays an important role in a discussion of Ellison's novel and of McPherson's fiction. This is particularly so in light of my use of White's notion of "persuasive communities," for the act of taking responsibility for presentation to an audience is, in effect, an attempt to create a coherent community that shares a language and a history.

11. Gerald L. Davis, "*I got the Word in me.*" Davis makes the following observation regarding Afro-American sermonic performance:

> It is not the linking together of analogous phrases that gives the African-American sermon its distinctive character. It is the utilization of independent narrative units held together through the use of theme-related bridges. In this discussion the thematic bridge is a category of formula that has the specialized function of bridging the sermon's independent units through restatements of the sermon's theme and by providing temporary closure for the preceding formula and entry into the next formula. (56)

12. If this sounds similar to the way the blues evokes an audience response, it could well be that the blues are the secular version of the kind of reflection the sermon is designed to elicit. One of the finest explications of this similarity can be found in James H. Cone's book, *The Spirituals and the Blues.* Indeed, Cone refers to the blues as a "secular spiritual."

13. The narrator sites himself as one who has transcended the need to engage in the denial of pleasure; using Bledsoe as the sign of repression and secrecy, he meditates on the power of shame. There is much to be unpacked here, for Ellison suggests that African American identity is mediated by the sense that pleasure is a resource for the racial Other to denigrate African American citizenship. Such an attitude is based on the premise that this pleasure is located in the body and therefore incapable of performing the tasks necessary to merit serious consideration within the body politic. For an example of this, see Thomas Jefferson's comments about African slaves in Notes on the State of Virginia. DuBois's concept of double-consciousness is also a discursive strategy meant to call attention to the machinery powering African American shame.

14. The act of reading the narrator performs is described in Wolfgang Iser's essay, "The Reading Process: A Phenomenological Approach."

15. James Alan McPherson, "An Act of Prostitution," *Hue and Cry,* 153–73.

16. One thinks here of William Harris's observation in Charles Johnson's *Oxherding Tale,* that the most lamentable thing about slavery was that it "epidermalized being," 12.

17. This is a theme McPherson returns to on a continued basis. Consider his story "A Solo Song: For Doc," where we find the same conflict between a reified set of rules and oral performance that often characterizes the American cultural space. For a more detailed discussion, see Chapter 4.

18. James Alan McPherson, "Problems of Art," *Elbow Room,* 94.

19. Though it may seem as if I am committing a kind of semantic "hairsplitting," the difference I draw between "testifying" and "testimony" rests on varying approaches to narration as those differences crystallize within the context of a courtroom. The former has to do with an approach to narrative where the teller aligns the "text" to the context. Mrs. Farragot's admonition does not intrude on Winfield's narrative so much as it suggests the collaborative nature of African American storytelling. The latter rests on the fragmentation of narrative. Thus Milford, as Mrs. Farragot's legal counsel, is empowered to assign meaning to Winfield's narrative and, in arbitrary fashion, include or exclude details based on his perception of the most "important" facts. The result, of course, is that testimony is not a narrative unified by the teller; rather, unity is achieved through a channel of discourse that makes the teller into object. The lawyer, empowered to ask questions, is the subject in a courtroom; the witness, in a position where she or he can only respond, is object. The lawyer offers a model of narrative unity to the jury in his or her summation, the act of unifying narrative strands into a conceptual whole that rests on coherence rather than truth.

20. Robert B. Stepto, *From Behind the Veil.* As I have noted elsewhere, the critical foundation for many of the ideas I work out in this discussion of law and narrative grows from Stepto's notion of authorial control.

21. James Alan McPherson, "A Sense of Story," *Elbow Room.*

22. Ralph Ellison, "Twentieth Century Fiction and the Black Mask of Humanity," *Shadow and Act,* 25.

23. Steven Cohan and Linda M. Shires, *Telling Stories: A Theoretical Analysis of Narrative Fiction,* 1.

24. This slippage serves to highlight the convergence of written and oral forms of discourse and suggests an imperfect "fit" between the two. Hence, as readers, we are forced to make the conceptual leap to consider a performative culture as we function within a textually biased culture. As the legal confrontation continues to enact an oral confrontation where performance can influence the jury's perception of the facts, the performance inevitably rests on the legal code and the facts, which are most powerful when they appear in tangible, material form.

25. I would argue that this story is often read as an anti-racist narrative, rather than as a self-reflexive rumination on the nature of the artist in society. Though Wright chooses class as a deconstructive site, both stories offer men whom McPherson might describe as "desperadoes," men who travel through despair in order to find "heroic hope, absurd hope, mad hope."

26. Ronald Dworkin, "Law as Interpretation," *The Politics of Interpretation,* 263.

27. Richard Delgado, "Storytelling for Oppositionists and Others: A Plea for Narrative," 2412 (Delgado's emphasis).

28. Robert B. Stepto, "Distrust of the Reader in Afro-American Narrative."

29. In addition to "Perspective of Literature," we see call and response in terms of McPherson's response to Ellison's "Brave Words for a Startling Occasion." Hence, McPherson's legal trilogy can be seen as a meditation on the state of American democracy.

30. John F. Callahan, *In the African-American Grain,* 17.

31. Peter Brooks, *Reading for the Plot,* 11–12. As Brooks demonstrates, the complexity to be found in the definition of the word "plot" is useful for my task here:

> 1.(a) A small piece of ground, generally used for a specific purpose; (b) a measured area of land; lot.
> 2. A ground plan, as for a building; chart; diagram.
> 3. The series of events consisting of the outline of the action of a narrative or drama.
> 4. A secret plan to accomplish a hostile or illegal purpose; scheme.

32. As such, we need to be mindful of John Hope Franklin's observations regarding the growth of "separate-but-equal" in the United States. Franklin notes:

> A survey of the history of the United States in the nineteenth century gives one the distinct impression that Jim Crow is the creature of a so-called free society. In the North, where freedom came relatively early, Jim Crow had an early birth and was nurtured, oddly enough, even by those who were committed to a loosely defined principle of universal freedom. The separation or exclusion of Negroes from the militia in several Northern states, their segregation in the schools of such states as Massachusetts and Ohio, and the clear-cut policy of excluding them altogether from certain other free states are cases in point. Such practices reflect at times a view widely held even among those who were opposed to slavery, that Negroes were inferior and deserved special, separate treatment.

John Hope Franklin, "Jim Crow Goes to School: The Genesis of Legal Segregation in the South," 135–48. One thinks, in addition here, of that moment in *The Great Gatsby* where Tom Buchanan, citing evidence found in a pseudo-scientific study called the *Rise of the Colored Empires,* asserts, "Civilization's going to pieces" and observes, "It's up to us, who are the dominant race, to watch or these other races will have control of things."

33. Guion Griffin Johnson, "Southern Paternalism After Emancipation," 131–32. When this is weighed against the South's leap into modernity through its post-Civil War enactment of Jim Crow laws, we see reflected the deep concern over racial contamination, the fear that racial equality would ultimately pollute the white body via miscegenation, and thus initiate the fall of American civilization. The stories unmask the anxiety being played out over the acquisition of status and suggest the manner in which whiteness simultaneously became the code key to the American dream-myth and a labyrinth where whiteness and "opportunity" became synonymous.

34. As numerous commentators have argued, the short story is a literary genre which has historically charted the transformative qualities inherent in a predicament.

35. This is most certainly the case in "An Act of Prostitution." By using humor to direct the reader away from indignation and anger at Philomena's exploitation, McPherson suggests that it is only through a more active form of reading, which resists the seductiveness of plot, that the reader can avoid being complicit in her exploitation. What this suggests is that in lieu of Philomena being able to tell her story, the reader needs to understand that in order for her presence in the courtroom to possess narrative centrality, a narration of her desire to find "honest" work is required. Because Mulligan never allows her to escape the confinement of spectacle, we never hear this. As the site of sexual transactions whose ethnicity is reread through the lens of race, Philomena is victimized because she lacks authorial control.

36. Wolfgang Iser, "Interaction Between Text and Reader." Iser intimates the merits of this conclusion when he argues that "central to the reading of every literary work is the interaction between its structure and its recipient." Iser continues:

> we may conclude that the literary work has two poles, which we might call the artistic and the aesthetic: the artistic pole is the author's text, and the aesthetic is the realization accomplished by the reader. In view of this polarity, it is clear that the work cannot be identical with the text or with its actualization but must be situated somewhere between the two. It must inevitably be virtual in character, as it cannot be reduced to the reality of the text or to the subjectivity of the reader, and it is from this virtuality that it derives its dynamism.

Conclusion

1. James Alan McPherson, "Junior and John Doe."

2. Interestingly, McPherson posits the comedian Richard Pryor as the only force capable of safeguarding the group idiom. Indeed, when one considers the differences between Pryor and his successor, Eddie Murphy, McPherson's observations achieve great clarity. Pryor's early work not only demonstrates a willingness to be self-critical but also situates McPherson's "group idiom" as a positive energy which he uses to critique white supremacy. Murphy, conversely, often lampoons African American identity as a way of setting himself apart from the group. His comedy, while drawing from Pryor, often situates the individual as a figure at risk among the masses. For a deeper discussion on these two comedians, see my essay on Pryor and Murphy in Sticopolous and Uebel, *The Color of Manhood,* entitled "The Cool Pose: Intersectionality, Masculinity, and Quiescence in the Comedy and Films of Richard Pryor and Eddie Murphy."

Bibliography

Abrahams, Roger D. *African-American Folklore: Stories from Black Traditions in the New World.* New York: Pantheon Books, 1985.

———. "Patterns of Performance in the West Indies." In *Afro-American Anthropology: Contemporary Perspectives,* ed. John F. Szwed and Norman E. Whitten. New York: Free Press, 1970.

———. "A Performance-Centered Approach to Gossip." *Man* n.s. 5 (1970): 290–301.

Baker, Houston A. *Blues, Ideology, and Afro-American Literature: A Vernacular Theory.* Chicago: University of Chicago Press, 1984.

———. *The Journey Back: Issues in Black Literature and Criticism.* Chicago: University of Chicago Press, 1984.

———. "To Move Without Moving: Creativity and Commerce in Ralph Ellison's Trueblood Episode." In Gates, ed., *Black Literature and Literary Theory,* 221–48.

Baldwin, James. "Going to Meet the Man." In *Going to Meet the Man.* New York: Laurel Publishing, 1981.

Barthes, Roland. *Mythologies.* Trans. Annette Lavers. New York: Hill and Wang, 1972.

Barthold, Bonnie J. *Black Time: Fiction of Africa, the Caribbean, and the United States.* New Haven, CT: Yale University Press, 1981.

Bascom, William R. "Verbal Art." *Journal of American Folklore* 68 (April/June 1955): 242–55.

Bauman, Richard. "Verbal Art as Performance." *American Anthropologist* 77 (June 1975): 290–311.

———. *Verbal Art as Performance.* Rowley, MA: Newbury House, 1977.

Beavers, Herman. "The Cool Pose: Intersectionality, Masculinity, and Quiescence in the Comedy and Films of Richard Pryor and Eddie Murphy." In *The Color of Manhood,* ed. Harry Sticopoulos and Michael Uebel. Durham, NC: Duke University Press, 1994.

———. "I Yam What You Is and You Is What I Yam: Rhetorical Invisibility in James A. McPherson's 'The Story of a Dead Man.'" *Callaloo* 9, 4 (Spring 1987): 535–47.

———. "Shared Centers of Ease: Healing and Kinship in James A. McPherson's 'The Story of a Scar.'" Unpublished essay.

Ben-Amos, Dan and Kenneth Goldstein. *Folklore: Performance and Communication.* The Hague: Mouton, 1975.

Benjamin, Walter. *Illuminations.* Trans. Harry Zohn. New York: Schocken Books, 1968.

Benston, Kimberly. "I Yam What I Am: The Topos of (Un)Naming in African-American Literature." In Gates, ed., *Black Literature and Literary Theory,* 151–72.

——, ed. *Speaking for You: The Vision of Ralph Ellison.* Washington, DC: Howard University Press, 1987.

Blaustein, Alpert P. and Robert L. Zagrando. *Civil Rights and the Black American.* New York: Washington Square Press, 1970.

Blicksilver, Edith. "The Image of Women in Selected Short Stories by James Alan McPherson." *College Language Association Journal* 22 (1978): 390–401.

Bluestein, Gene. "The Blues as Literary Theme." *Massachusetts Review* 8 (1967): 593–617.

Bontemps, Arna. "A Summer Tragedy." In *Calling the Wind: Twentieth-Century African-American Short Stories,* ed. Clarence Major. New York: Harper Perennial Books, 1993.

Boorstin, Daniel. *The Americans: The Democratic Experience.* New York: Vintage Books, 1974.

Booth, Wayne. *The Rhetoric of Fiction.* Chicago: University of Chicago Press, 1961. Reprint 1982.

Bradley, David. *The Chaneysville Incident.* New York: Avon Books, 1982.

Brooks, Peter. *Reading for the Plot: Design and Intention in Narrative.* New York: Knopf, 1984. Reprint Cambridge, MA: Harvard University Press, 1992.

Brown, Sterling A. *The Collected Poems of Sterling A. Brown.* New York: Harper and Row, 1980.

——. "Negro Characters as Seen by White Authors." *Journal of Negro Education* (April 1933): 179–203.

Brown, Sterling A., Arthur P. Davis, and Ulysses Lee. *The Negro Caravan.* New York: Dryden Press, 1941.

Burke, Kenneth. *The Philosophy of Literary Form: Studies in Symbolic Action.* 1941. Berkeley: University of California Press, 1971.

Byerman, Keith E. *Fingering the Jagged Grain: Tradition and Form in Recent Black Fiction.* Athens: University of Georgia Press, 1986.

Cahan, Abraham. *Yekl and the Imported Bridegroom and Other Stories of the New York Ghetto.* 1896. Reprint New York: Dover, 1970.

Callahan, John F. *In the African-American Grain: The Pursuit of Voice in Twentieth-Century Black Fiction.* Urbana: University of Illinois Press, 1988.

——. "Image-Making: Tradition and the Two Versions of *The Autobiography of Miss Jane Pitman.*" *Chicago Review* 28, 4 (Fall 1976): 45–62.

——. "'Riffing' and Paradigm Building: The Anomaly of Tradition and Innovation in *Invisible Man* and *The Structure of Scientific Revolutions.*" *Callaloo* 10, 1 (Summer 1987): 91–102.

Campbell, Joseph. *The Hero with a Thousand Faces.* Princeton, NJ: Princeton University Press, 1949. Reprint 1967.

Campbell, Mary Schmidt. "History and the Art of Romare Bearden." In *Memory and Metaphor: The Art of Romare Bearden, 1940–1987.* New York: Studio Museum in Harlem and Oxford University Press, 1991.

Chapman, Abraham. "Concepts of the Black Aesthetic." In *The Black Writer in Africa and the Americas,* ed. Lloyd Brown. Los Angeles: Hennessey and Ingalls, 1973.

——. "An Interview with Michael S. Harper." *Arts in Society* 11, 3 (1974): 462–71.
Chatman, Seymour. *Story and Discourse: Narrative Structure in Fiction and Film.* Ithaca, NY: Cornell University Press, 1978.
——. "The Structure of Narrative Transmission." In *Style and Structure in Literature: Essays in the New Stylistics,* ed. Roger Fowler. Ithaca, NY: Cornell University Press, 1975.
Christian, Barbara. *Black Women Novelists: The Development of a Tradition, 1892–1976.* Westport, CT: Greenwood Press, 1980.
Clarke, John Henrik. "The Visible Dimensions of *Invisible Man.*" *Black World* (December 1970): 30–34.
Cohan, Steven and Linda M. Shires. *Telling Stories: A Theoretical Analysis of Narrative Fiction.* New York and London: Routledge, 1988.
Cone, James H. *The Spirituals and the Blues: An Interpretation.* New York: Seabury Press, 1972.
Cooke, Michael. *Afro-American Literature in the Twentieth Century: The Achievement of Intimacy.* New Haven, CT: Yale University Press, 1984.
Cnudde, Charles F. *Democracy in the American South.* Chicago: Markham, 1971.
Cornell, Drucilla, Michel Rosenfeld, and David Gray Carlson, eds. *Deconstruction and the Possibility of Justice.* New York: Routledge, Chapman, and Hall, 1992.
Crow, Bill. *Jazz Anecdotes.* New York: Oxford University Press, 1990.
Culler, Jonathan. *Framing the Sign: Criticism and Its Institutions.* Norman: University of Oklahoma Press, 1989.
Davis, Gerald I. *"I got the Word in me and I can sing it, you know": A Study of the Performed African-American Sermon.* Philadelphia: University of Pennsylvania Press, 1985.
Delgado, Richard. "Storytelling for Oppositionists and Others: A Plea for Narrative." *Michigan Law Review* 87 (August 1989): 2411.
deTocqueville, Alexis. *Democracy in America.* 1833. Reprint New York: Knopf, 1976.
Dixon, Melvin. "O Mary Rambo Don't You Weep." *Carleton Miscellany* 18, 3 (Winter 1980): 98–104.
——. *Ride Out the Wilderness: Geography and Identity in Afro-American Literature.* Urbana: University of Illinois Press, 1987.
Domnarski, William. "The Voices of Misery and Despair in the Fictions of James Alan McPherson." *Arizona Quarterly* 42, 1 (Spring 1986): 39–44.
Donaldson, Scott. *By Force of Will: The Life and Art of Ernest Hemingway.* New York: Penguin Books, 1977.
Douglass, Frederick. *Narrative of the Life of Frederick Douglass, An American Slave.* 1845. Reprint New York: Anchor Books, 1973.
DuBois, William Edward Burghardt. *The Souls of Black Folk.* 1903. Reprint New York: Avon Books, 1965.
Dundes, Alan. "Metafolklore and Oral Literary Criticism." *Monist* 50 (October 1966): 505–16.
Dworkin, Ronald. "Law as Interpretation." In *The Politics of Interpretation,* ed. W. J. T. Mitchell. Chicago: University of Chicago Press, 1983.
Eagleton, Terry. *Literary Theory: An Introduction.* Oxford: Basil Blackwell, 1983.
Ellison, Ralph. "A Coupla Scalped Indians." *New World Writing* 9 (1956).
——. "Did You Ever Dream Lucky?" *New World Writing* 5 (1954).

——. "Flying Home." In *Best Stories by Negro Writers: An Anthology,* ed. Langston Hughes. Boston: Little, Brown, 1967.

——. *Going to the Territory.* New York: Random House, 1985. Reprint New York: Vintage Books, 1987.

——. *Invisible Man.* New York: Random House, 1952. Reprint New York: Vintage Books, 1990.

——. "King of the Bingo Game." In *Norton Anthology of Short Fiction,* ed. R. V. Cassell. New York: W. W. Norton, 1981.

——. *Shadow and Act.* New York: Random House, 1964. Reprint New York: Vintage Books, 1972.

Evans, Mari, ed. *Black Women Writers (1850–1980): A Critical Evaluation.* Garden City, NY: Anchor Books, 1983.

Fabre, Michel. "Bayonne, or the Yoknapatawpha of Ernest Gaines." *Callaloo* 1, 3 (May 1978): 110–24.

Fagunwa, D. O. *The Forest of a Thousand Daemons: A Hunter's Saga.* Trans. Wole Soyinka. New York: Random House, 1982.

Faulkner, William. *Absalom, Absalom.* 1936. Reprint New York: Modern Library, 1964.

——. *Go Down, Moses and Other Stories.* 1940. Reprint New York: Vintage Books, 1972.

——. *The Hamlet.* 1931. New York: Vintage Books, 1972.

——. *Light in August.* 1932. Reprint New York: Vintage Books, 1972.

——. *The Sound and the Fury.* 1929. Reprint New York: Vintage Books, 1972.

Fikes, Robert, Jr. "The Works of an 'American Writer': A James Alan McPherson Bibliography." *College Language Association Journal* 22 (1979): 415–23.

Fitzgerald, F. Scott. *The Great Gatsby.* 1925. Reprint New York: Scribner, 1953.

Foley, Barbara. *Telling the Truth: The Theory and Practice of Documentary Fiction.* Ithaca, NY: Cornell University Press, 1986.

Forrest, Leon. "Luminosity from the Lower Frequencies." *Carleton Miscellany* 18, 3 (Winter 1980): 82–97.

Franklin, John Hope. "Jim Crow Goes to School: The Genesis of Legal Separation in the South." In *The Negro in the South Since 1865: Selected Essays in American Negro History,* ed. Charles E. Wynes. New York: Harper Colophon, 1965.

Gaines, Ernest J. *The Autobiography of Miss Jane Pittman.* New York: Dial Press, 1971. Reprint New York: Doubleday, 1987.

——. *Bloodline.* New York: W. W. Norton, 1968. Reprint 1976.

——. *Catherine Carmier.* New York: W. W. Norton, 1964. Reprint San Francisco: North Point Press, 1981.

——. *A Gathering of Old Men.* New York: Vintage Books, 1984. Reprint New York: Alfred Knopf, 1992.

——. "Home: A Photo-Essay." *Callaloo* 1, 3 (May 1978): 52–67.

——. *In My Father's House.* New York: W. W. Norton, 1978. Reprint 1992.

——. *A Lesson Before Dying.* New York: Alfred Knopf, 1993.

——. "Miss Jane and I." *Callaloo* 1, 3 (May 1978).

——. *Of Love and Dust.* New York: Dial Press, 1967. Reprint 1979.

Gates, Henry-Louis, Jr., ed. *Black Literature and Literary Theory.* New York: Methuen, 1984.

——. *Loose Canons: Notes on the Culture Wars.* New York: Oxford University Press, 1992.

——. *The Signifying Monkey: A Theory of Afro-American Literary Criticism.* New York: Oxford University Press, 1987.

Gaudet, Marcia and Carl D. Wooten. "Conversation with Ernest J. Gaines." *Callaloo* 11, 2 (Spring 1987): 228–40. Included in Gaudet and Wooten, *Porch Talk.*

——. *Porch Talk with Ernest J. Gaines: Conversations on the Writer's Craft.* Baton Rouge: Louisiana State University Press, 1990.

Gleeson, Judith. *Of Leaf and Bone.* New York: Random House, 1980.

Gray, Richard. *The Literature of Memory: Modern Writers of the American South.* Baltimore: Johns Hopkins University Press, 1977.

Hadas, Moses. Introduction to *The Complete Plays of Sophocles.* New York: Bantam Books, 1967. Reprint 1979.

Haltunen, Karen. "Gothic Imagination and Social Reform: The Haunted Houses of Lyman Beecher, Henry Ward Beecher, and Harriet Beecher Stowe." In Sundquist, ed., *New Essays on Uncle Tom's Cabin.*

Harper, Michael S. "Certainties" (poem). *Ploughshares* 13, 1 (1987): 62–63.

——. *Healing Song for the Inner Ear: Poems.* Urbana: University of Illinois Press, 1985.

——. *Images of Kin: New and Selected Poems.* Urbana: University of Illinois Press, 1985.

——. *Nightmare Begins Responsibility.* Urbana: University of Illinois Press, 1972.

Harper, Michael S. and Robert B. Stepto. "Study and Experience: An Interview with Ralph Ellison." In Harper and Stepto, eds., *Chant of Saints,* 451–69.

——, eds. *Chant of Saints: A Gathering of Afro-American Literature, Art, and Scholarship.* Urbana: University of Illinois Press, 1986.

Harper, Michael S., Larry Kart, and Al Young. "Jazz and Letters: A Colloquy." *TriQuarterly68* (Winter 1987).

Hayden, Robert. *Angle of Ascent: New and Selected Poems.* New York: Liveright, 1975.

Hemingway, Ernest. *The Short Stories of Ernest Hemingway.* 1938. Reprint New York: Scribner's, 1966.

——. *The Sun Also Rises.* New York: Scribner's 1926.

Hentoff, Nat. *The Jazz Life.* New York: Da Capo Press, 1975.

Hofheins, Roger and Dan Tooker. *Fiction! Interviews with Northern California Novelists.* New York: Harcourt, 1976.

Howe, Irving. "Of Black Boys and Native Sons." *Dissent* (Autumn 1963). Reprinted in *Criticism: Some Major American Writers.* New York: Holt, Rinehart, Winston, 1971.

——. "Mass Society and Postmodern Fiction." In *Practising Postmodernism, Reading Modernism,* ed. Patricia Waugh. London: Edward Arnold, 1992.

Hunter, Jefferson. *Image and Word: The Interaction of Twentieth-Century Photographs and Texts.* Cambridge MA: Harvard University Press, 1987.

Hurston, Zora Neale. *Mules and Men.* 1935. Reprint New York: Harper Perennial Library, 1970.

——. *Dust Tracks on a Road: An Autobiography.* Urbana: University of Illinois Press, 1970. Reprint 1985.

——. *Their Eyes Were Watching God.* 1937. Reprint Urbana: University of Illinois Press, 1976.

Hymes, Dell. *"In vain I tried to tell you": Essays in Native American Ethnopoetics.* Philadelphia: University of Pennsylvania Press, 1982.

Iser, Wolfgang. *The Implied Reader: Patterns of Communication in Prose Fiction from Bunyan to Beckett.* Baltimore: Johns Hopkins University Press, 1974.

——. "Interaction Between Text and Reader." In Suleiman and Crosman, eds., *The Reader in the Text.*

——. "The Reading Process: A Phenomenological Approach." In Tompkins, ed., *Reader-Response Criticism.*

Johnson, Abby Arthur and Ronald Maberry Johnson. *Propaganda and Aesthetics: The Literary Politics of Afro-American Magazines in the Twentieth Century.* Amherst: University of Massachusetts Press, 1979.

Johnson, Charles Richard. *Being and Race: Black Writing Since 1970.* Bloomington: Indiana University Press, 1988.

——. *Oxherding Tale.* New York: Grove Press, 1982. Reprint 1986.

Johnson, Guion Griffin. "Southern Paternalism After Emancipation." In *The Negro in the South Since 1865: Selected Essays,* ed. Charles E. Wynes. 1965. Reprint New York: Harper Colophon, 1968.

Jones, Leroi and Larry Neal, eds. *Black Fire: An Anthology of Afro-American Writing.* New York: William Morrow, 1968.

Karst, Kenneth L. *Belonging to America: Equal Citizenship and the Constitution.* New Haven, CT: Yale University Press, 1980.

Kavanaugh, James. "Benito Cereno and the Liberal Hero." In *Ideology and Classic American Literature,* ed. Sacvan Bercovitch and Myra Jehlen. Cambridge: Cambridge University Press, 1989.

Kent, George E. *Blackness and the Adventure of Western Culture.* Chicago: Third World Press, 1972.

Kerr, Elizabeth M. *William Faulkner's Gothic Domain.* Port Washington, NY: Kennikat Press, 1979.

Killens, John Oliver and Jerry W. Ward, Jr., eds. *Black Southern Voices: An Anthology.* New York: Meridian Books, 1992.

Kuhn, Thomas S. *The Structure of Scientific Revolutions.* Chicago: University of Chicago Press, 1962. Reprint 1970.

——. *The Essential Tension: Selected Studies in Scientific Tension and Change.* Chicago: University of Chicago Press, 1977.

Landon, Ephraim, ed. *The Law as Literature.* New York: Simon and Schuster, 1960.

Levine, Lawrence. *Black Culture and Black Consciousness: Afro-American Folk Thought from Slavery to Freedom.* New York: Oxford University Press, 1977.

Lewis, R. W. B. *The American Adam: Innocence, Tragedy, and Tradition in the Nineteenth Century.* Chicago: University of Chicago Press, 1959.

Lewis. *The Great Gatsby.*

Mackey, Nathaniel. "Sound and Sentiment, Sound and Symbol." *Callaloo* 10, 1 (Winter 1987): 29–54.

Marshall, Paule. *Brown Girl, Brownstones.* 1959. Reprint Old Westbury, NY: Feminist Press, 1981.

——. *Praisesong for the Widow.* 1983. Reprint New York: Random House, 1985.

Martin, Wallace. *Recent Theories of Narrative.* Ithaca, NY: Cornell University Press, 1986.

Mbiti, John S. *African Religions and Philosophy.* 1969. Reprint Oxford: Heinemann, 1990.

Maclean, Marie. *Narrative as Performance: The Beaudelairean Experiment.* London: Methuen, 1987.

McFeeley, William S. *Frederick Douglass.* New York: Touchstone Books, 1991.

McPherson, James Alan. *Elbow Room: Stories.* Boston: Little, Brown, 1977. Reprint New York: Scribner's 1987.

——. *Hue and Cry: Short Stories.* Boston: Little, Brown, 1968. Reprint New York: Ballantine Books, 1979.
——. "Indivisible Man" (interview with Ralph Ellison). *Atlantic Monthly* (December 1969).
——. "Junior and John Doe." In *Lure and Loathing: Essays on Race, Identity, and the Ambivalence of Assimilation,* ed. Gerald Early. New York: Allen Lane, 1993.
——. "On Becoming an American Writer." *Atlantic Monthly* (December 1978).
Melville, Herman. "Bartleby the Scrivener"; "Benito Cereno." Reprinted in *Heath Anthology of American Literature,* ed. Paul Lauter et al. Lexington, MA: D. C. Heath, 1994.
——. *Moby Dick.* 1851. Reprint New York: New American Library, 1980.
Morrison, Toni. *Playing in the Dark: Whiteness and the Literary Imagination.* Cambridge, MA: Harvard University Press, 1992.
——. *Song of Solomon.* New York: Knopf, 1977. Reprint 1987.
——. *Sula.* New York: Knopf, 1973. Reprint 1978.
Murray, Albert. *The Hero and the Blues.* Columbia: University of Missouri Press, 1974.
——. *The Omni-Americans: New Perspectives on Black Experience and American Culture.* 1970. Reprint New York: Vintage Books, 1983.
——. *South to a Very Old Place.* New York: McGraw-Hill, 1971.
——. *Stomping the Blues.* 1976. Reprint New York: Vintage Books, 1982.
Nadel, Alan. *Invisible Criticism: Ralph Ellison and the American Canon.* Iowa City: University of Iowa Press, 1988.
Neal, Larry. "Ellison's Zoot Suit." *Black World* (December 1970). Reprinted in Benston, ed., *Speaking for You.*
Oates, Stephen B. *Faulkner: The Man and the Artist.* New York: Harper and Row, 1987.
O'Brien, John. *Interviews with Black Writers.* New York: Liveright, 1973.
Okpewho, Isidore. *The Epic in Africa: Toward a Poetics of the Oral Performance.* New York: Columbia University Press, 1979.
O'Meally, Robert G. *The Craft of Ralph Ellison.* Cambridge, MA: Harvard University Press, 1980.
——. "The Rules of Magic: Hemingway as Ellison's 'Ancestor.'" In Benston, ed., *Speaking for You.*
——, ed. *New Essays on Invisible Man.* Cambridge: Cambridge University Press, 1988.
Ong, Walter J. *Orality and Literacy: The Technology of the Word.* London: Methuen, 1982.
Ostendorf, Berndt. *Black Literature in White America.* Totowa, NJ: Barnes and Noble, 1982.
O'Rourke, David, O.P. "The Experience of Conversion." In *The Human Experience of Conversion: Persons and Structures in Transformation,* ed. Francis A. Eigo. Villanova, PA: Villanova University Press, 1987.
Outlaw, Lucius. "Language and Consciousness: Toward a Hermeneutic of Black Culture." *Cultural Hermeneutics* 1 (1974): 403–13.
Patton, Sharon F. "Memory and Metaphor: The Art of Romare Bearden, 1940–1987." In *Memory and Metaphor: The Art of Romare Bearden, 1940–1987.* New York: Studio Museum in Harlem and Oxford University Press, 1991.
Paz, Octavio. "The Tree of Life." In Paz, *Convergences: Essays on Art and Literature.* New York: Harcourt Brace, Jovanovich, 1987.

Pelton, Robert D. *The Trickster in West Africa: A Study of Mythic Irony and Sacred Delight.* Berkeley: University of California Press, 1980.

Petry, Ann. *The Street.* 1946. Reprint Boston: Beacon Press, 1985.

Prince, Gerard. "Introduction to the Study of the Narratee." In Tompkins, ed., *Reader-Response Criticism.*

Pryse, Marjorie and Hortense Spillers. *Conjuring: Black Women, Fiction, and Literary Tradition.* Bloomington: Indiana University Press, 1987.

Raglan, Fitzroy Richard Somerset, Baron. *The Hero: A Study in Tradition, Myth, and Drama.* London: Watts, 1949.

Reed, Ishmael. *Conjure: Selected Poems, 1963–1970.* Amherst: University of Massachusetts Press, 1972.

——. *Yellow Back Radion Broke-Down.* 1969. Reprint New York: Atheneum, 1988.

Reilly, John, ed. *Twentieth-Century Interpretations of Invisible Man: A Collection of Critical Essays.* Englewood Cliffs, NJ: Prentice-Hall, 1969.

Roberts, John W. *From Trickster to Badman: The Black Folk Hero in Slavery and Freedom.* Philadelphia: University of Pennsylvania Press, 1989.

——. "The Individual and the Community in Two Short Stories by Ernest J. Gaines." *Black American Literature Forum* 18 (Summer 1984).

Rowell, Charles H. "This Louisiana Thing That Drives Me: An Interview with Ernest J. Gaines." *Callaloo* 1, 3 (May 1978): 39–51.

Sadler, Lynn Veach. "Ralph Ellison and the Bird Artist." *South Atlantic Bulletin* 44, 4 (November 1979).

Schraufnagel, Neal A. *From Apology to Protest: The Black American Novel.* Deland, FL: Everett/Edwards, 1973.

Schultz, Elizabeth A. "The Heirs of Ralph Ellison." *College Language Association Journal* 22 (1978–79): 101–22.

Schwartz, Delmore. *In Dreams Begin Responsibilities.* 1938. Reprint New York: New Directions, 1978.

Sedgwick, Eve Kosofsky. *The Coherence of Gothic Conventions.* New York: Arno Press, 1980.

Sheffey, Ruth T. "Antaeus Revisited: James Alan McPherson and Elbow Room." In *Amid Visions and Revisions: Poetry and Criticism on Literature and the Arts,* ed. Burney J. Hollis. Baltimore: Morgan State University Press, 1985.

Sidran, Ben. *Black Talk.* New York: Holt, Rinehart, and Winston, 1971.

Silko, Leslie Marmon. *Storyteller.* New York: Seaver Books, 1981.

Simpson, Lewis. *The Dispossessed Garden: Pastoral and History in Southern Literature.* 1975. Reprint Baton Rouge: Louisiana State University Press, 1983.

Smith, Valerie. *Self-Discovery and Authority in African-American Narrative.* Cambridge, MA: Harvard University Press, 1987.

Sollors, Werner. *Beyond Ethnicity: Consent and Descent in American Culture.* New York: Oxford University Press, 1986.

Sontag, Susan. *Illness as Metaphor.* New York: Farrar, Strauss, Giroux, 1978.

Sophocles. *Philoctetes.* In *The Complete Plays of Sophocles.* New York: Bantam Books, 1967. Reprint 1979.

Stepto, Robert B. "After Modernism, After Hibernation: Michael S. Harper, Robert Hayden, and Jay Wright." In Harper and Stepto, eds., *Chant of Saints,* 470–86.

——. "Distrust of the Reader in Afro-American Narrative." In *Reconstructing*

American Literary History, ed. Sacvan Bercovitch. Cambridge, MA: Harvard University Press, 1986.
——. *From Behind the Veil: A Study of Afro-American Narrative*. Urbana: University of Illinois Press, 1979. Reprint 1991.
——. "I Thought I Knew These People: Richard Wright and the Afro-American Literary Tradition." In Harper and Stepto, eds., *Chant of Saints*, 192–213.
Stewart, James T. "The Development of the Black Revolutionary Artist." In Jones and Neal, eds., *Black Fire*, 3–10.
Suleiman, Susan and Inge Crosman, eds. *The Reader in the Text: Essays on Audience and Interpretation*. Princeton, NJ: Princeton University Press, 1980.
Sundquist, Eric J., ed. *New Essays on Uncle Tom's Cabin*. Cambridge: Cambridge University Press, 1986.
Todorov, Tzvetan. *The Poetics of Prose*. Ithaca, NY: Cornell University Press, 1977.
Tompkins, Jane P., ed. *Reader-Response Criticism: From Formalism to Post-Structuralism*. Baltimore: Johns Hopkins University Press, 1980.
——. *Sensational Designs: The Cultural Work of American Fiction, 1760–1860*. New York: Oxford University Press, 1985.
Toomer, Jean. *Cane*. New York: Liveright, 1923. Reprint New York: Norton, 1975.
Turner, Victor. *The Anthropology of Performance*. New York: PAJ Publications, 1988.
——. *Dramas, Fields, and Metaphors: Symbolic Action in Human Society*. Ithaca, NY: Cornell University Press, 1974.
——. *The Ritual Process: Structure and Anti-Structure*. 1969. Reprint. Ithaca, NY: Cornell University Press, 1978.
Twain, Mark. *The Adventures of Huckleberry Finn*. Reprint New York: Airmont Books, 1962.
——. *Pudd'nhead Wilson*. Reprint New York: New American Library, 1964.
Twelve Southerners. *I'll Take My Stand: The South and the Agrarian Tradition*. New York: Harper, 1962.
Walker, Alice. *The Color Purple*. New York: Harcourt Brace Jovanovich, 1982.
——. *In Love and Trouble: Stories of Black Women*. New York: Harcourt Brace Jovanovich, 1973.
——. *Meridian*. New York: Avon Books, 1976.
Ward, Douglas Turner. *Day of Absence*. In *The New Black Playwrights: An Anthology*, ed. William Couch. Baton Rouge: Louisiana State University Press, 1968.
Waugh, Patricia. *Metafiction: The Theory and Practice of Self-Conscious Fiction*. London: Methuen, 1984.
Wellman, Francis L. *The Art of Cross-Examination: With the Cross-Examinations of Important Witnesses in Some Celebrated Cases*. 1945. Reprint Birmingham, AL: Legal Classical Library, 1983.
Welty, Eudora. *The Collected Stories of Eudora Welty*. New York: Harcourt Brace Jovanovich, 1980.
Werner, Craig. "Tell Old Pharoah: The Afro-American Response to Faulkner." *Southern Review* (Winter 1982): 711–35.
White, Hayden. "The Literary Form of History." In *The Writing of History: Literary Form and Historical Understanding*, ed. Robert H. Canary and Henry Kozicki. Madison: University of Wisconsin Press, 1978.

White, James Boyd. *Heracles' Bow: Essays on the Rhetoric and the Poetics of Law.* Madison: University of Wisconsin Press, 1985.

Williams, Sherley Anne. *Give Birth to Brightness: A Thematic Study in Neo-Black Literature.* New York: Dial Press, 1973.

——. "The Blues Roots of Poetry." In Harper and Stepto, eds., *Chant of Saints,* 123–35.

Williams, William Carlos. *In the American Grain: Essays.* 1925. Reprint New York: New Directions, 1956.

Wright, John. "Dedicated Dreamer, Consecrated Acts: Shadowing Ellison." *Carleton Miscellany* 18, 3 (Winter 1980). Abridged version, "Shadowing Ellison," in Benston, ed., *Speaking for You.*

Wright, Richard. *Black Boy: A Record of Childhood and Youth.* New York: Harper and Row, 1945.

——. *Native Son.* New York: Harper and Row, 1940.

——. *Uncle Tom's Children.* New York: Harper and Row, 1937.

Index

Penn Studies in Contemporary American Fiction
A Series Edited by Emory Elliott, University of California at Riverside

Dennis Barone. *Beyond the Red Notebook: Essays on Paul Auster.* 1995
Herman Beavers. *Wrestling Angels into Song: The Fictions of Ernest J. Gaines and James Alan McPherson.* 1994
Alicia Borinsky. *Theoretical Fables: The Pedagogical Dream in Contemporary Latin American Fiction.* 1994
Marc Chénetier. *Beyond Suspicion: The New American Fiction from 1960 to the Present.* 1995
Silvio Gaggi. *Modern/Postmodern: A Study in Twentieth-Century Arts and Ideas.* 1989
John Johnston. *Carnival of Repetition: Gaddis's* The Recognitions *and Postmodern Theory.* 1990
Paul Maltby. *Dissident Postmodernists: Barthelme, Coover, Pynchon.* 1991
Ellen Pifer. *Saul Bellow Against the Grain.* 1990
Arthur M. Saltzman. *Designs of Darkness in Contemporary American Fiction.* 1990
Brian Stonehill. *The Self-Conscious Novel: Artifice in Fiction from Joyce to Pynchon.* 1988
Patricia Tobin. *John Barth and the Anxiety of Continuance.* 1992
Alan Wilde. *Middle Grounds: Studies in Contemporary American Fiction.* 1987

This book was set in Baskerville and Eras typefaces. Baskerville was designed by John Baskerville at his private press in Birmingham, England, in the eighteenth century. The first typeface to depart from oldstyle typeface design, Baskerville has more variation between thick and thin strokes. In an effort to insure that the thick and thin strokes of his typeface reproduced well on paper, John Baskerville developed the first wove paper, the surface of which was much smoother than the laid paper of the time. The development of wove paper was partly responsible for the introduction of typefaces classified as modern, which have even more contrast between thick and thin strokes.

Eras was designed in 1969 by Studio Hollenstein in Paris for the Wagner Typefoundry. A contemporary script-like version of a sans-serif typeface, the letters of Eras have a monotone stroke and are slightly inclined.

Printed on acid-free paper.